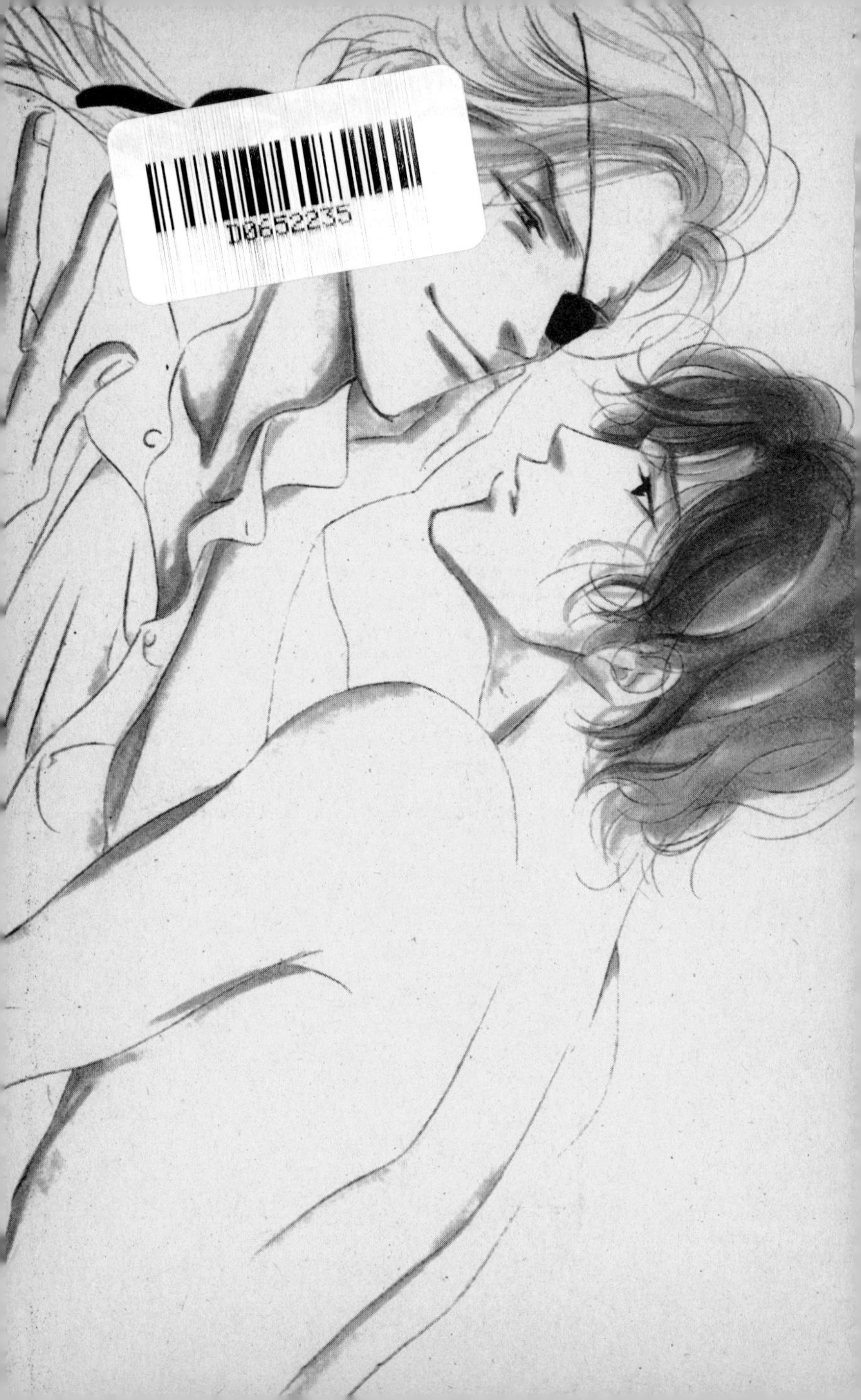

Gerard and Jacques

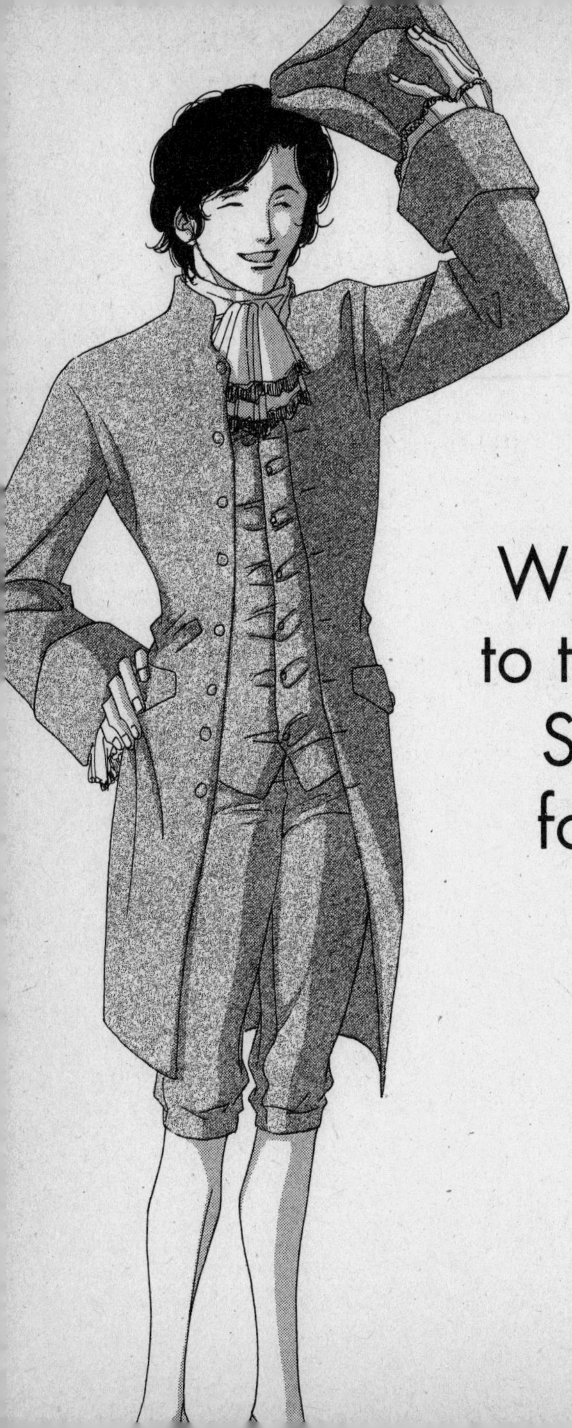

What I Do to the Child Striving for Love

WAS THERE EVER
A CHILD WHO WAS
AS LOVED BY HIS
PARENTS AS I
WAS, GROWING UP?

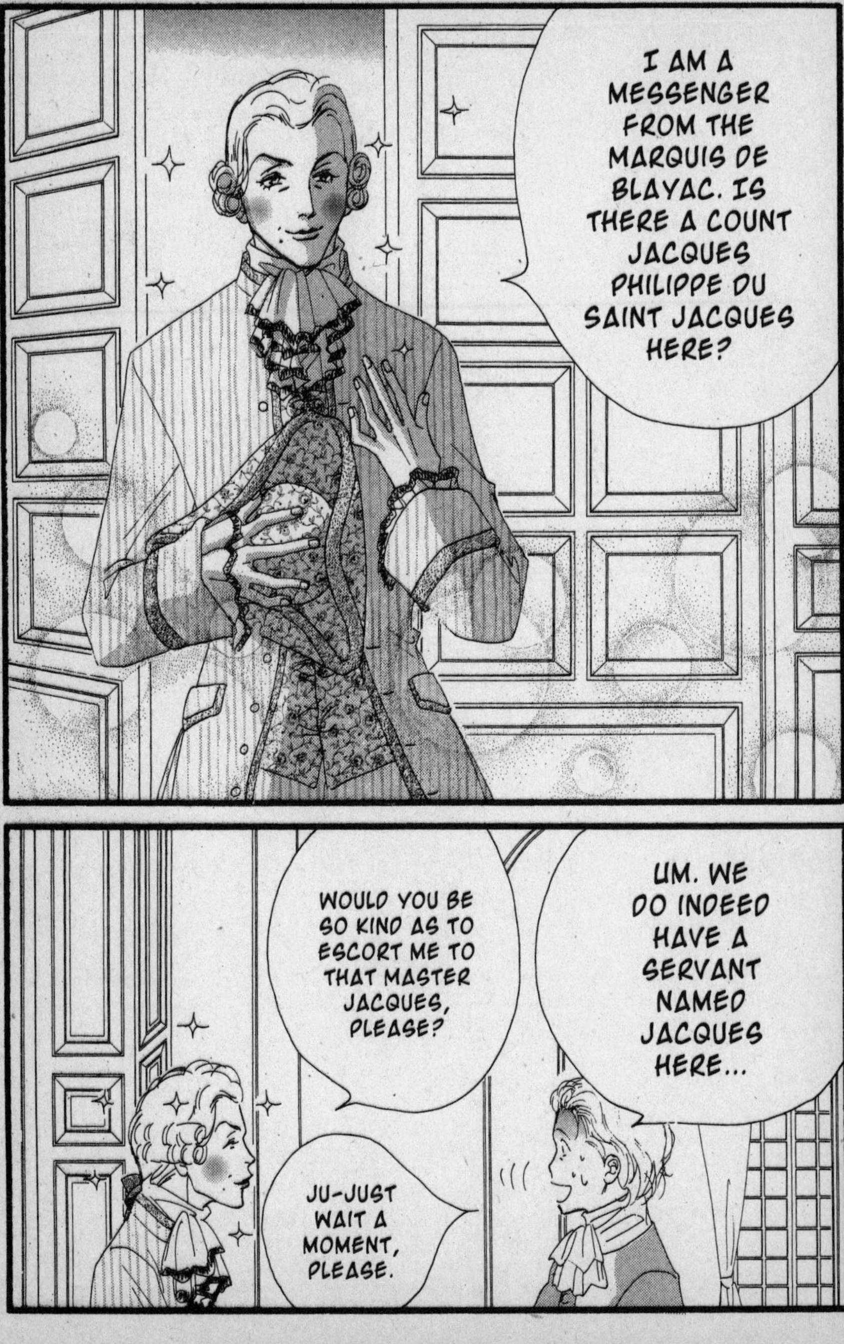
I AM A MESSENGER FROM THE MARQUIS DE BLAYAC. IS THERE A COUNT JACQUES PHILIPPE DU SAINT JACQUES HERE?
UM. WE DO INDEED HAVE A SERVANT NAMED JACQUES HERE...
WOULD YOU BE SO KIND AS TO ESCORT ME TO THAT MASTER JACQUES, PLEASE?
JU-JUST WAIT A MOMENT, PLEASE.

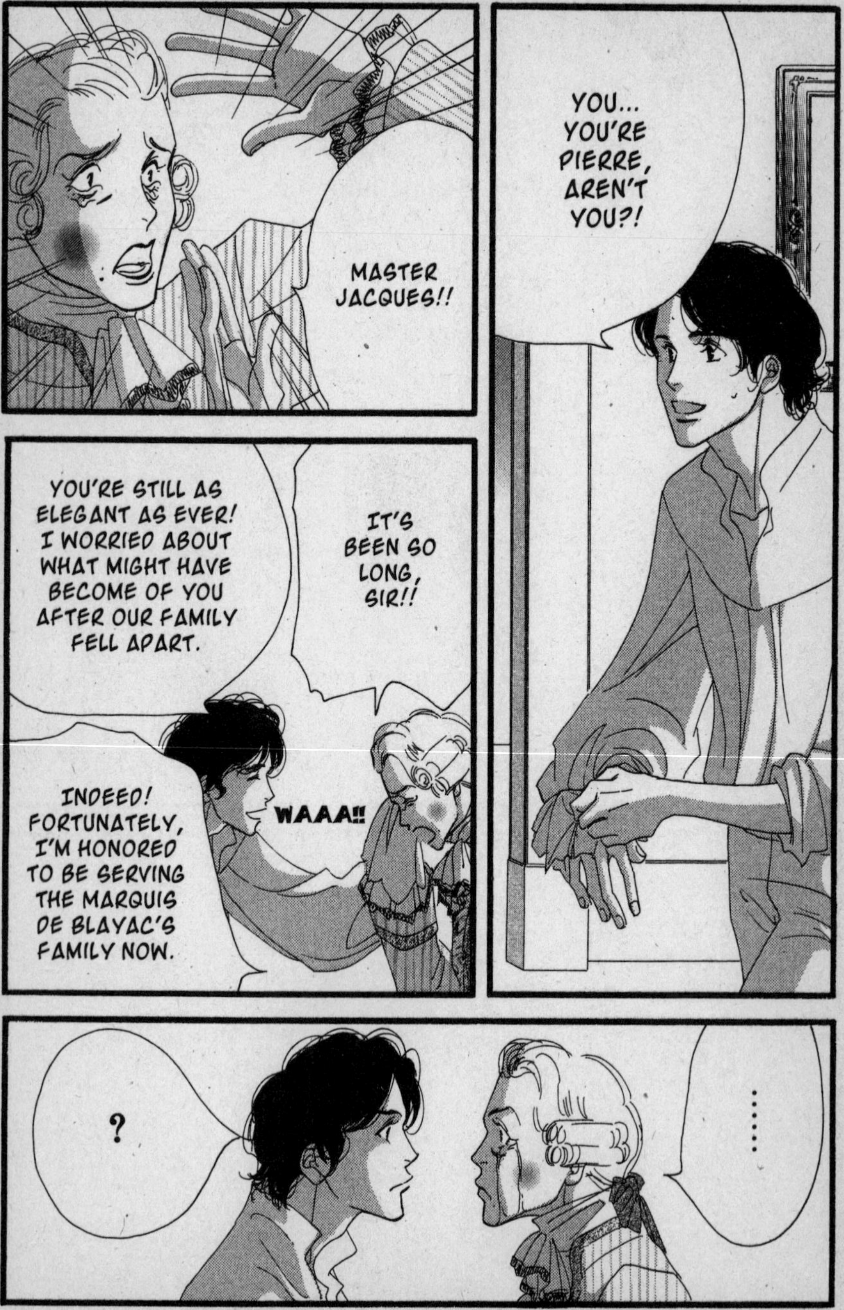
YOU... YOU'RE PIERRE, AREN'T YOU?!
MASTER JACQUES!!
IT'S BEEN SO LONG, SIR!!
YOU'RE STILL AS ELEGANT AS EVER! I WORRIED ABOUT WHAT MIGHT HAVE BECOME OF YOU AFTER OUR FAMILY FELL APART.
WAAA!!
INDEED! FORTUNATELY, I'M HONORED TO BE SERVING THE MARQUIS DE BLAYAC'S FAMILY NOW.
......
?

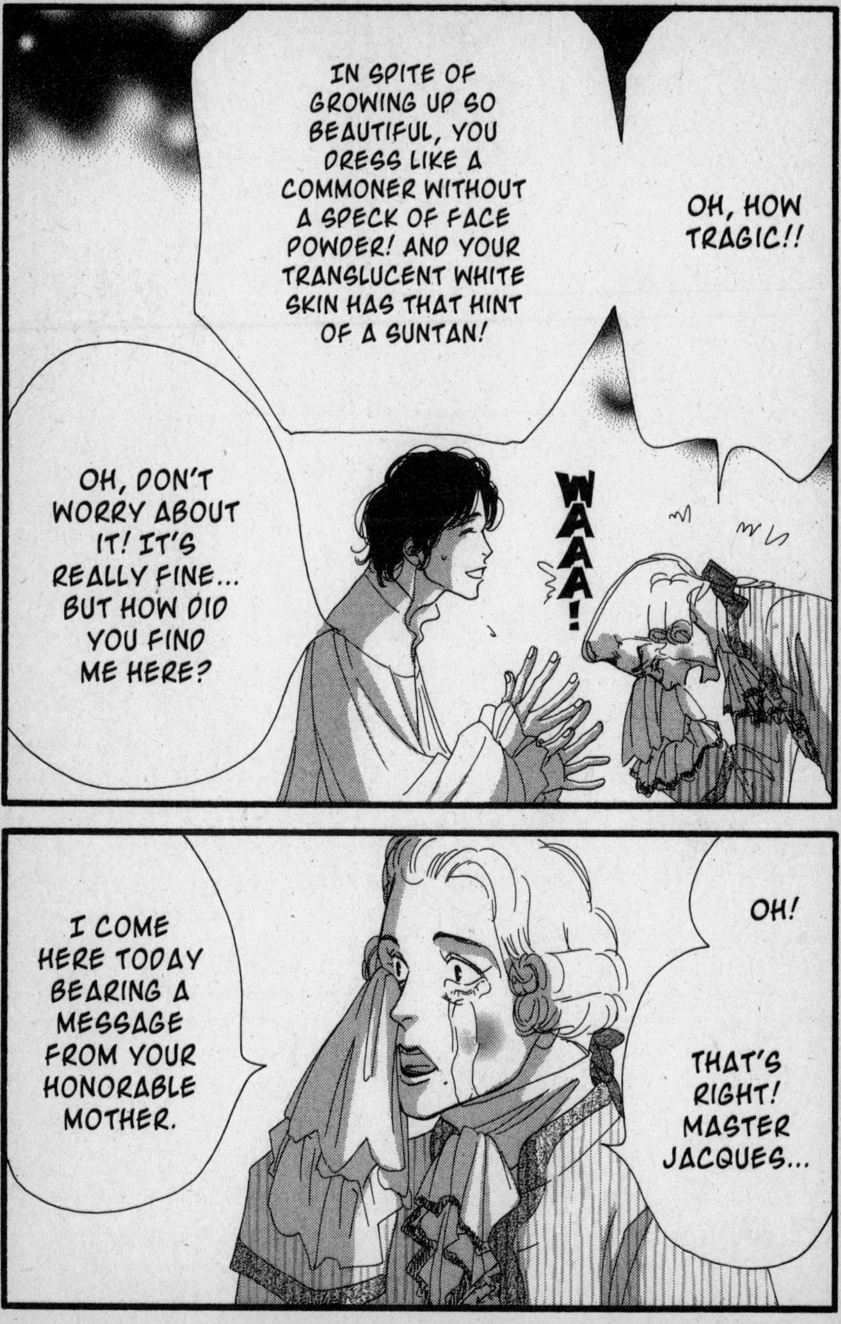
IN SPITE OF GROWING UP SO BEAUTIFUL, YOU DRESS LIKE A COMMONER WITHOUT A SPECK OF FACE POWDER! AND YOUR TRANSLUCENT WHITE SKIN HAS THAT HINT OF A SUNTAN!
OH, HOW TRAGIC!!
WAAAA!
OH, DON'T WORRY ABOUT IT! IT'S REALLY FINE... BUT HOW DID YOU FIND ME HERE?
OH!
THAT'S RIGHT! MASTER JACQUES...
I COME HERE TODAY BEARING A MESSAGE FROM YOUR HONORABLE MOTHER.

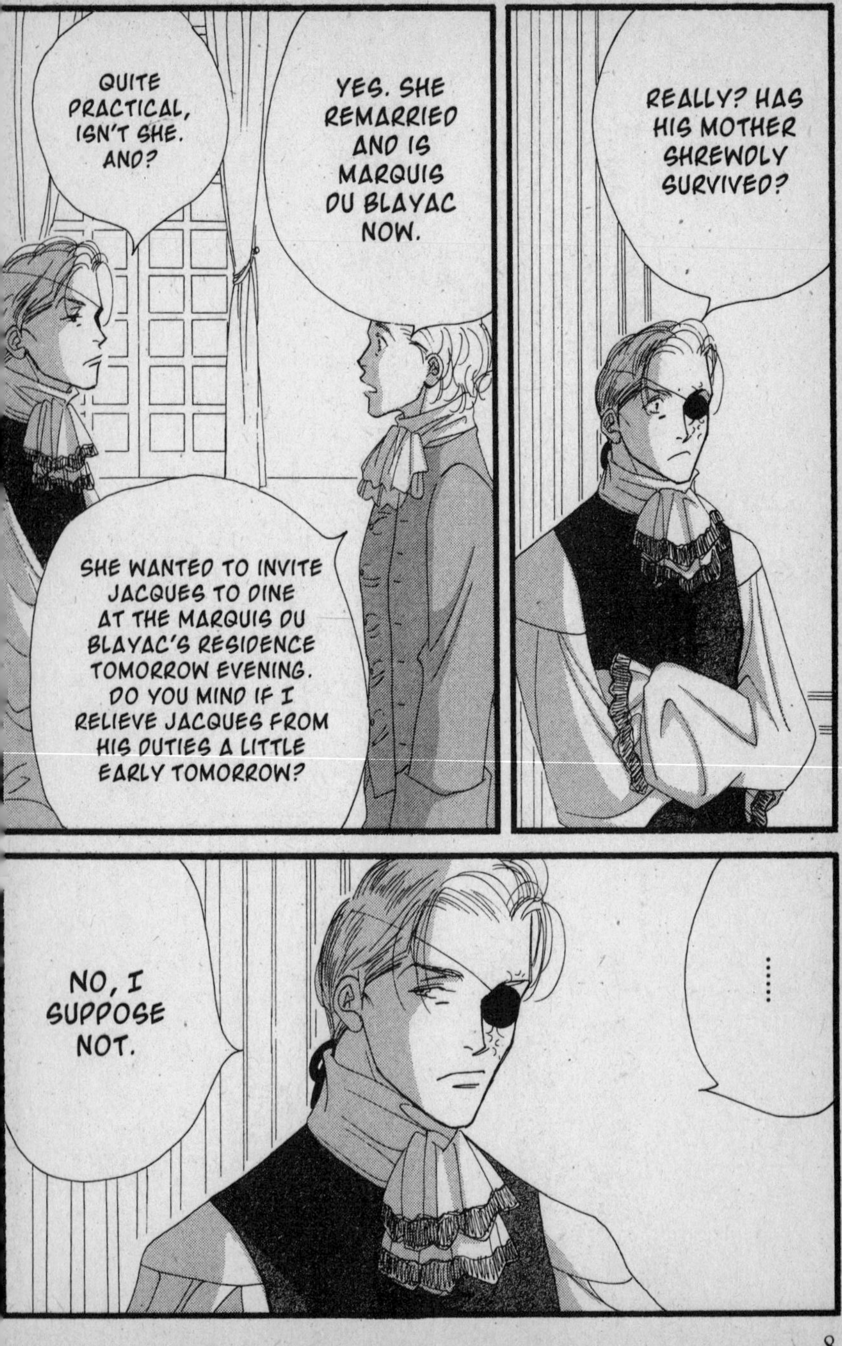
REALLY? HAS HIS MOTHER SHREWDLY SURVIVED?
YES. SHE REMARRIED AND IS MARQUIS DU BLAYAC NOW.
QUITE PRACTICAL, ISN'T SHE. AND?
SHE WANTED TO INVITE JACQUES TO DINE AT THE MARQUIS DU BLAYAC'S RESIDENCE TOMORROW EVENING. DO YOU MIND IF I RELIEVE JACQUES FROM HIS DUTIES A LITTLE EARLY TOMORROW?
……
NO, I SUPPOSE NOT.

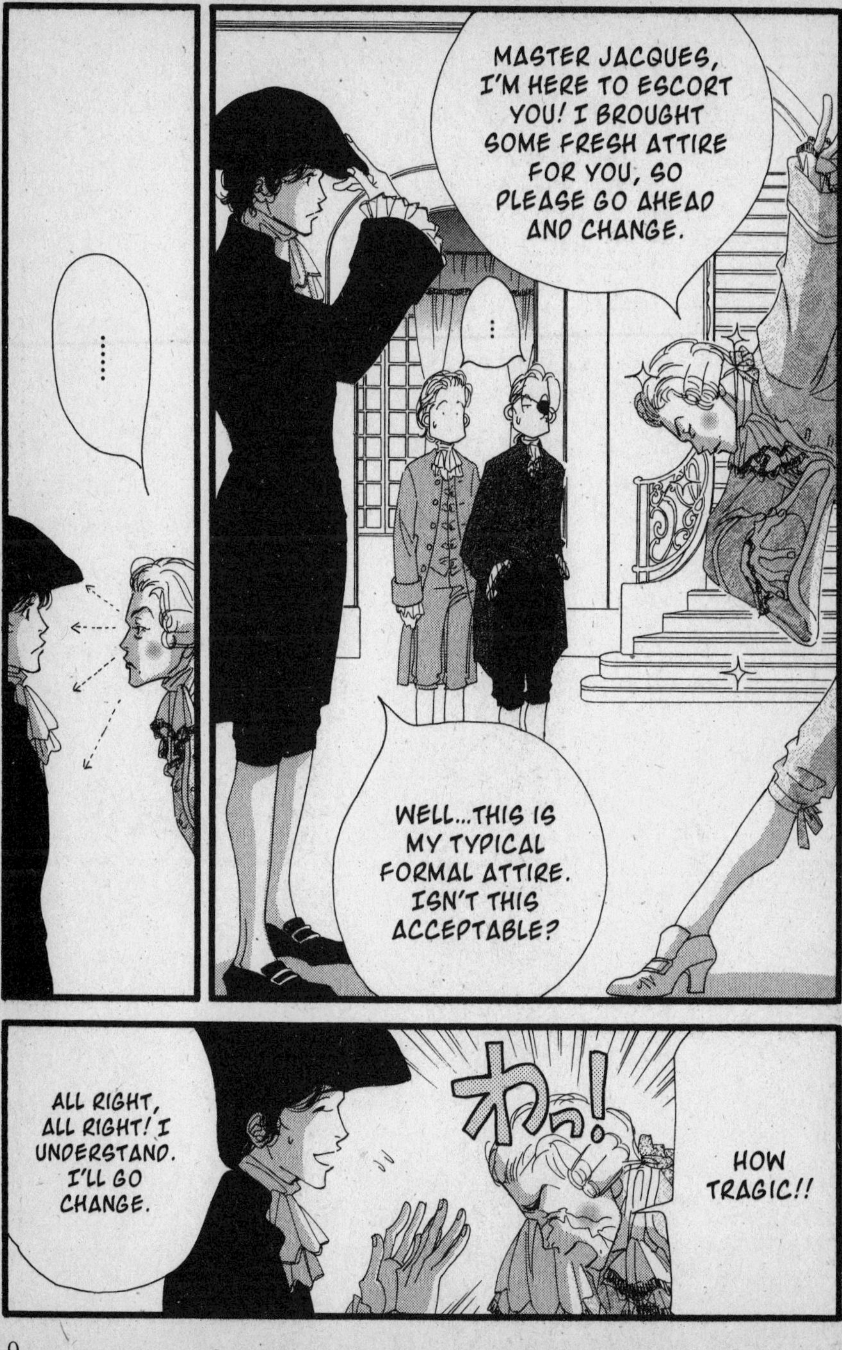
MASTER JACQUES, I'M HERE TO ESCORT YOU! I BROUGHT SOME FRESH ATTIRE FOR YOU, SO PLEASE GO AHEAD AND CHANGE.
...
WELL...THIS IS MY TYPICAL FORMAL ATTIRE. ISN'T THIS ACCEPTABLE?
......
HOW TRAGIC!!
わっ!
ALL RIGHT, ALL RIGHT! I UNDERSTAND. I'LL GO CHANGE.

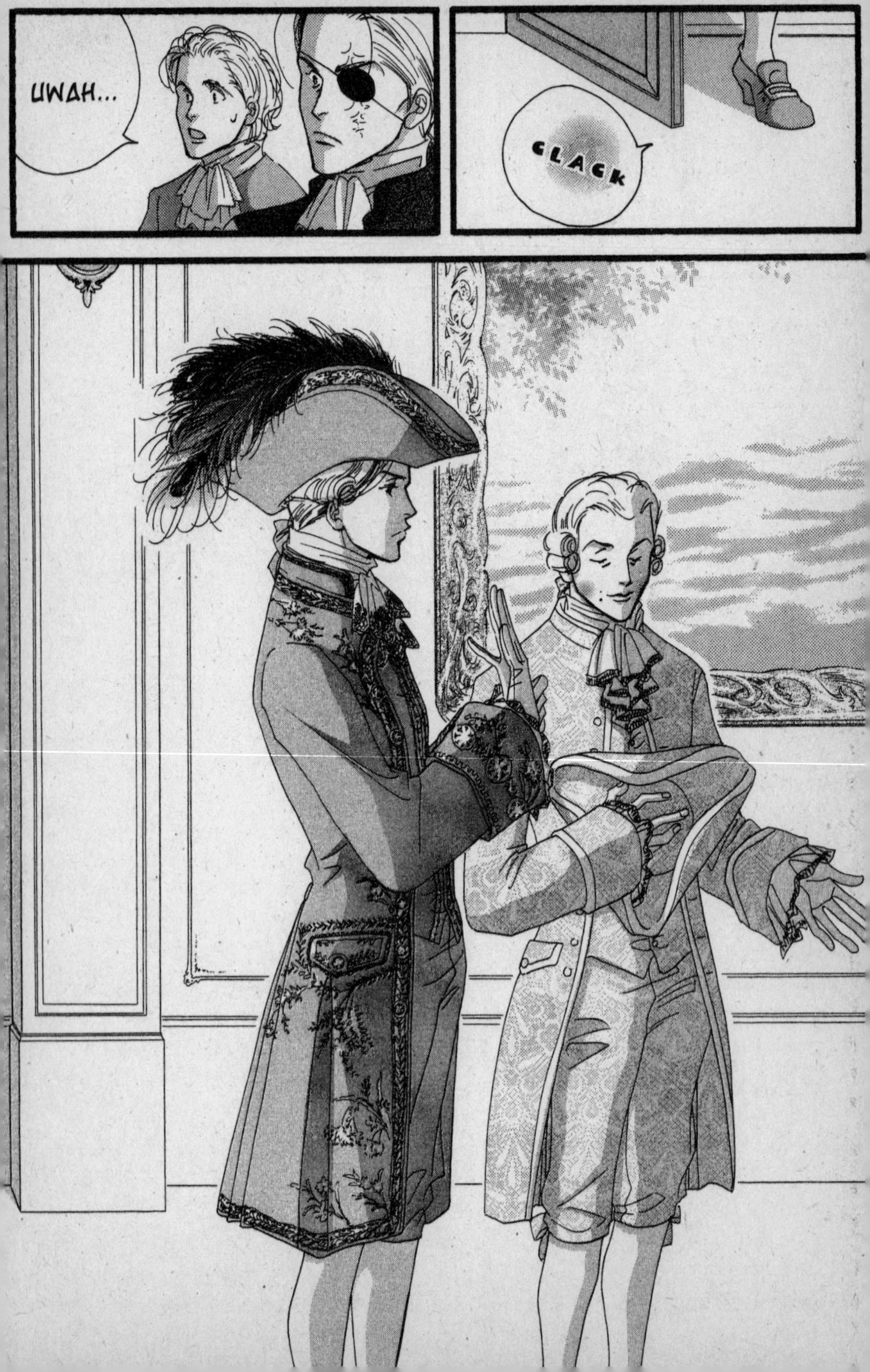
CLACK
UWAH...

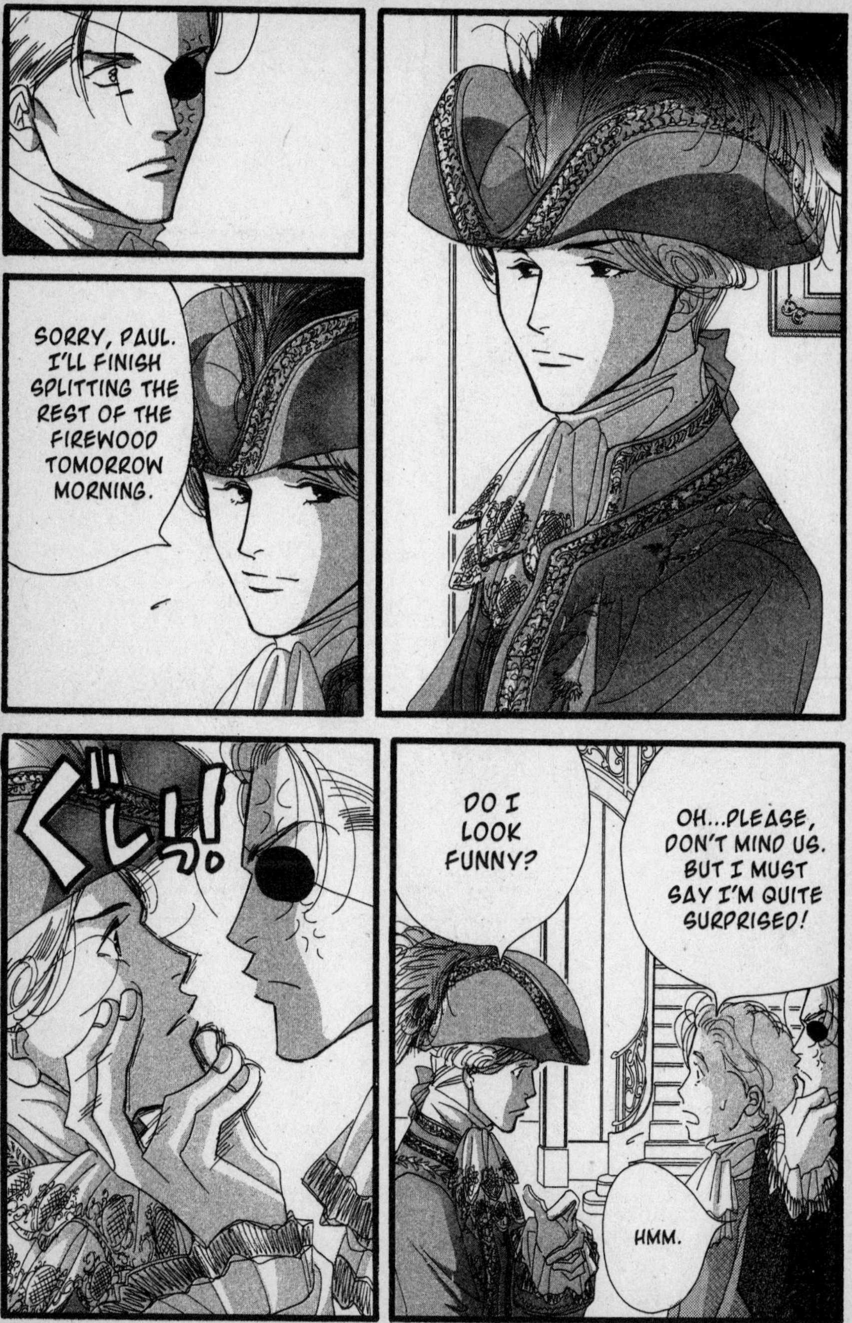
SORRY, PAUL. I'LL FINISH SPLITTING THE REST OF THE FIREWOOD TOMORROW MORNING.
OH...PLEASE, DON'T MIND US. BUT I MUST SAY I'M QUITE SURPRISED!
DO I LOOK FUNNY?
HMM.
ぐいっ!

WHAT ARE YOU DOING?!
IT'S TERRIFYING HOW WELL THIS SUITS YOU.
HUH?!
IT'S TRUE.
I'M REALLY RATHER SHOCKED AT HOW WELL YOU FIT THE SHOES OF A CHILD OF THE NOBILITY, MY LORD COUNT.
IF YOU TAKE AFTER YOUR MOTHER, SHE MUST BE STUNNING.

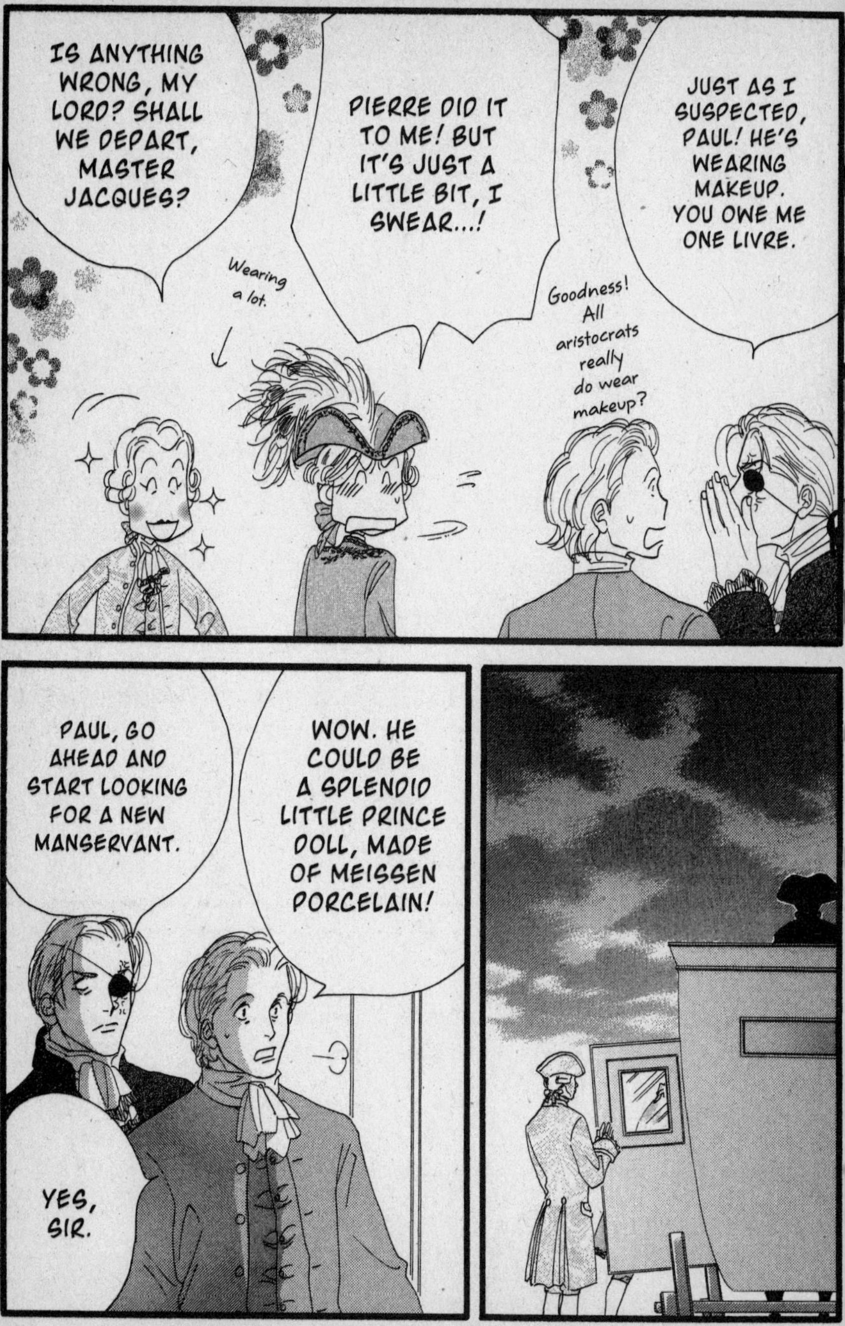
JUST AS I SUSPECTED, PAUL! HE'S WEARING MAKEUP. YOU OWE ME ONE LIVRE.
Goodness! All aristocrats really do wear makeup?
PIERRE DID IT TO ME! BUT IT'S JUST A LITTLE BIT, I SWEAR...!
Wearing a lot.
IS ANYTHING WRONG, MY LORD? SHALL WE DEPART, MASTER JACQUES?
WOW. HE COULD BE A SPLENDID LITTLE PRINCE DOLL, MADE OF MEISSEN PORCELAIN!
PAUL, GO AHEAD AND START LOOKING FOR A NEW MANSERVANT.
YES, SIR.

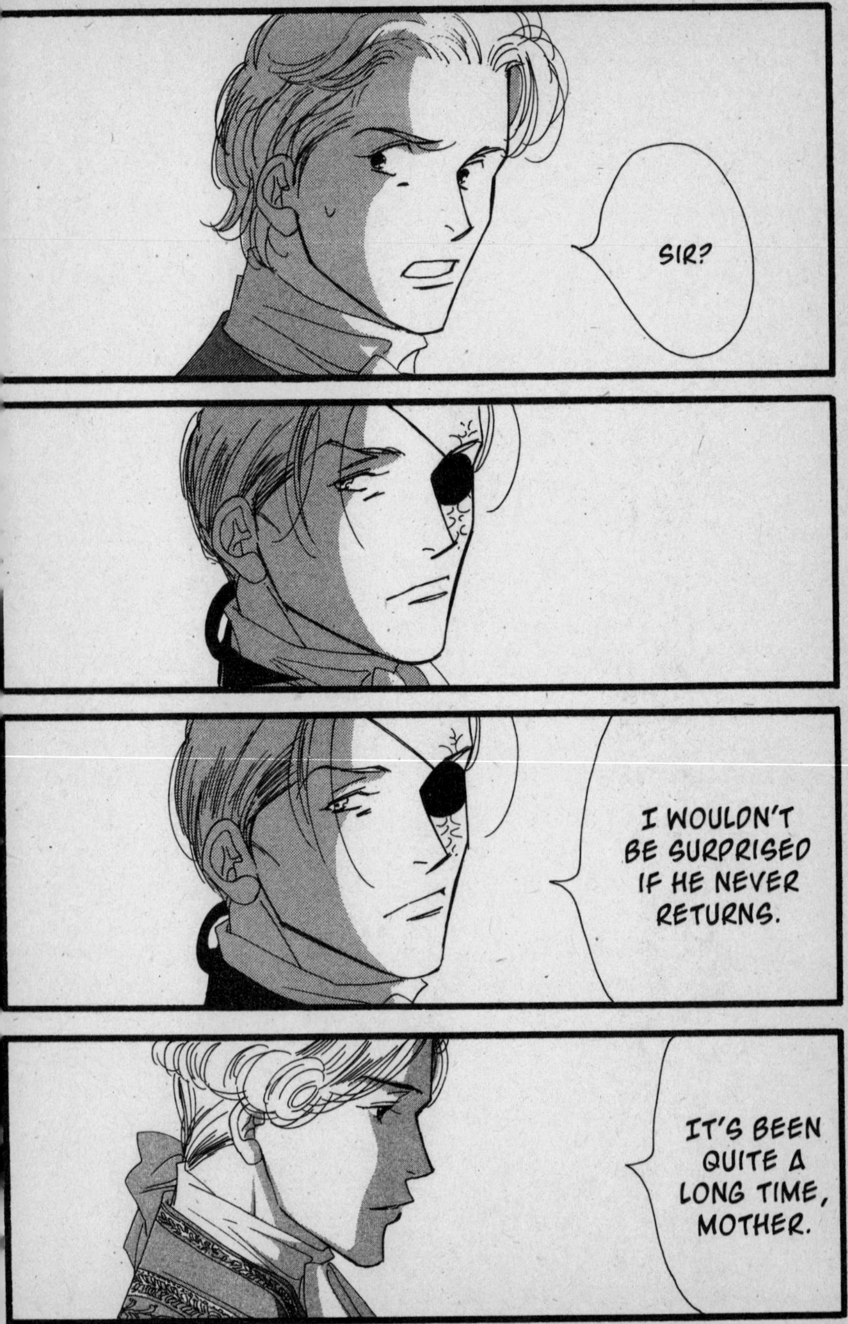
SIR?
I WOULDN'T BE SURPRISED IF HE NEVER RETURNS.
IT'S BEEN QUITE A LONG TIME, MOTHER.

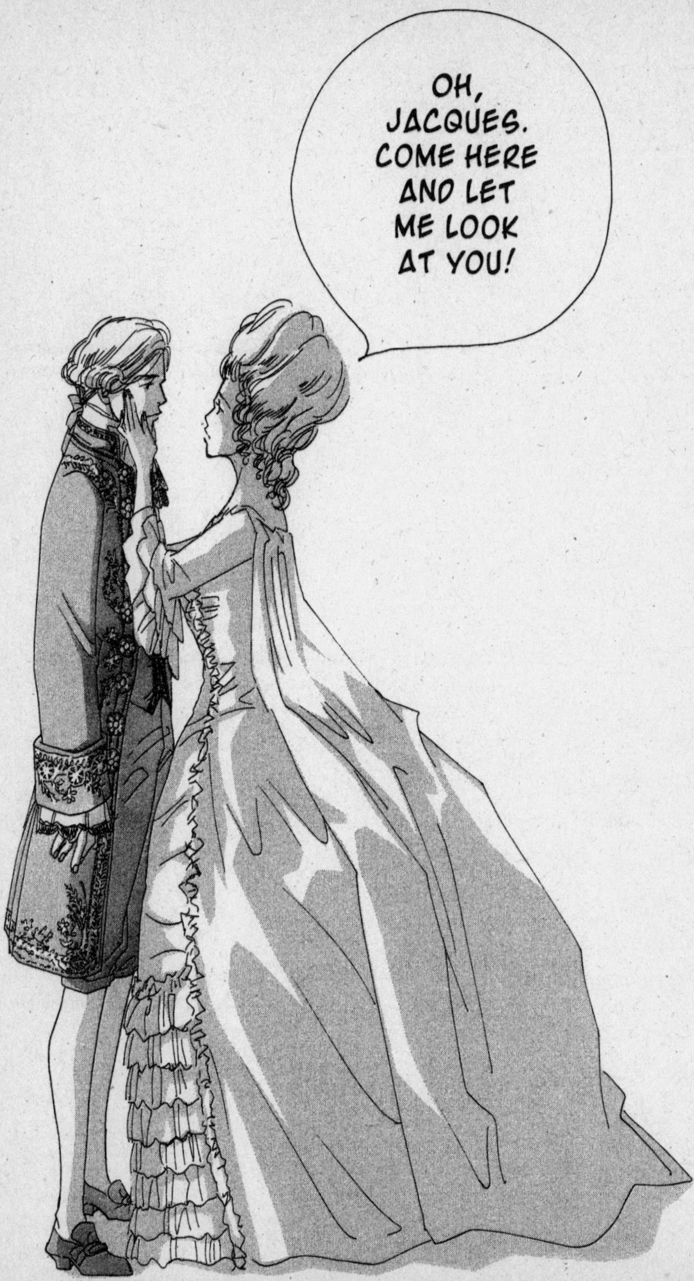
OH, JACQUES. COME HERE AND LET ME LOOK AT YOU!

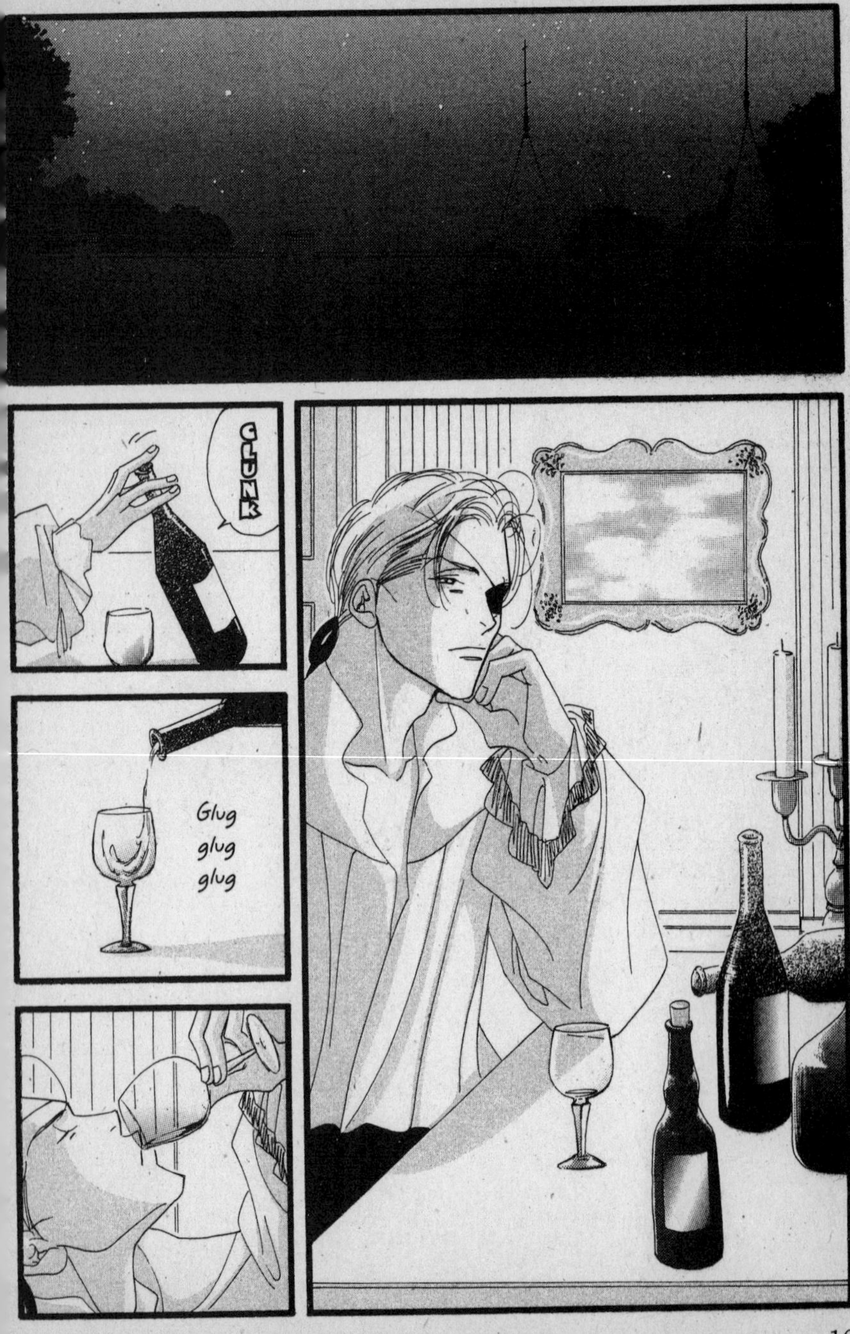
CLUNK
Glug glug glug

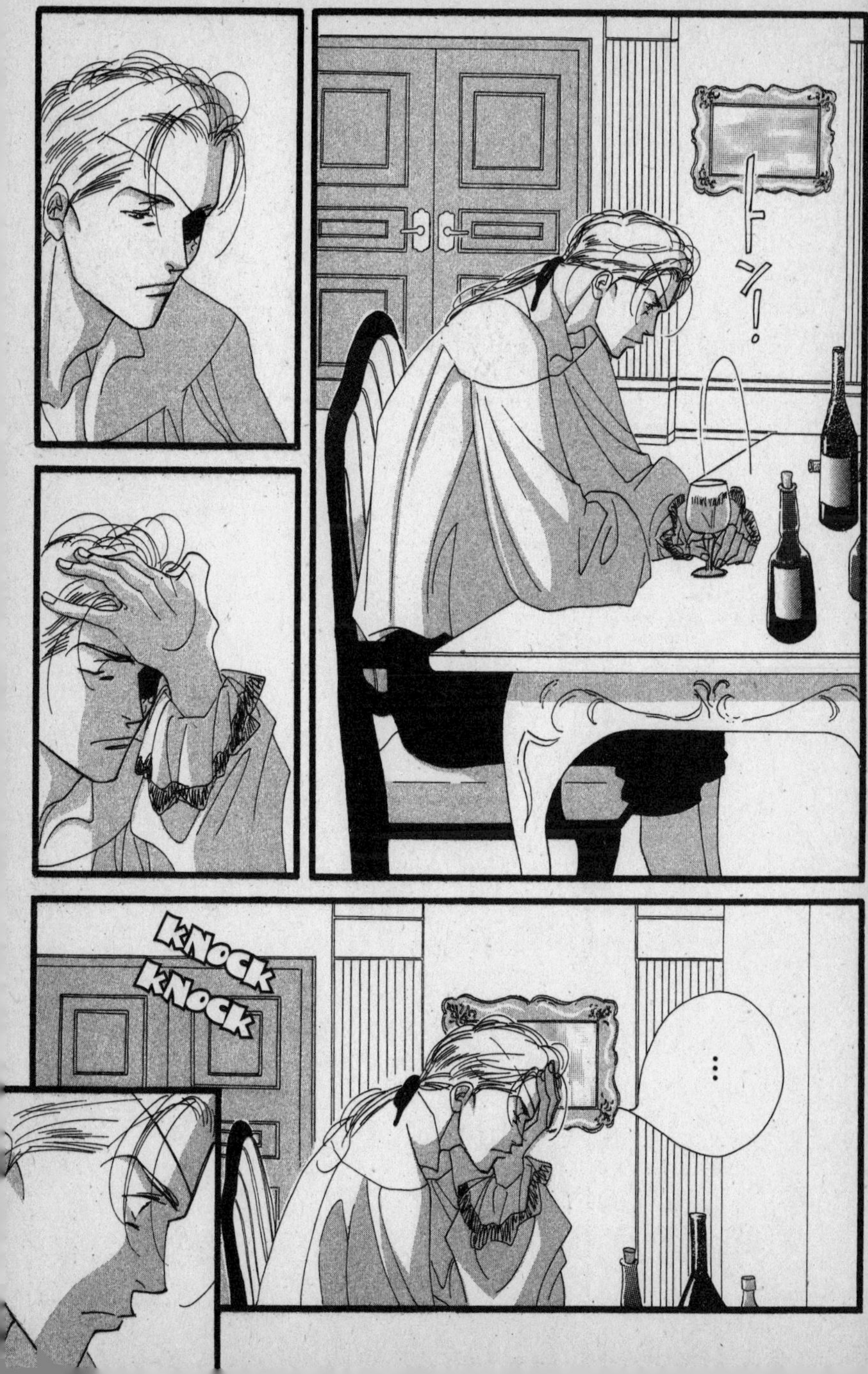

トン!
KNOCK KNOCK
...

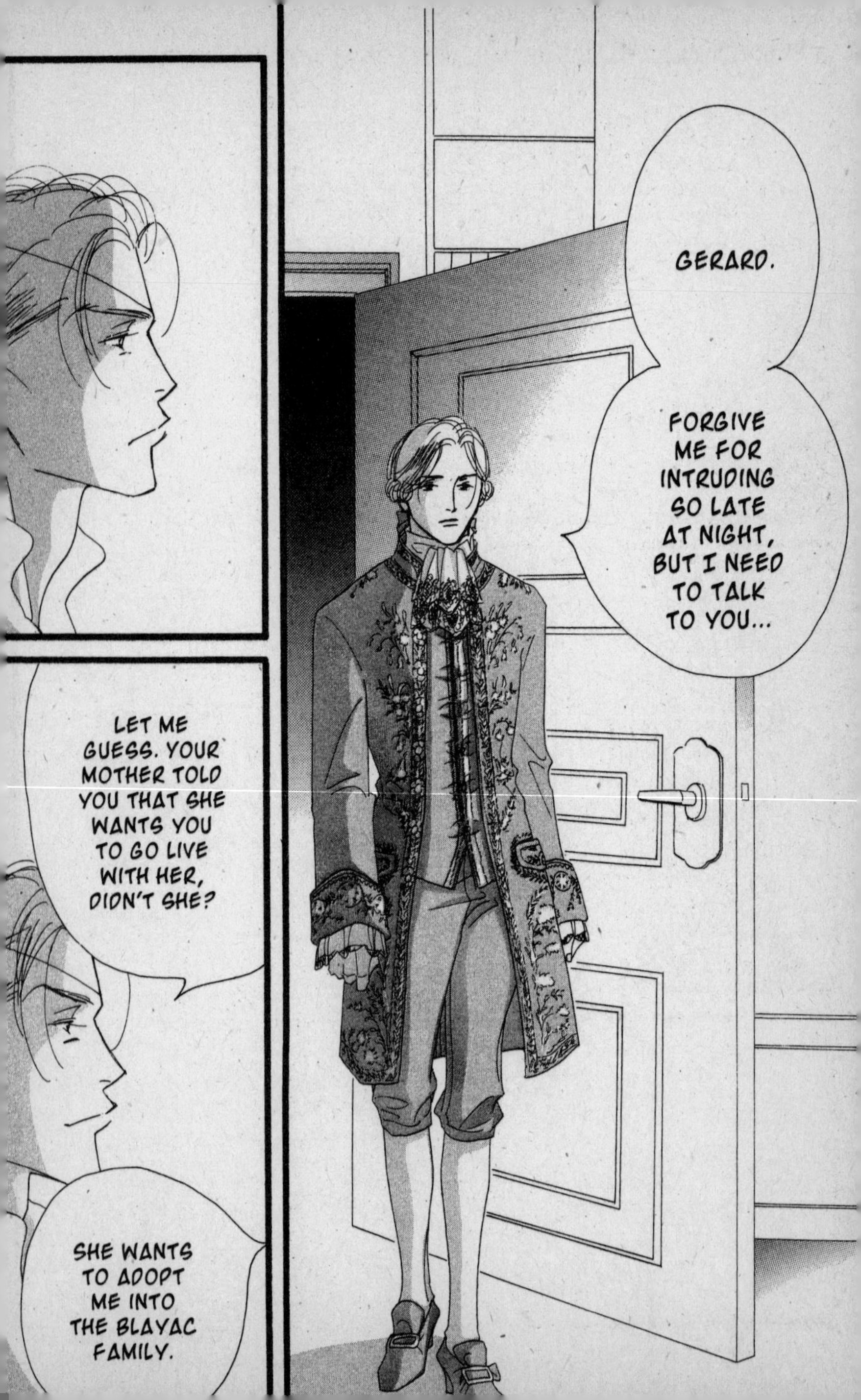
GERARD.
FORGIVE ME FOR INTRUDING SO LATE AT NIGHT, BUT I NEED TO TALK TO YOU...
LET ME GUESS. YOUR MOTHER TOLD YOU THAT SHE WANTS YOU TO GO LIVE WITH HER, DIDN'T SHE?
SHE WANTS TO ADOPT ME INTO THE BLAYAC FAMILY.

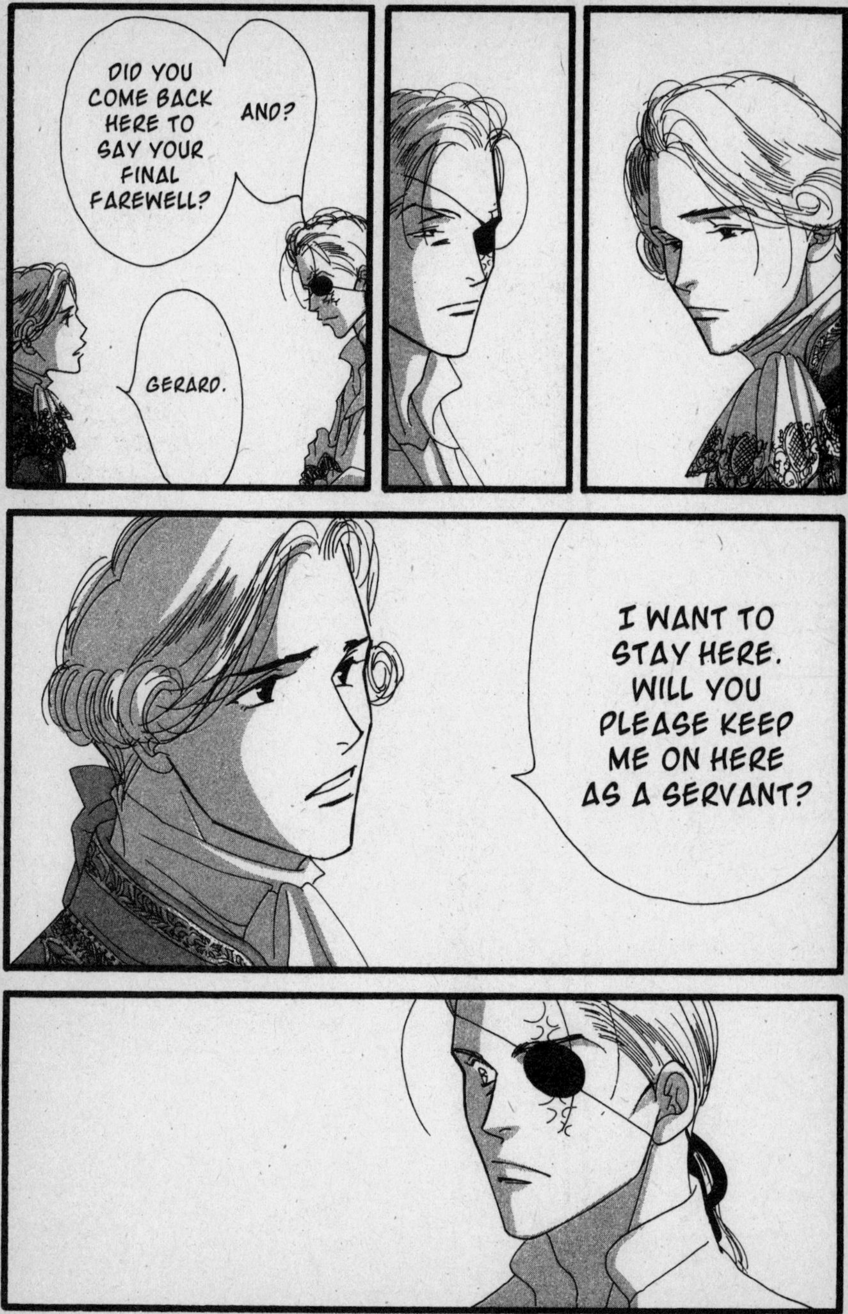
AND?
DID YOU COME BACK HERE TO SAY YOUR FINAL FAREWELL?
GERARD.
I WANT TO STAY HERE. WILL YOU PLEASE KEEP ME ON HERE AS A SERVANT?

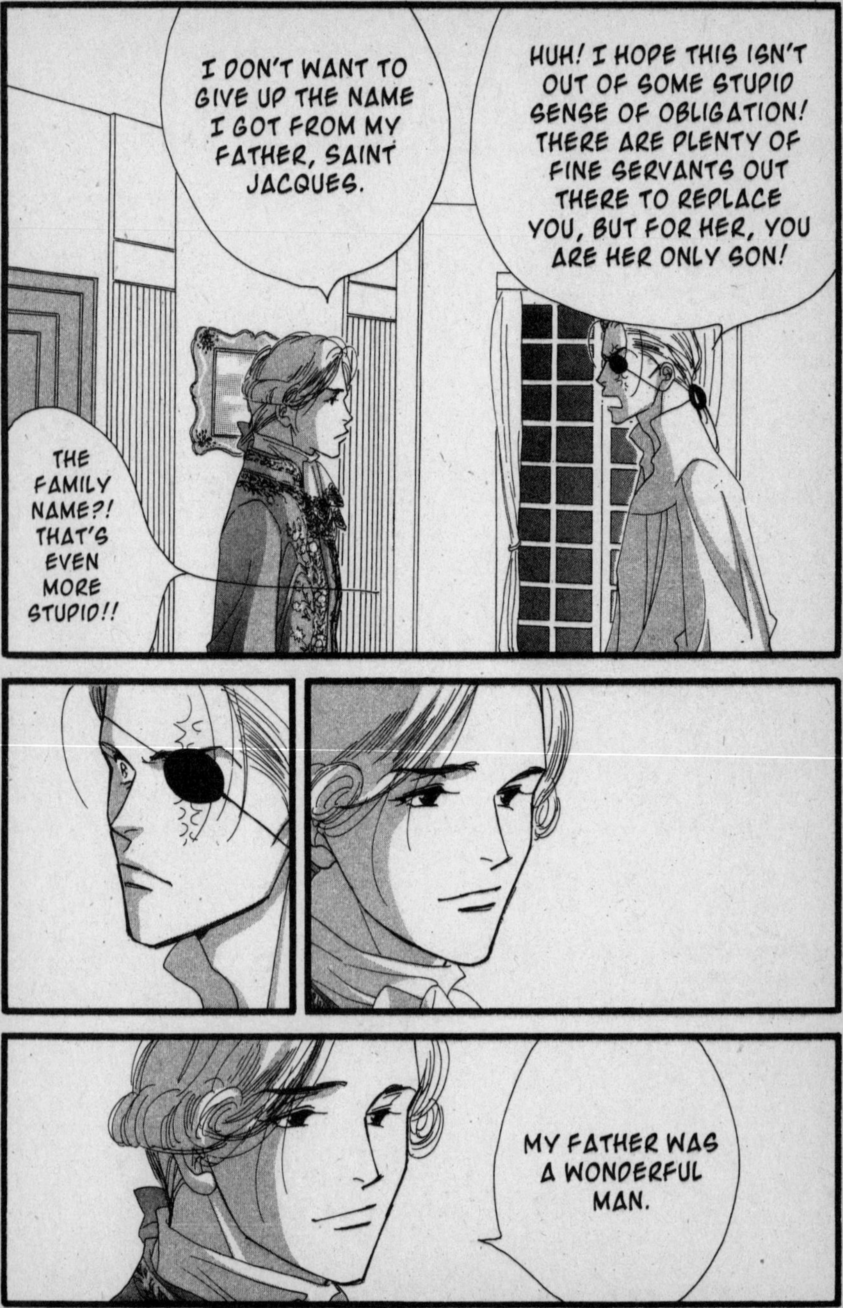
HUH! I HOPE THIS ISN'T OUT OF SOME STUPID SENSE OF OBLIGATION! THERE ARE PLENTY OF FINE SERVANTS OUT THERE TO REPLACE YOU, BUT FOR HER, YOU ARE HER ONLY SON!
I DON'T WANT TO GIVE UP THE NAME I GOT FROM MY FATHER, SAINT JACQUES.
THE FAMILY NAME?! THAT'S EVEN MORE STUPID!!
MY FATHER WAS A WONDERFUL MAN.

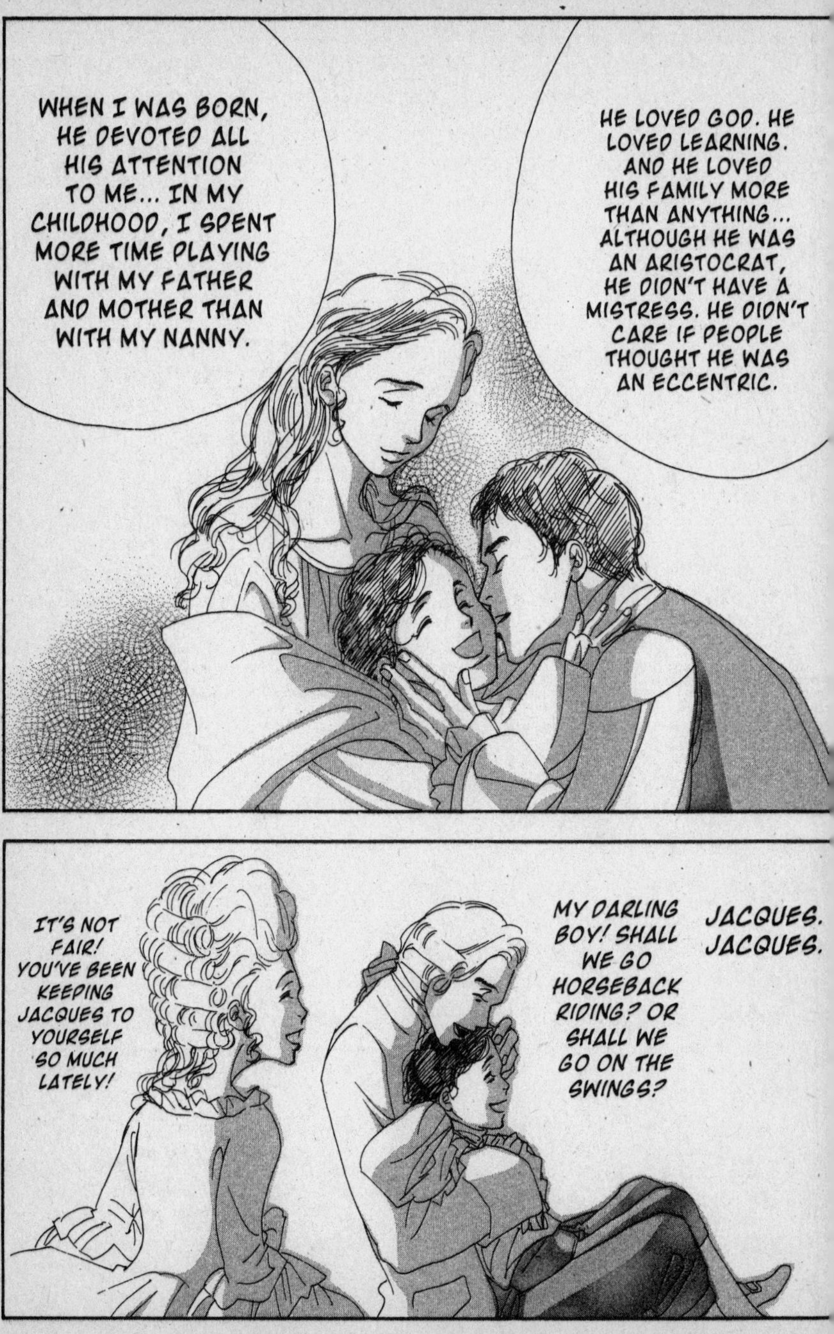
HE LOVED GOD. HE LOVED LEARNING. AND HE LOVED HIS FAMILY MORE THAN ANYTHING... ALTHOUGH HE WAS AN ARISTOCRAT, HE DIDN'T HAVE A MISTRESS. HE DIDN'T CARE IF PEOPLE THOUGHT HE WAS AN ECCENTRIC.
WHEN I WAS BORN, HE DEVOTED ALL HIS ATTENTION TO ME... IN MY CHILDHOOD, I SPENT MORE TIME PLAYING WITH MY FATHER AND MOTHER THAN WITH MY NANNY.
JACQUES. JACQUES.
MY DARLING BOY! SHALL WE GO HORSEBACK RIDING? OR SHALL WE GO ON THE SWINGS?
IT'S NOT FAIR! YOU'VE BEEN KEEPING JACQUES TO YOURSELF SO MUCH LATELY!

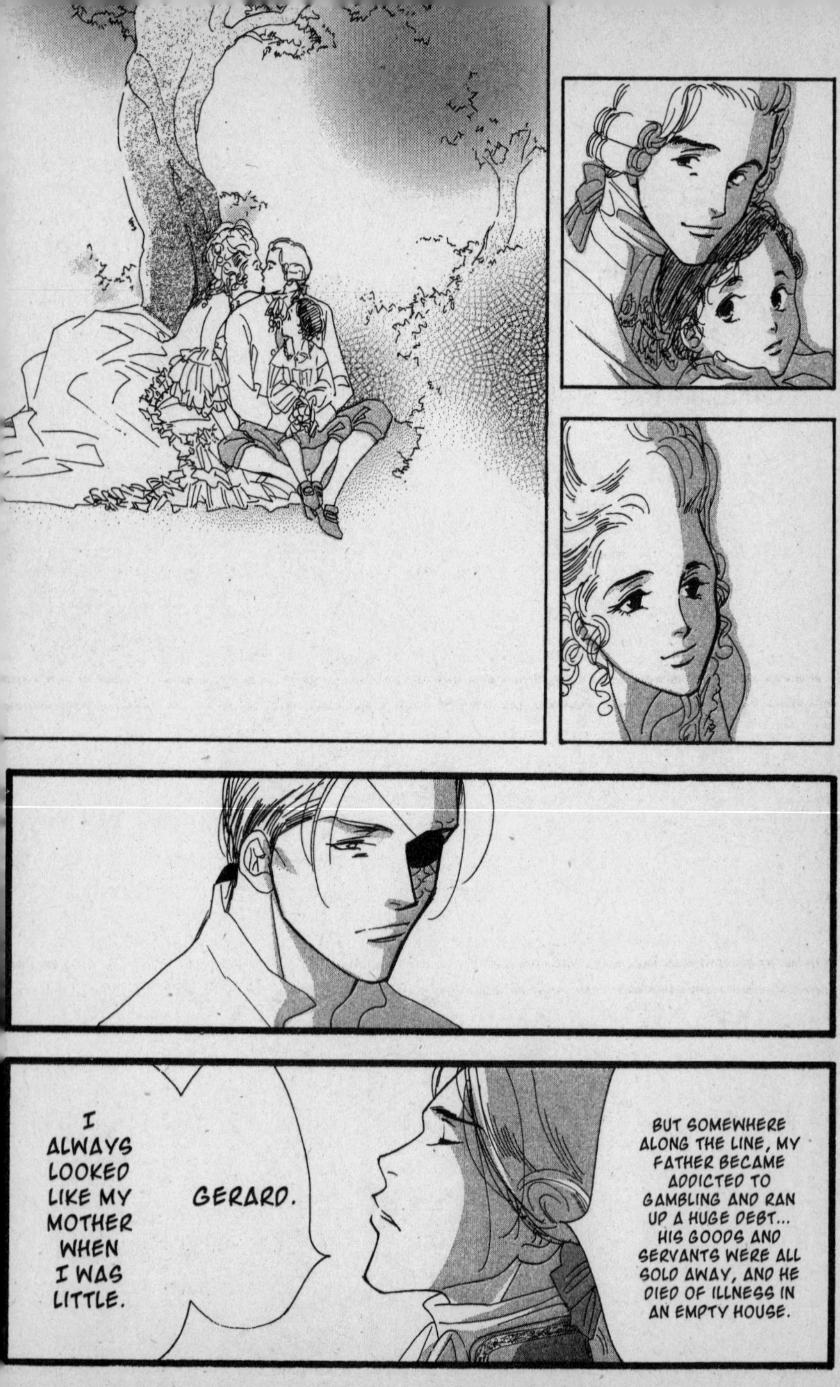
BUT SOMEWHERE ALONG THE LINE, MY FATHER BECAME ADDICTED TO GAMBLING AND RAN UP A HUGE DEBT... HIS GOODS AND SERVANTS WERE ALL SOLD AWAY, AND HE DIED OF ILLNESS IN AN EMPTY HOUSE.
GERARD.
I ALWAYS LOOKED LIKE MY MOTHER WHEN I WAS LITTLE.

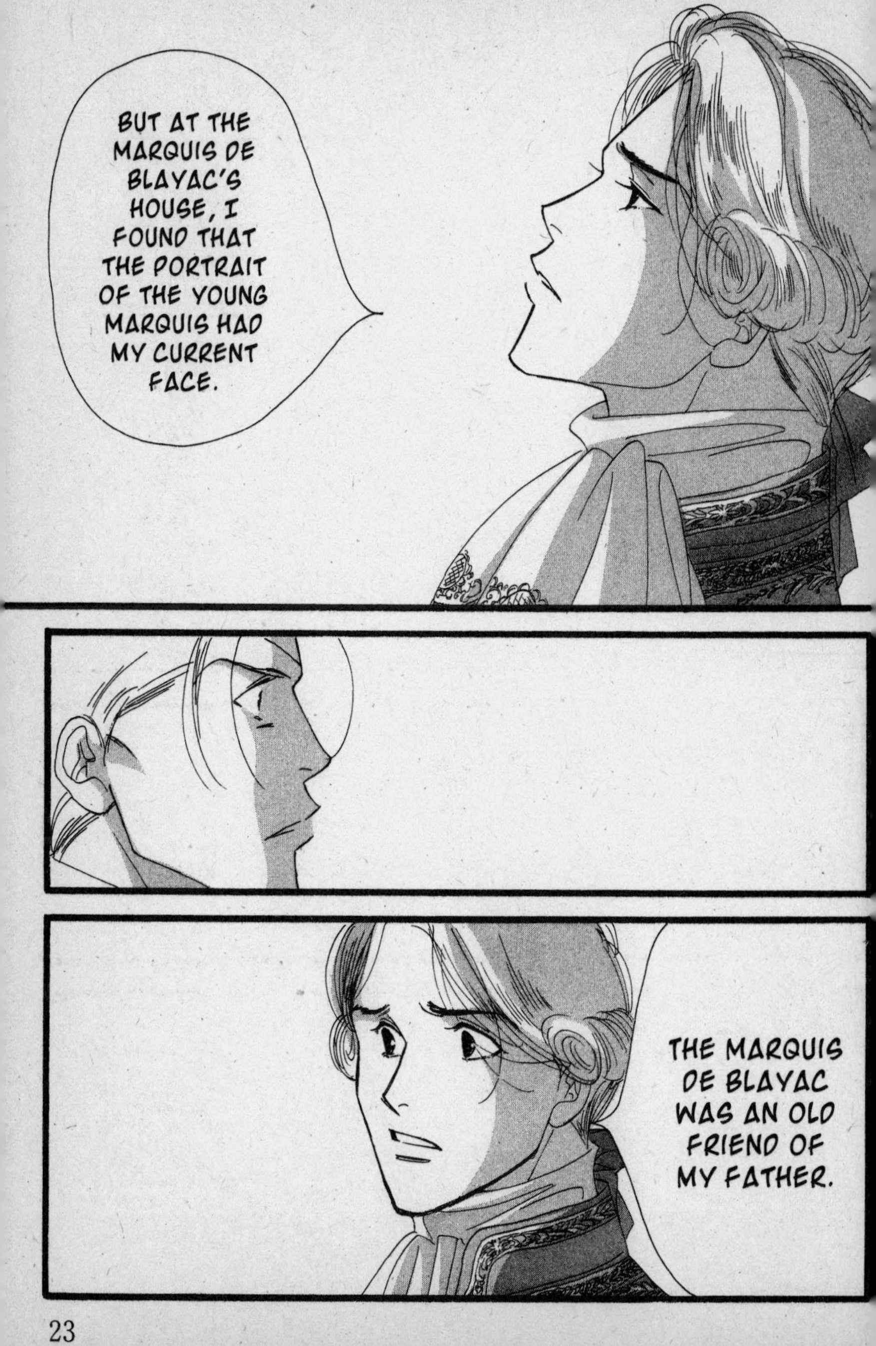
BUT AT THE MARQUIS DE BLAYAC'S HOUSE, I FOUND THAT THE PORTRAIT OF THE YOUNG MARQUIS HAD MY CURRENT FACE.
THE MARQUIS DE BLAYAC WAS AN OLD FRIEND OF MY FATHER.

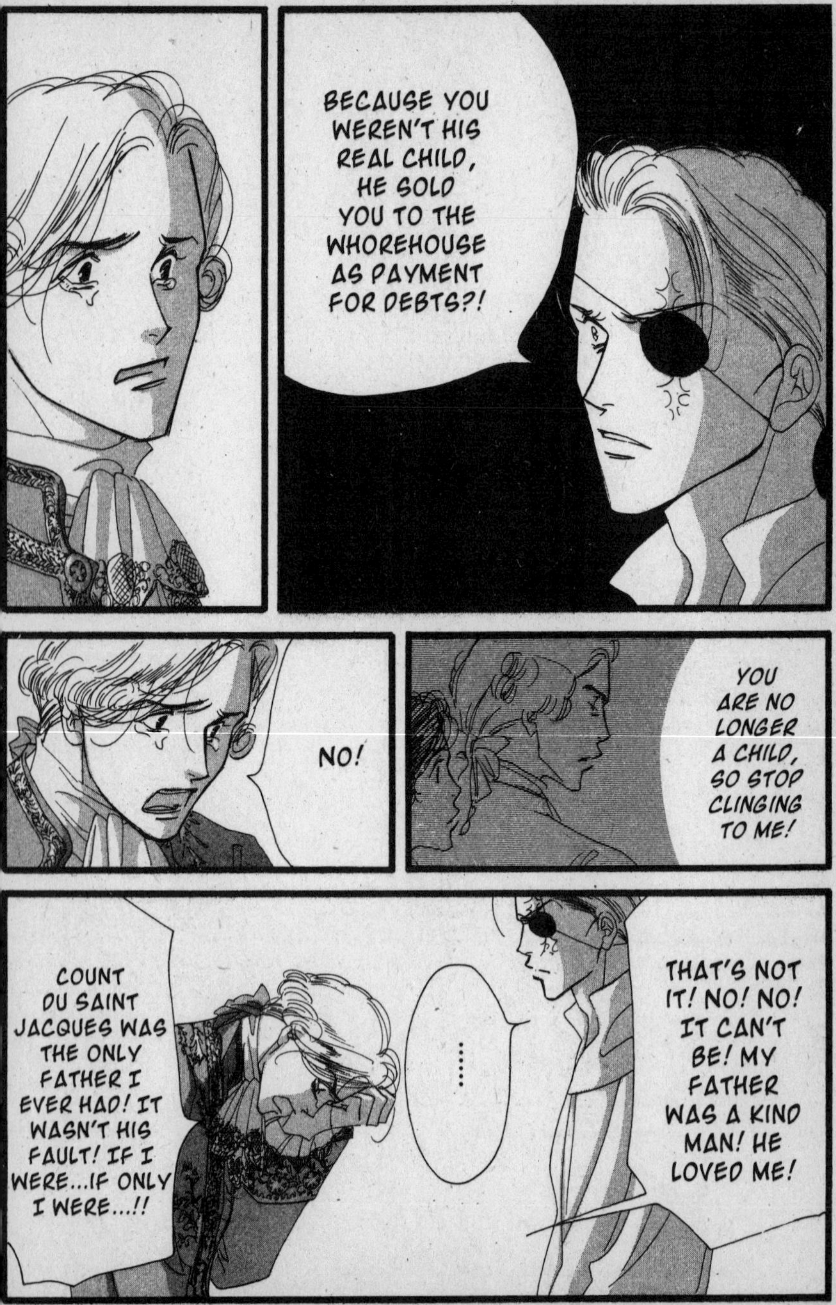
BECAUSE YOU WEREN'T HIS REAL CHILD, HE SOLD YOU TO THE WHOREHOUSE AS PAYMENT FOR DEBTS?!
YOU ARE NO LONGER A CHILD, SO STOP CLINGING TO ME!
NO!
THAT'S NOT IT! NO! NO! IT CAN'T BE! MY FATHER WAS A KIND MAN! HE LOVED ME!
......
COUNT DU SAINT JACQUES WAS THE ONLY FATHER I EVER HAD! IT WASN'T HIS FAULT! IF I WERE...IF ONLY I WERE...!!

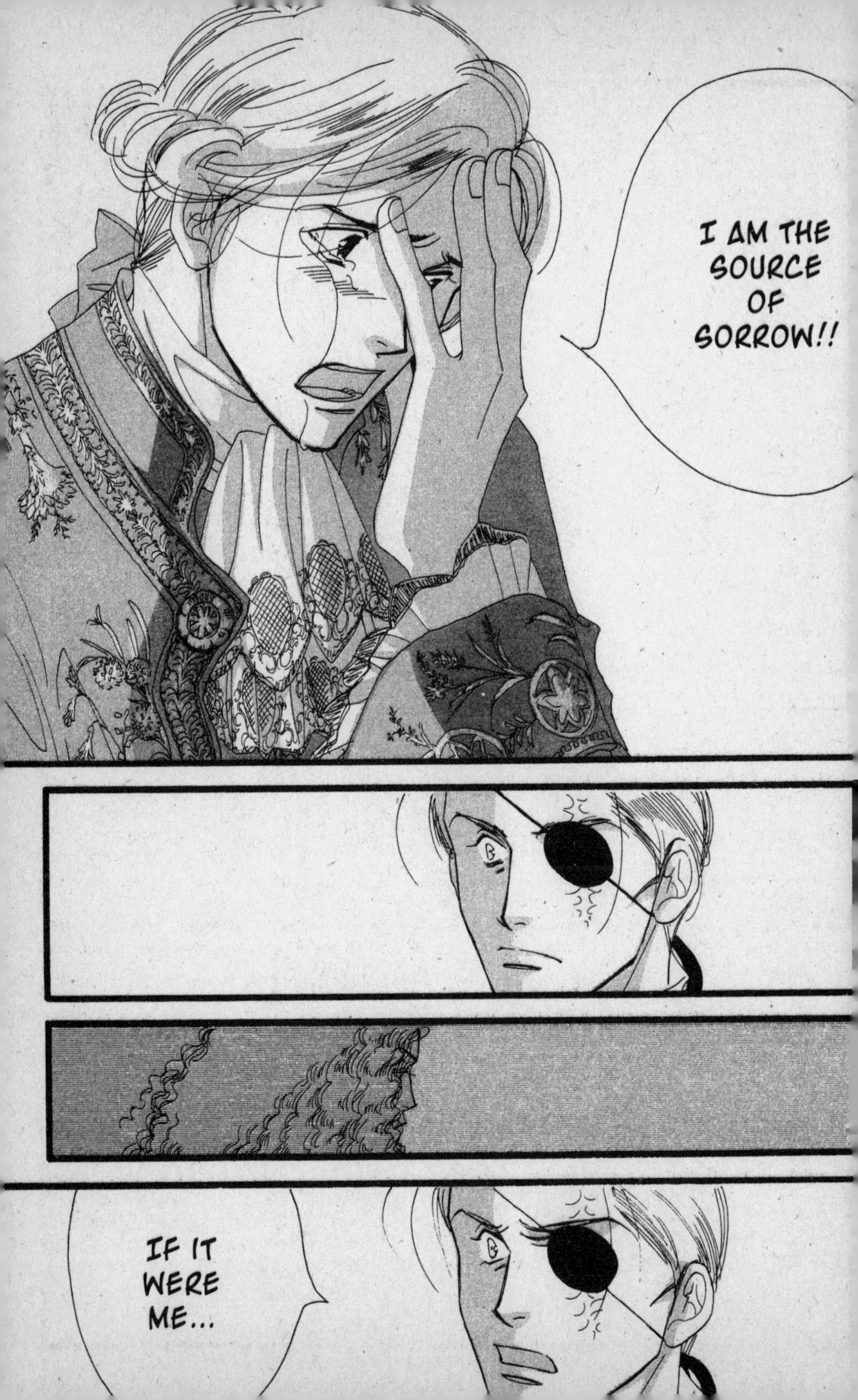
I AM THE SOURCE OF SORROW!!
IF IT WERE ME...

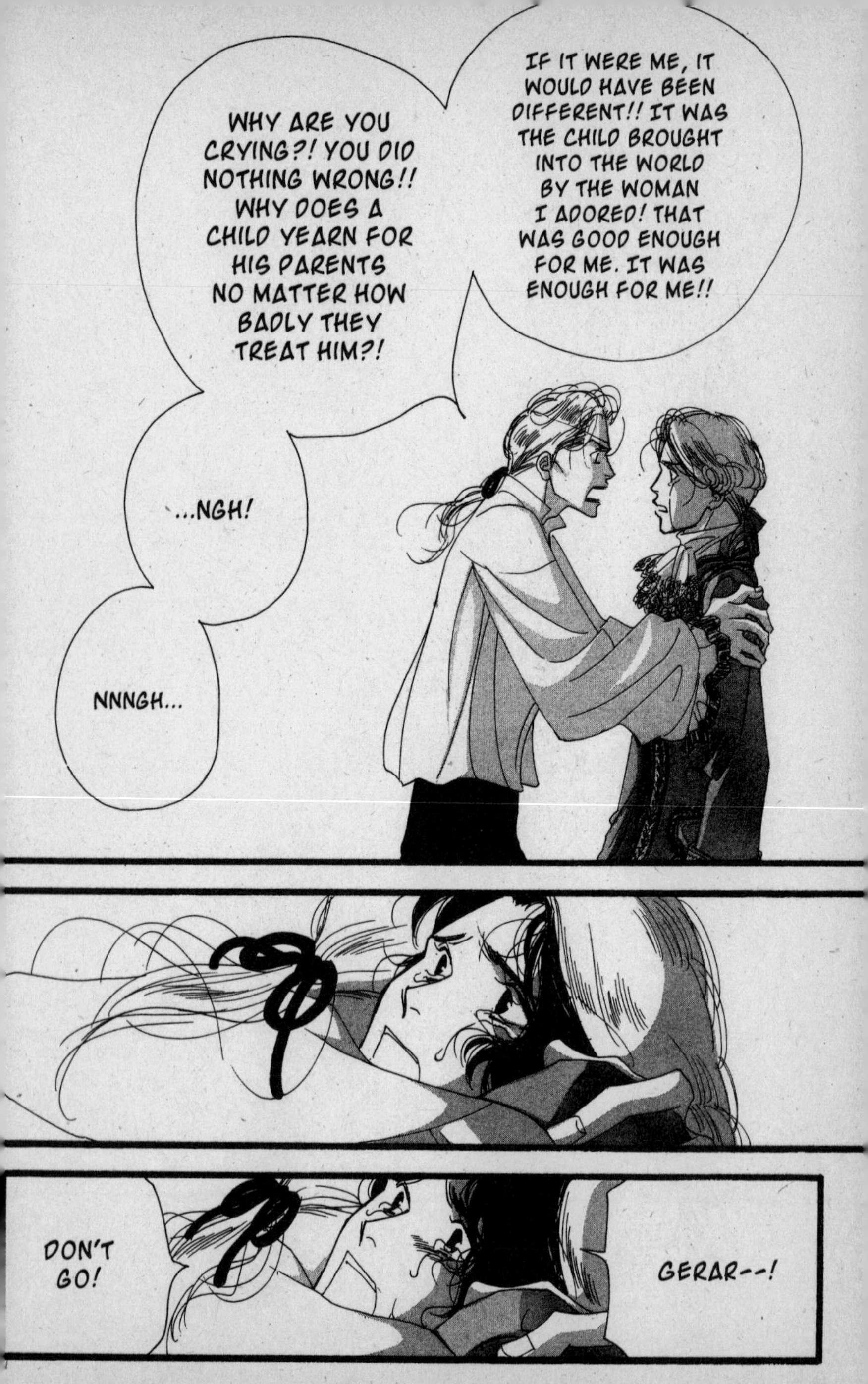
IF IT WERE ME, IT WOULD HAVE BEEN DIFFERENT!! IT WAS THE CHILD BROUGHT INTO THE WORLD BY THE WOMAN I ADORED! THAT WAS GOOD ENOUGH FOR ME. IT WAS ENOUGH FOR ME!!
WHY ARE YOU CRYING?! YOU DID NOTHING WRONG!! WHY DOES A CHILD YEARN FOR HIS PARENTS NO MATTER HOW BADLY THEY TREAT HIM?!
...NGH!
NNNGH...
GERAR--!
DON'T GO!

I WON'T LET YOU GO! MORE THAN YOUR REAL FATHER, MORE THAN YOUR REAL MOTHER, I PROMISE I'LL LOVE YOU THE MOST!

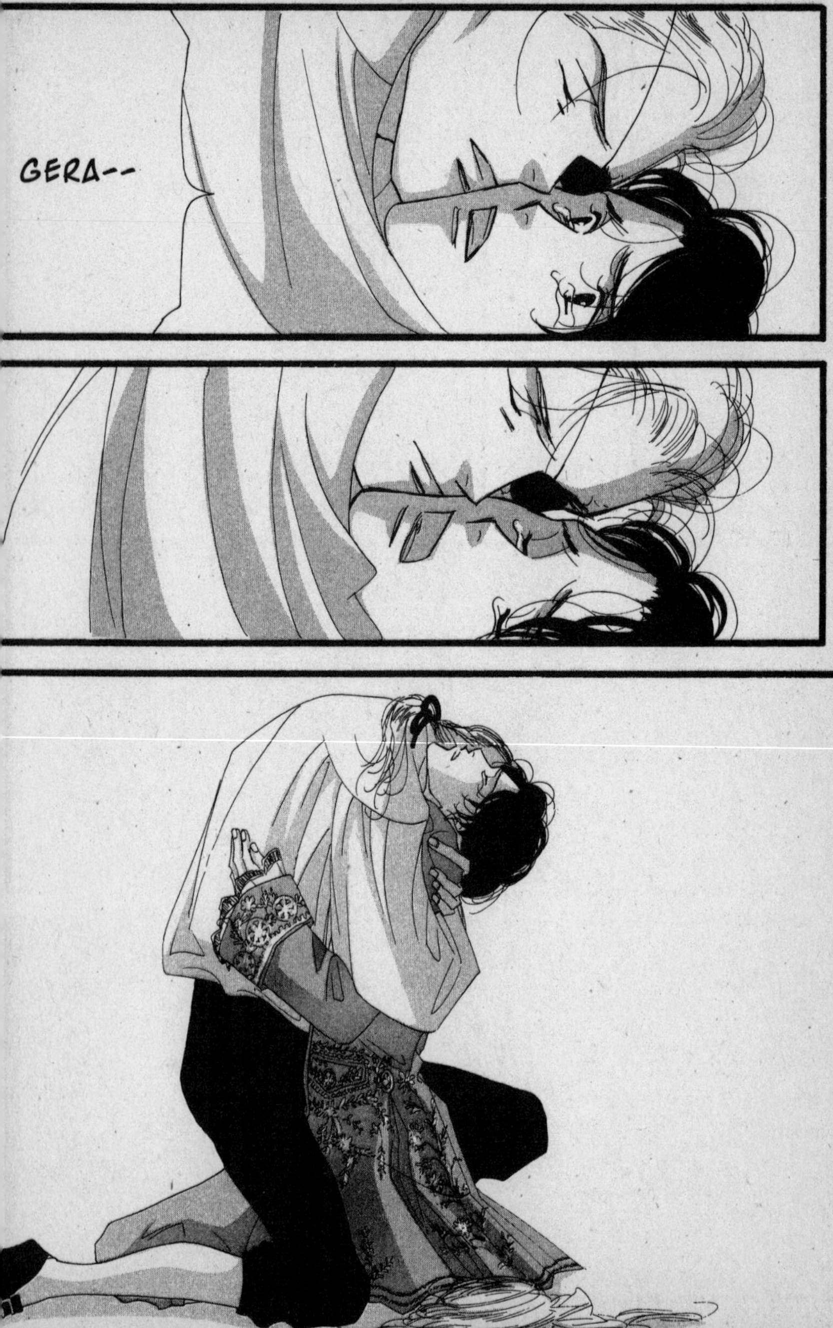
GERA--

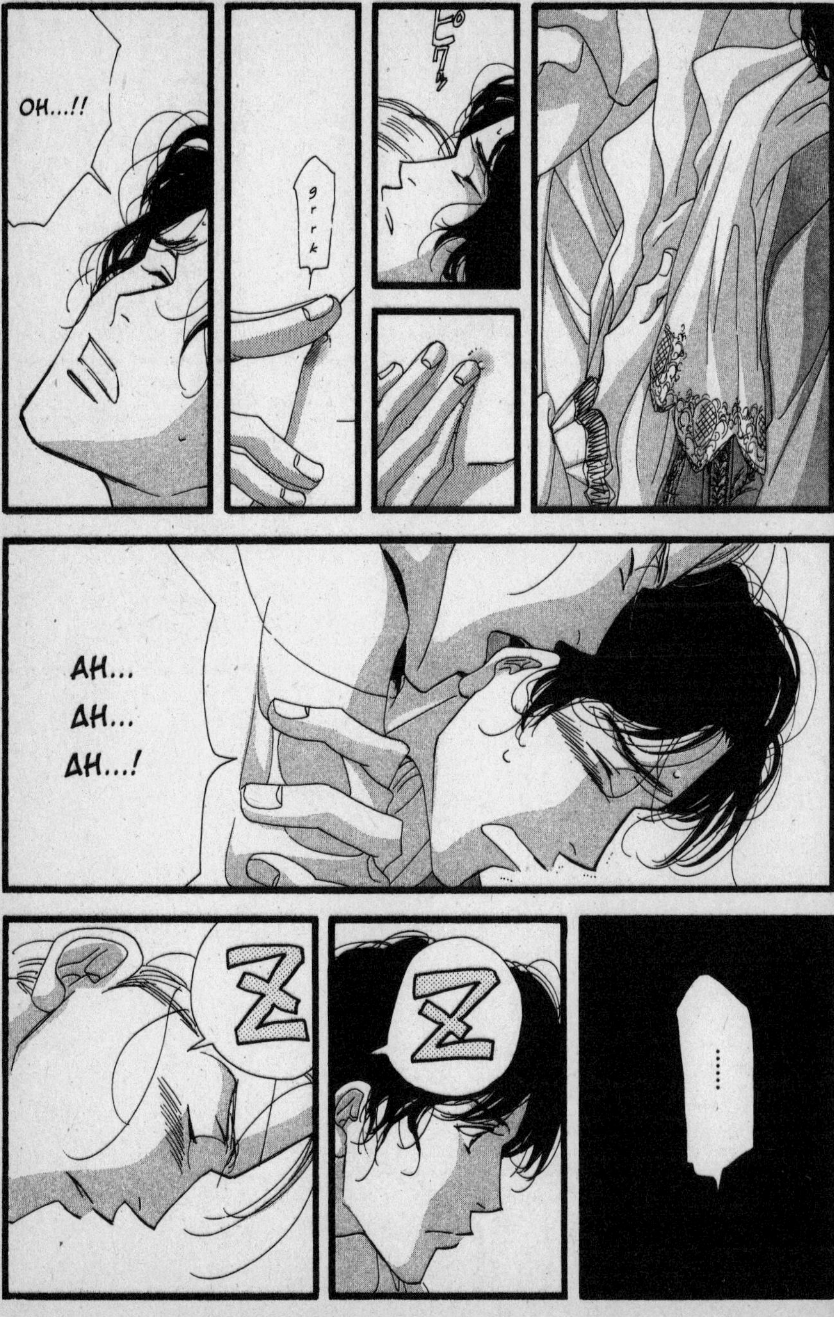

ピクッ
grrk
OH...!!
AH...
AH...
AH...!
......
Z
Z

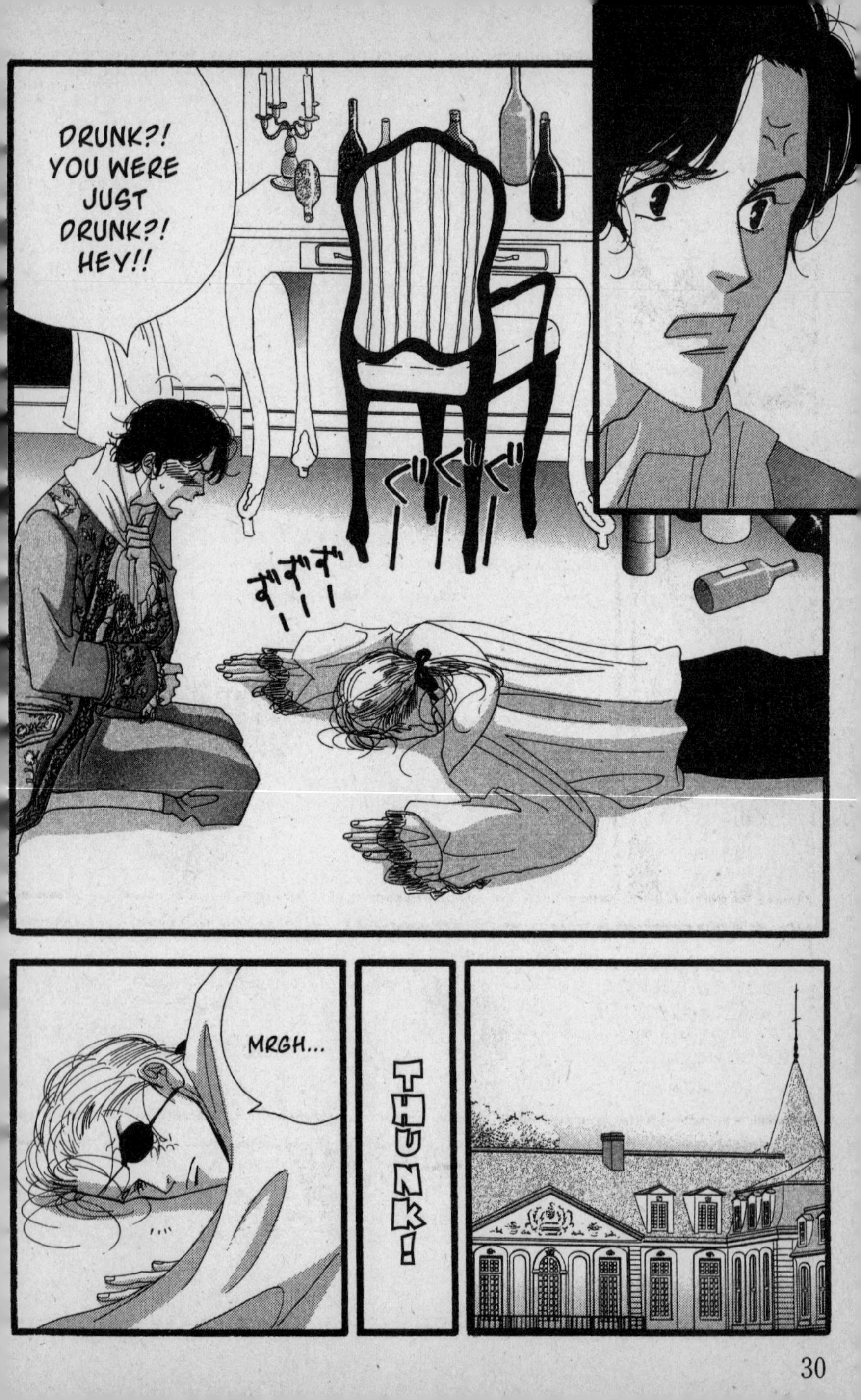
DRUNK?! YOU WERE JUST DRUNK?! HEY!!
ぐぐぐ
ずずず
THUNK!
MRGH...

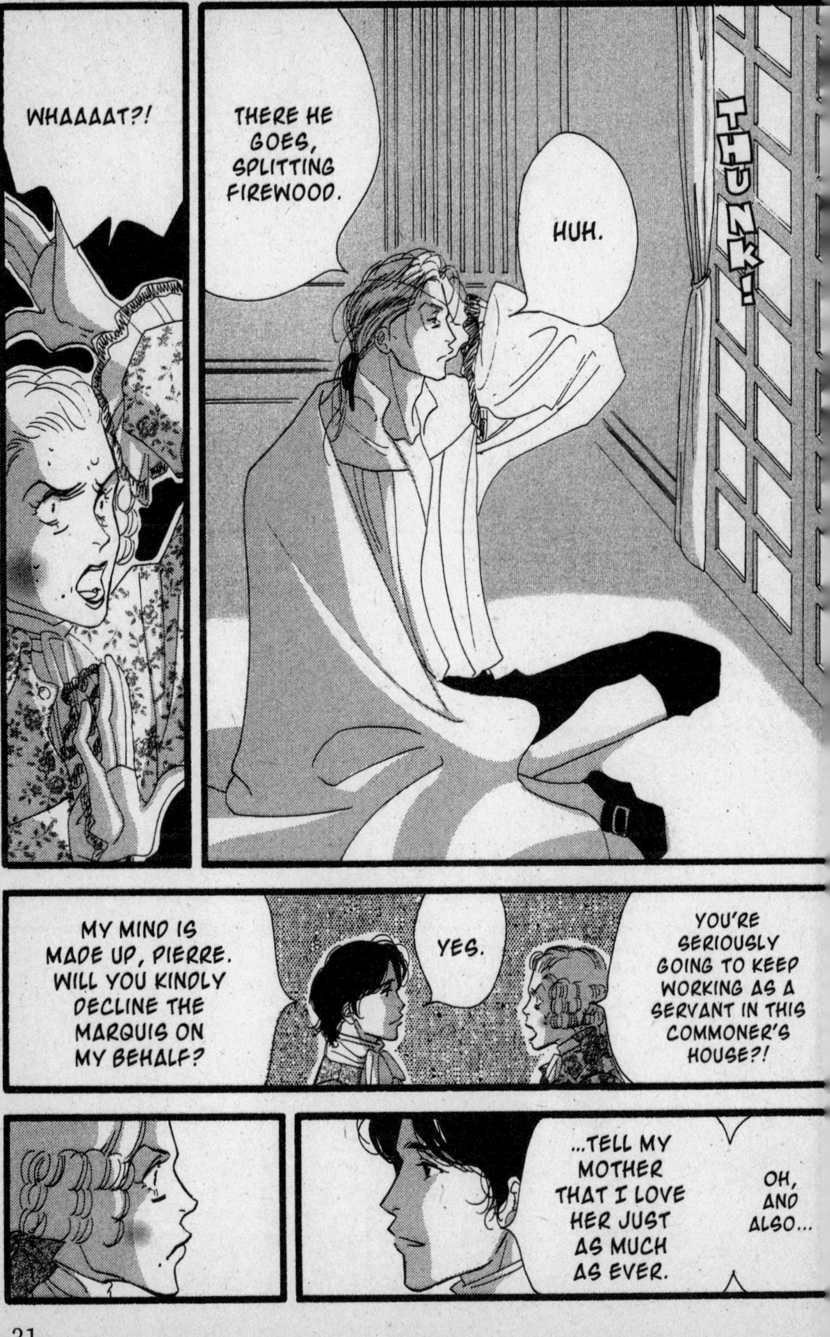
THUNK!
HUH.
THERE HE GOES, SPLITTING FIREWOOD.
WHAAAAT?!
YOU'RE SERIOUSLY GOING TO KEEP WORKING AS A SERVANT IN THIS COMMONER'S HOUSE?!
YES.
MY MIND IS MADE UP, PIERRE. WILL YOU KINDLY DECLINE THE MARQUIS ON MY BEHALF?
OH, AND ALSO...
...TELL MY MOTHER THAT I LOVE HER JUST AS MUCH AS EVER.

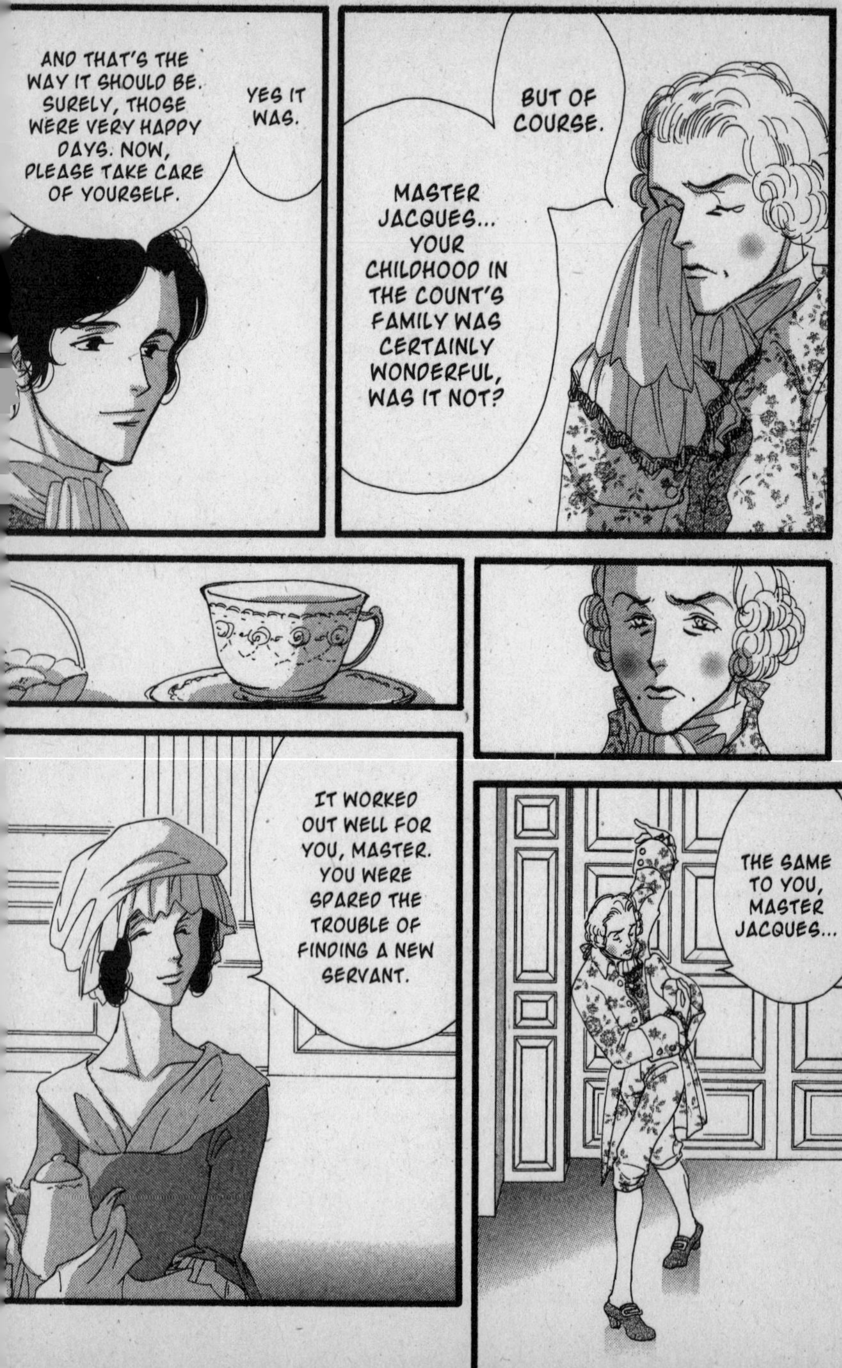
BUT OF COURSE.
MASTER JACQUES... YOUR CHILDHOOD IN THE COUNT'S FAMILY WAS CERTAINLY WONDERFUL, WAS IT NOT?
YES IT WAS.
AND THAT'S THE WAY IT SHOULD BE. SURELY, THOSE WERE VERY HAPPY DAYS. NOW, PLEASE TAKE CARE OF YOURSELF.
THE SAME TO YOU, MASTER JACQUES...
IT WORKED OUT WELL FOR YOU, MASTER. YOU WERE SPARED THE TROUBLE OF FINDING A NEW SERVANT.

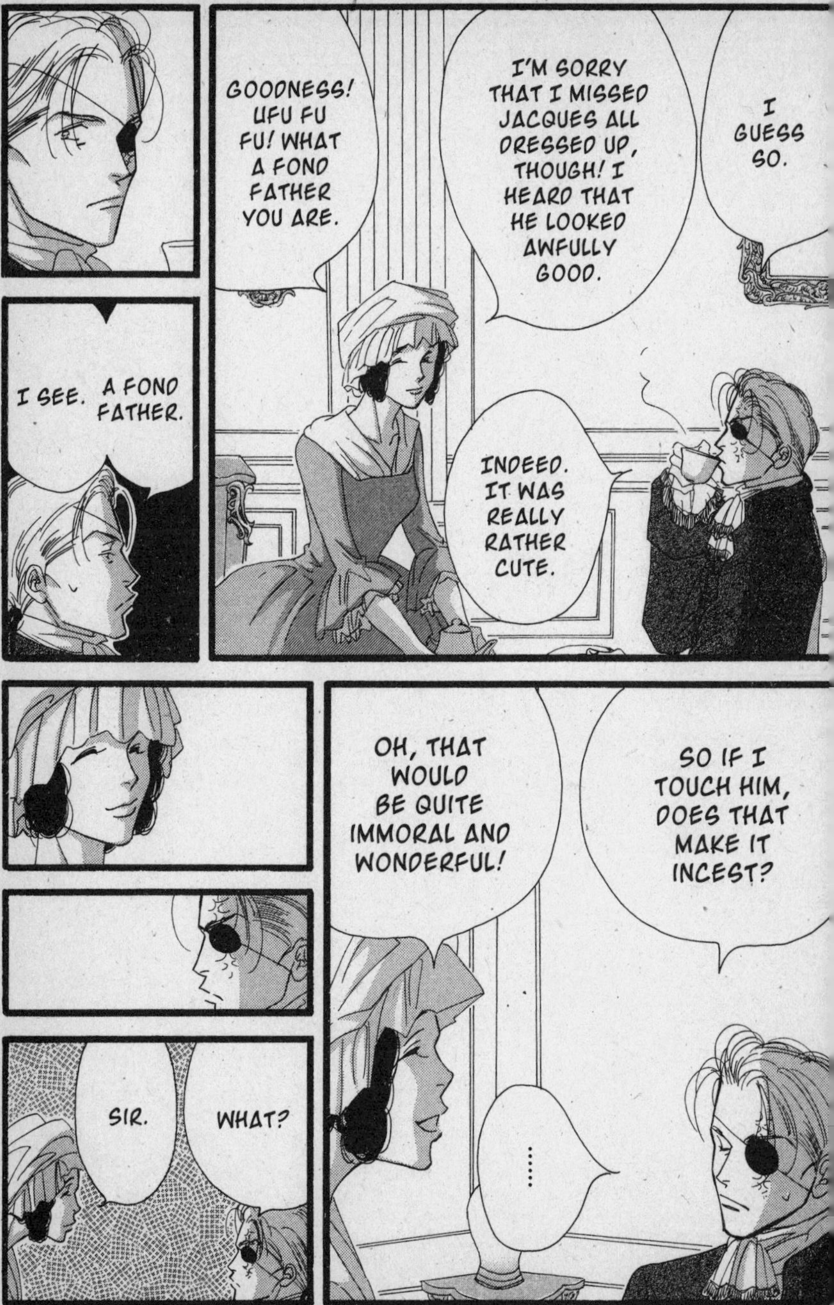
I GUESS SO.
I'M SORRY THAT I MISSED JACQUES ALL DRESSED UP, THOUGH! I HEARD THAT HE LOOKED AWFULLY GOOD.
GOODNESS! UFU FU FU! WHAT A FOND FATHER YOU ARE.
INDEED. IT WAS REALLY RATHER CUTE.
I SEE. A FOND FATHER.
SO IF I TOUCH HIM, DOES THAT MAKE IT INCEST?
OH, THAT WOULD BE QUITE IMMORAL AND WONDERFUL!
......
WHAT?
SIR.

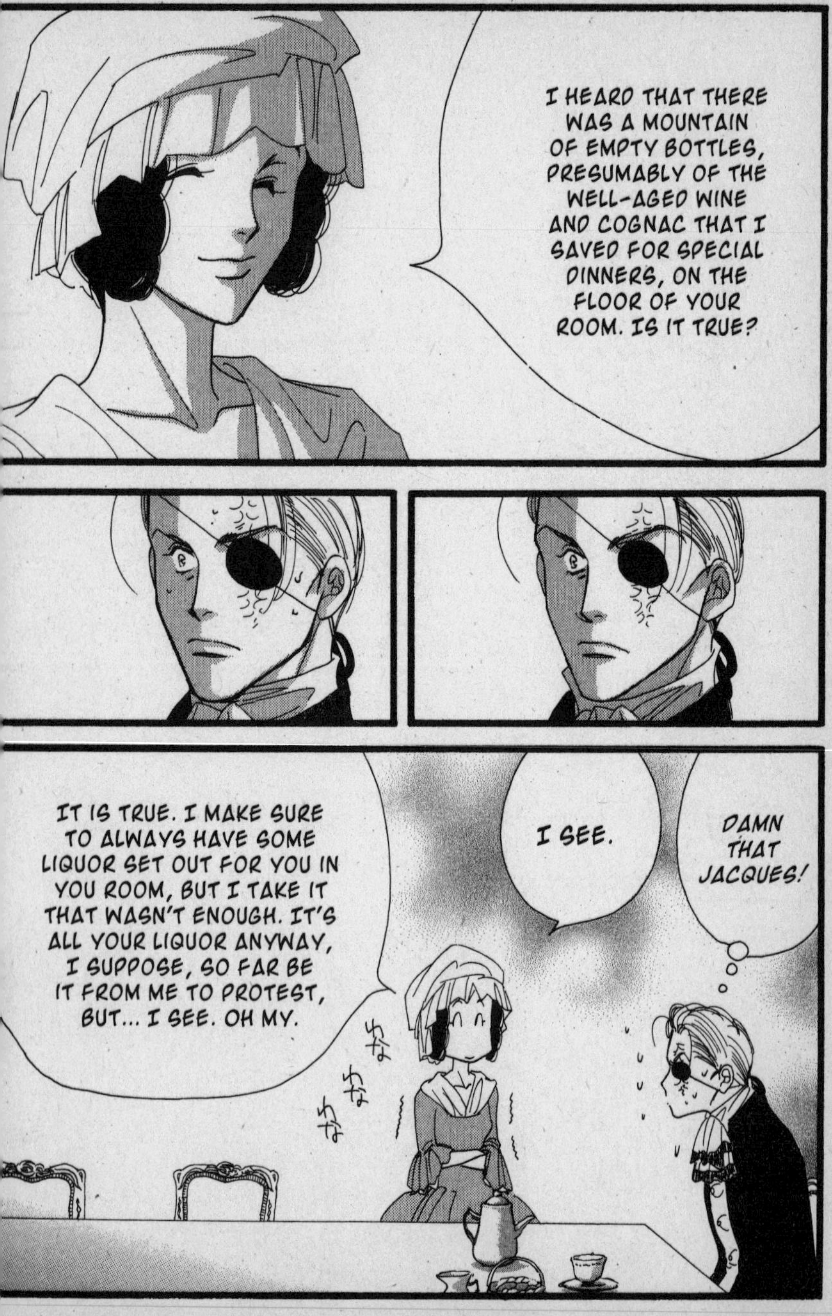
I HEARD THAT THERE WAS A MOUNTAIN OF EMPTY BOTTLES, PRESUMABLY OF THE WELL-AGED WINE AND COGNAC THAT I SAVED FOR SPECIAL DINNERS, ON THE FLOOR OF YOUR ROOM. IS IT TRUE?
DAMN THAT JACQUES!
I SEE.
IT IS TRUE. I MAKE SURE TO ALWAYS HAVE SOME LIQUOR SET OUT FOR YOU IN YOU ROOM, BUT I TAKE IT THAT WASN'T ENOUGH. IT'S ALL YOUR LIQUOR ANYWAY, I SUPPOSE, SO FAR BE IT FROM ME TO PROTEST, BUT... I SEE. OH MY.

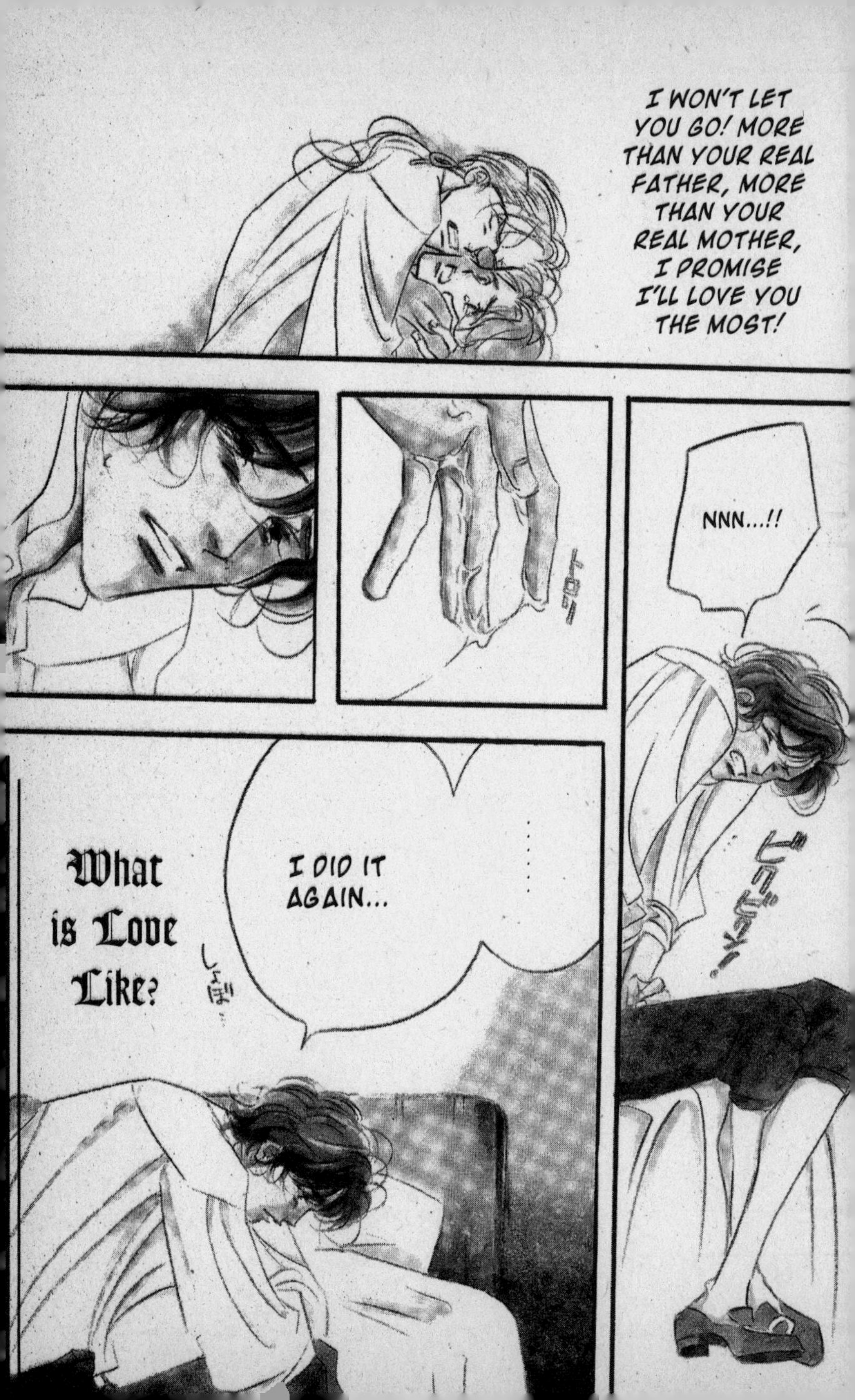
I WON'T LET YOU GO! MORE THAN YOUR REAL FATHER, MORE THAN YOUR REAL MOTHER, I PROMISE I'LL LOVE YOU THE MOST!
NNN...!!
I DID IT AGAIN...
.....
What is Love Like?

What is Love Like?

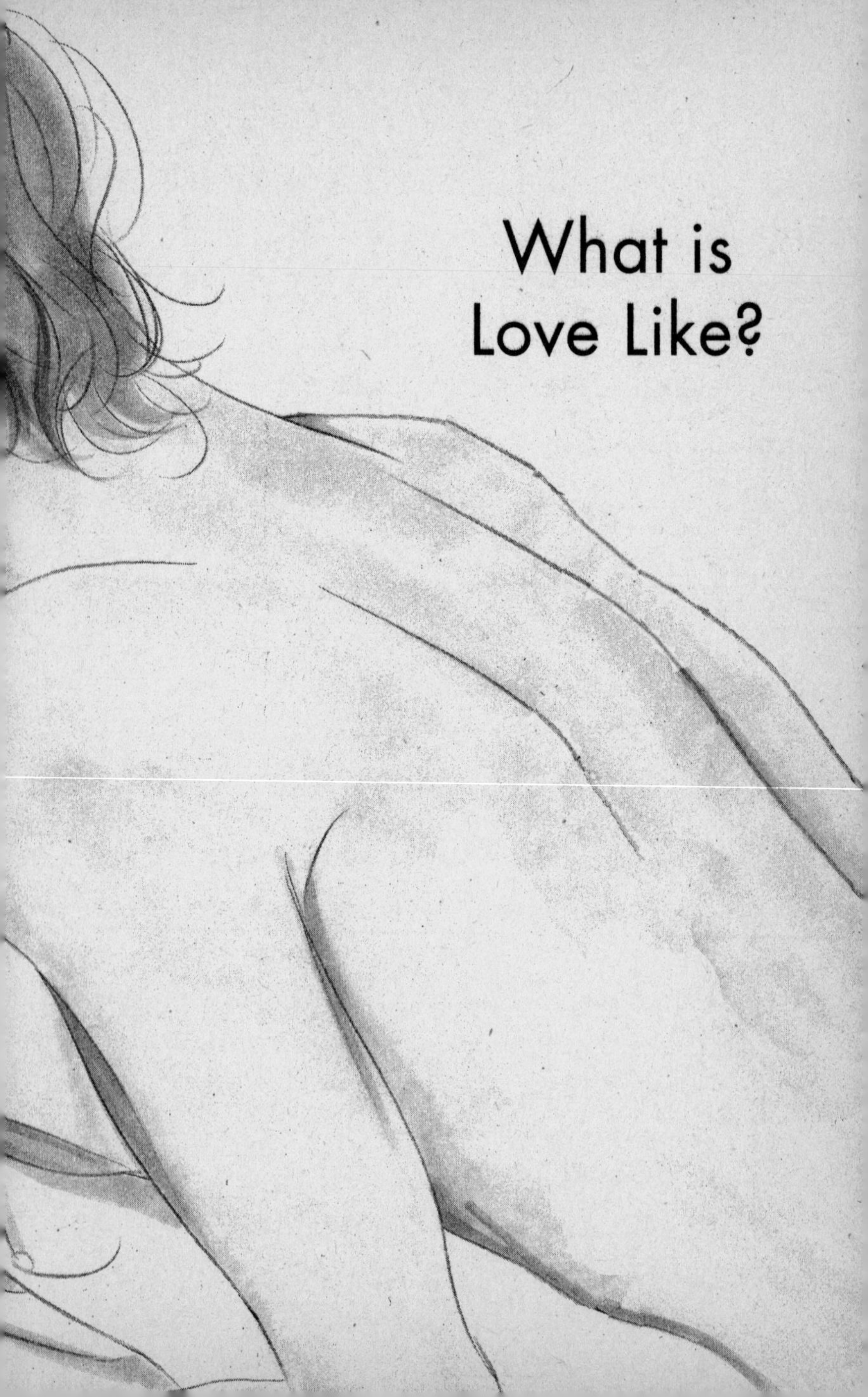

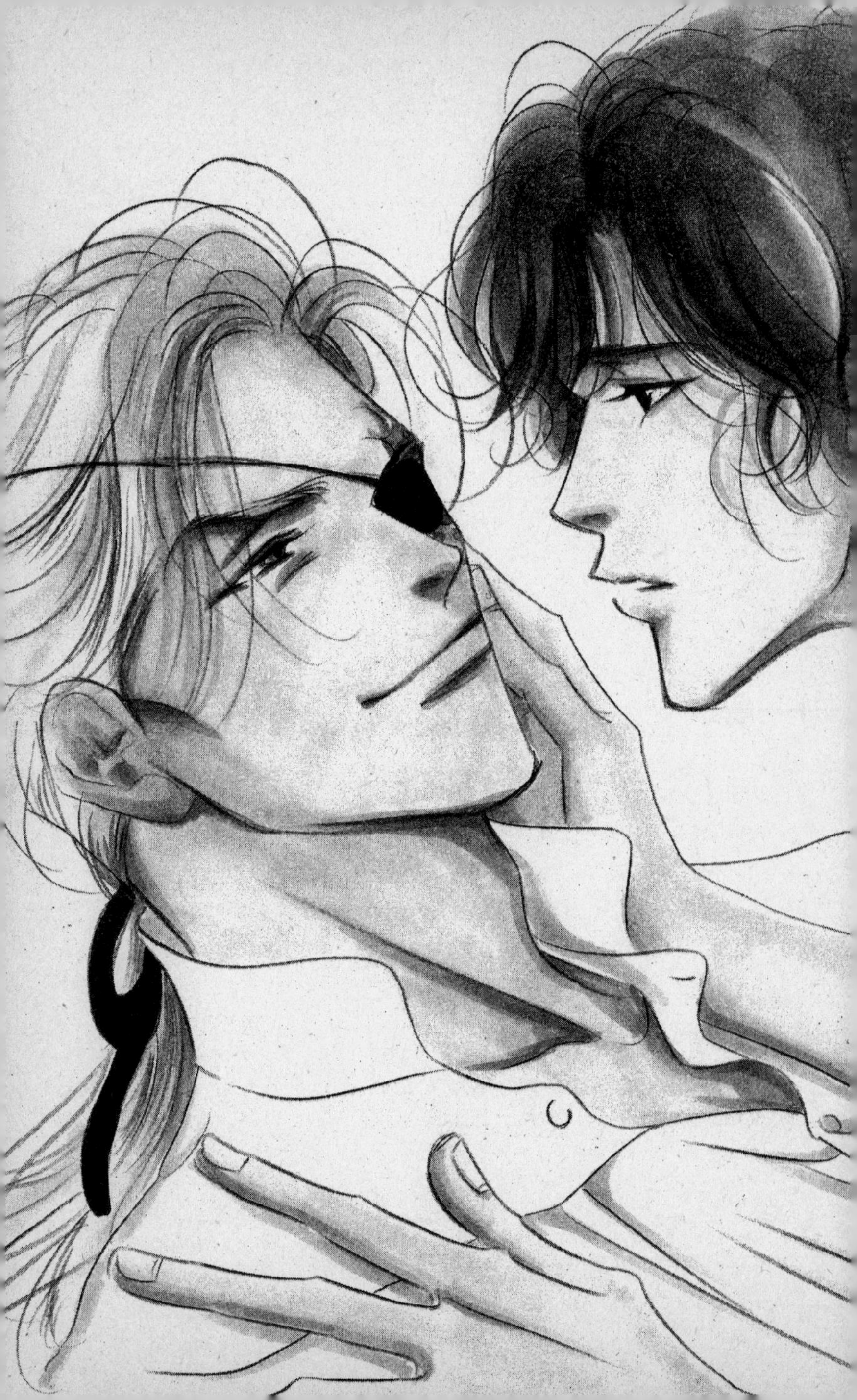

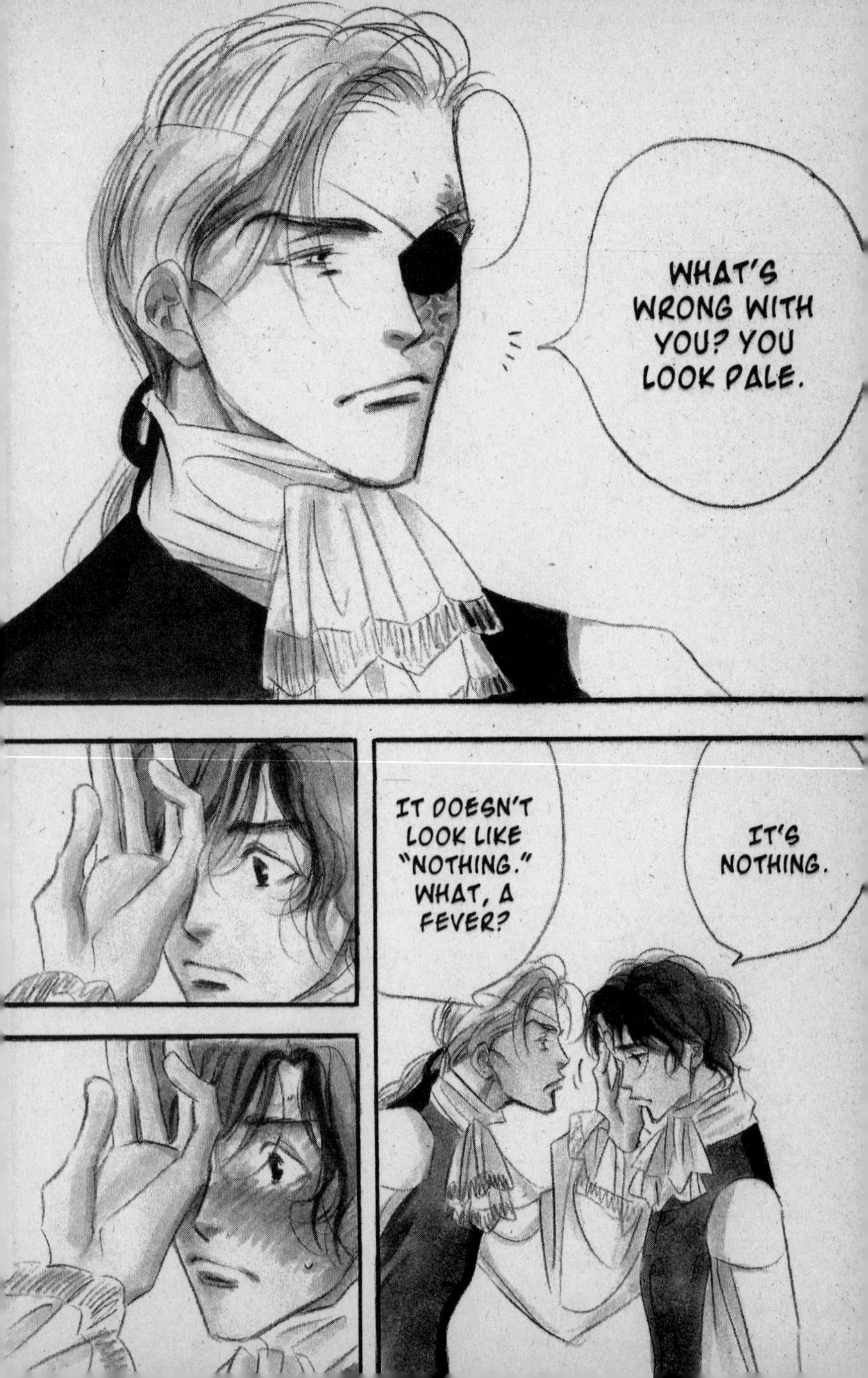
WHAT'S WRONG WITH YOU? YOU LOOK PALE.
IT'S NOTHING.
IT DOESN'T LOOK LIKE "NOTHING." WHAT, A FEVER?

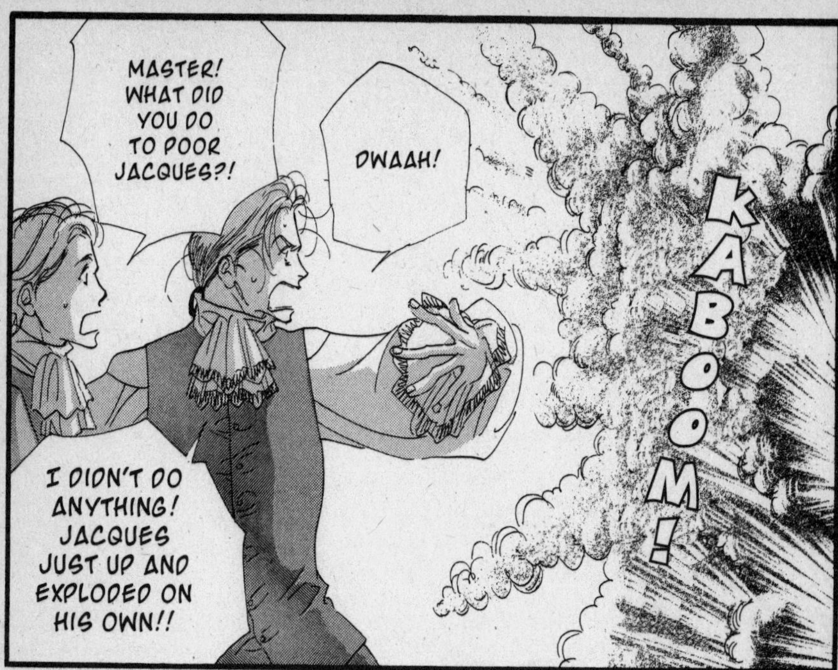
KABOOM!
DWAAH!
MASTER! WHAT DID YOU DO TO POOR JACQUES?!
I DIDN'T DO ANYTHING! JACQUES JUST UP AND EXPLODED ON HIS OWN!!

Wow. How nostalgic!!

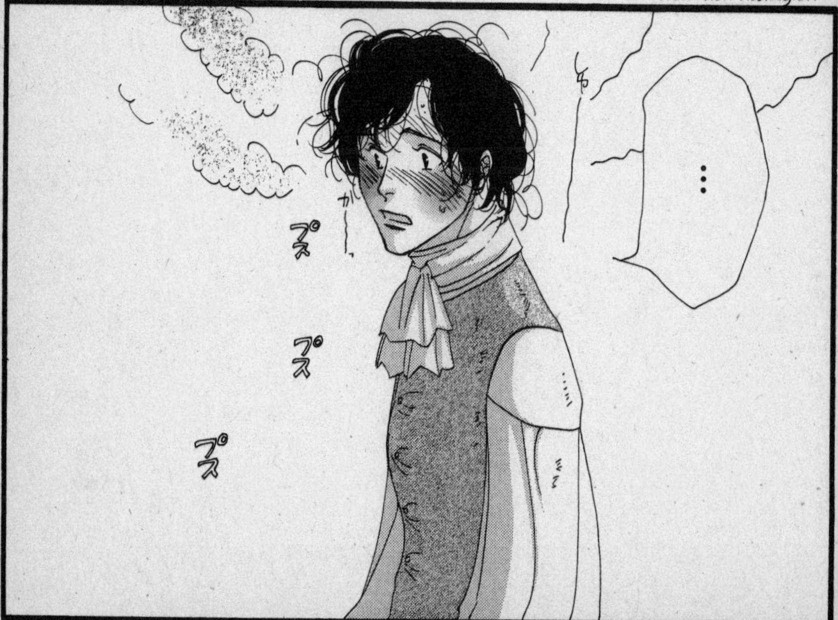
...
プス
プス
プス

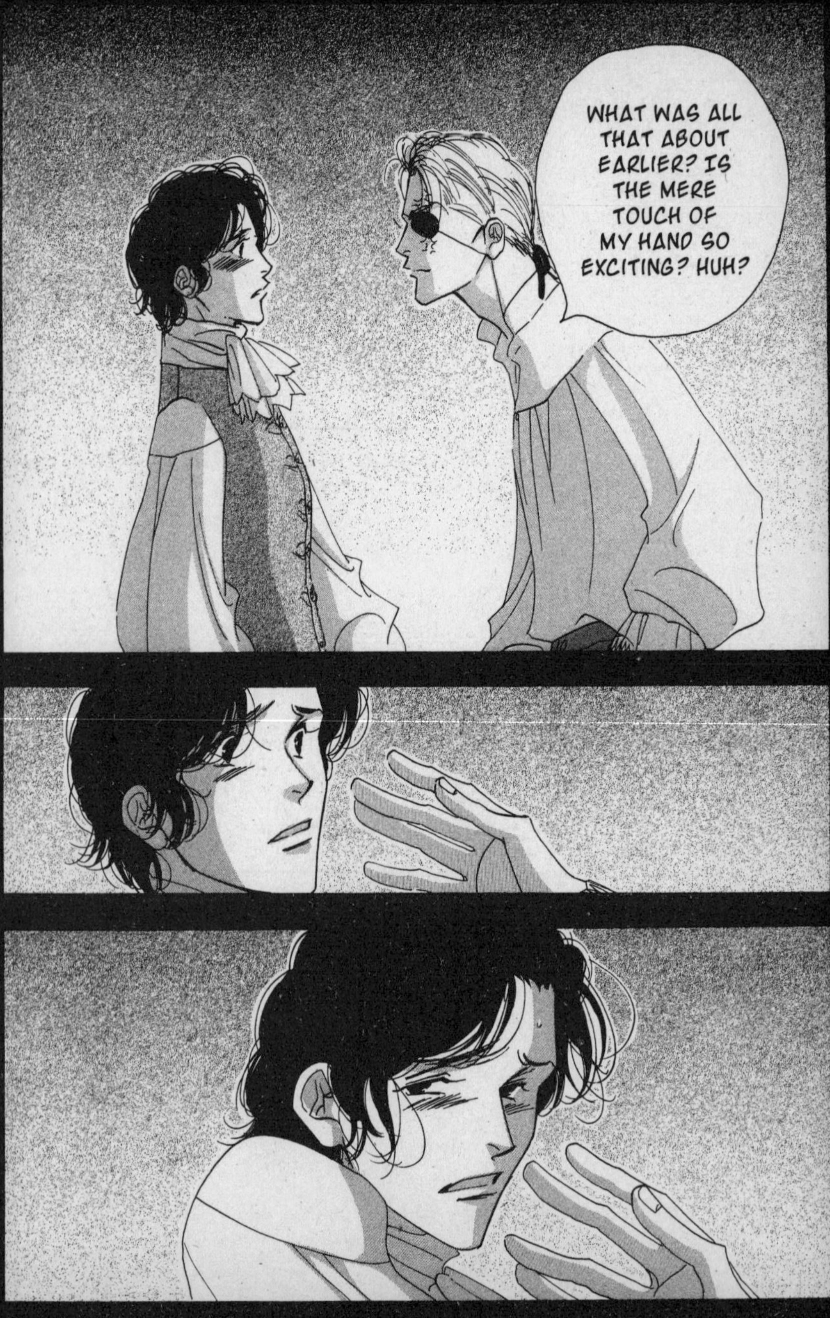
WHAT WAS ALL THAT ABOUT EARLIER? IS THE MERE TOUCH OF MY HAND SO EXCITING? HUH?

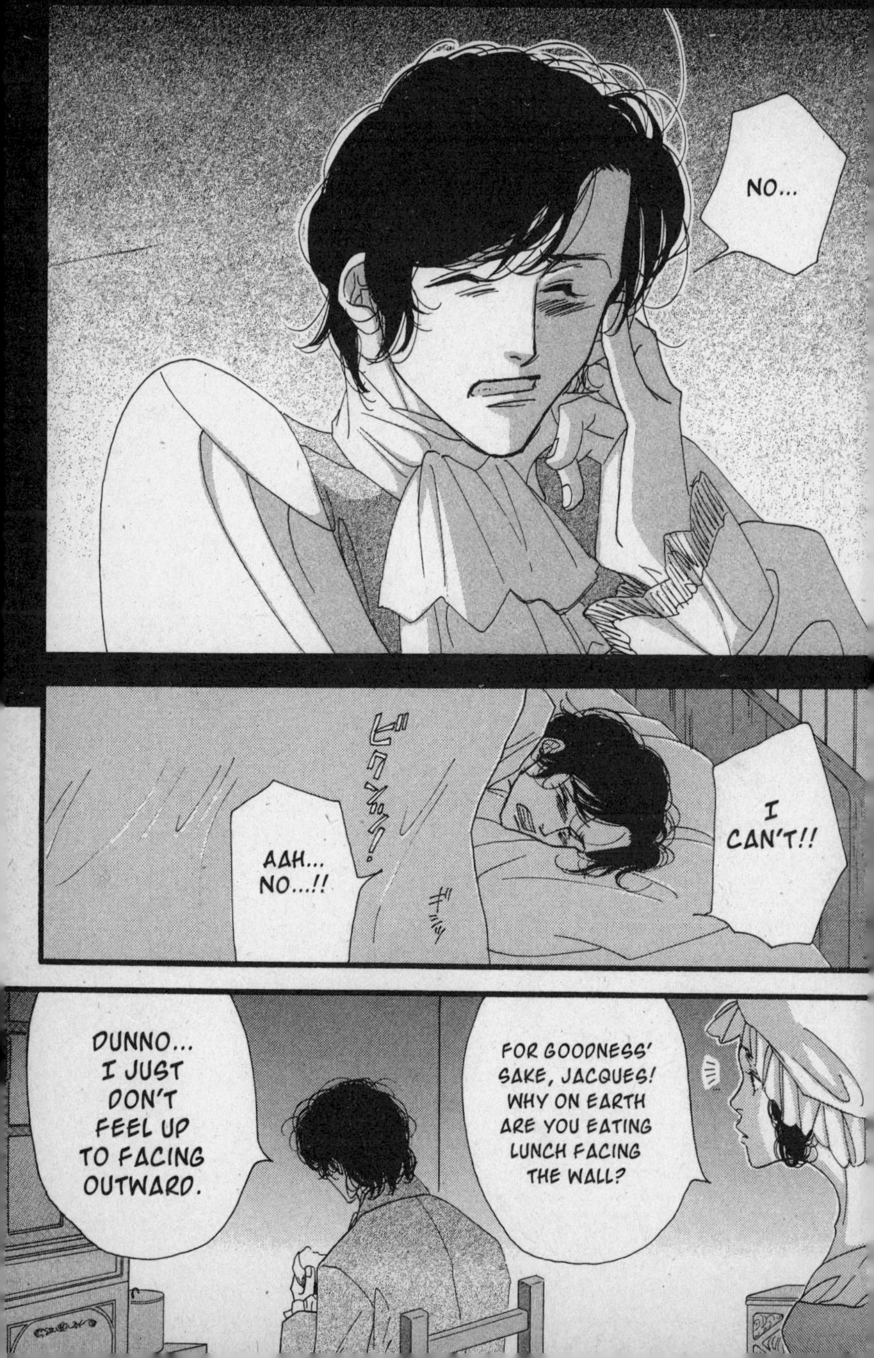
NO...
I CAN'T!!
AAH... NO...!!
FOR GOODNESS' SAKE, JACQUES! WHY ON EARTH ARE YOU EATING LUNCH FACING THE WALL?
DUNNO... I JUST DON'T FEEL UP TO FACING OUTWARD.

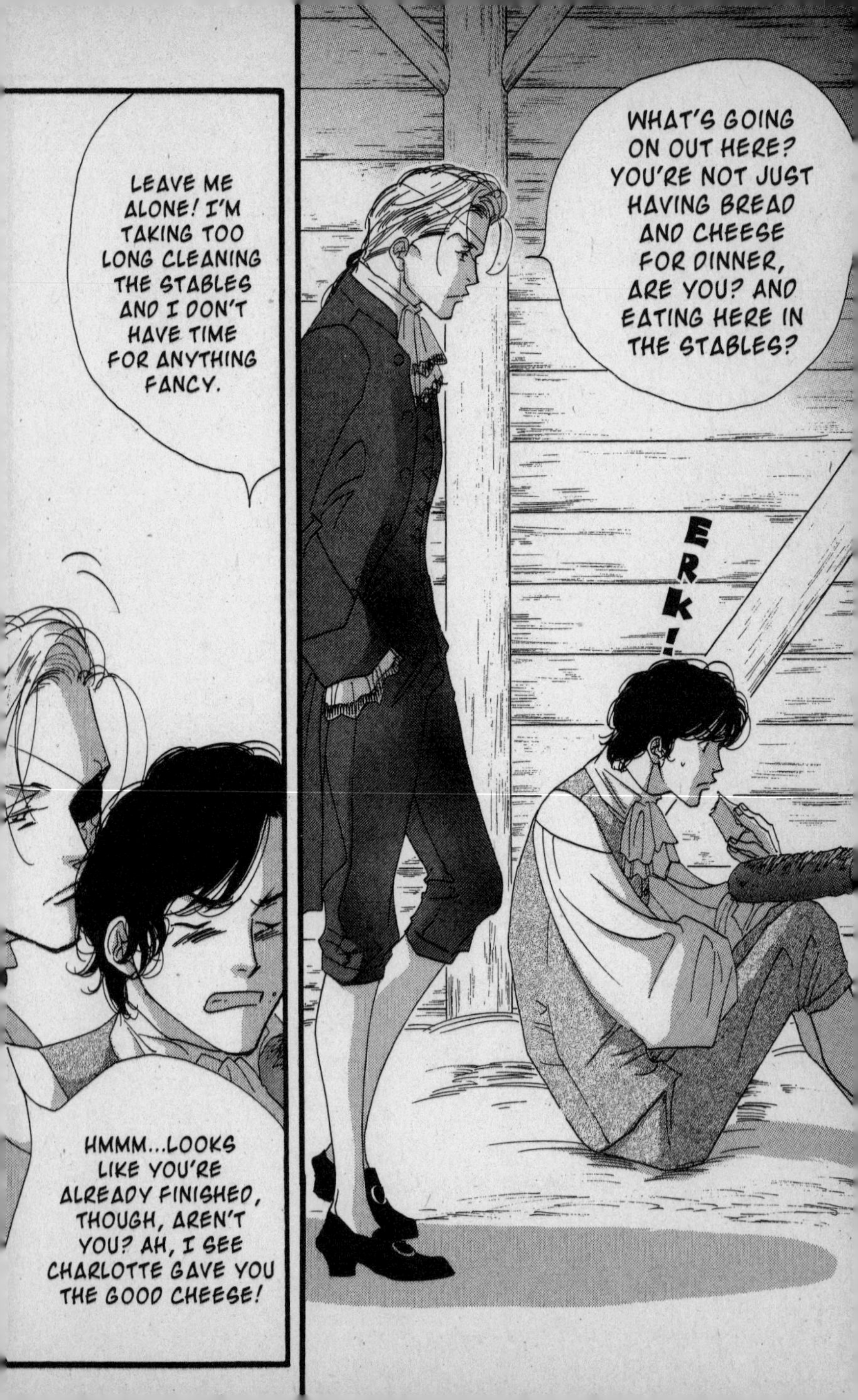
WHAT'S GOING ON OUT HERE? YOU'RE NOT JUST HAVING BREAD AND CHEESE FOR DINNER, ARE YOU? AND EATING HERE IN THE STABLES?
ERK!!
LEAVE ME ALONE! I'M TAKING TOO LONG CLEANING THE STABLES AND I DON'T HAVE TIME FOR ANYTHING FANCY.
HMMM...LOOKS LIKE YOU'RE ALREADY FINISHED, THOUGH, AREN'T YOU? AH, I SEE CHARLOTTE GAVE YOU THE GOOD CHEESE!

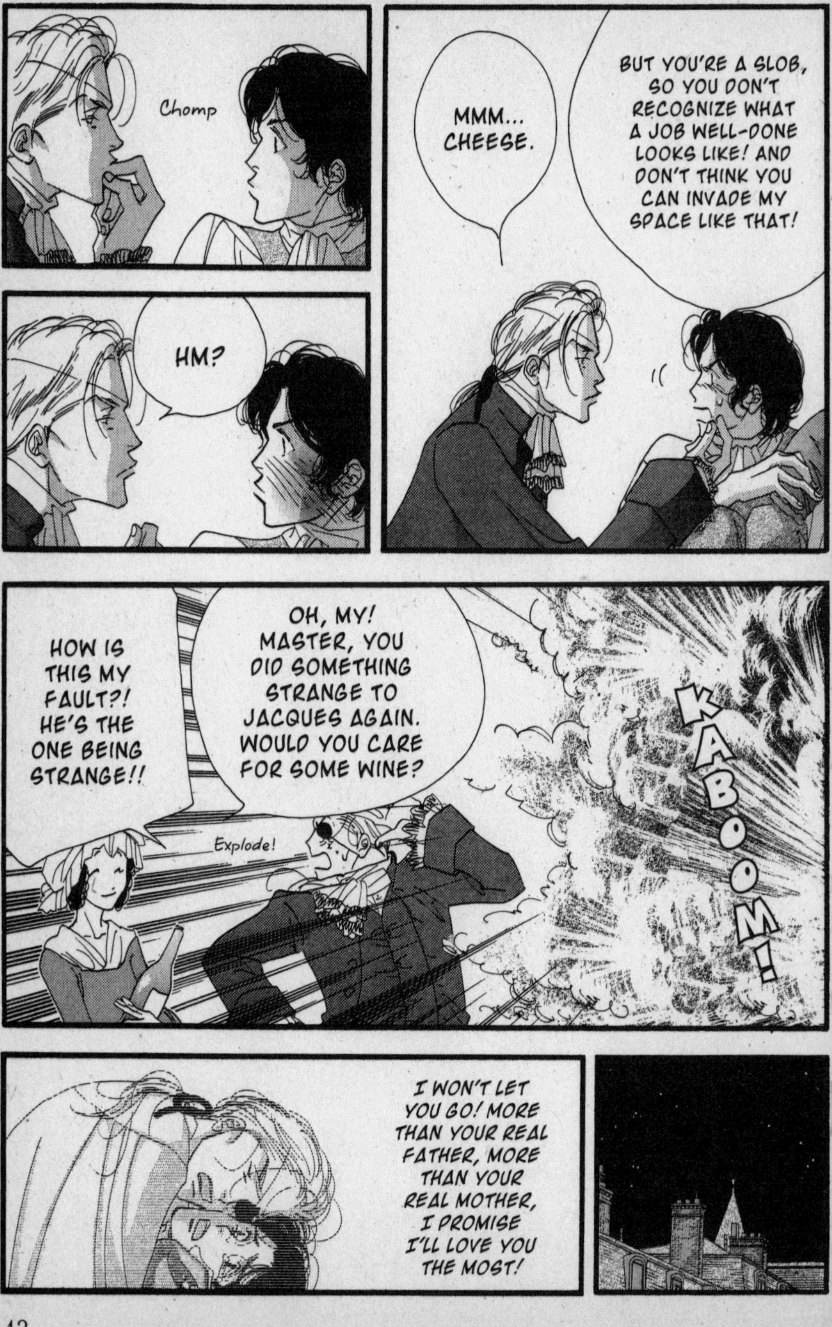
BUT YOU'RE A SLOB, SO YOU DON'T RECOGNIZE WHAT A JOB WELL-DONE LOOKS LIKE! AND DON'T THINK YOU CAN INVADE MY SPACE LIKE THAT!
MMM... CHEESE.
Chomp
HM?
KABOOM!
OH, MY! MASTER, YOU DID SOMETHING STRANGE TO JACQUES AGAIN. WOULD YOU CARE FOR SOME WINE?
HOW IS THIS MY FAULT?! HE'S THE ONE BEING STRANGE!!
Explode!
I WON'T LET YOU GO! MORE THAN YOUR REAL FATHER, MORE THAN YOUR REAL MOTHER, I PROMISE I'LL LOVE YOU THE MOST!

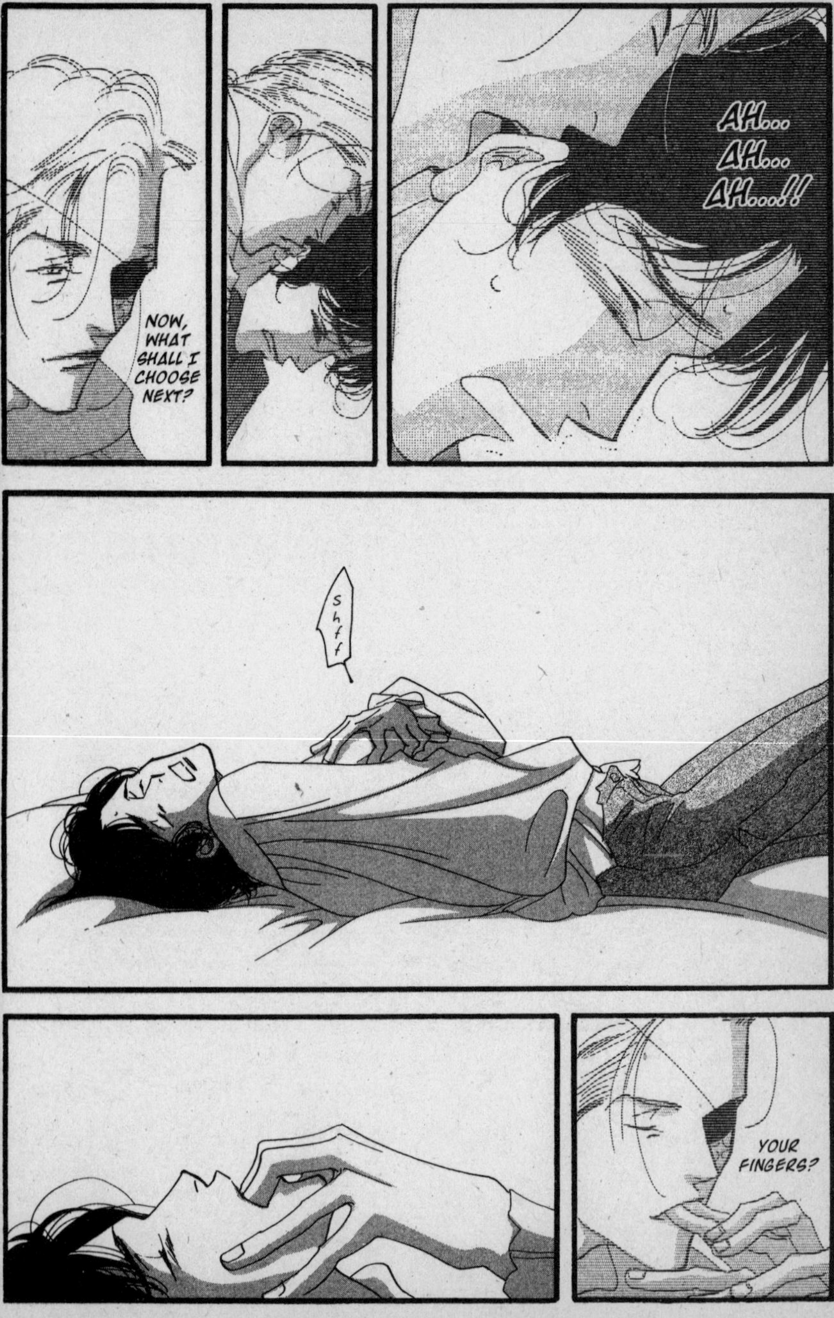
AH... AH... AH...!!
NOW, WHAT SHALL I CHOOSE NEXT?
shff
YOUR FINGERS?

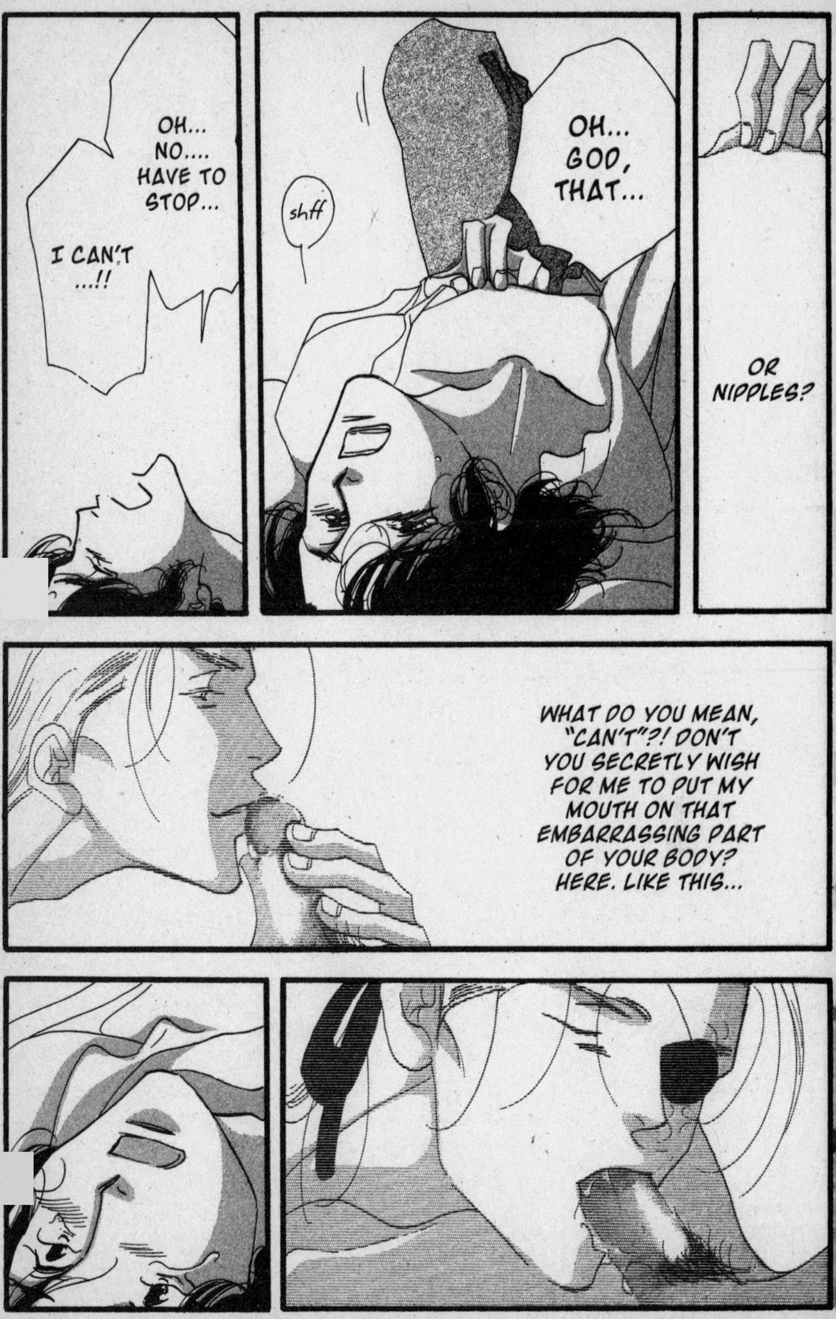
OR NIPPLES?
OH... GOD, THAT...
shff
OH... NO.... HAVE TO STOP...
I CAN'T ...!!
WHAT DO YOU MEAN, "CAN'T"?! DON'T YOU SECRETLY WISH FOR ME TO PUT MY MOUTH ON THAT EMBARRASSING PART OF YOUR BODY? HERE. LIKE THIS...

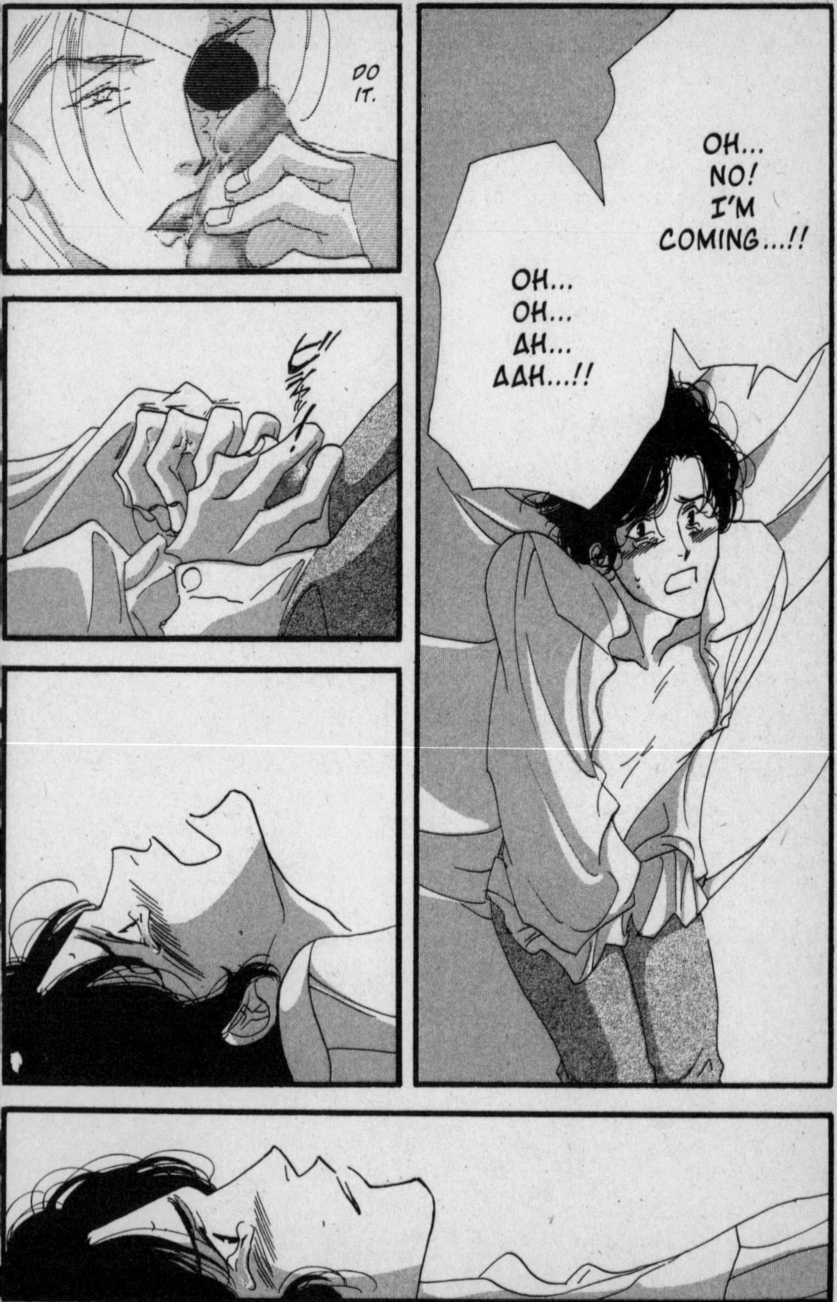
OH... NO! I'M COMING...!!
OH... OH... AH... AAH...!!
DO IT.

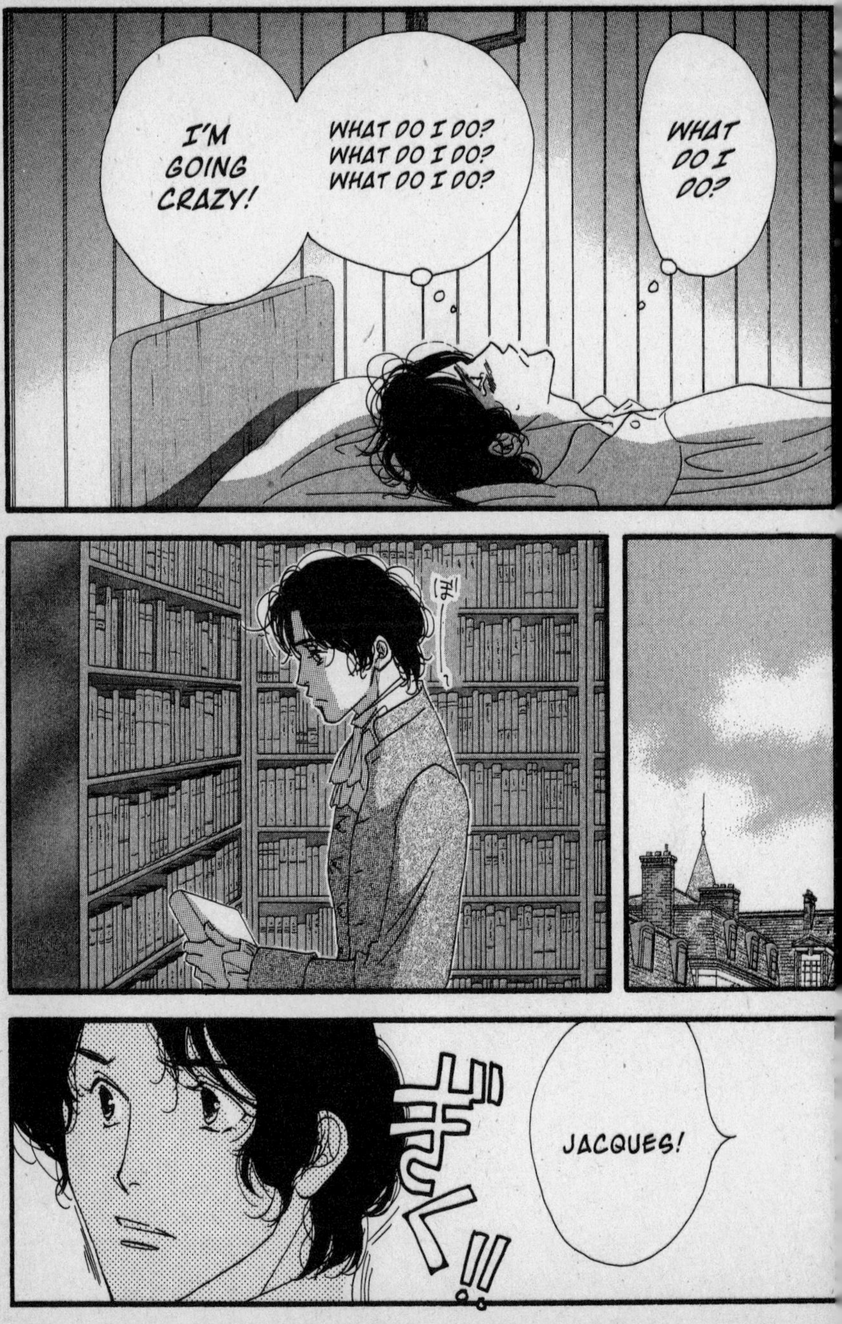
WHAT DO I DO?
WHAT DO I DO? WHAT DO I DO? WHAT DO I DO?
I'M GOING CRAZY!
JACQUES!
ぎく!!

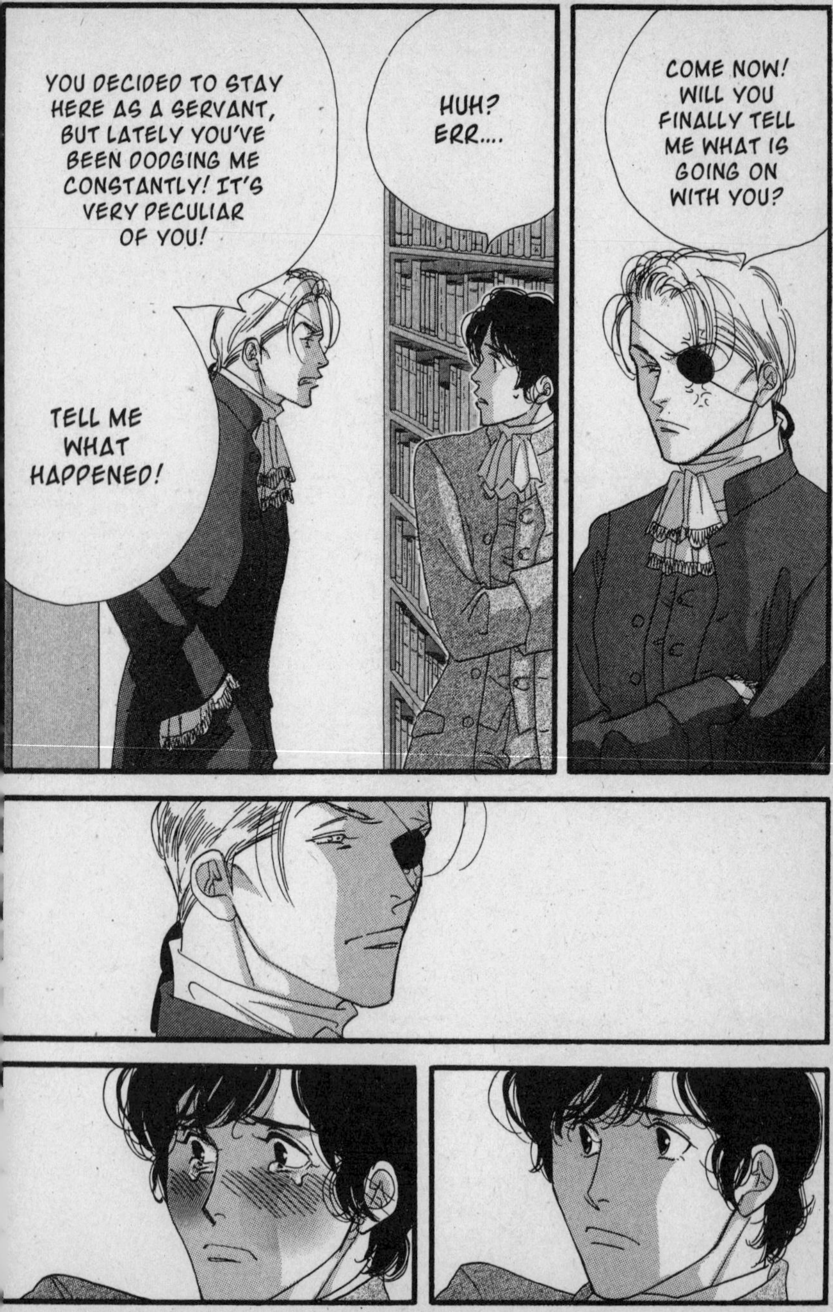
COME NOW! WILL YOU FINALLY TELL ME WHAT IS GOING ON WITH YOU?
HUH? ERR....
YOU DECIDED TO STAY HERE AS A SERVANT, BUT LATELY YOU'VE BEEN DODGING ME CONSTANTLY! IT'S VERY PECULIAR OF YOU!
TELL ME WHAT HAPPENED!

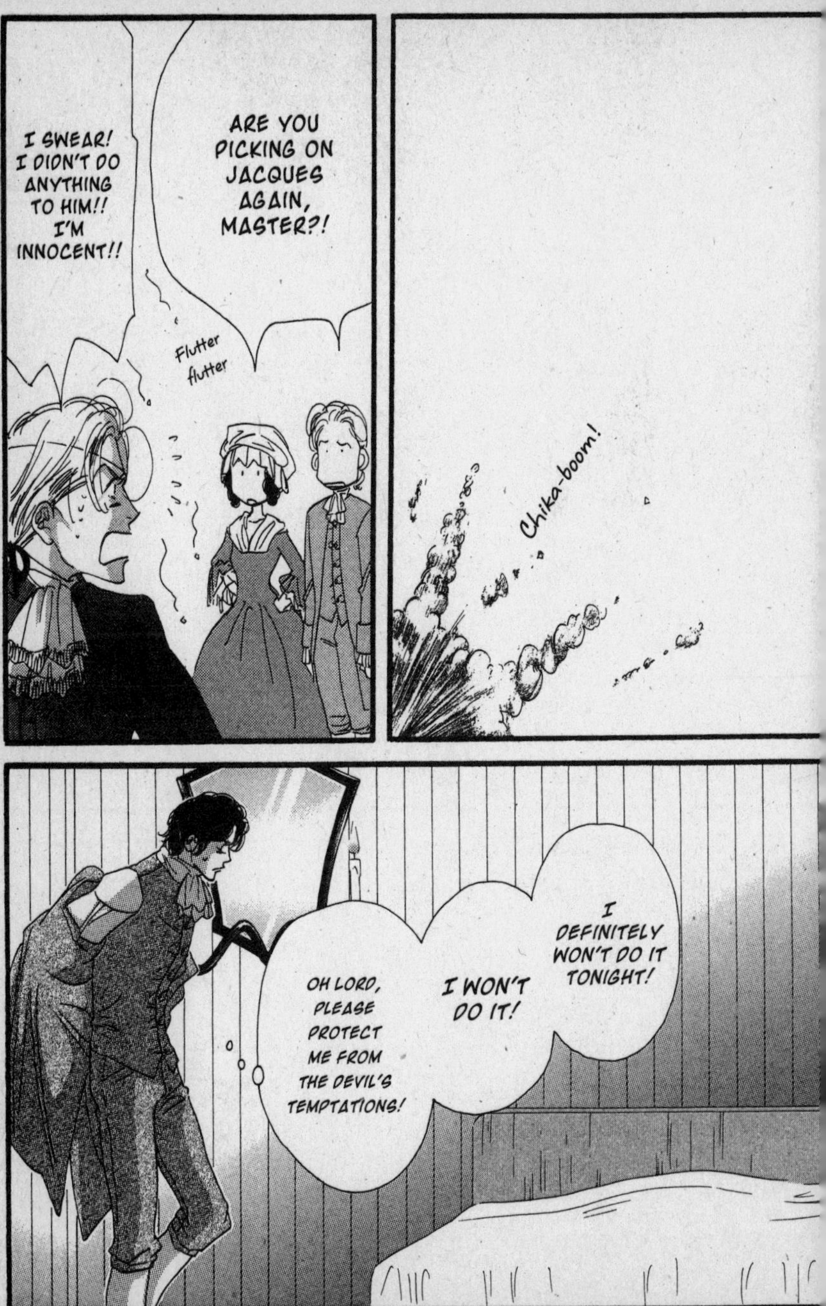
Chika-boom!
ARE YOU PICKING ON JACQUES AGAIN, MASTER?!
I SWEAR! I DIDN'T DO ANYTHING TO HIM!! I'M INNOCENT!!
Flutter flutter
I DEFINITELY WON'T DO IT TONIGHT!
I WON'T DO IT!
OH LORD, PLEASE PROTECT ME FROM THE DEVIL'S TEMPTATIONS!

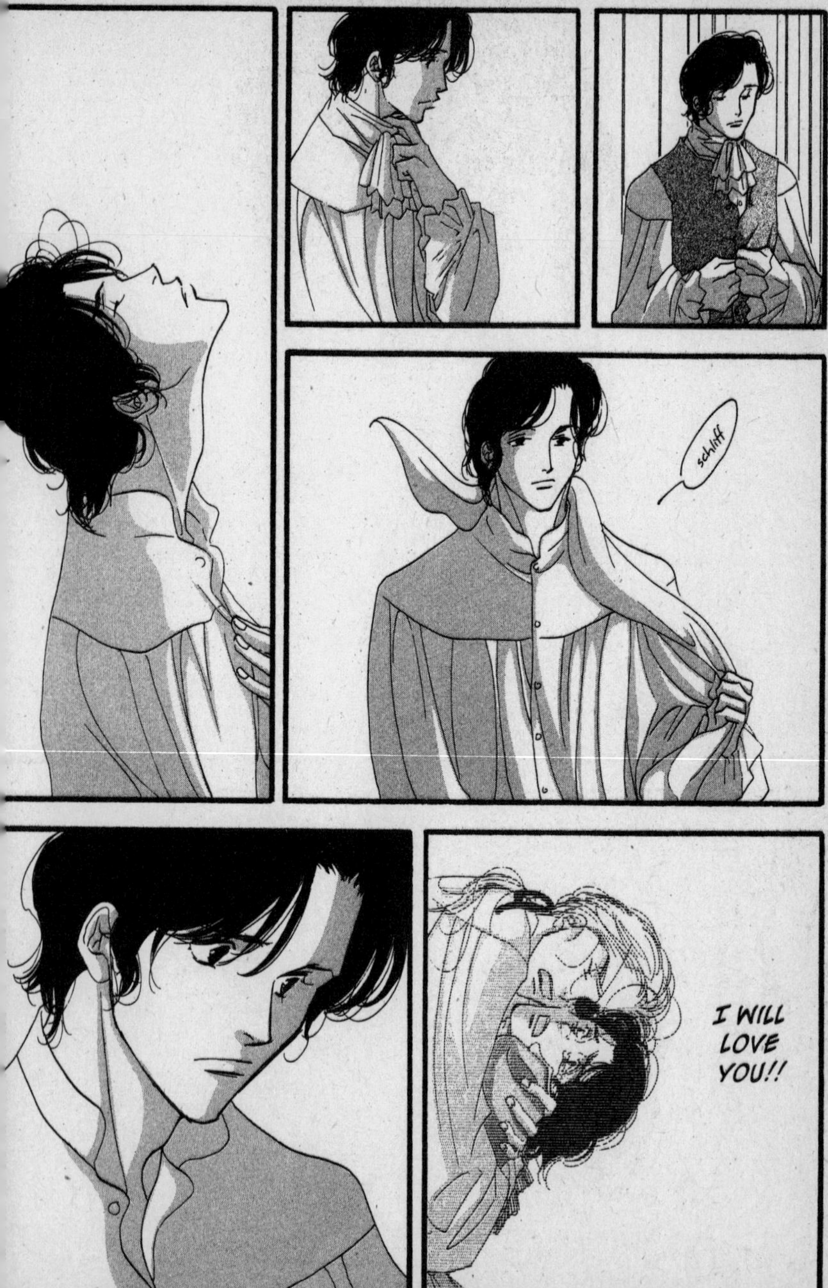
schliff
I WILL LOVE YOU!!

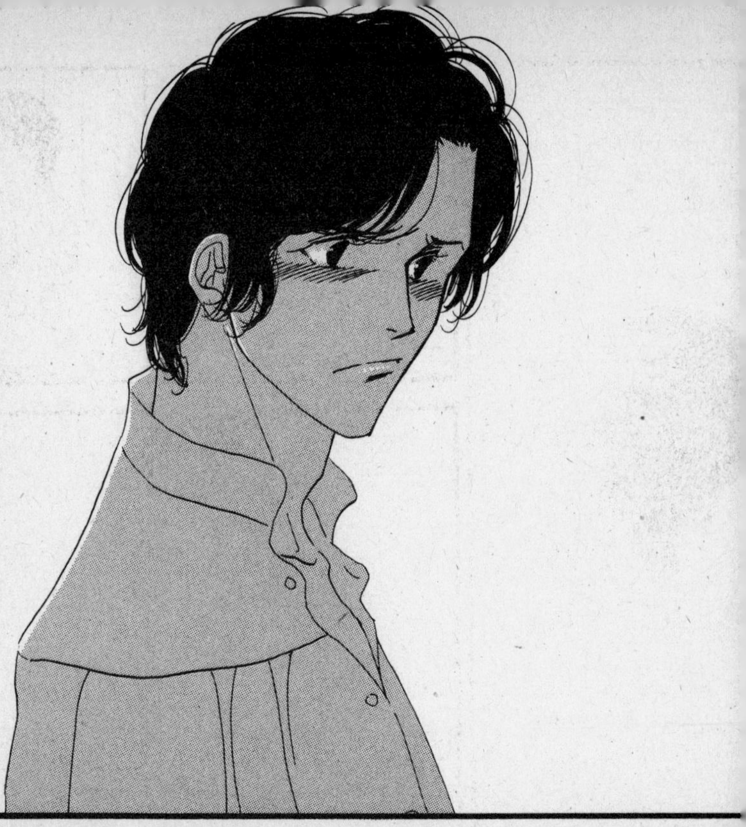
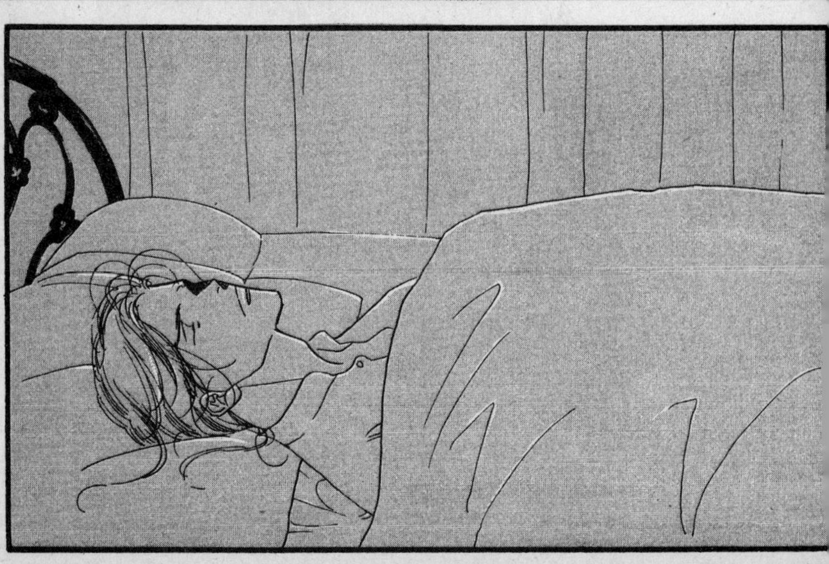

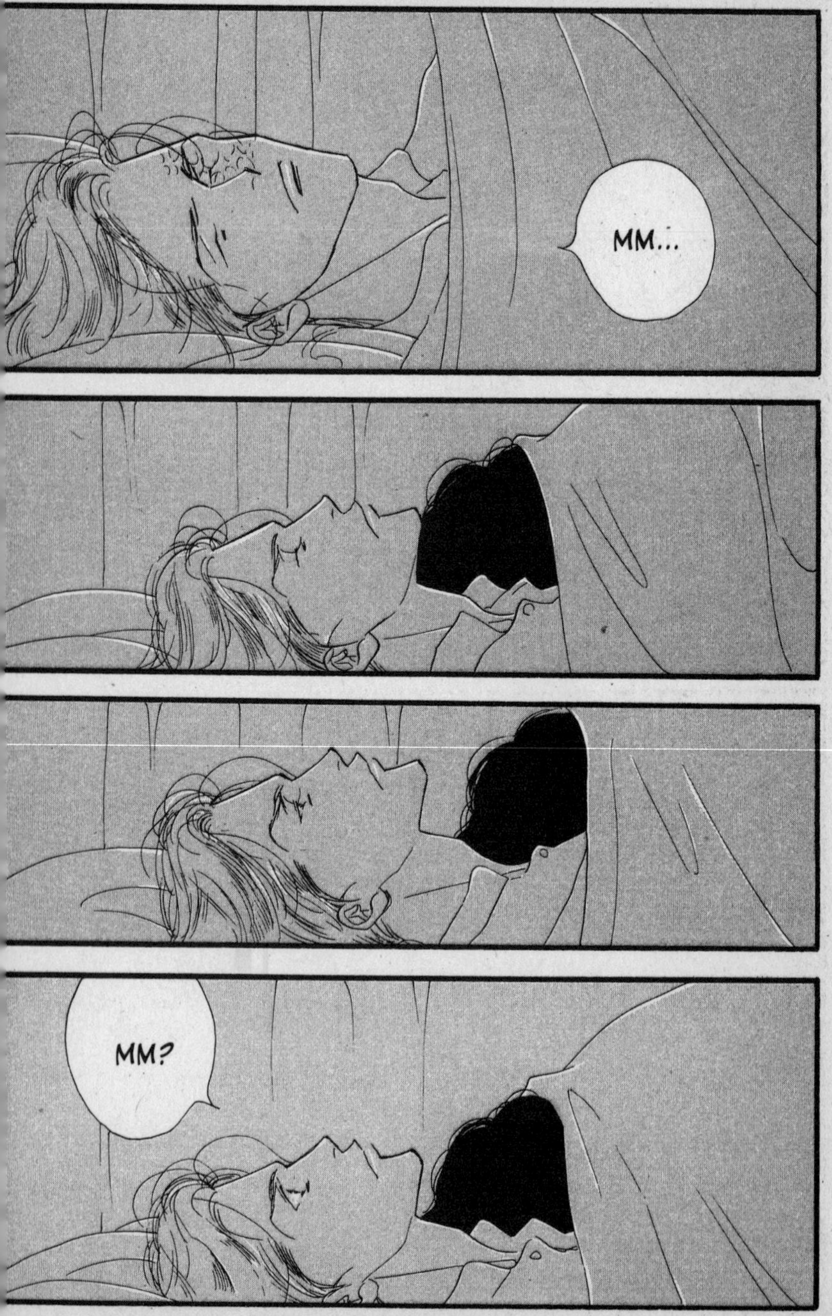
MM...
MM?

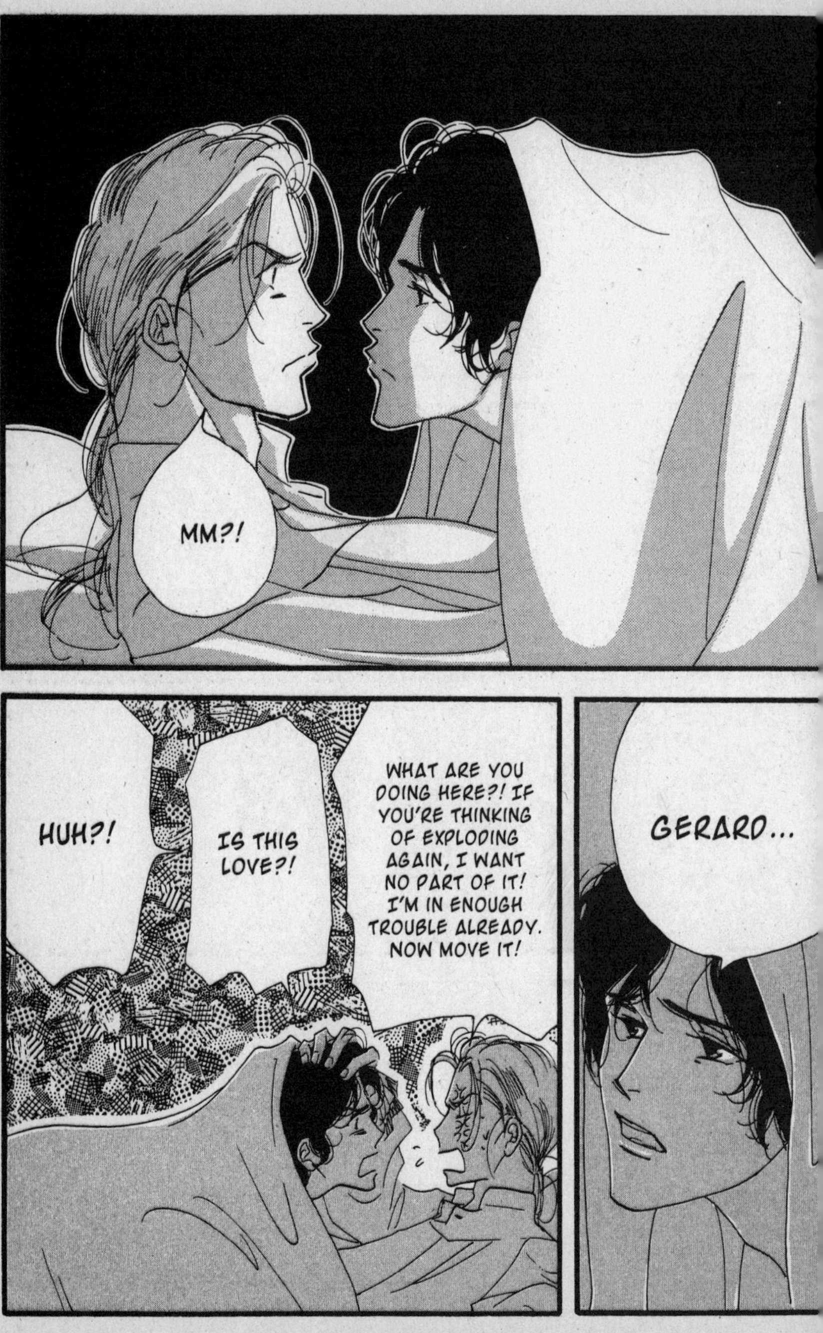
MM?!
GERARD...
WHAT ARE YOU DOING HERE?! IF YOU'RE THINKING OF EXPLODING AGAIN, I WANT NO PART OF IT! I'M IN ENOUGH TROUBLE ALREADY. NOW MOVE IT!
IS THIS LOVE?!
HUH?!

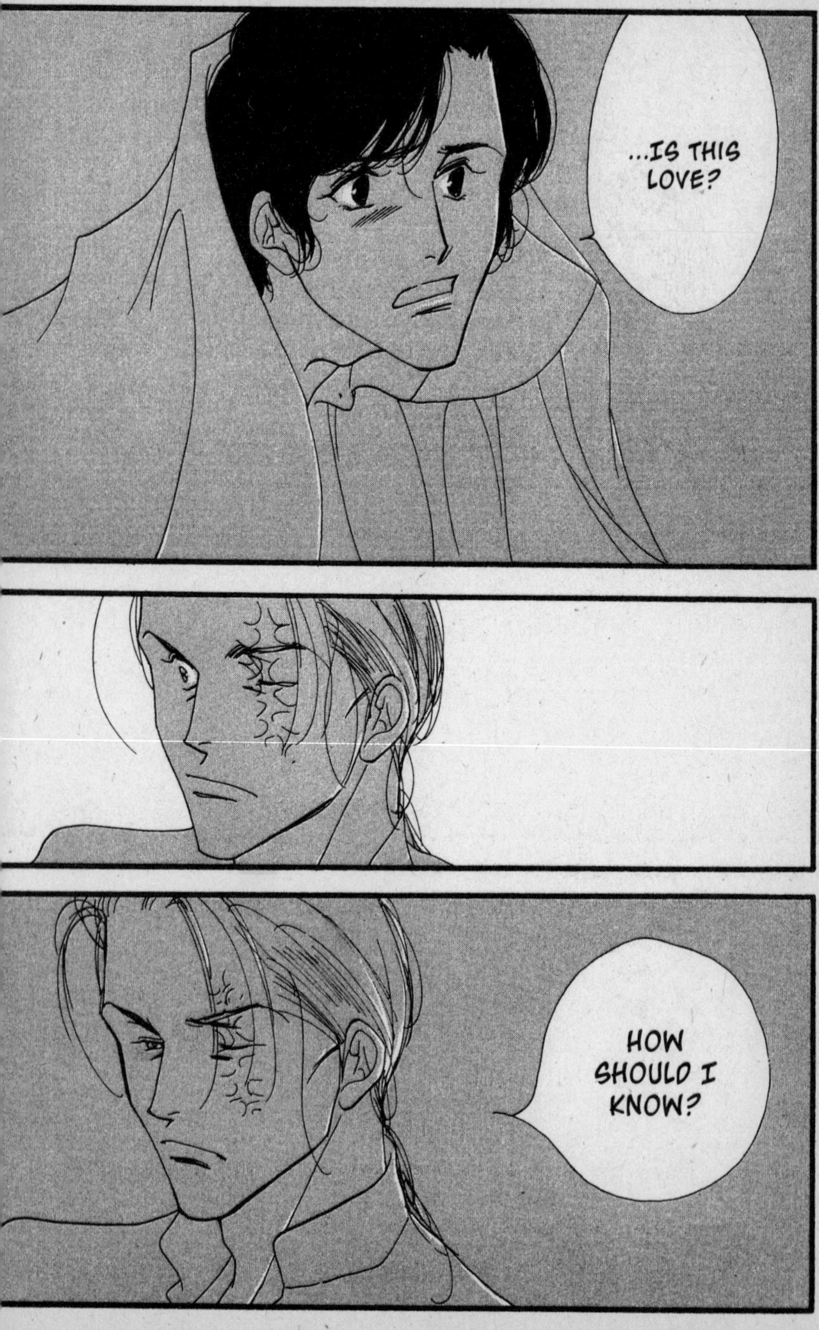
...IS THIS LOVE?
HOW SHOULD I KNOW?

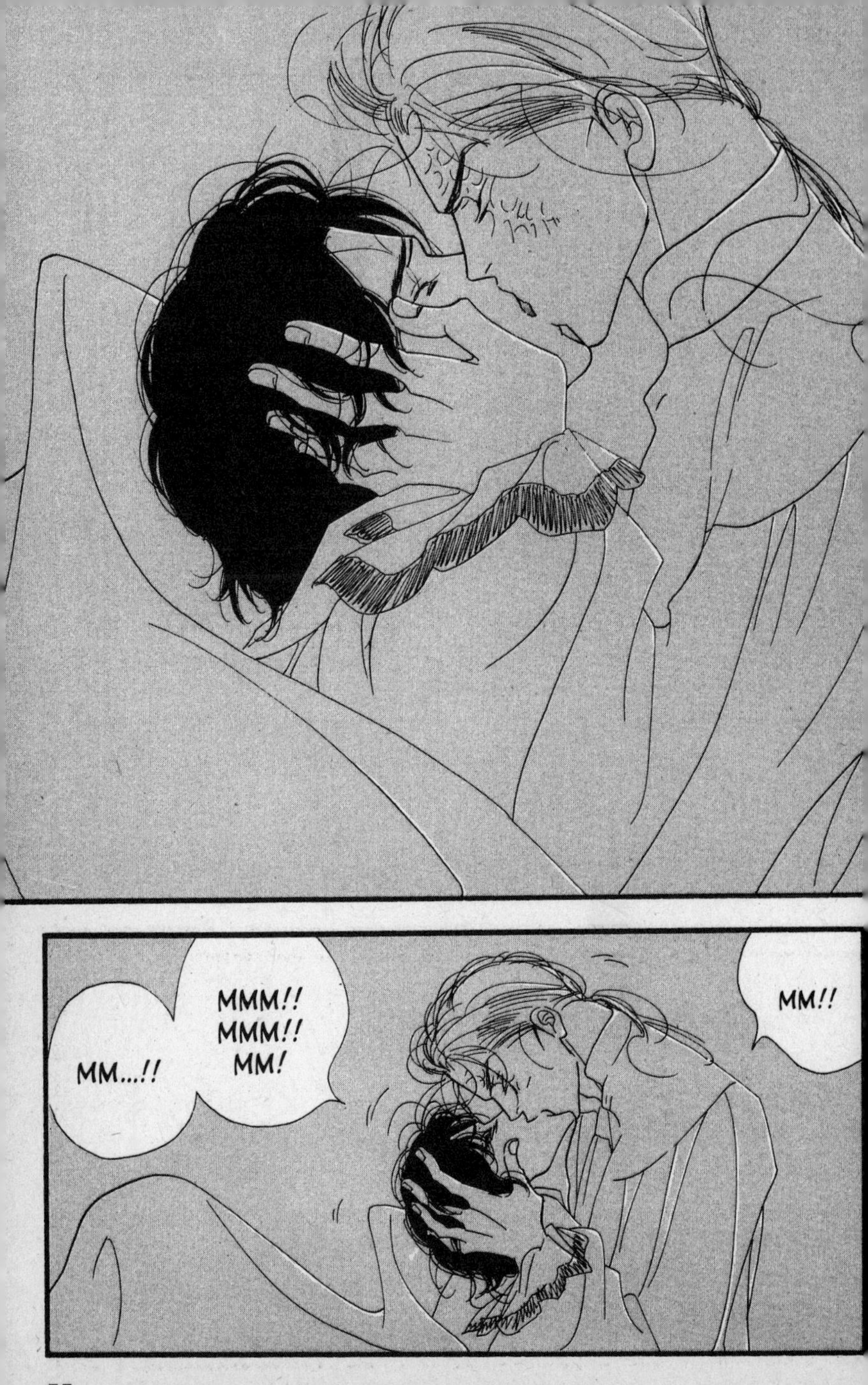
MM!!
MMM!! MMM!! MM!
MM...!!

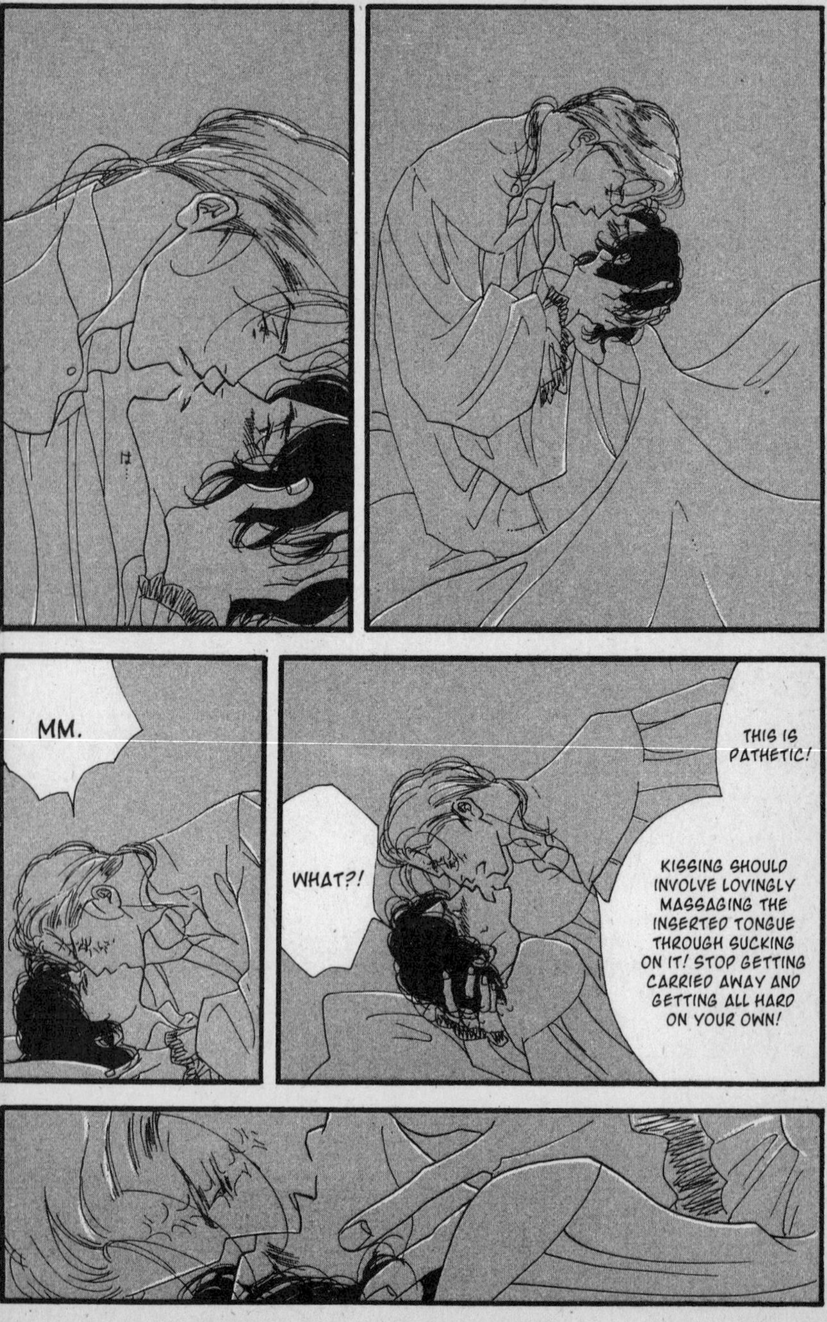
MM.
WHAT?!
THIS IS PATHETIC!
KISSING SHOULD INVOLVE LOVINGLY MASSAGING THE INSERTED TONGUE THROUGH SUCKING ON IT! STOP GETTING CARRIED AWAY AND GETTING ALL HARD ON YOUR OWN!

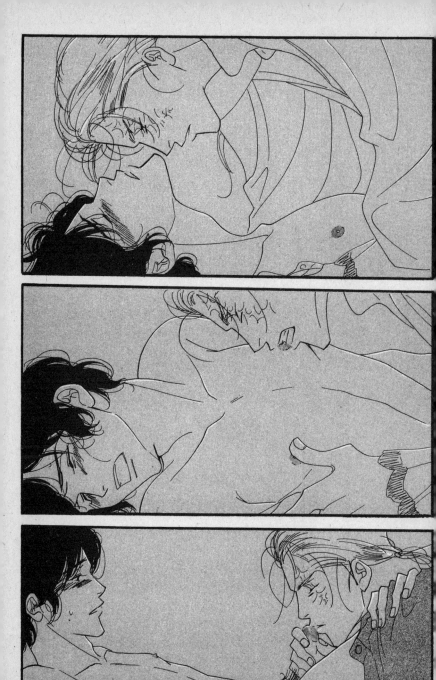

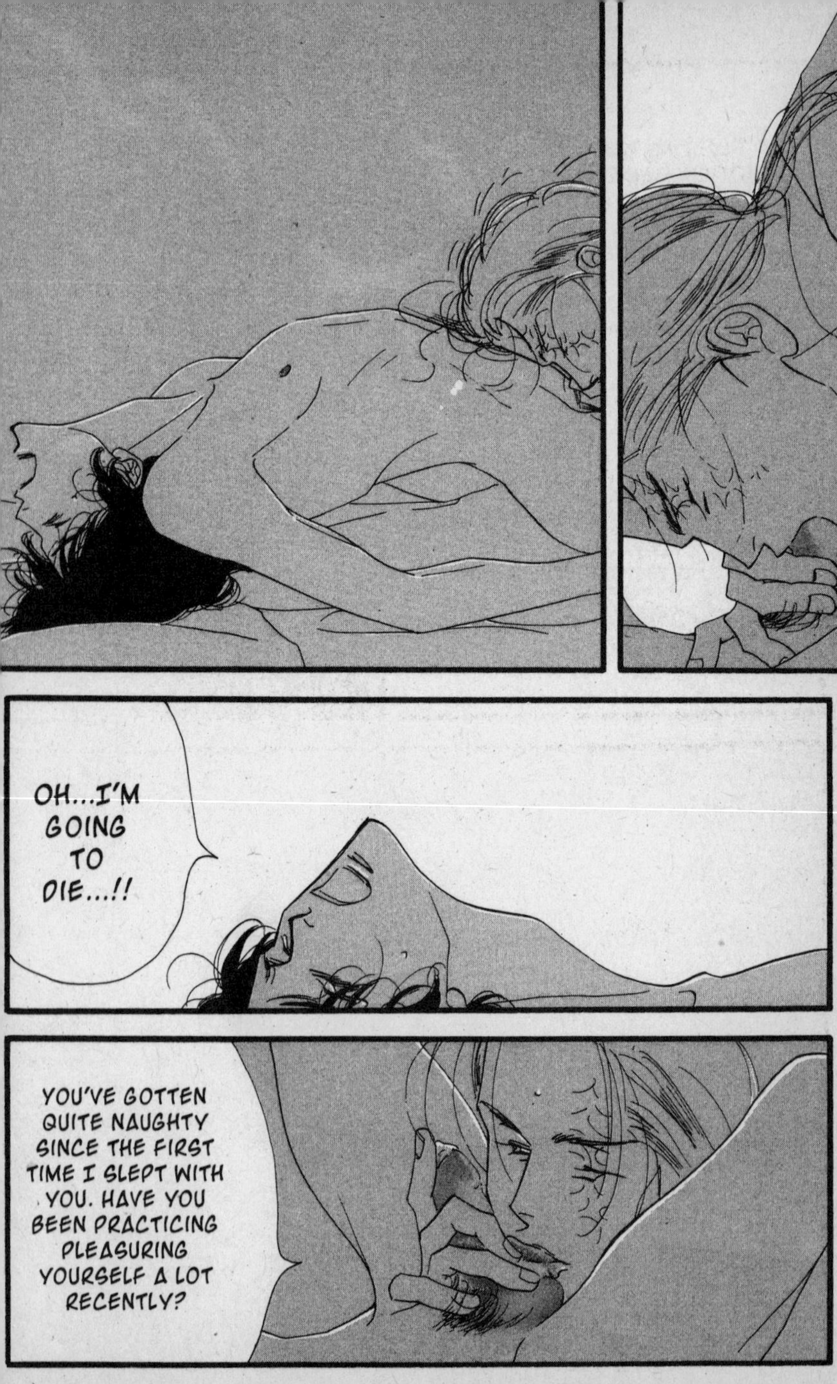
OH...I'M GOING TO DIE...!!
YOU'VE GOTTEN QUITE NAUGHTY SINCE THE FIRST TIME I SLEPT WITH YOU. HAVE YOU BEEN PRACTICING PLEASURING YOURSELF A LOT RECENTLY?

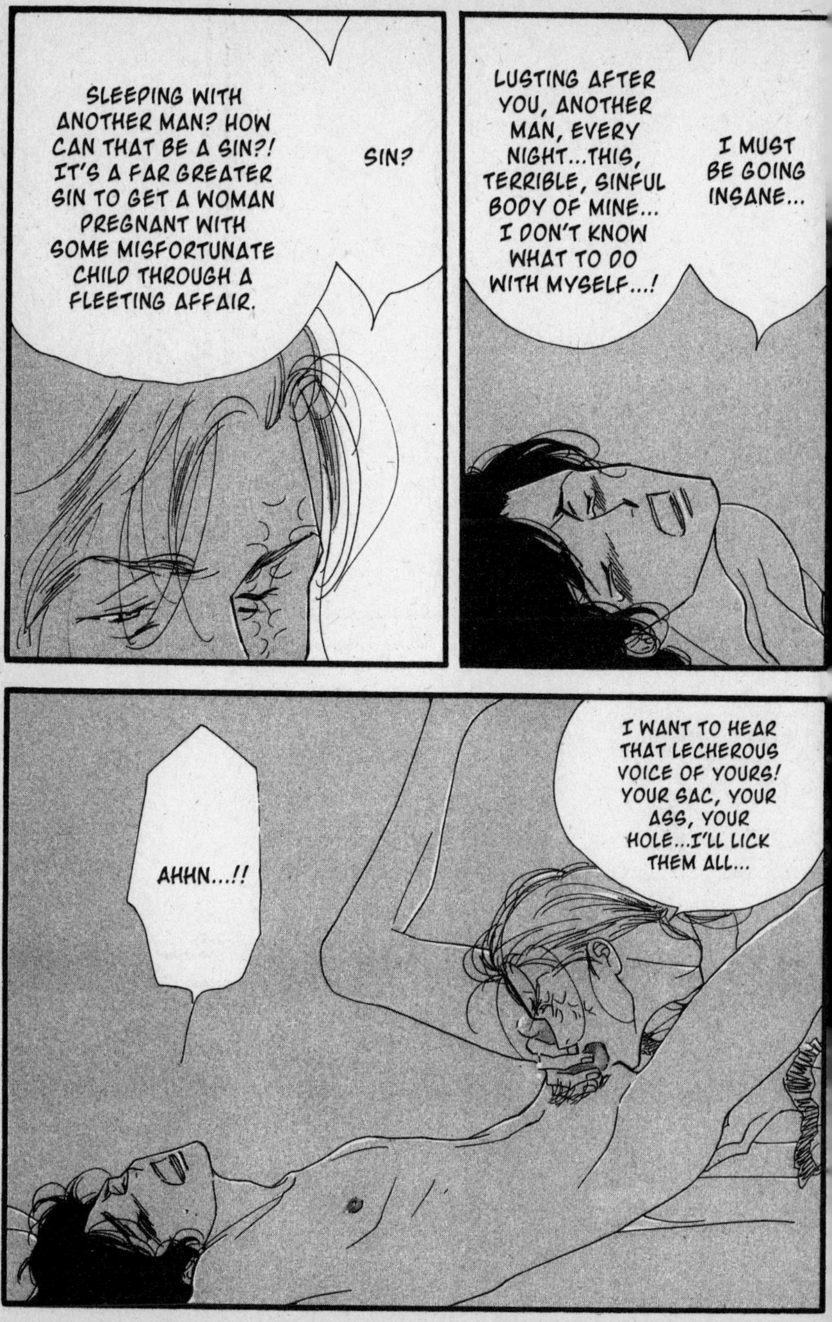
I MUST BE GOING INSANE...
LUSTING AFTER YOU, ANOTHER MAN, EVERY NIGHT...THIS, TERRIBLE, SINFUL BODY OF MINE... I DON'T KNOW WHAT TO DO WITH MYSELF...!
SIN?
SLEEPING WITH ANOTHER MAN? HOW CAN THAT BE A SIN?! IT'S A FAR GREATER SIN TO GET A WOMAN PREGNANT WITH SOME MISFORTUNATE CHILD THROUGH A FLEETING AFFAIR.
I WANT TO HEAR THAT LECHEROUS VOICE OF YOURS! YOUR SAC, YOUR ASS, YOUR HOLE...I'LL LICK THEM ALL...
AHHN...!!

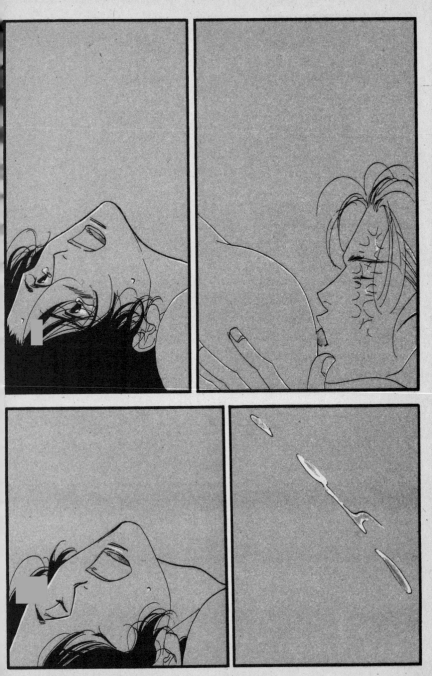

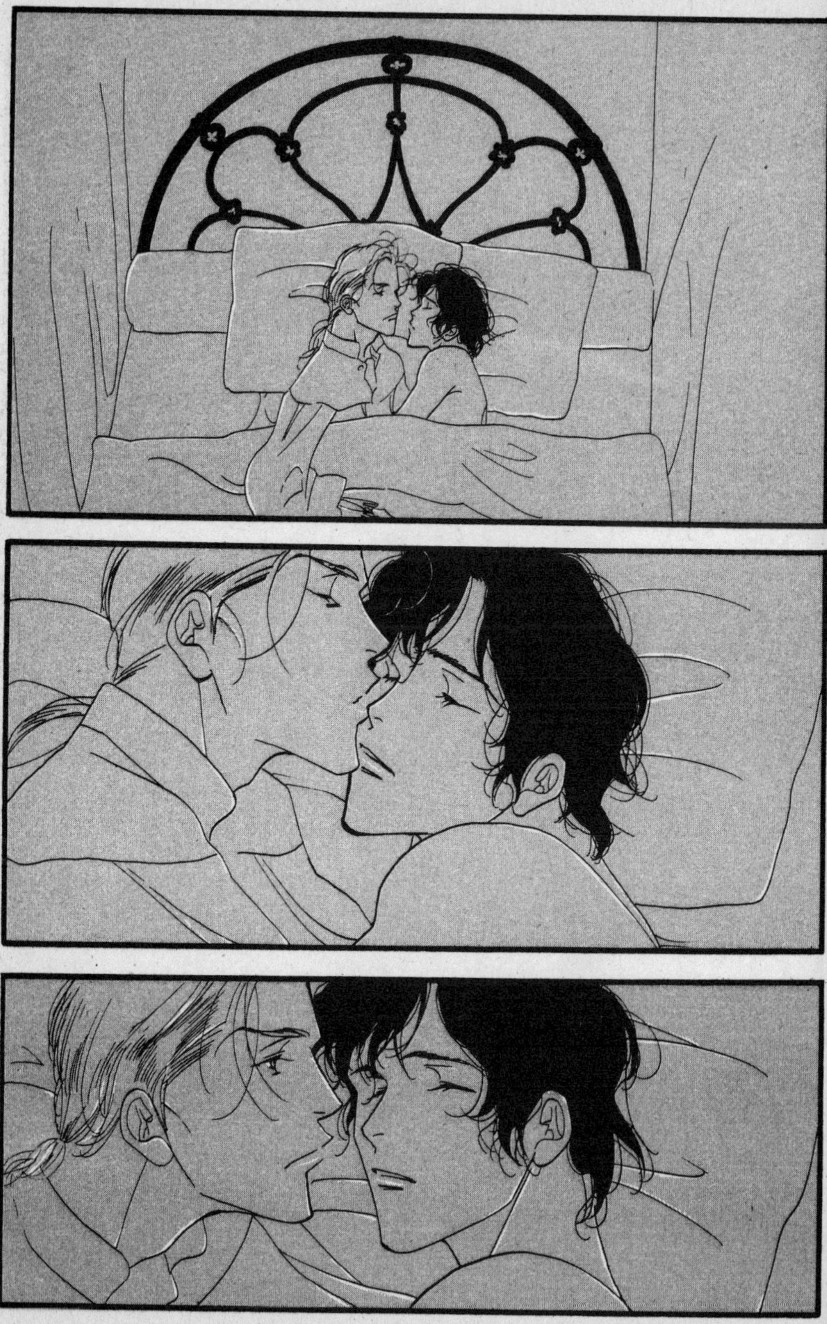

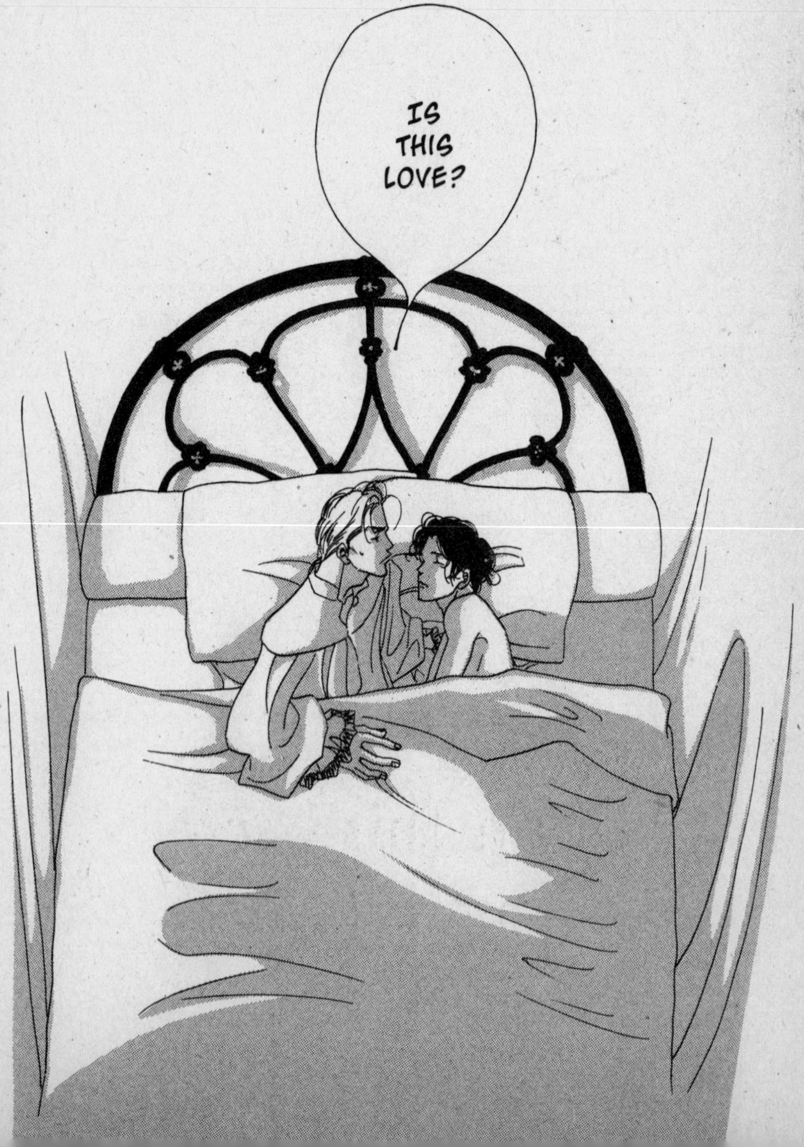
IS THIS LOVE?

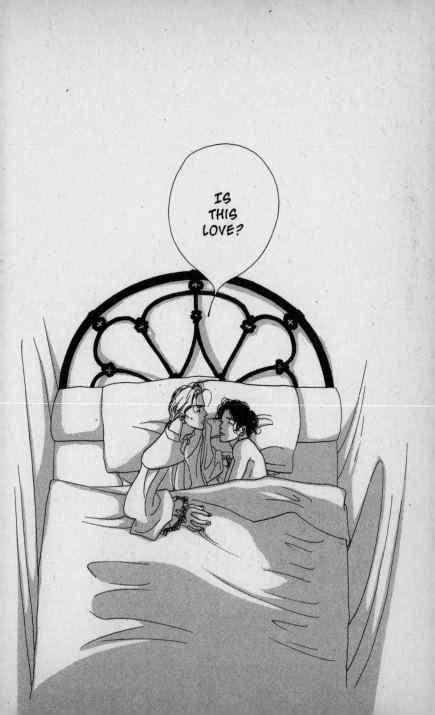

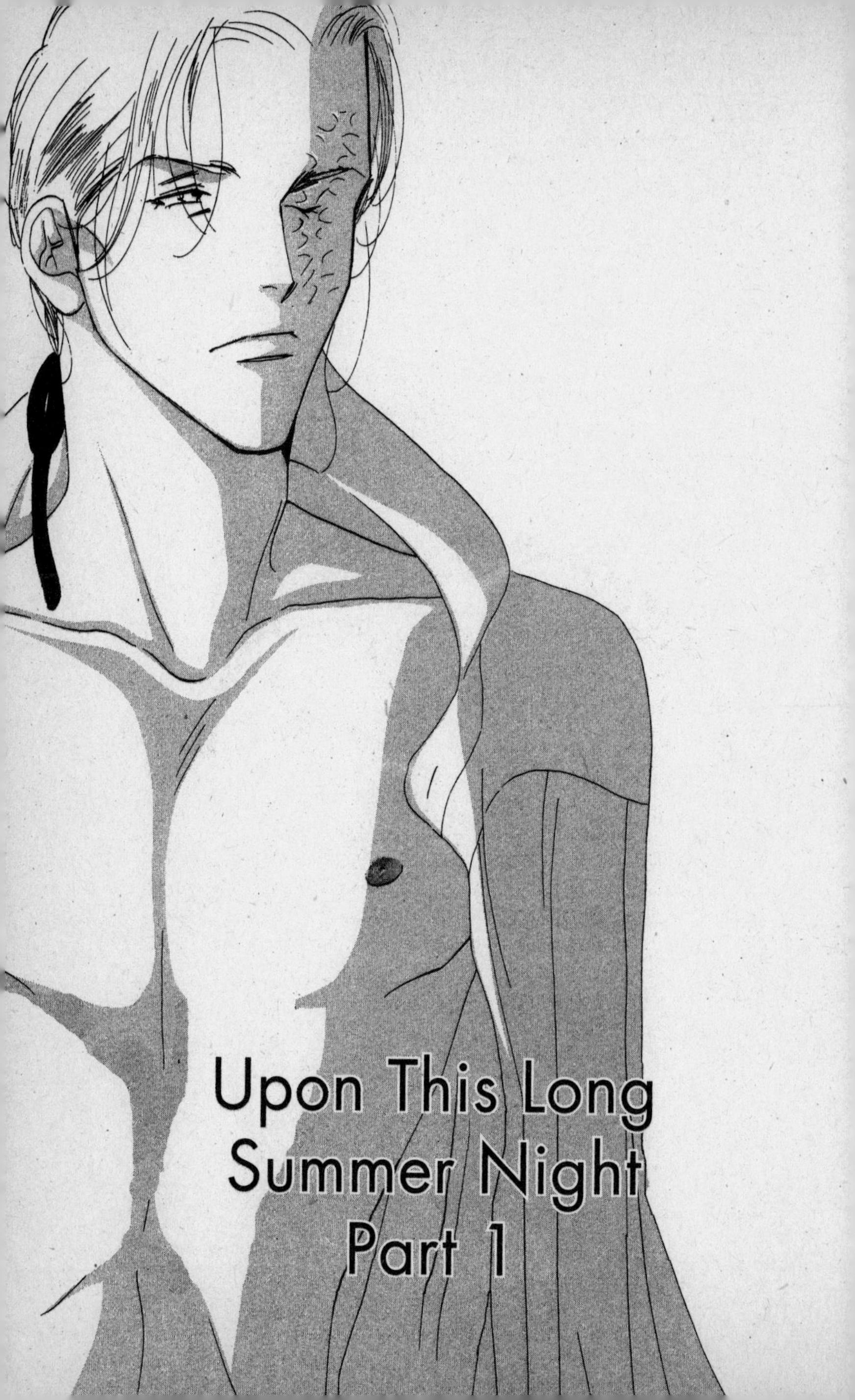

Upon This Long Summer Night Part 1

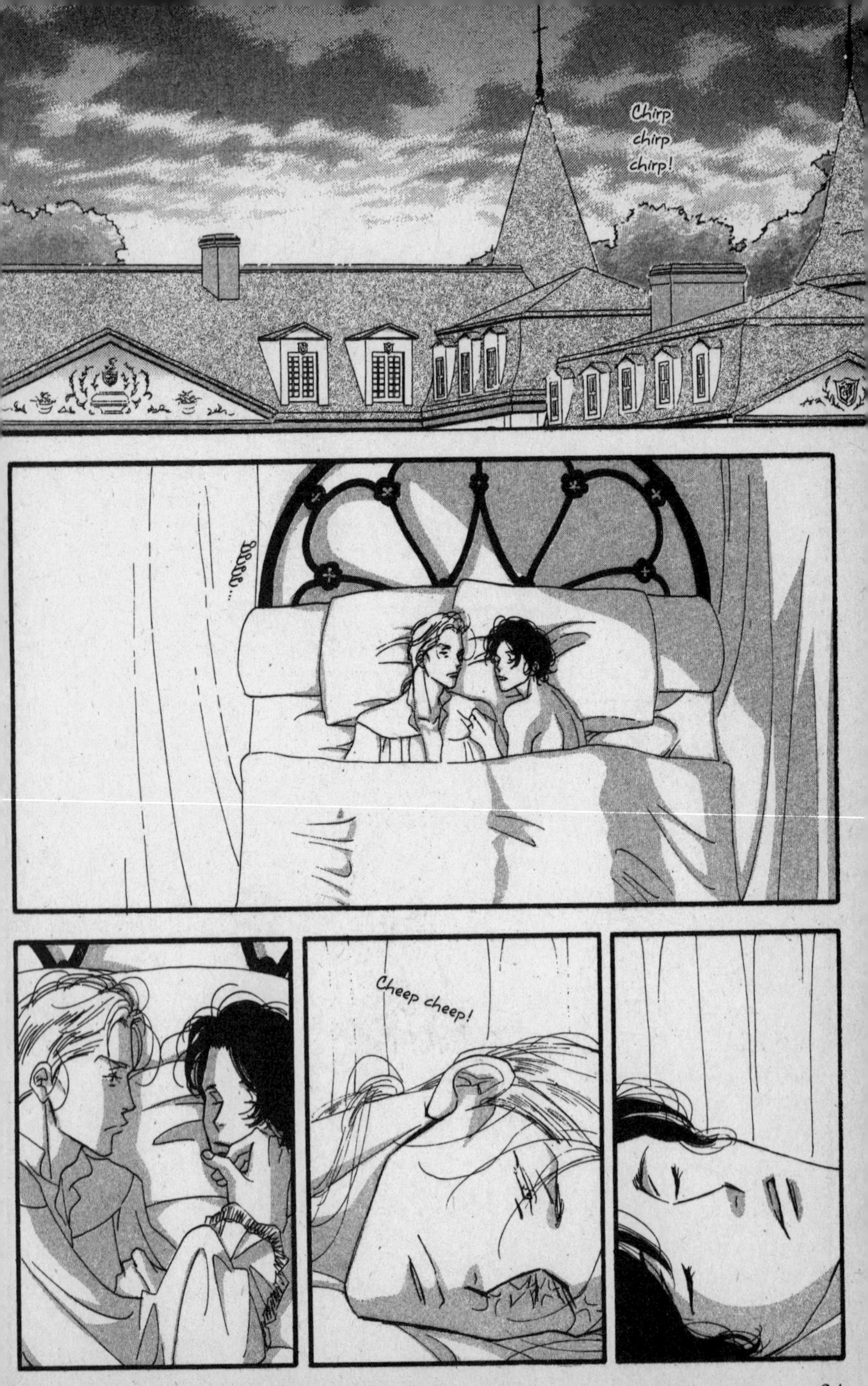
Chirp chirp chirp!
Cheep cheep!

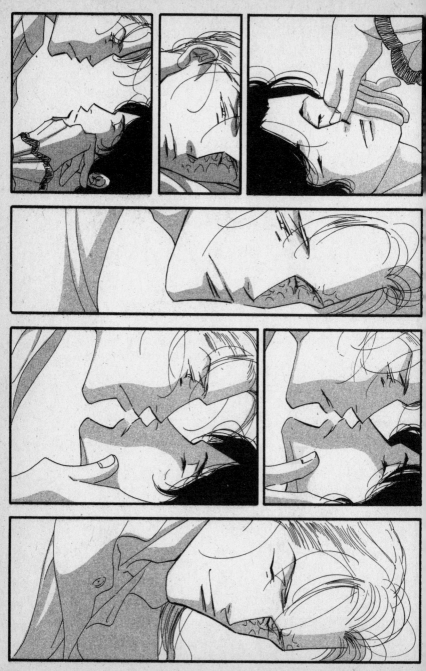

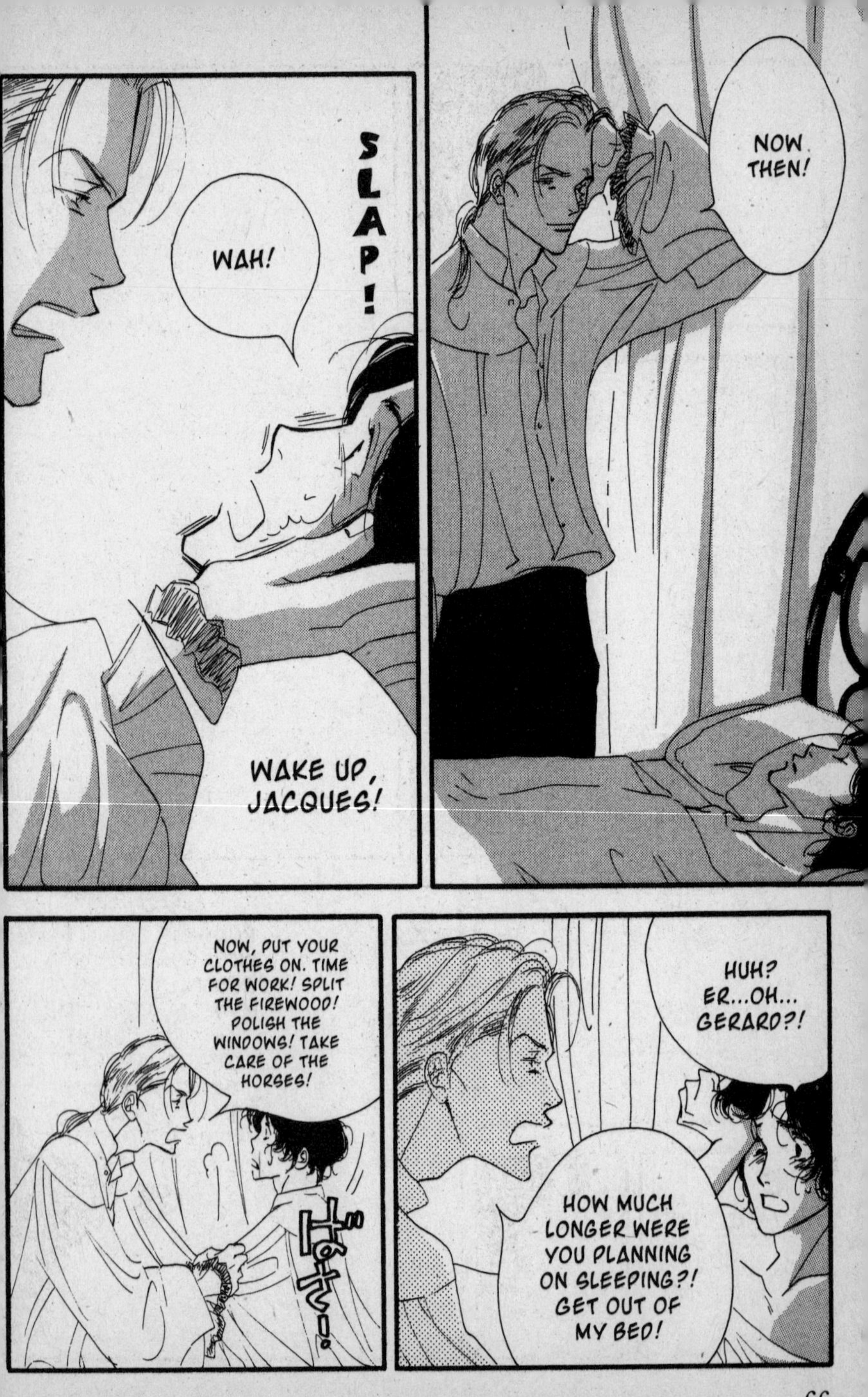
NOW THEN!
SLAP!
WAH!
WAKE UP, JACQUES!
HUH? ER...OH... GERARD?!
HOW MUCH LONGER WERE YOU PLANNING ON SLEEPING?! GET OUT OF MY BED!
NOW, PUT YOUR CLOTHES ON. TIME FOR WORK! SPLIT THE FIREWOOD! POLISH THE WINDOWS! TAKE CARE OF THE HORSES!

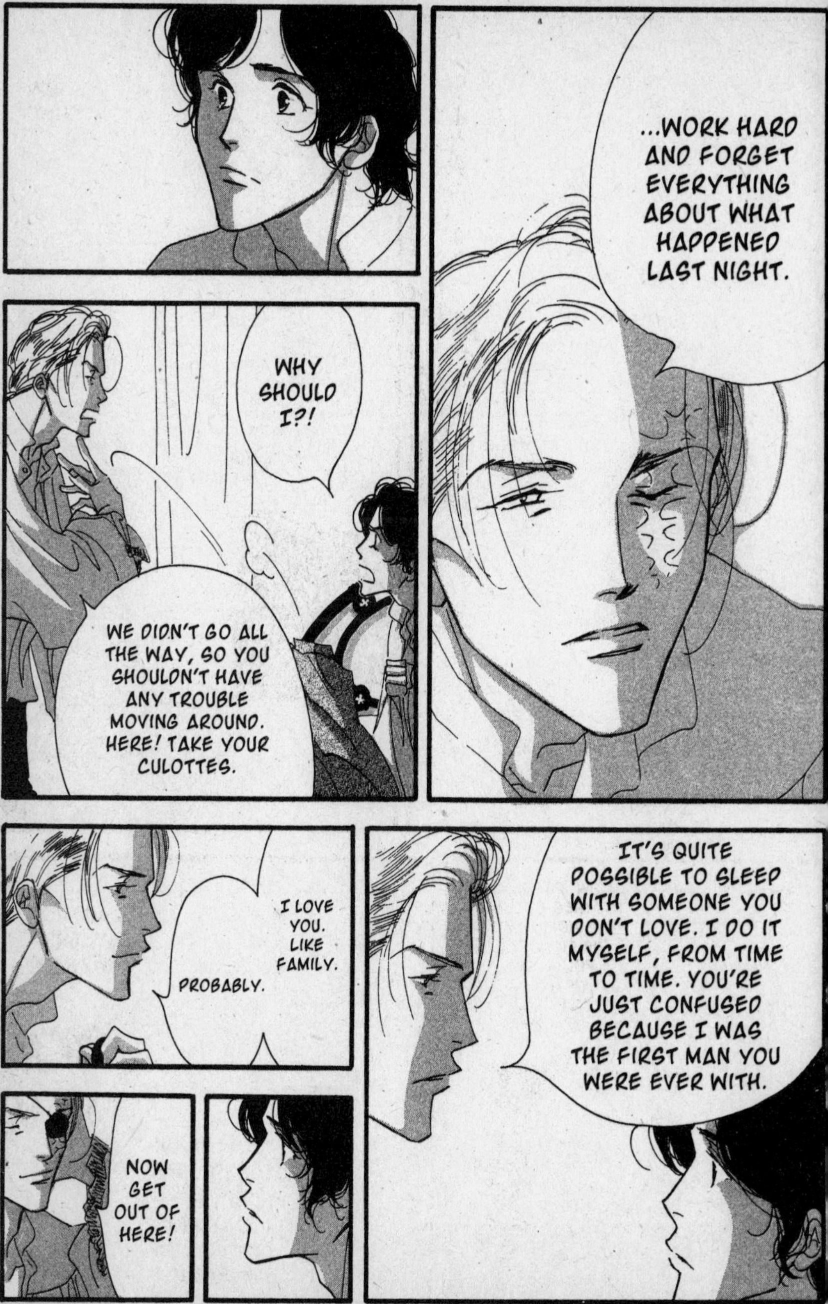
...WORK HARD AND FORGET EVERYTHING ABOUT WHAT HAPPENED LAST NIGHT.
WHY SHOULD I?!
WE DIDN'T GO ALL THE WAY, SO YOU SHOULDN'T HAVE ANY TROUBLE MOVING AROUND. HERE! TAKE YOUR CULOTTES.
IT'S QUITE POSSIBLE TO SLEEP WITH SOMEONE YOU DON'T LOVE. I DO IT MYSELF, FROM TIME TO TIME. YOU'RE JUST CONFUSED BECAUSE I WAS THE FIRST MAN YOU WERE EVER WITH.
I LOVE YOU. LIKE FAMILY.
PROBABLY.
NOW GET OUT OF HERE!

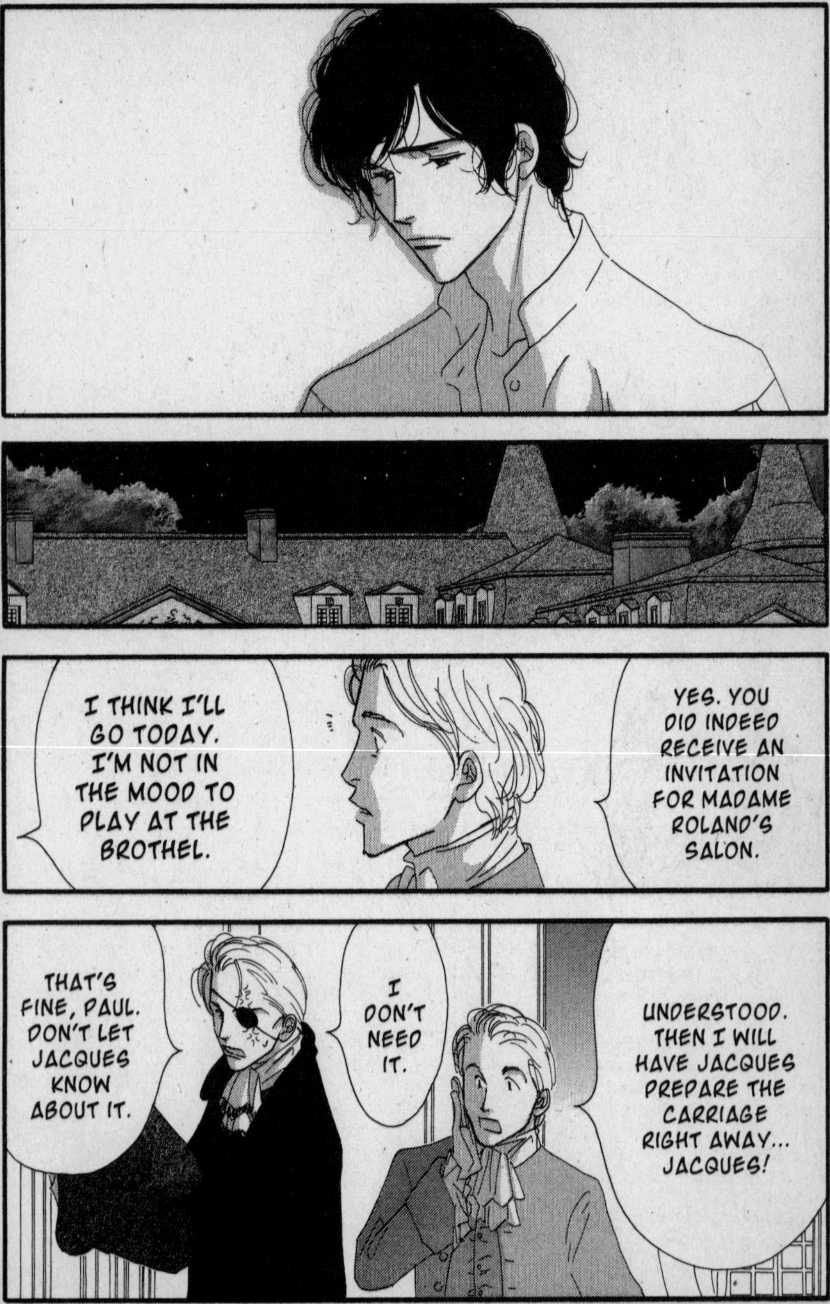
YES. YOU DID INDEED RECEIVE AN INVITATION FOR MADAME ROLAND'S SALON.
I THINK I'LL GO TODAY. I'M NOT IN THE MOOD TO PLAY AT THE BROTHEL.
UNDERSTOOD. THEN I WILL HAVE JACQUES PREPARE THE CARRIAGE RIGHT AWAY... JACQUES!
I DON'T NEED IT.
THAT'S FINE, PAUL. DON'T LET JACQUES KNOW ABOUT IT.

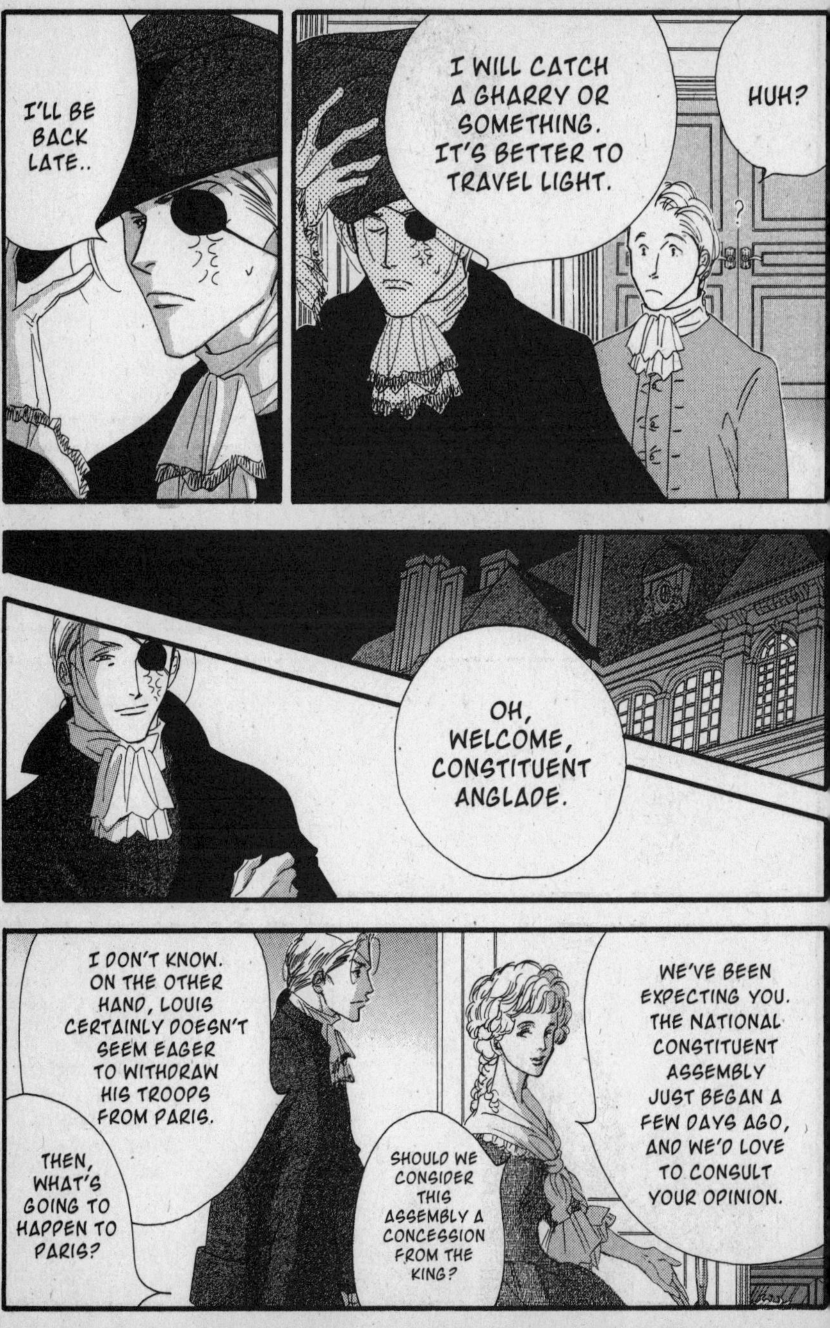
HUH?
I WILL CATCH A GHARRY OR SOMETHING. IT'S BETTER TO TRAVEL LIGHT.
I'LL BE BACK LATE..
OH, WELCOME, CONSTITUENT ANGLADE.
WE'VE BEEN EXPECTING YOU. THE NATIONAL CONSTITUENT ASSEMBLY JUST BEGAN A FEW DAYS AGO, AND WE'D LOVE TO CONSULT YOUR OPINION.
SHOULD WE CONSIDER THIS ASSEMBLY A CONCESSION FROM THE KING?
I DON'T KNOW. ON THE OTHER HAND, LOUIS CERTAINLY DOESN'T SEEM EAGER TO WITHDRAW HIS TROOPS FROM PARIS.
THEN, WHAT'S GOING TO HAPPEN TO PARIS?

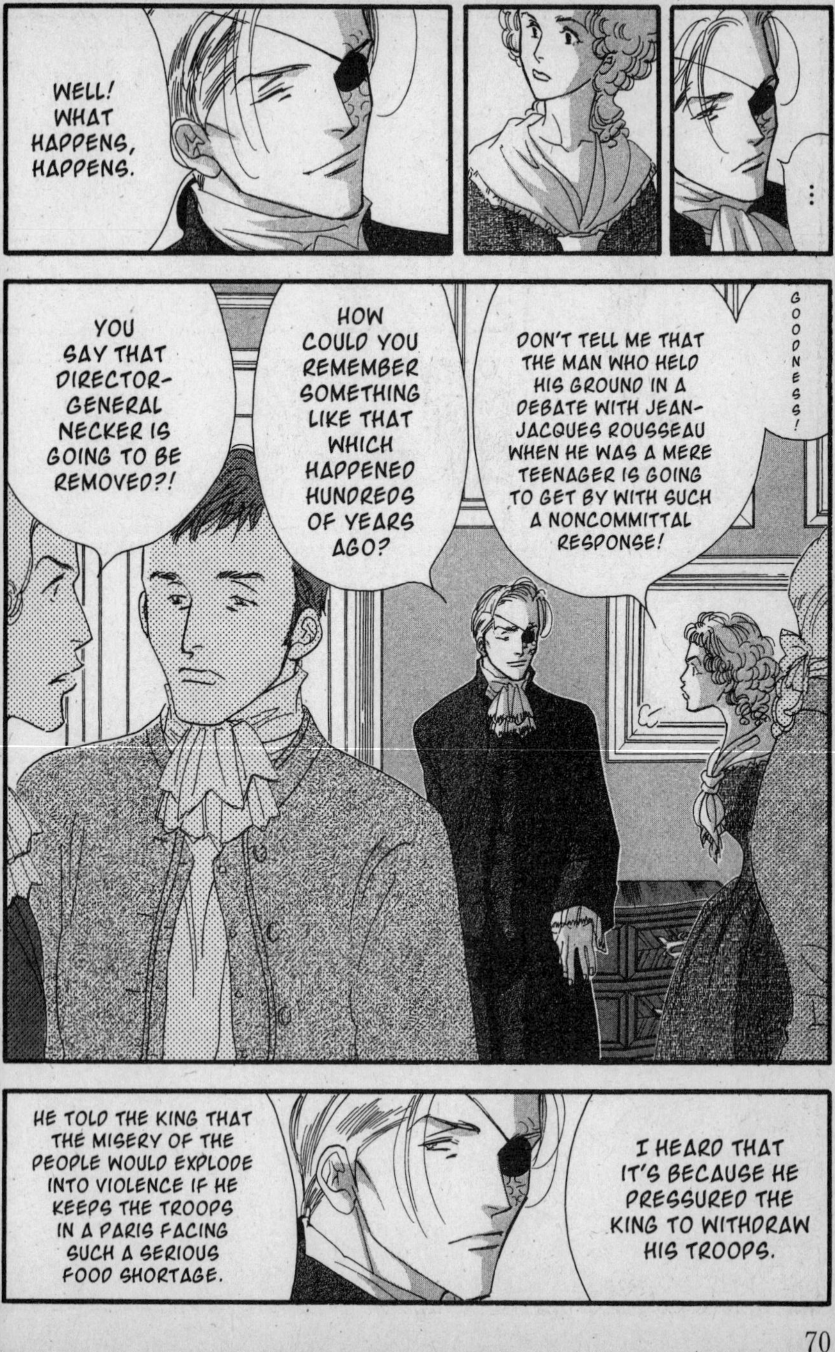
...
WELL! WHAT HAPPENS, HAPPENS.
GOODNESS!
DON'T TELL ME THAT THE MAN WHO HELD HIS GROUND IN A DEBATE WITH JEAN-JACQUES ROUSSEAU WHEN HE WAS A MERE TEENAGER IS GOING TO GET BY WITH SUCH A NONCOMMITTAL RESPONSE!
HOW COULD YOU REMEMBER SOMETHING LIKE THAT WHICH HAPPENED HUNDREDS OF YEARS AGO?
YOU SAY THAT DIRECTOR-GENERAL NECKER IS GOING TO BE REMOVED?!
I HEARD THAT IT'S BECAUSE HE PRESSURED THE KING TO WITHDRAW HIS TROOPS.
HE TOLD THE KING THAT THE MISERY OF THE PEOPLE WOULD EXPLODE INTO VIOLENCE IF HE KEEPS THE TROOPS IN A PARIS FACING SUCH A SERIOUS FOOD SHORTAGE.

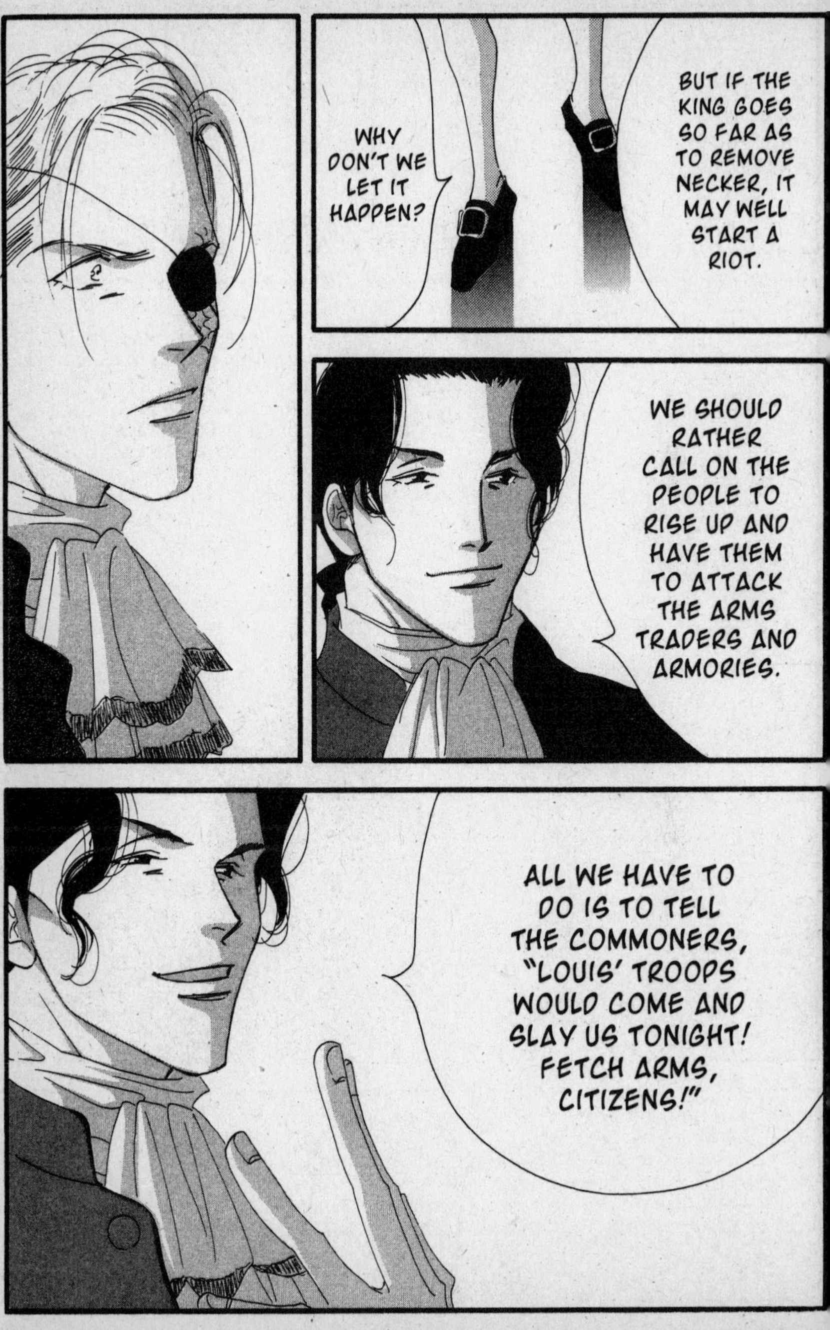
BUT IF THE KING GOES SO FAR AS TO REMOVE NECKER, IT MAY WELL START A RIOT.
WHY DON'T WE LET IT HAPPEN?
WE SHOULD RATHER CALL ON THE PEOPLE TO RISE UP AND HAVE THEM TO ATTACK THE ARMS TRADERS AND ARMORIES.
ALL WE HAVE TO DO IS TO TELL THE COMMONERS, "LOUIS' TROOPS WOULD COME AND SLAY US TONIGHT! FETCH ARMS, CITIZENS!"

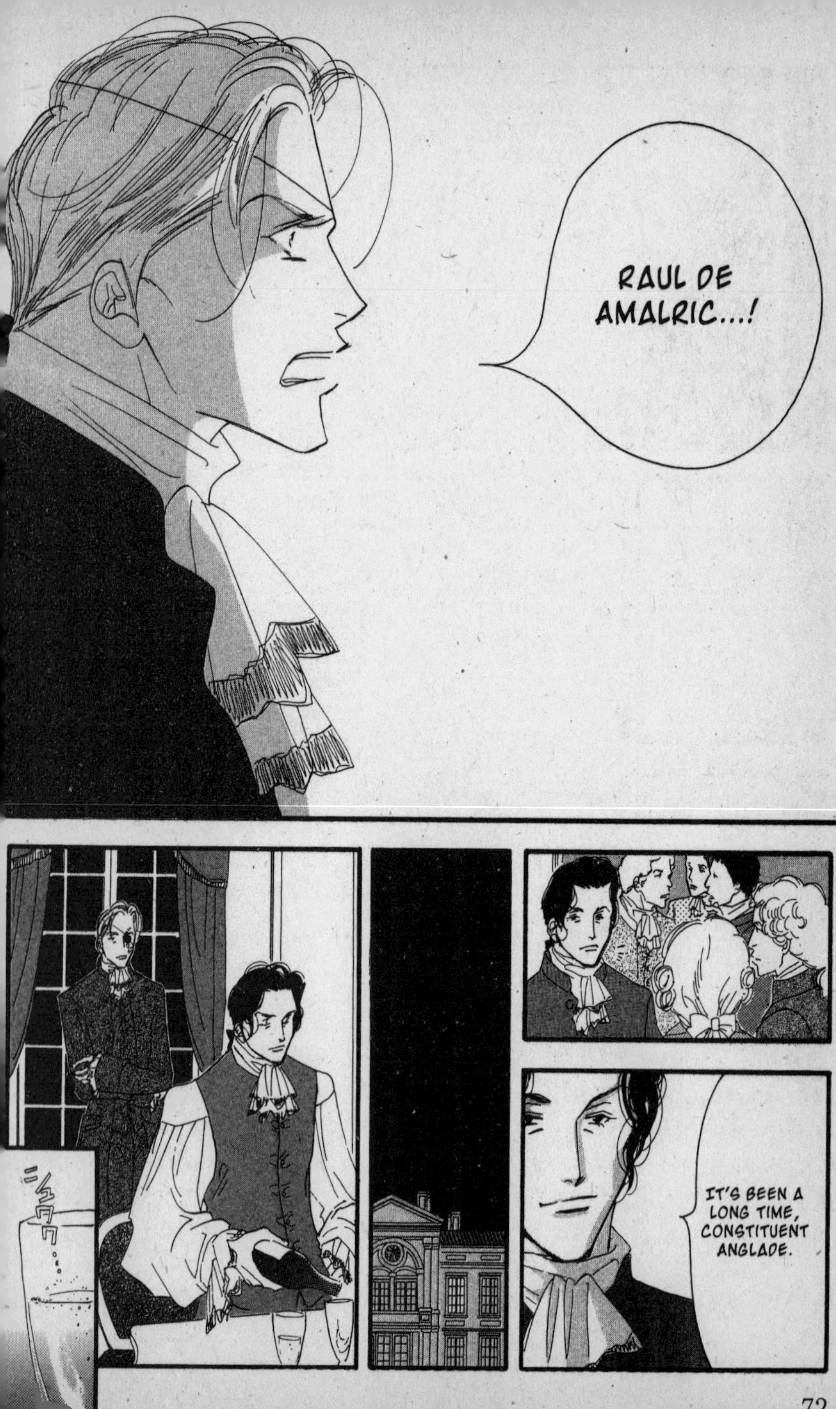
RAUL DE AMALRIC...!
IT'S BEEN A LONG TIME, CONSTITUENT ANGLADE.

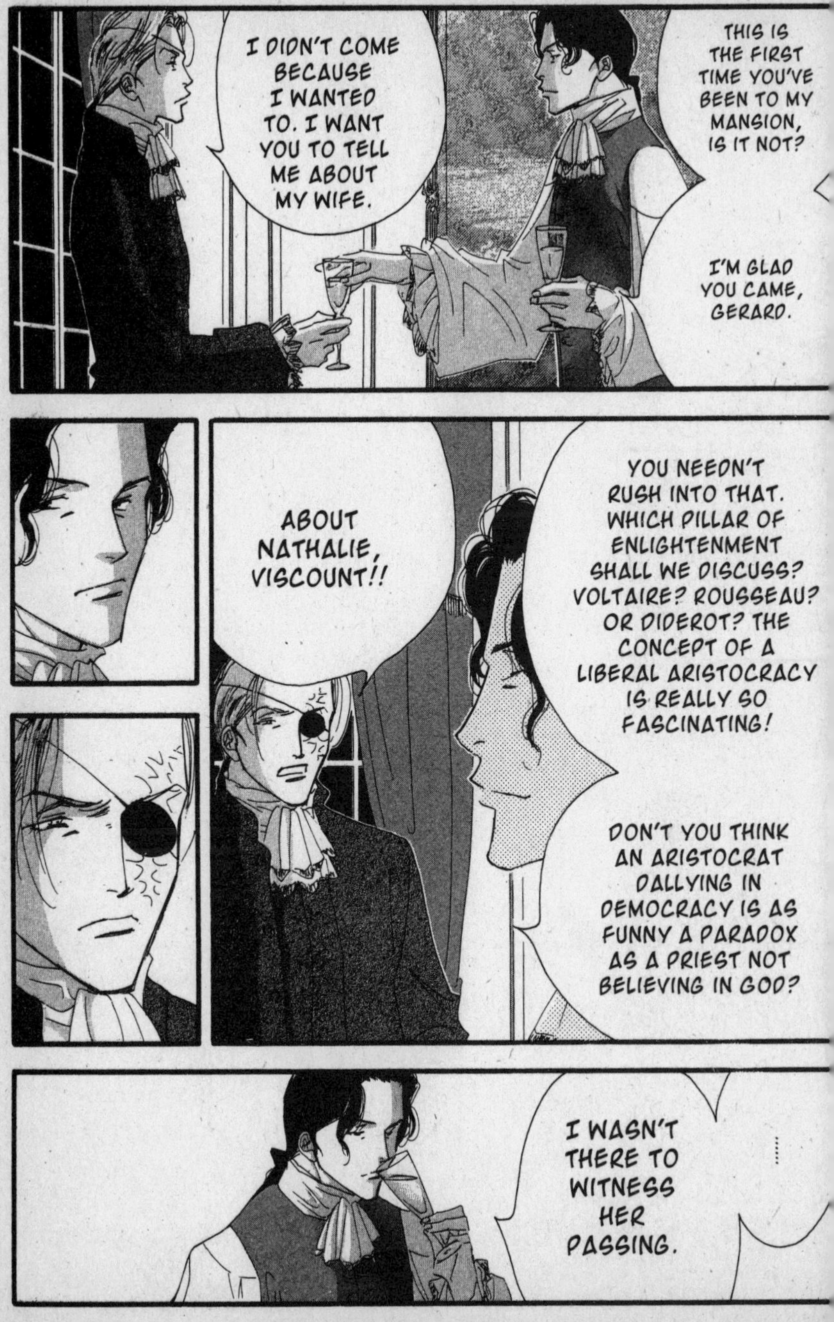
THIS IS THE FIRST TIME YOU'VE BEEN TO MY MANSION, IS IT NOT?
I DIDN'T COME BECAUSE I WANTED TO. I WANT YOU TO TELL ME ABOUT MY WIFE.
I'M GLAD YOU CAME, GERARD.
YOU NEEDN'T RUSH INTO THAT. WHICH PILLAR OF ENLIGHTENMENT SHALL WE DISCUSS? VOLTAIRE? ROUSSEAU? OR DIDEROT? THE CONCEPT OF A LIBERAL ARISTOCRACY IS REALLY SO FASCINATING!
ABOUT NATHALIE, VISCOUNT!!
DON'T YOU THINK AN ARISTOCRAT DALLYING IN DEMOCRACY IS AS FUNNY A PARADOX AS A PRIEST NOT BELIEVING IN GOD?
......
I WASN'T THERE TO WITNESS HER PASSING.

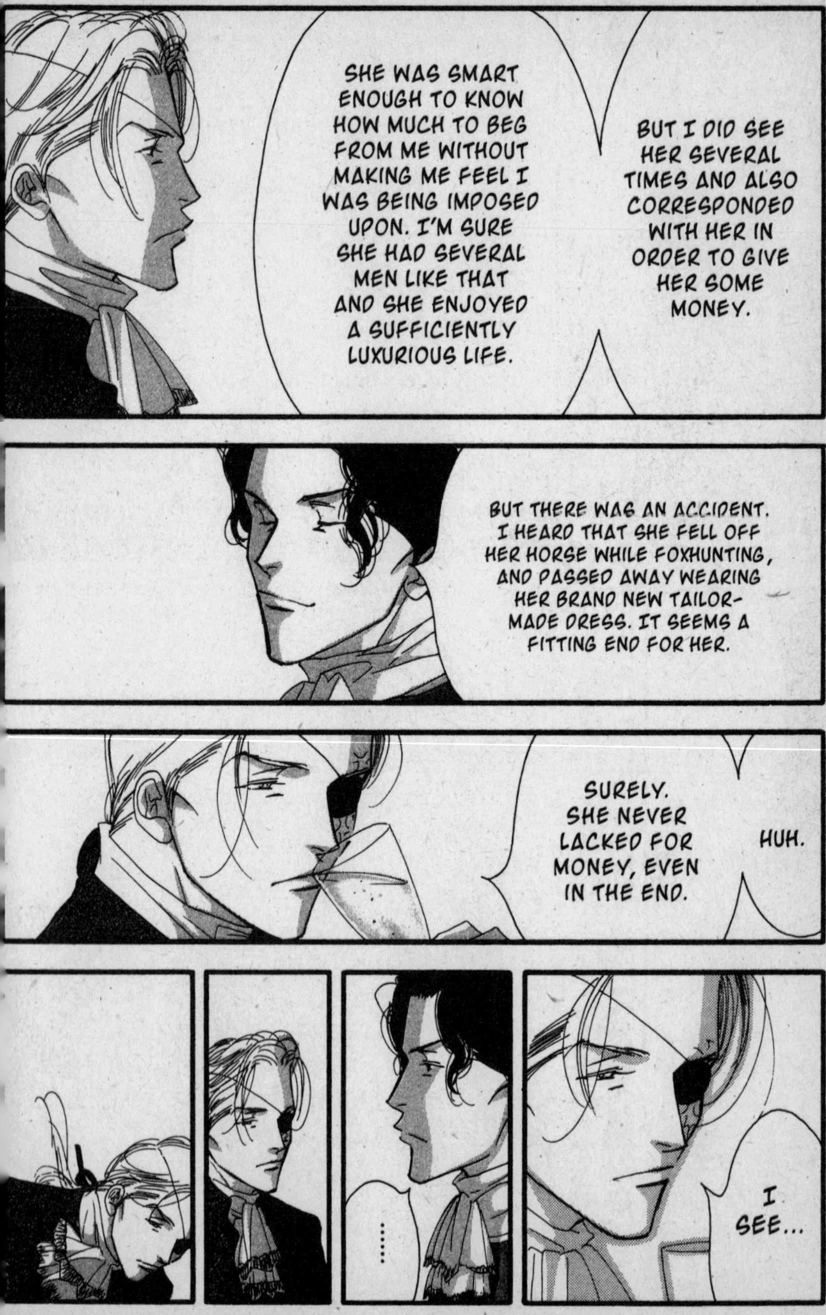
BUT I DID SEE HER SEVERAL TIMES AND ALSO CORRESPONDED WITH HER IN ORDER TO GIVE HER SOME MONEY.
SHE WAS SMART ENOUGH TO KNOW HOW MUCH TO BEG FROM ME WITHOUT MAKING ME FEEL I WAS BEING IMPOSED UPON. I'M SURE SHE HAD SEVERAL MEN LIKE THAT AND SHE ENJOYED A SUFFICIENTLY LUXURIOUS LIFE.
BUT THERE WAS AN ACCIDENT. I HEARD THAT SHE FELL OFF HER HORSE WHILE FOXHUNTING, AND PASSED AWAY WEARING HER BRAND NEW TAILOR-MADE DRESS. IT SEEMS A FITTING END FOR HER.
HUH.
SURELY. SHE NEVER LACKED FOR MONEY, EVEN IN THE END.
I SEE...
......

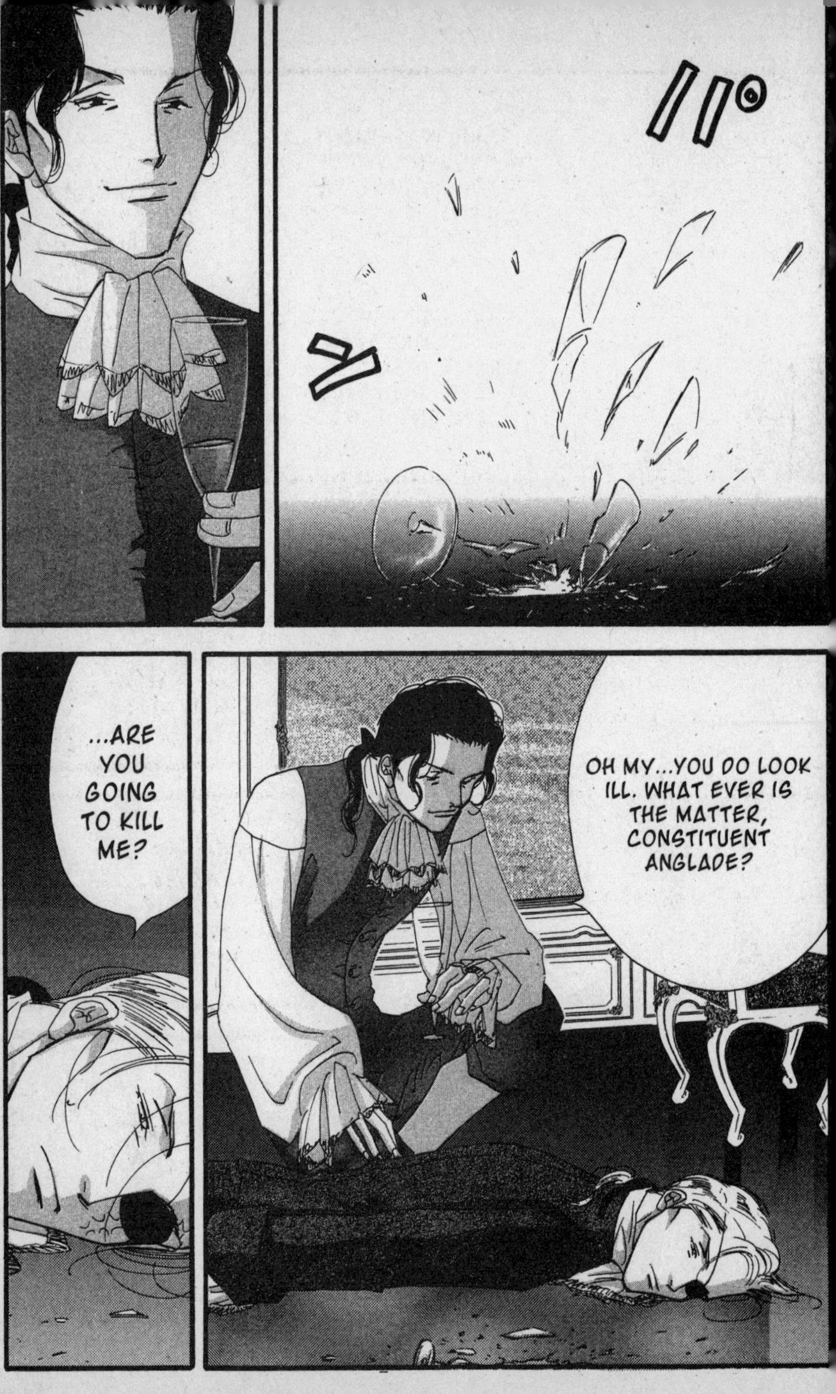

OH MY...YOU DO LOOK ILL. WHAT EVER IS THE MATTER, CONSTITUENT ANGLADE?
...ARE YOU GOING TO KILL ME?

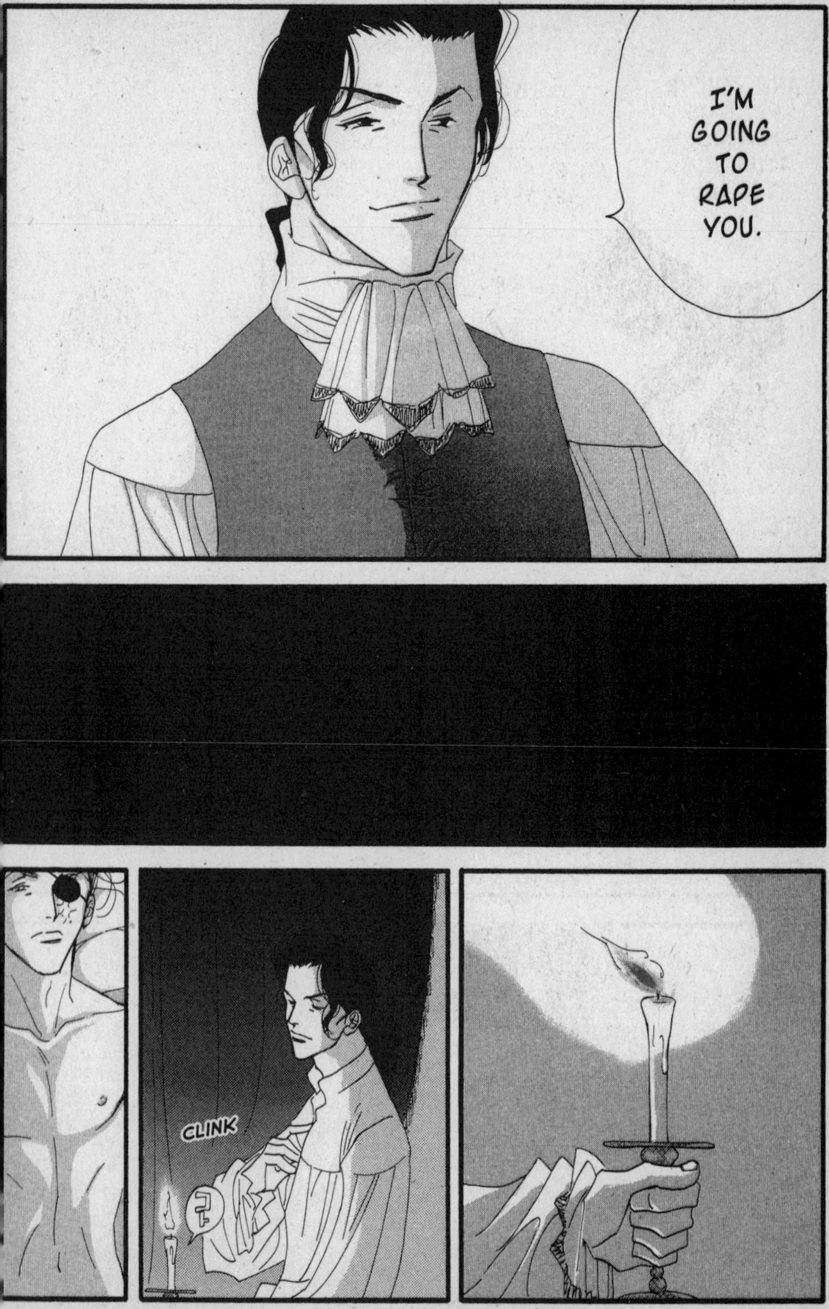
I'M GOING TO RAPE YOU.
CLINK

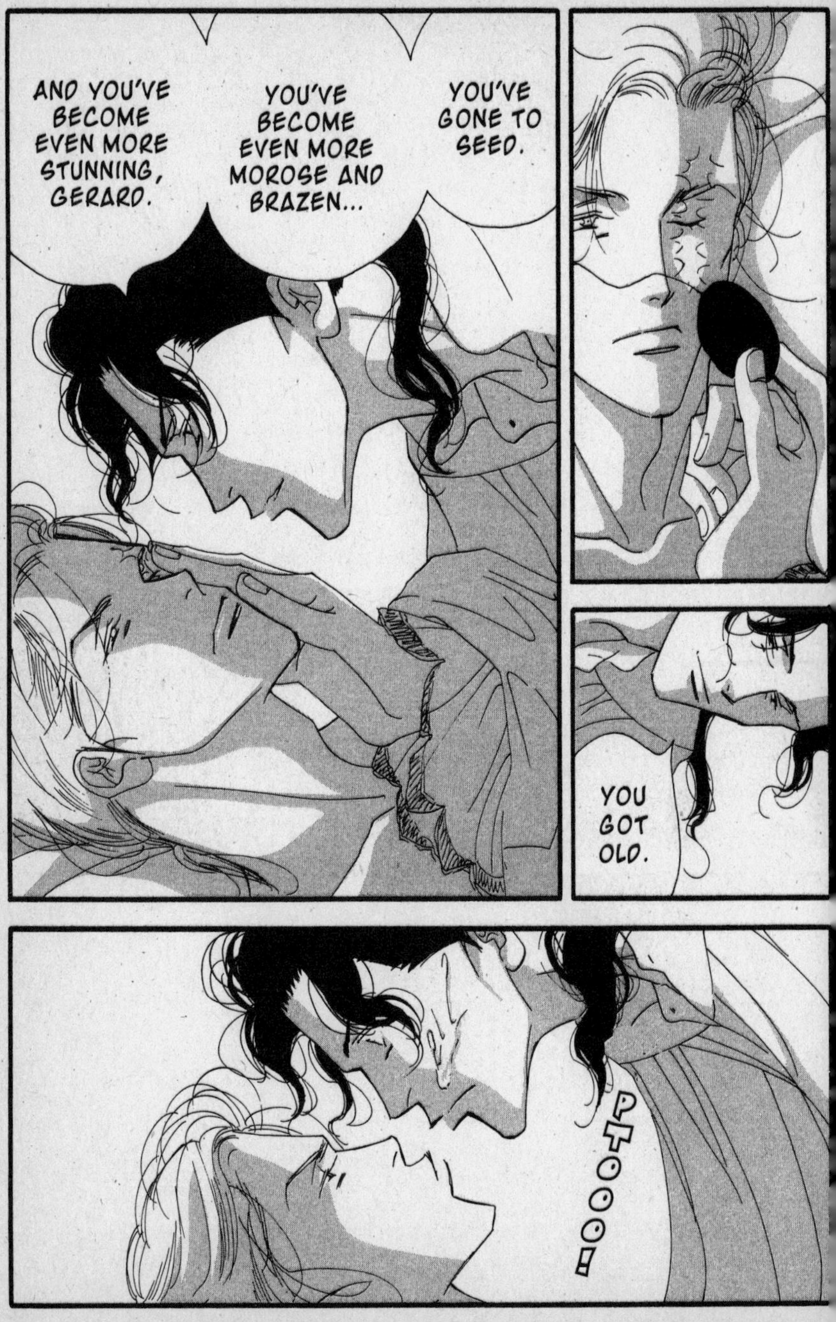
YOU GOT OLD.
YOU'VE GONE TO SEED.
YOU'VE BECOME EVEN MORE MOROSE AND BRAZEN...
AND YOU'VE BECOME EVEN MORE STUNNING, GERARD.
PTOOOOO!

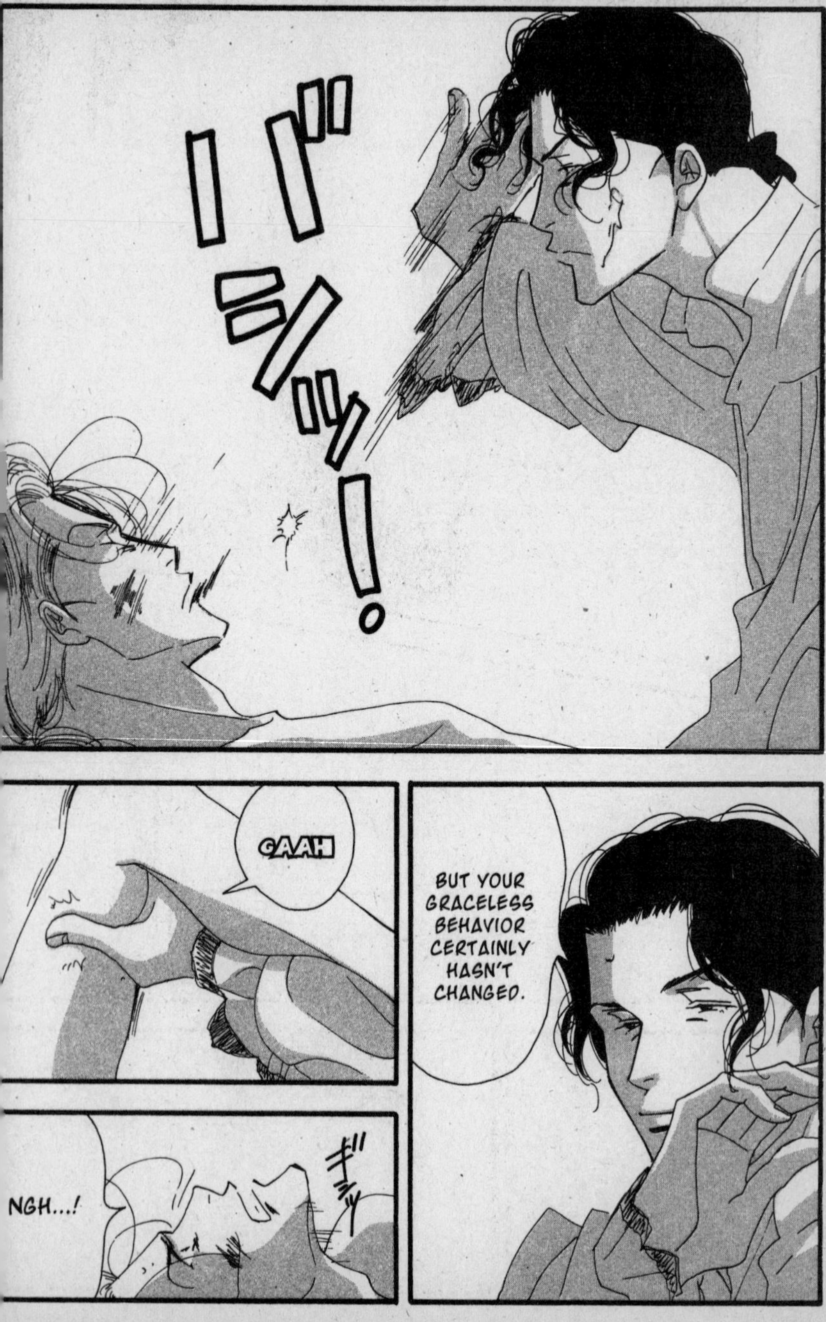
バシッー!
GAAH
BUT YOUR GRACELESS BEHAVIOR CERTAINLY HASN'T CHANGED.
NGH...!
ギリッ

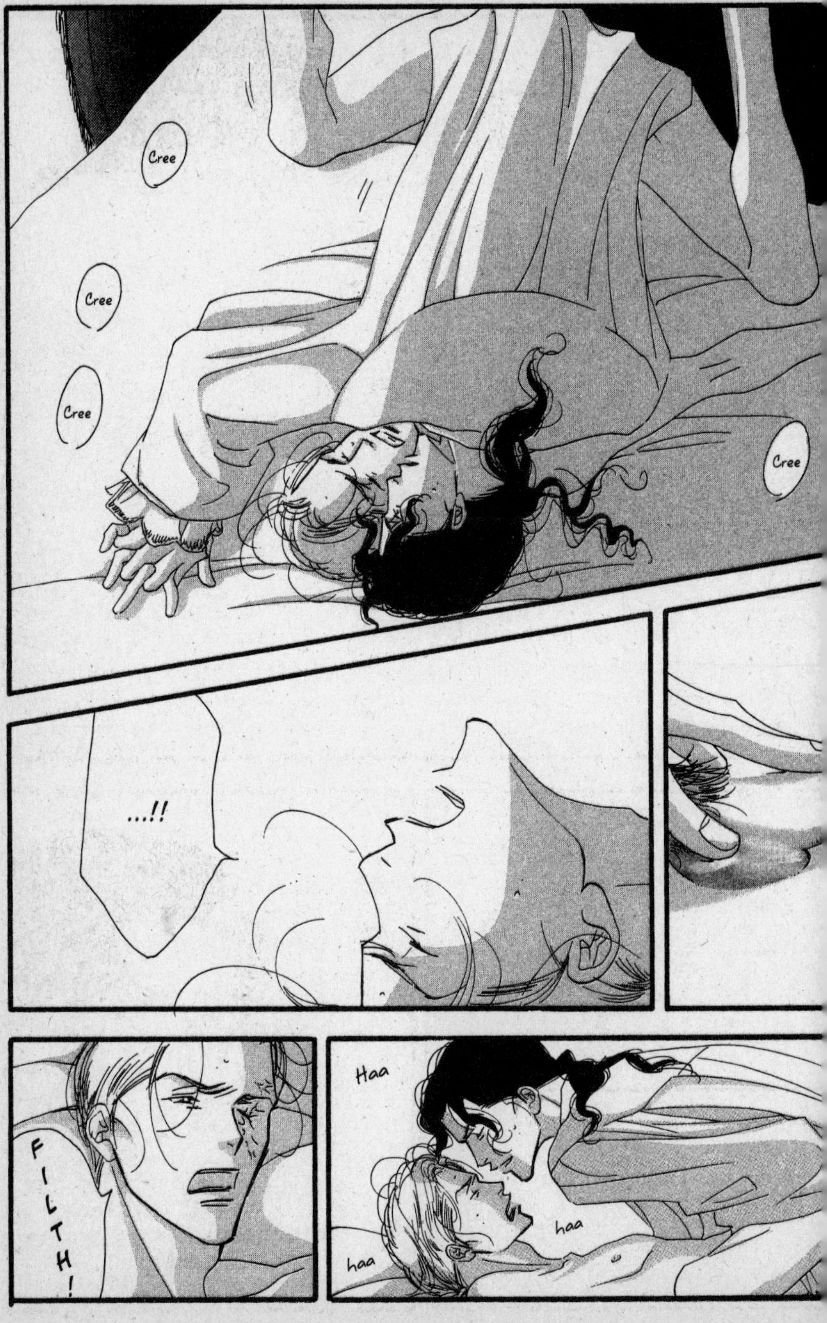
Cree
Cree
Cree
Cree
...!!
Haa
haa
haa
FILTH!

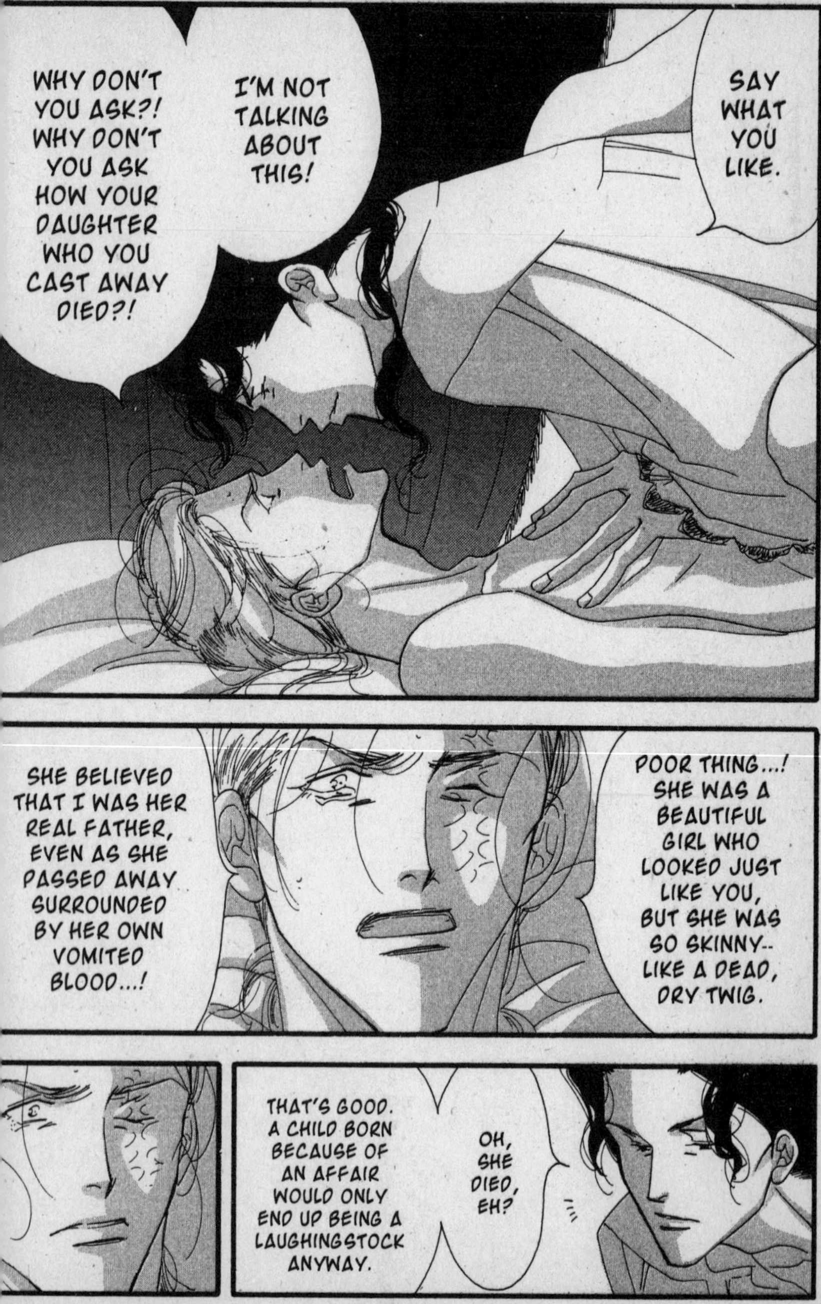
SAY WHAT YOU LIKE.
I'M NOT TALKING ABOUT THIS!
WHY DON'T YOU ASK?! WHY DON'T YOU ASK HOW YOUR DAUGHTER WHO YOU CAST AWAY DIED?!
POOR THING...! SHE WAS A BEAUTIFUL GIRL WHO LOOKED JUST LIKE YOU, BUT SHE WAS SO SKINNY-- LIKE A DEAD, DRY TWIG.
SHE BELIEVED THAT I WAS HER REAL FATHER, EVEN AS SHE PASSED AWAY SURROUNDED BY HER OWN VOMITED BLOOD...!
OH, SHE DIED, EH?
THAT'S GOOD. A CHILD BORN BECAUSE OF AN AFFAIR WOULD ONLY END UP BEING A LAUGHINGSTOCK ANYWAY.

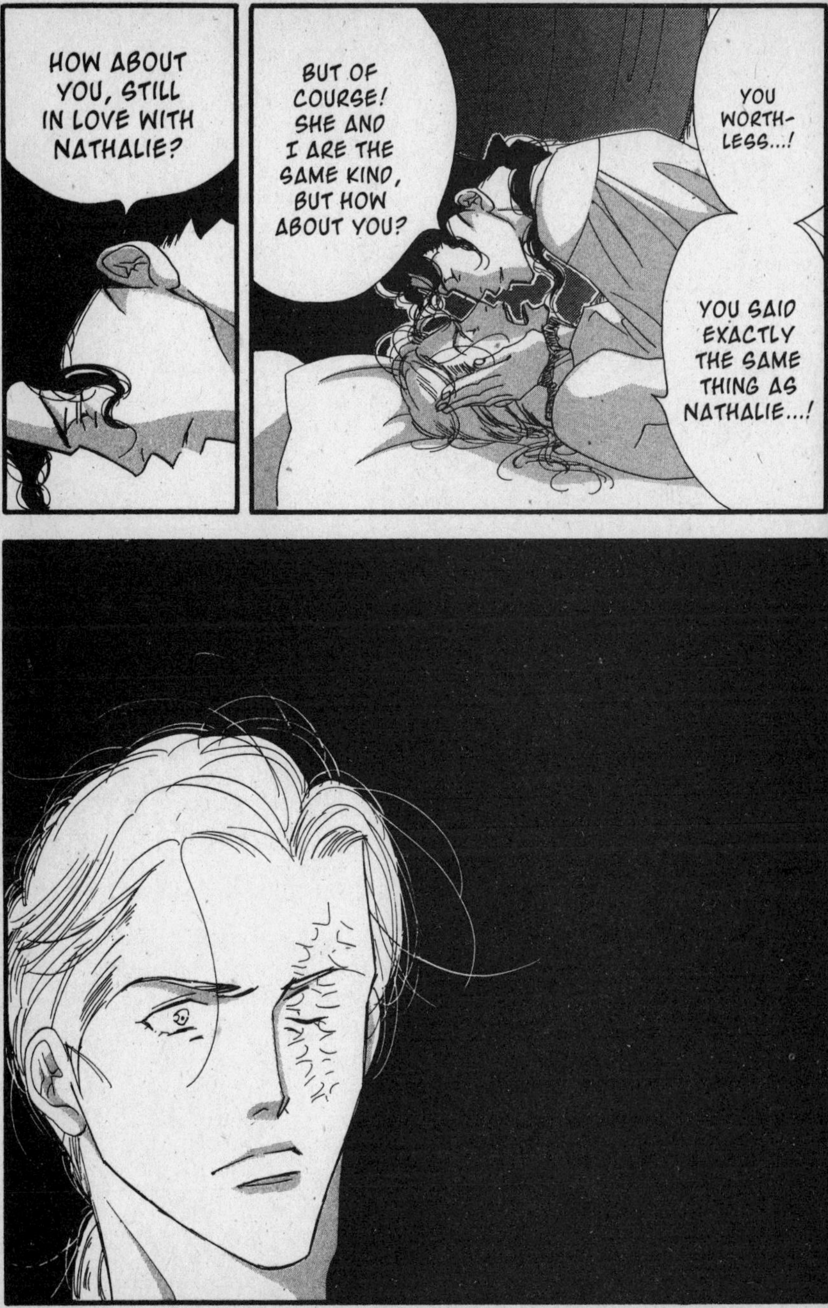

HOW ABOUT YOU, STILL IN LOVE WITH NATHALIE?
BUT OF COURSE! SHE AND I ARE THE SAME KIND, BUT HOW ABOUT YOU?
YOU WORTH-LESS...!
YOU SAID EXACTLY THE SAME THING AS NATHALIE...!

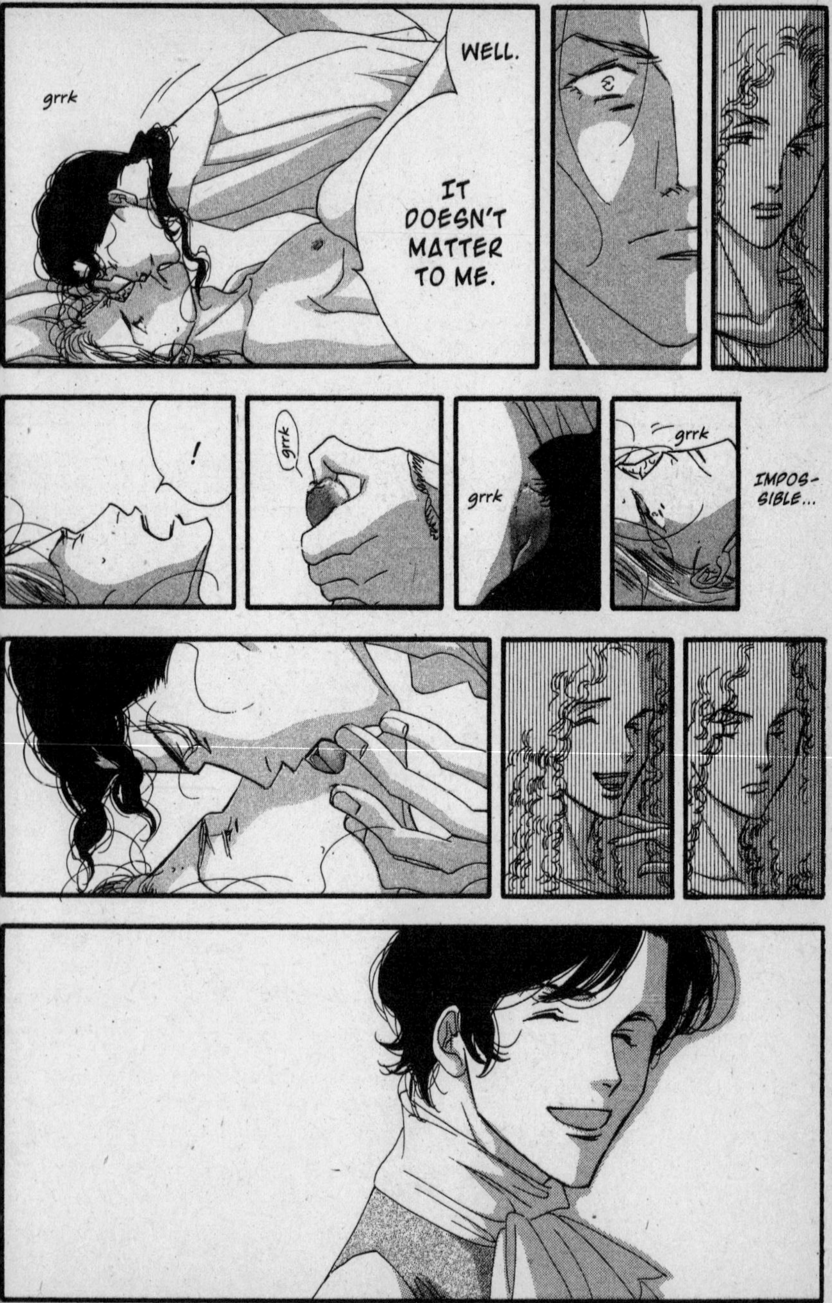
WELL.
grrk
IT DOESN'T MATTER TO ME.
IMPOS-SIBLE...
grrk
grrk
grrk
!

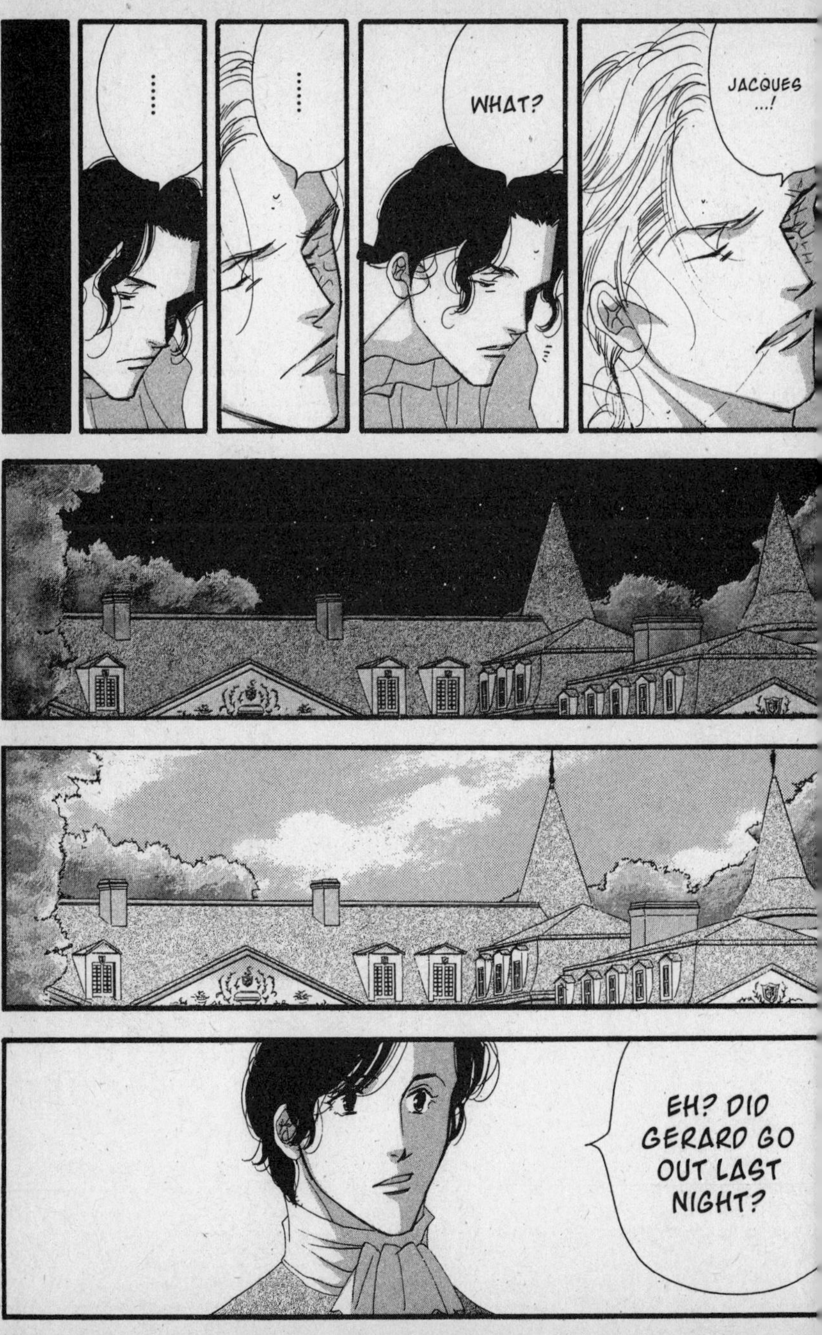
JACQUES ...!
WHAT?
......
......
EH? DID GERARD GO OUT LAST NIGHT?

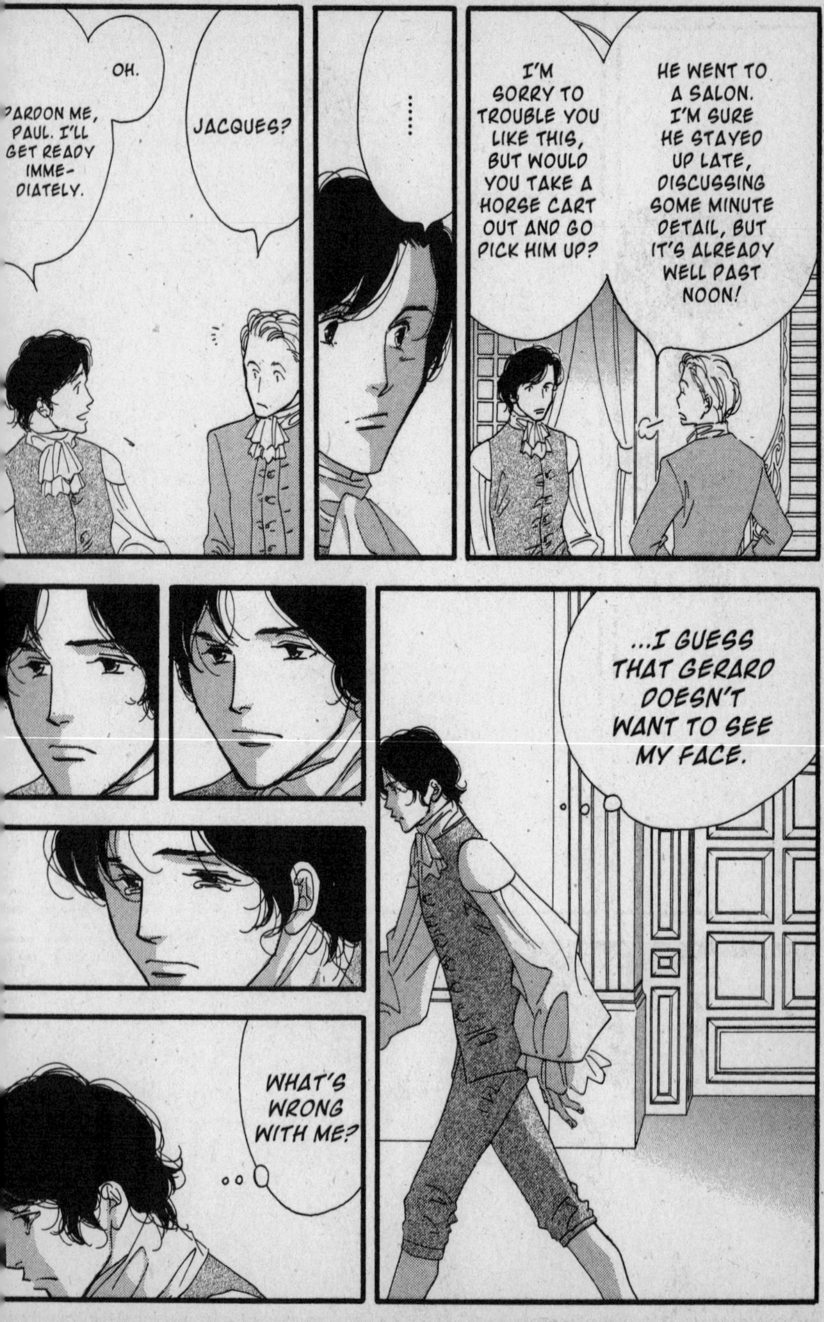
HE WENT TO A SALON. I'M SURE HE STAYED UP LATE, DISCUSSING SOME MINUTE DETAIL, BUT IT'S ALREADY WELL PAST NOON!
I'M SORRY TO TROUBLE YOU LIKE THIS, BUT WOULD YOU TAKE A HORSE CART OUT AND GO PICK HIM UP?
......
JACQUES?
OH.
PARDON ME, PAUL. I'LL GET READY IMME-DIATELY.
...I GUESS THAT GERARD DOESN'T WANT TO SEE MY FACE.
WHAT'S WRONG WITH ME?

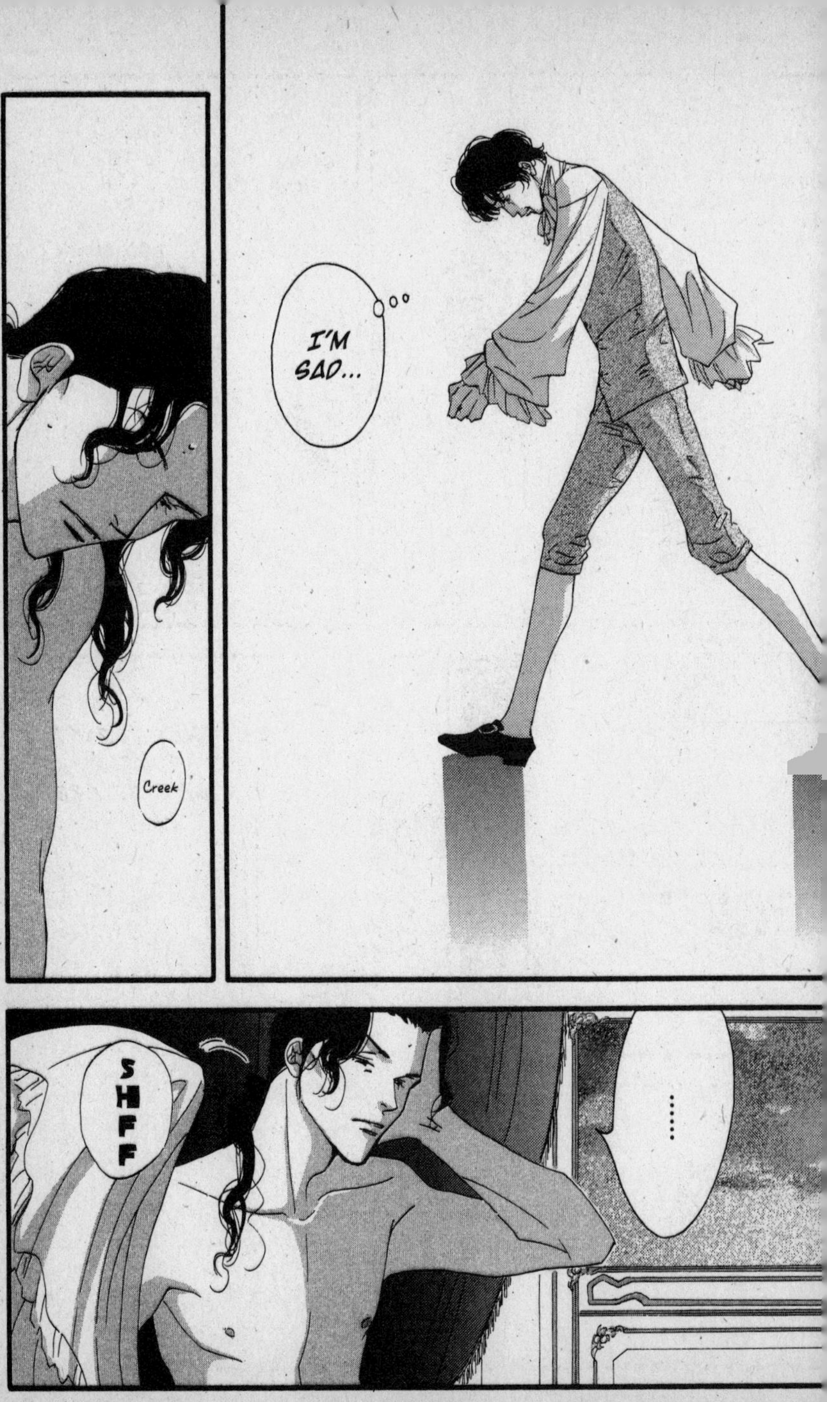
I'M SAD...
Creek
......
SHFF

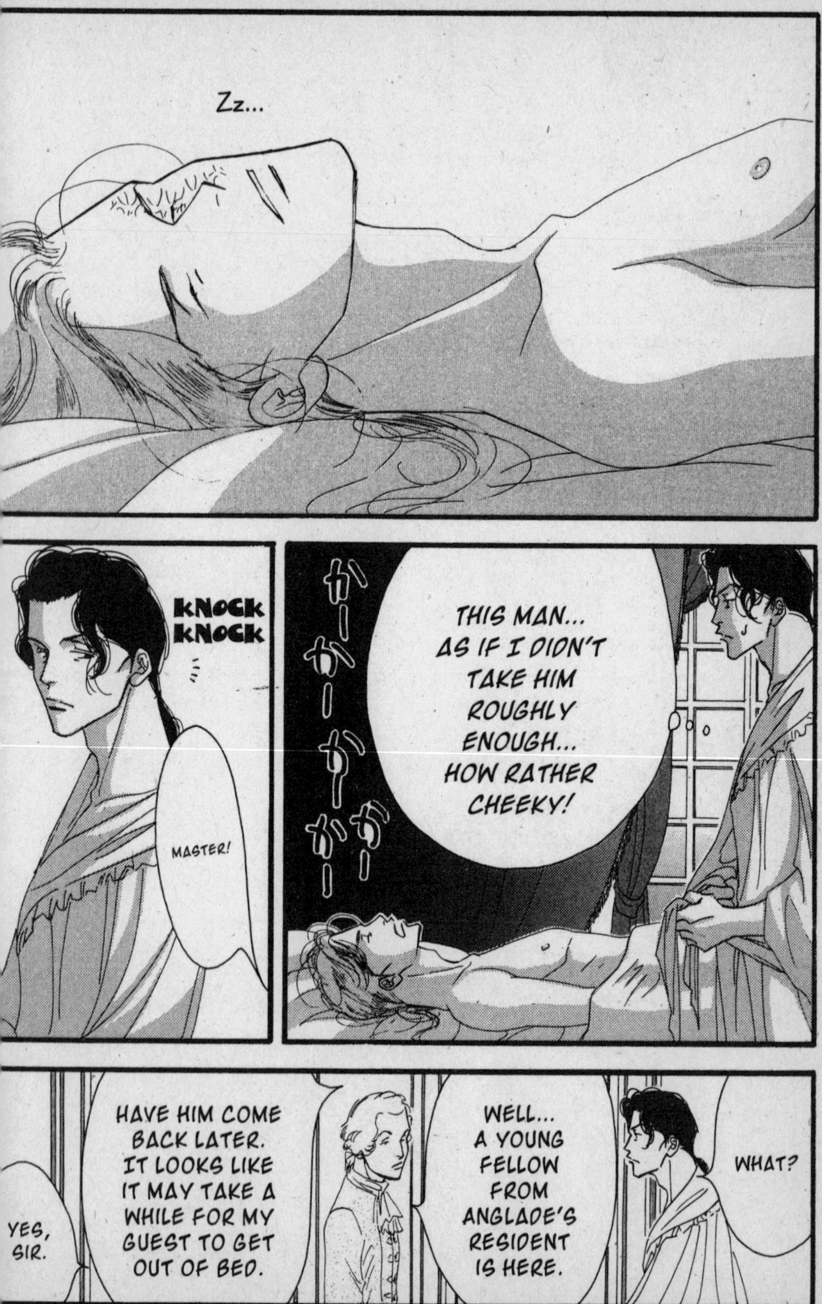
Zz...
かー
かーかーかーかー
THIS MAN... AS IF I DIDN'T TAKE HIM ROUGHLY ENOUGH... HOW RATHER CHEEKY!
KNOCK KNOCK
MASTER!
WHAT?
WELL... A YOUNG FELLOW FROM ANGLADE'S RESIDENT IS HERE.
HAVE HIM COME BACK LATER. IT LOOKS LIKE IT MAY TAKE A WHILE FOR MY GUEST TO GET OUT OF BED.
YES, SIR.

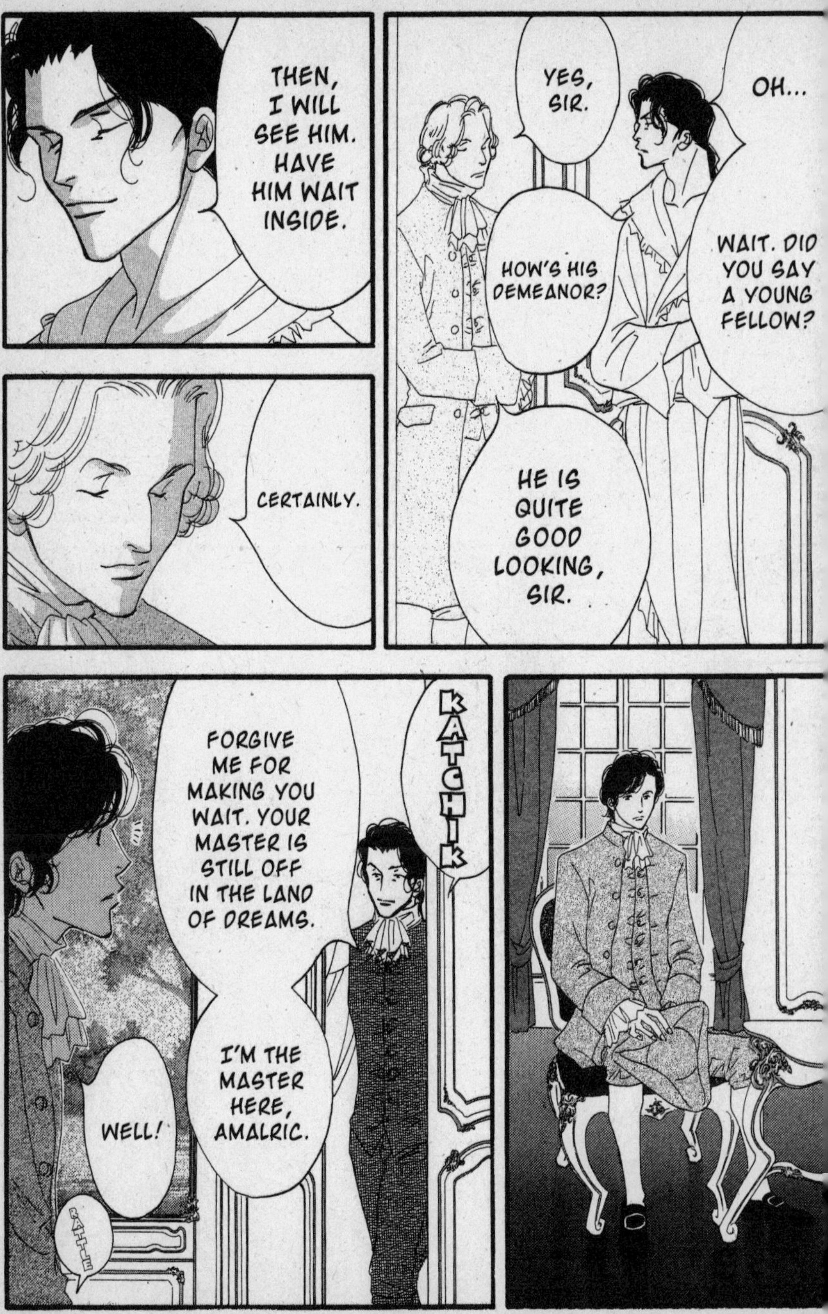
OH...
WAIT. DID YOU SAY A YOUNG FELLOW?
YES, SIR.
HOW'S HIS DEMEANOR?
HE IS QUITE GOOD LOOKING, SIR.
THEN, I WILL SEE HIM. HAVE HIM WAIT INSIDE.
CERTAINLY.
KATCHIK
FORGIVE ME FOR MAKING YOU WAIT. YOUR MASTER IS STILL OFF IN THE LAND OF DREAMS.
I'M THE MASTER HERE, AMALRIC.
WELL!
RATTLE

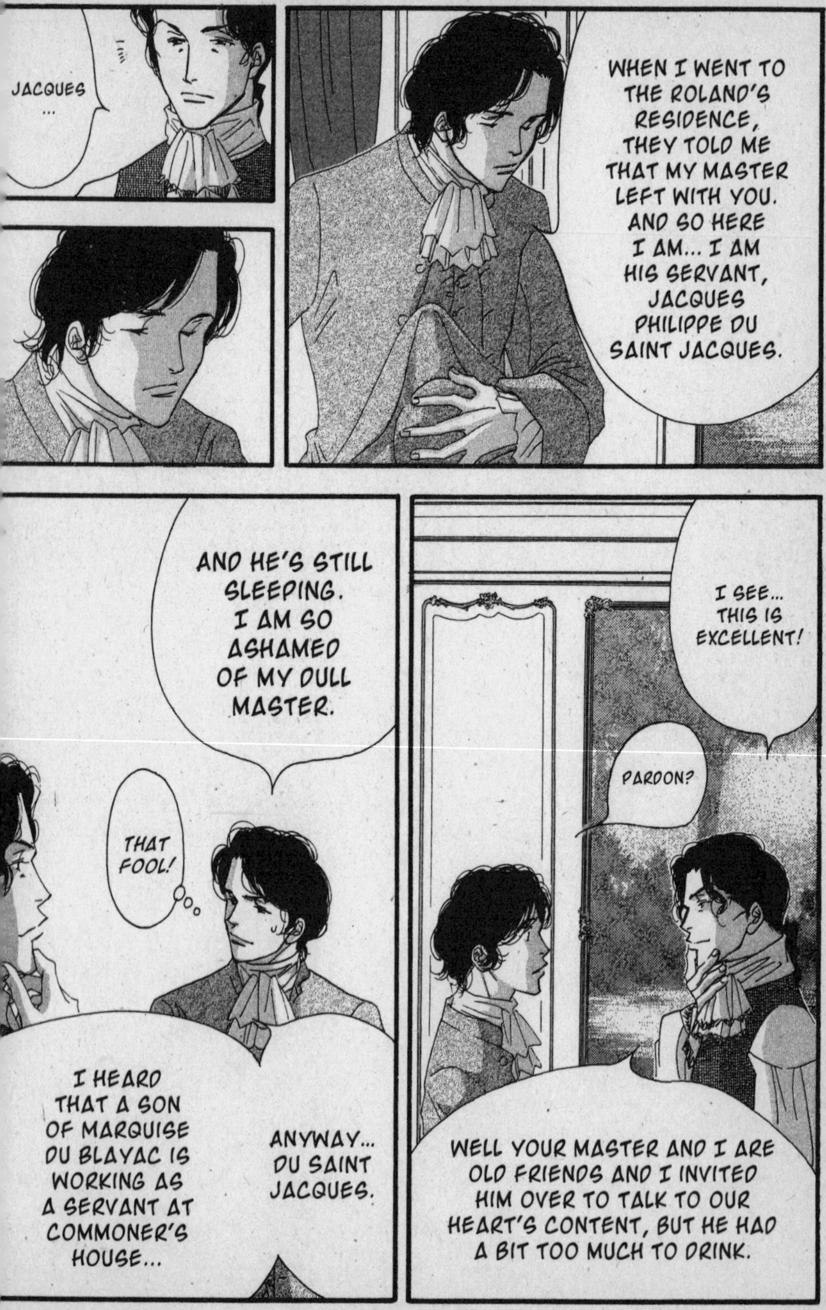

WHEN I WENT TO THE ROLAND'S RESIDENCE, THEY TOLD ME THAT MY MASTER LEFT WITH YOU. AND SO HERE I AM... I AM HIS SERVANT, JACQUES PHILIPPE DU SAINT JACQUES.
JACQUES ...
I SEE... THIS IS EXCELLENT!
PARDON?
WELL YOUR MASTER AND I ARE OLD FRIENDS AND I INVITED HIM OVER TO TALK TO OUR HEART'S CONTENT, BUT HE HAD A BIT TOO MUCH TO DRINK.
AND HE'S STILL SLEEPING. I AM SO ASHAMED OF MY DULL MASTER.
THAT FOOL!
ANYWAY... DU SAINT JACQUES.
I HEARD THAT A SON OF MARQUISE DU BLAYAC IS WORKING AS A SERVANT AT COMMONER'S HOUSE...

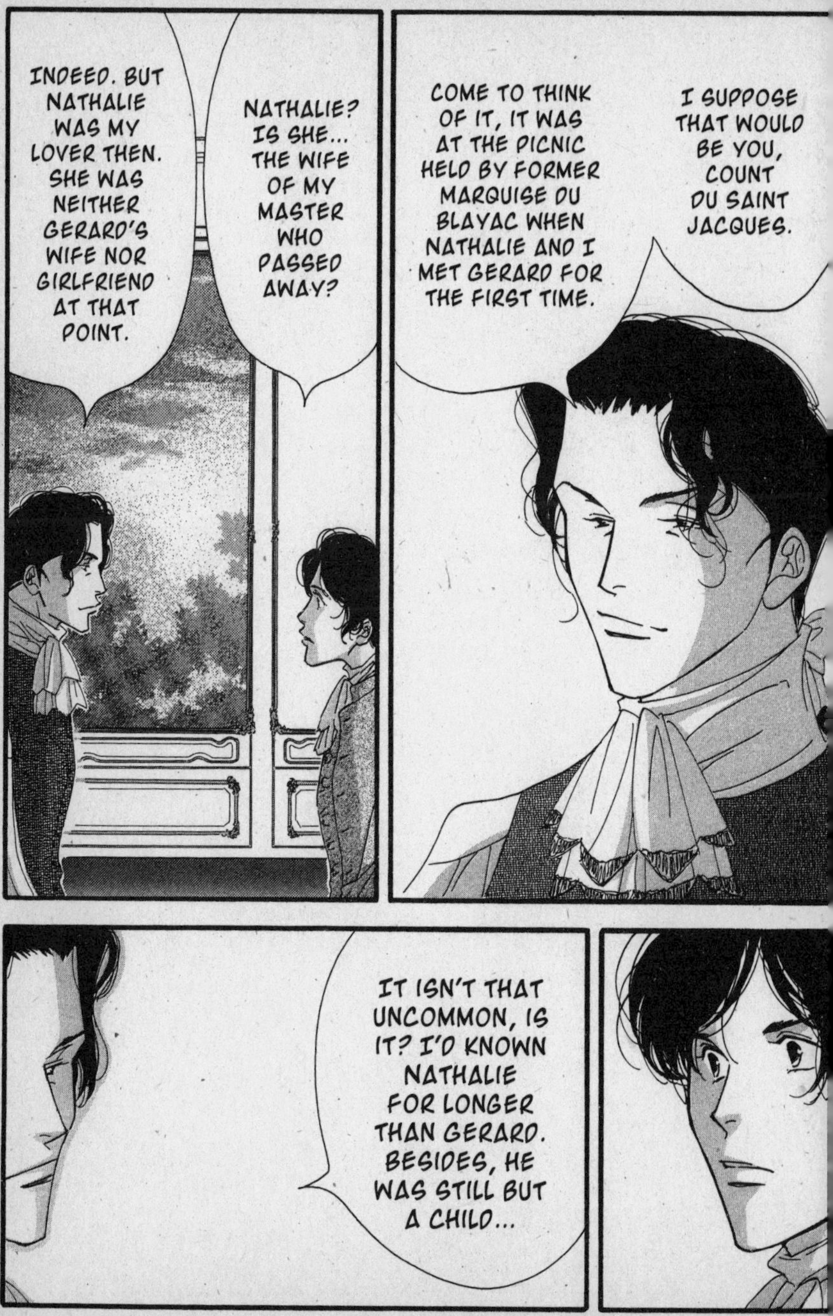

I SUPPOSE THAT WOULD BE YOU, COUNT DU SAINT JACQUES.
COME TO THINK OF IT, IT WAS AT THE PICNIC HELD BY FORMER MARQUISE DU BLAYAC WHEN NATHALIE AND I MET GERARD FOR THE FIRST TIME.
NATHALIE? IS SHE... THE WIFE OF MY MASTER WHO PASSED AWAY?
INDEED. BUT NATHALIE WAS MY LOVER THEN. SHE WAS NEITHER GERARD'S WIFE NOR GIRLFRIEND AT THAT POINT.
IT ISN'T THAT UNCOMMON, IS IT? I'D KNOWN NATHALIE FOR LONGER THAN GERARD. BESIDES, HE WAS STILL BUT A CHILD...

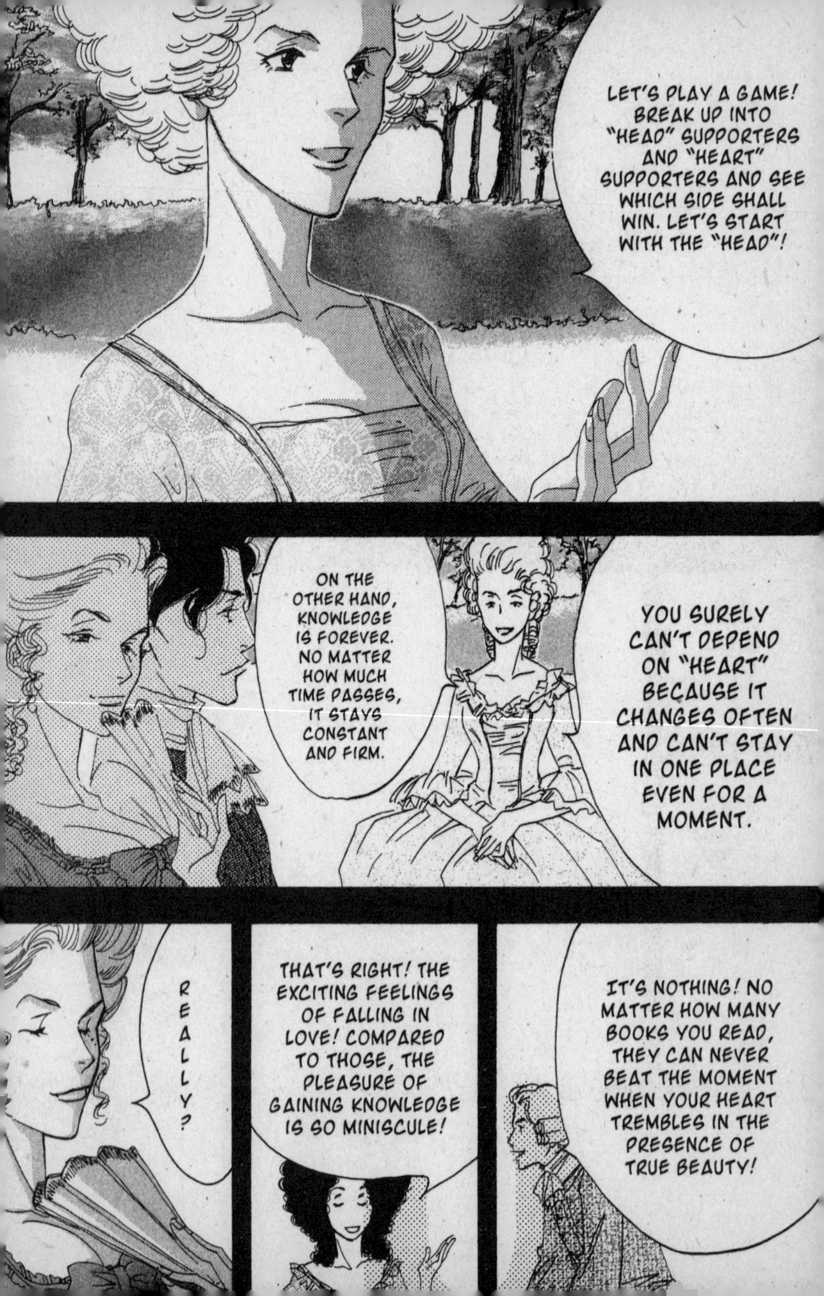
LET'S PLAY A GAME! BREAK UP INTO "HEAD" SUPPORTERS AND "HEART" SUPPORTERS AND SEE WHICH SIDE SHALL WIN. LET'S START WITH THE "HEAD"!
YOU SURELY CAN'T DEPEND ON "HEART" BECAUSE IT CHANGES OFTEN AND CAN'T STAY IN ONE PLACE EVEN FOR A MOMENT.
ON THE OTHER HAND, KNOWLEDGE IS FOREVER. NO MATTER HOW MUCH TIME PASSES, IT STAYS CONSTANT AND FIRM.
IT'S NOTHING! NO MATTER HOW MANY BOOKS YOU READ, THEY CAN NEVER BEAT THE MOMENT WHEN YOUR HEART TREMBLES IN THE PRESENCE OF TRUE BEAUTY!
THAT'S RIGHT! THE EXCITING FEELINGS OF FALLING IN LOVE! COMPARED TO THOSE, THE PLEASURE OF GAINING KNOWLEDGE IS SO MINISCULE!
REALLY?

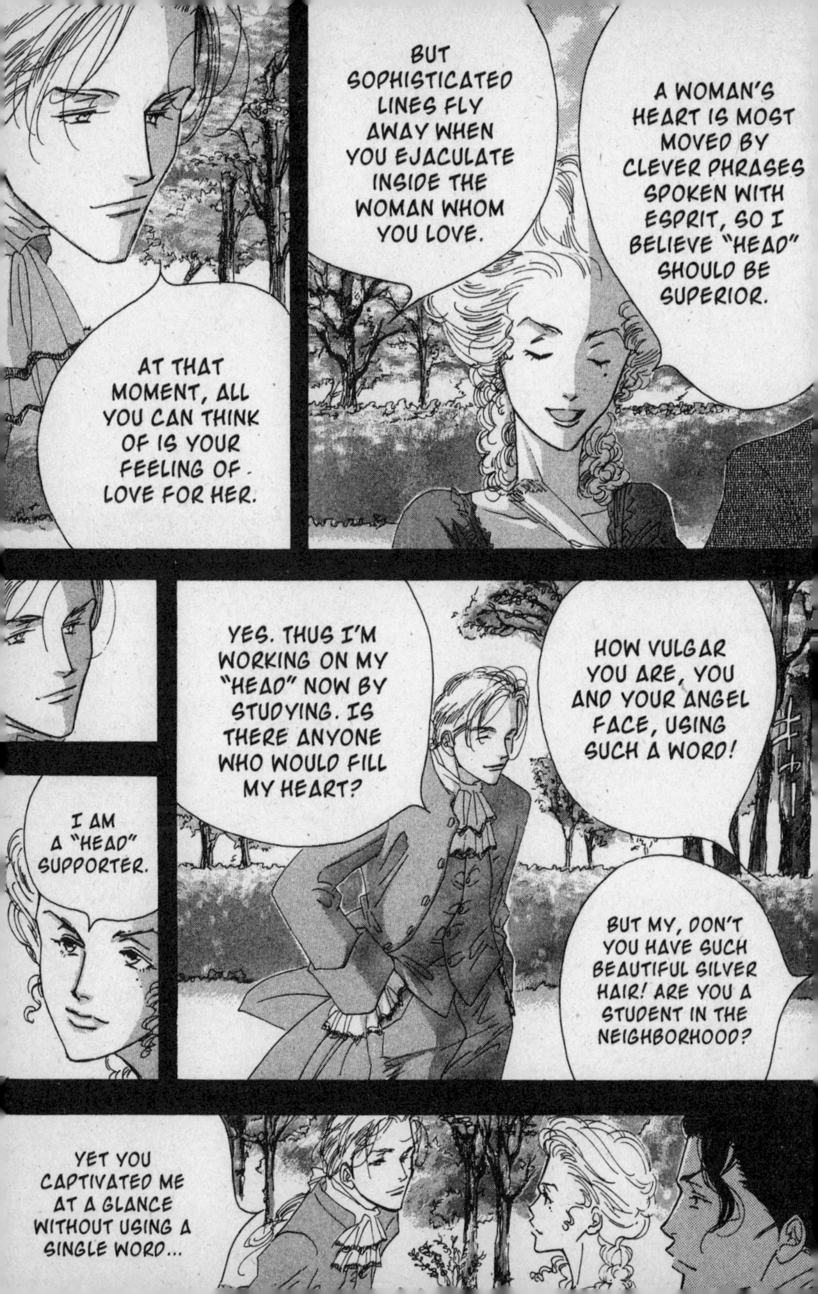
A WOMAN'S HEART IS MOST MOVED BY CLEVER PHRASES SPOKEN WITH ESPRIT, SO I BELIEVE "HEAD" SHOULD BE SUPERIOR.
BUT SOPHISTICATED LINES FLY AWAY WHEN YOU EJACULATE INSIDE THE WOMAN WHOM YOU LOVE.
AT THAT MOMENT, ALL YOU CAN THINK OF IS YOUR FEELING OF LOVE FOR HER.
HOW VULGAR YOU ARE, YOU AND YOUR ANGEL FACE, USING SUCH A WORD!
YES. THUS I'M WORKING ON MY "HEAD" NOW BY STUDYING. IS THERE ANYONE WHO WOULD FILL MY HEART?
BUT MY, DON'T YOU HAVE SUCH BEAUTIFUL SILVER HAIR! ARE YOU A STUDENT IN THE NEIGHBORHOOD?
I AM A "HEAD" SUPPORTER.
YET YOU CAPTIVATED ME AT A GLANCE WITHOUT USING A SINGLE WORD...

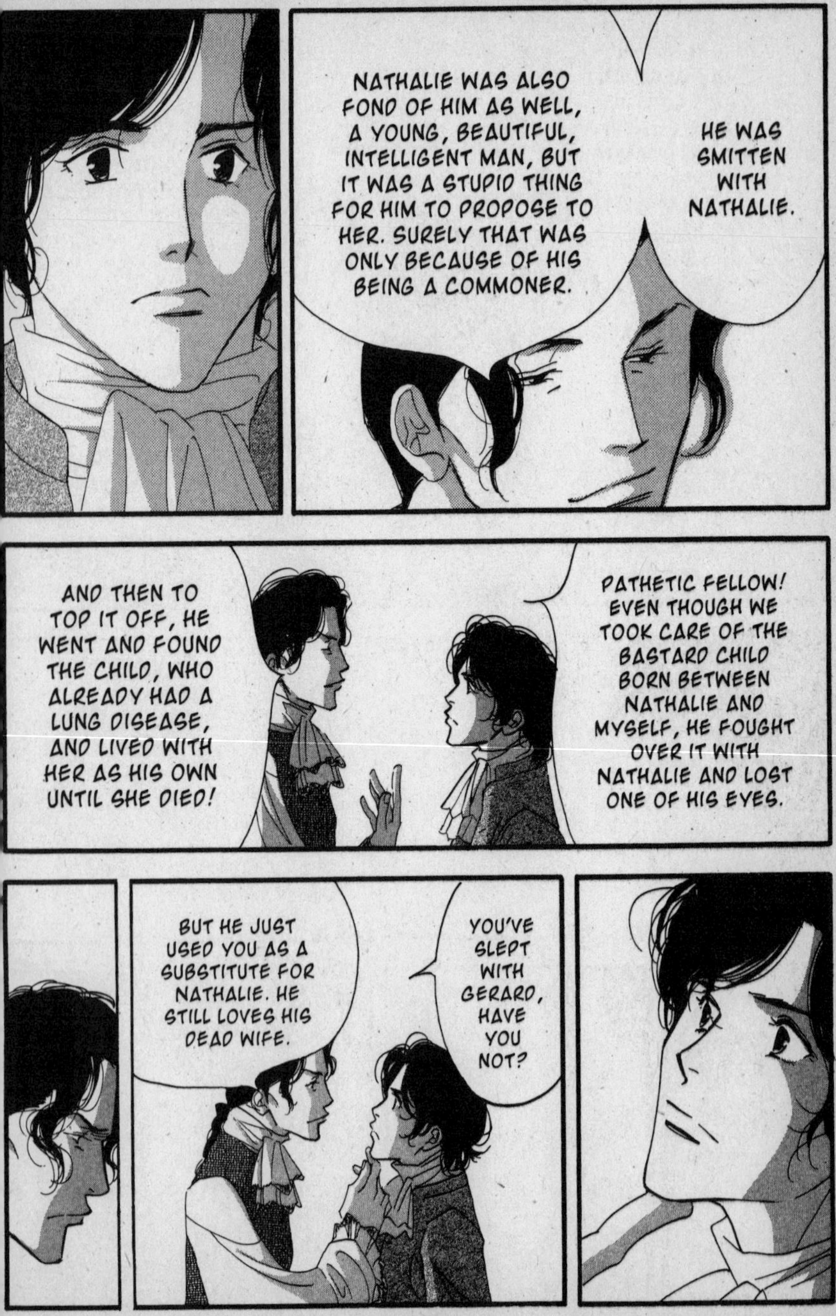
HE WAS SMITTEN WITH NATHALIE.
NATHALIE WAS ALSO FOND OF HIM AS WELL, A YOUNG, BEAUTIFUL, INTELLIGENT MAN, BUT IT WAS A STUPID THING FOR HIM TO PROPOSE TO HER. SURELY THAT WAS ONLY BECAUSE OF HIS BEING A COMMONER.
PATHETIC FELLOW! EVEN THOUGH WE TOOK CARE OF THE BASTARD CHILD BORN BETWEEN NATHALIE AND MYSELF, HE FOUGHT OVER IT WITH NATHALIE AND LOST ONE OF HIS EYES.
AND THEN TO TOP IT OFF, HE WENT AND FOUND THE CHILD, WHO ALREADY HAD A LUNG DISEASE, AND LIVED WITH HER AS HIS OWN UNTIL SHE DIED!
YOU'VE SLEPT WITH GERARD, HAVE YOU NOT?
BUT HE JUST USED YOU AS A SUBSTITUTE FOR NATHALIE. HE STILL LOVES HIS DEAD WIFE.

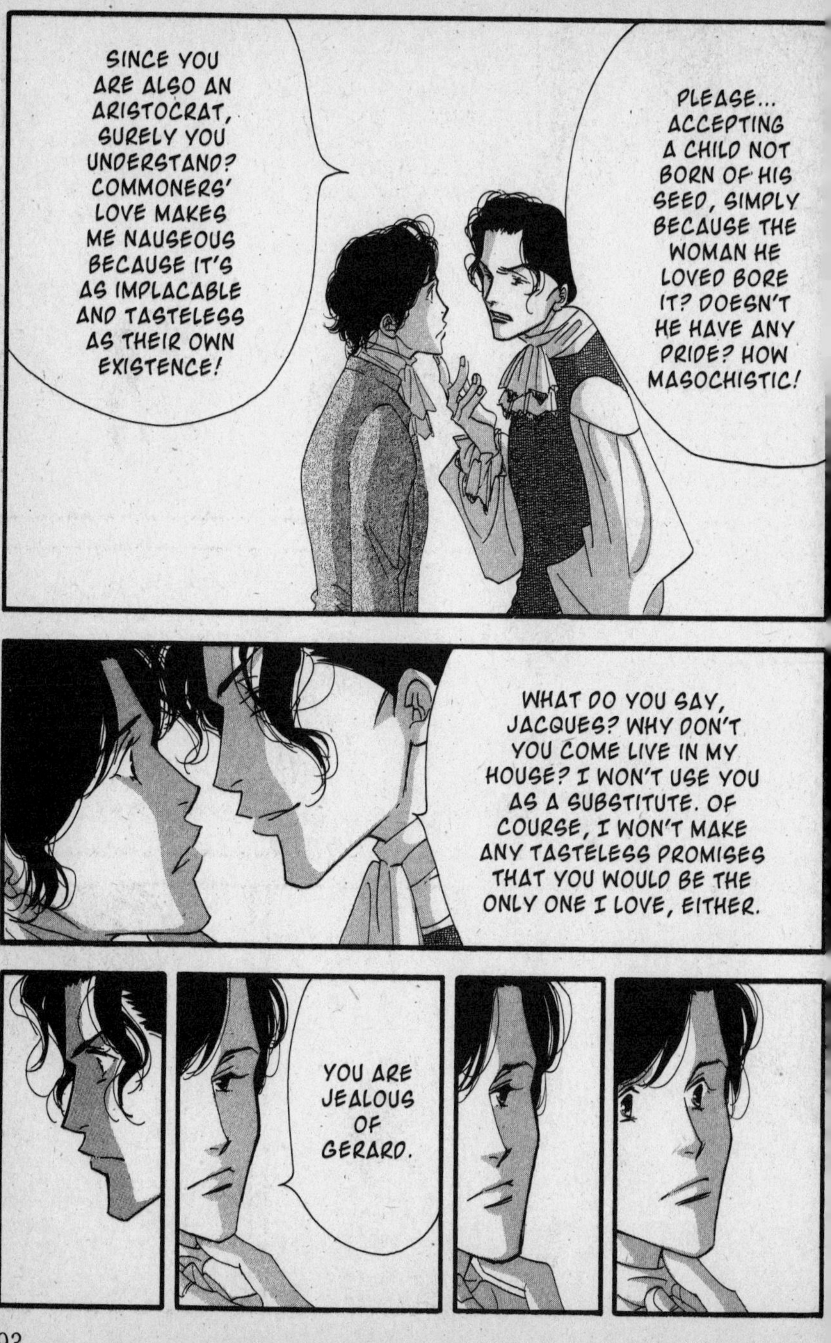
PLEASE... ACCEPTING A CHILD NOT BORN OF HIS SEED, SIMPLY BECAUSE THE WOMAN HE LOVED BORE IT? DOESN'T HE HAVE ANY PRIDE? HOW MASOCHISTIC!
SINCE YOU ARE ALSO AN ARISTOCRAT, SURELY YOU UNDERSTAND? COMMONERS' LOVE MAKES ME NAUSEOUS BECAUSE IT'S AS IMPLACABLE AND TASTELESS AS THEIR OWN EXISTENCE!
WHAT DO YOU SAY, JACQUES? WHY DON'T YOU COME LIVE IN MY HOUSE? I WON'T USE YOU AS A SUBSTITUTE. OF COURSE, I WON'T MAKE ANY TASTELESS PROMISES THAT YOU WOULD BE THE ONLY ONE I LOVE, EITHER.
YOU ARE JEALOUS OF GERARD.

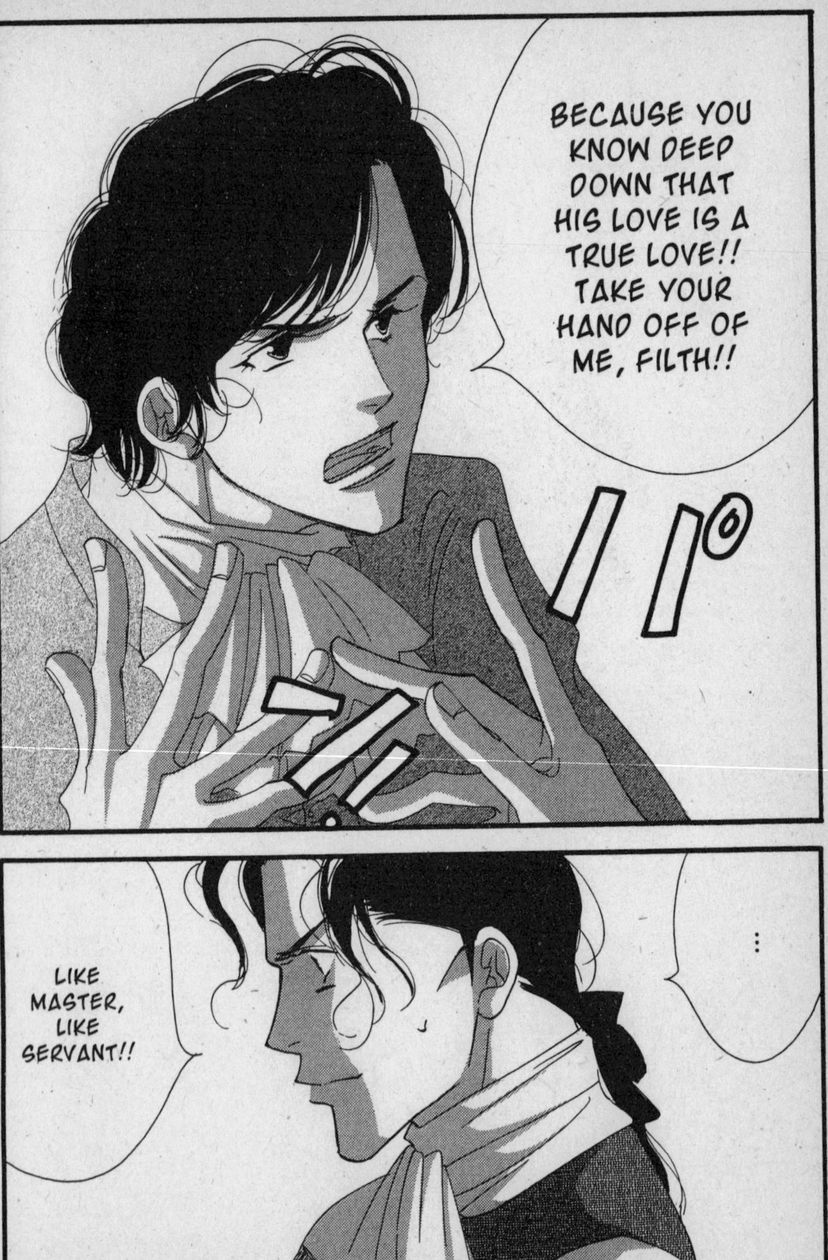
BECAUSE YOU KNOW DEEP DOWN THAT HIS LOVE IS A TRUE LOVE!! TAKE YOUR HAND OFF OF ME, FILTH!!
...
LIKE MASTER, LIKE SERVANT!!

Upon this long summer night Part II

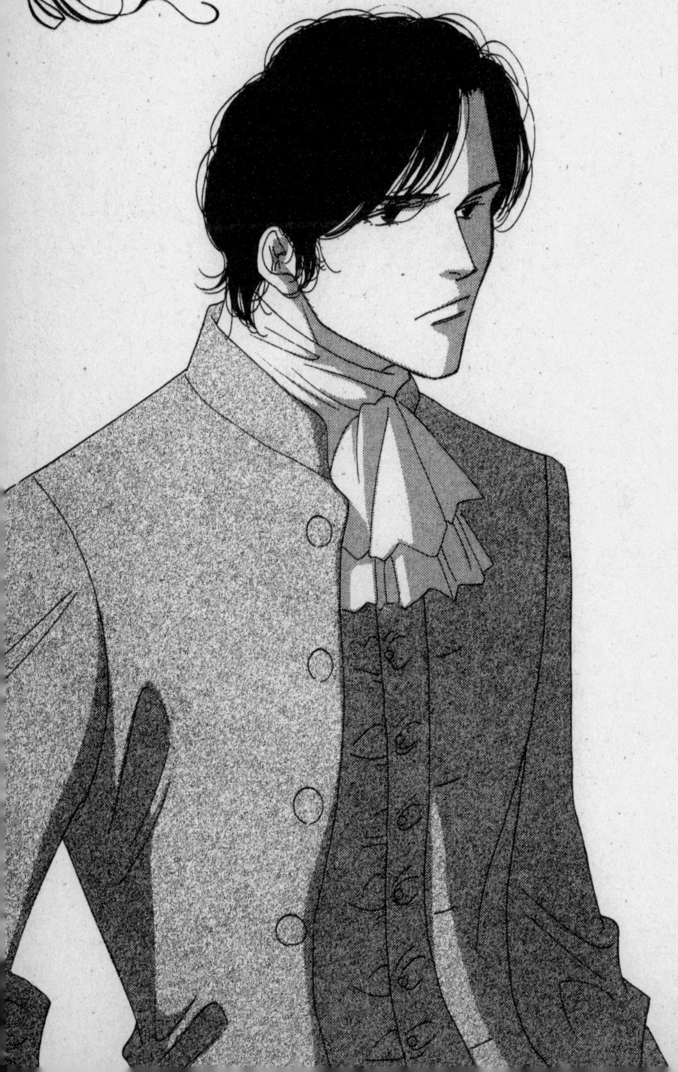

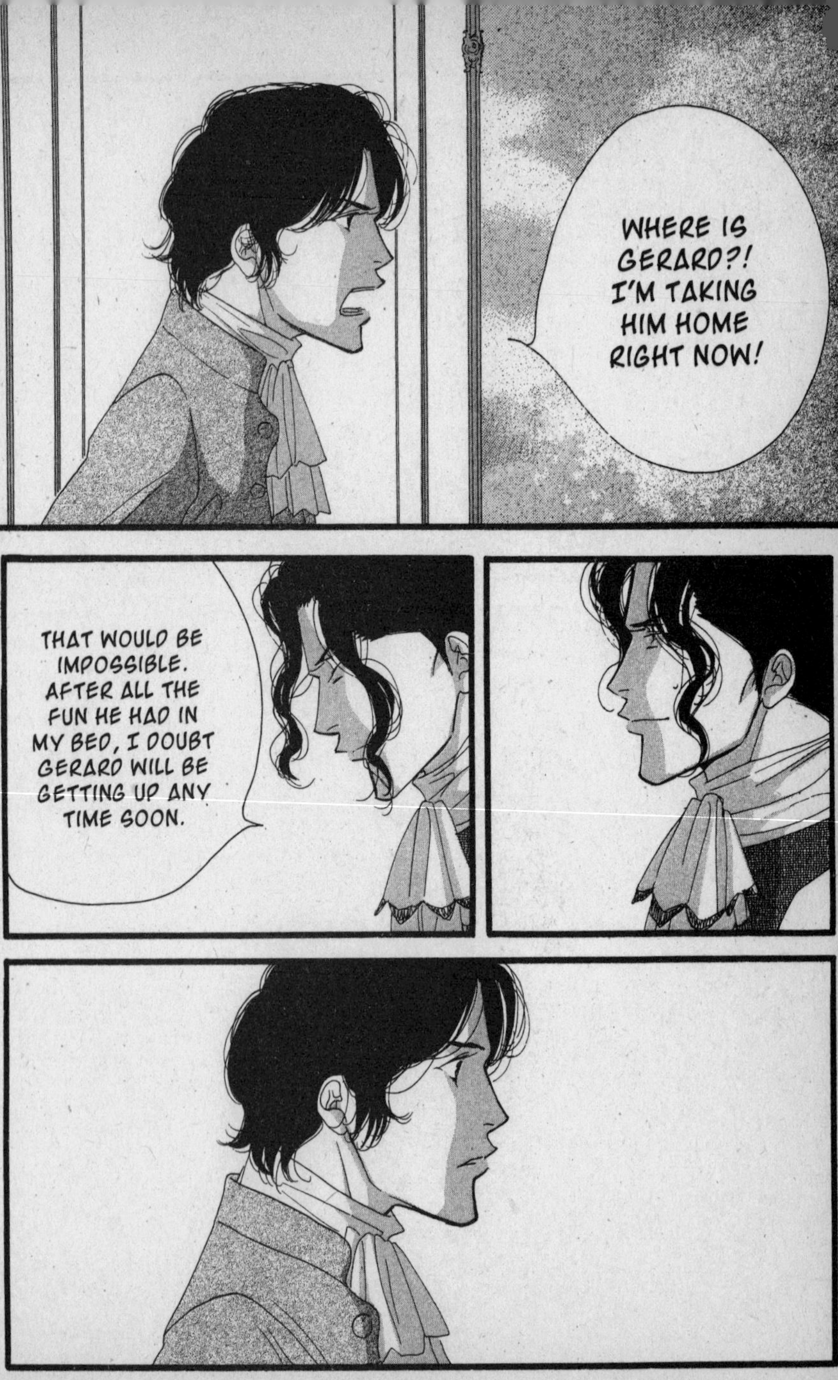
WHERE IS GERARD?! I'M TAKING HIM HOME RIGHT NOW!
THAT WOULD BE IMPOSSIBLE. AFTER ALL THE FUN HE HAD IN MY BED, I DOUBT GERARD WILL BE GETTING UP ANY TIME SOON.

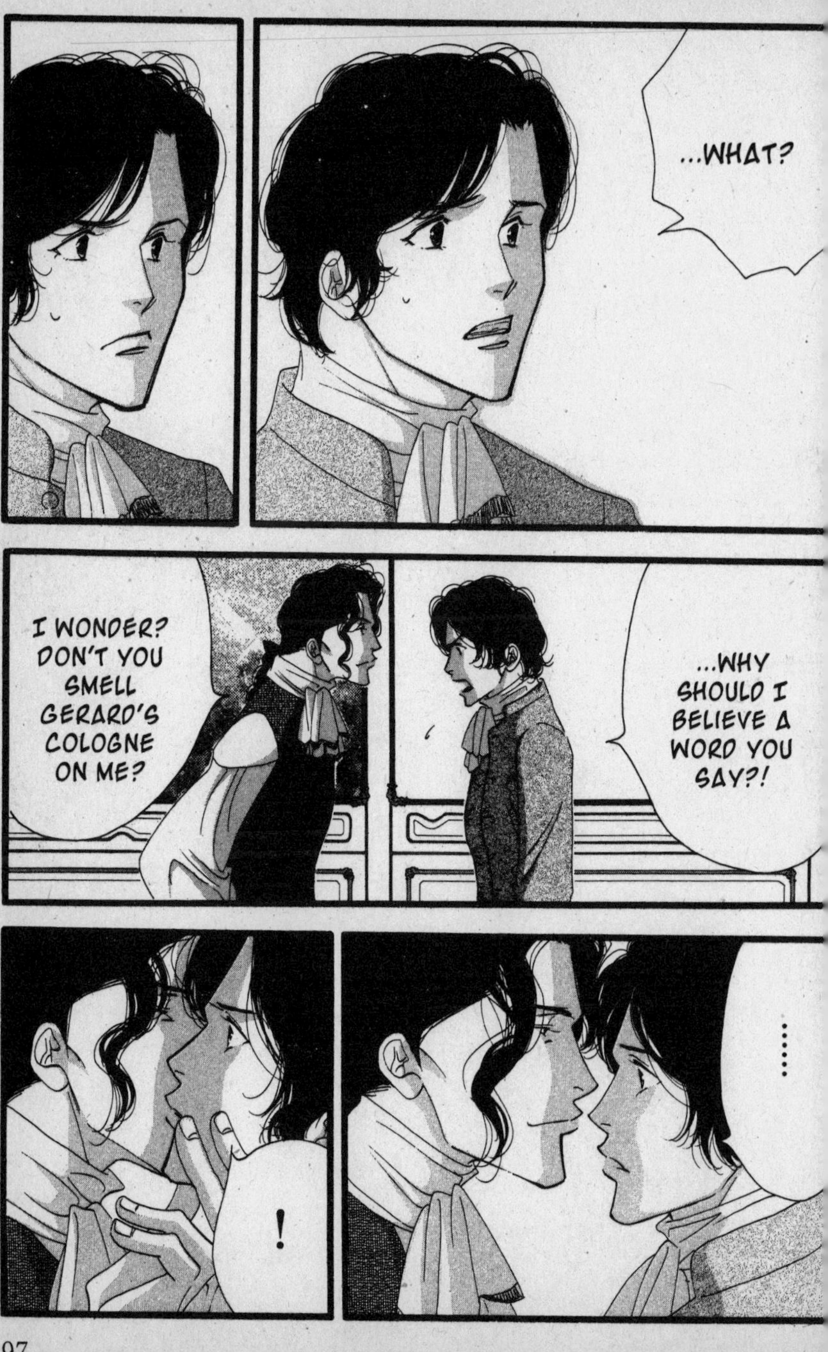
...WHAT?
...WHY SHOULD I BELIEVE A WORD YOU SAY?!
I WONDER? DON'T YOU SMELL GERARD'S COLOGNE ON ME?
......
!

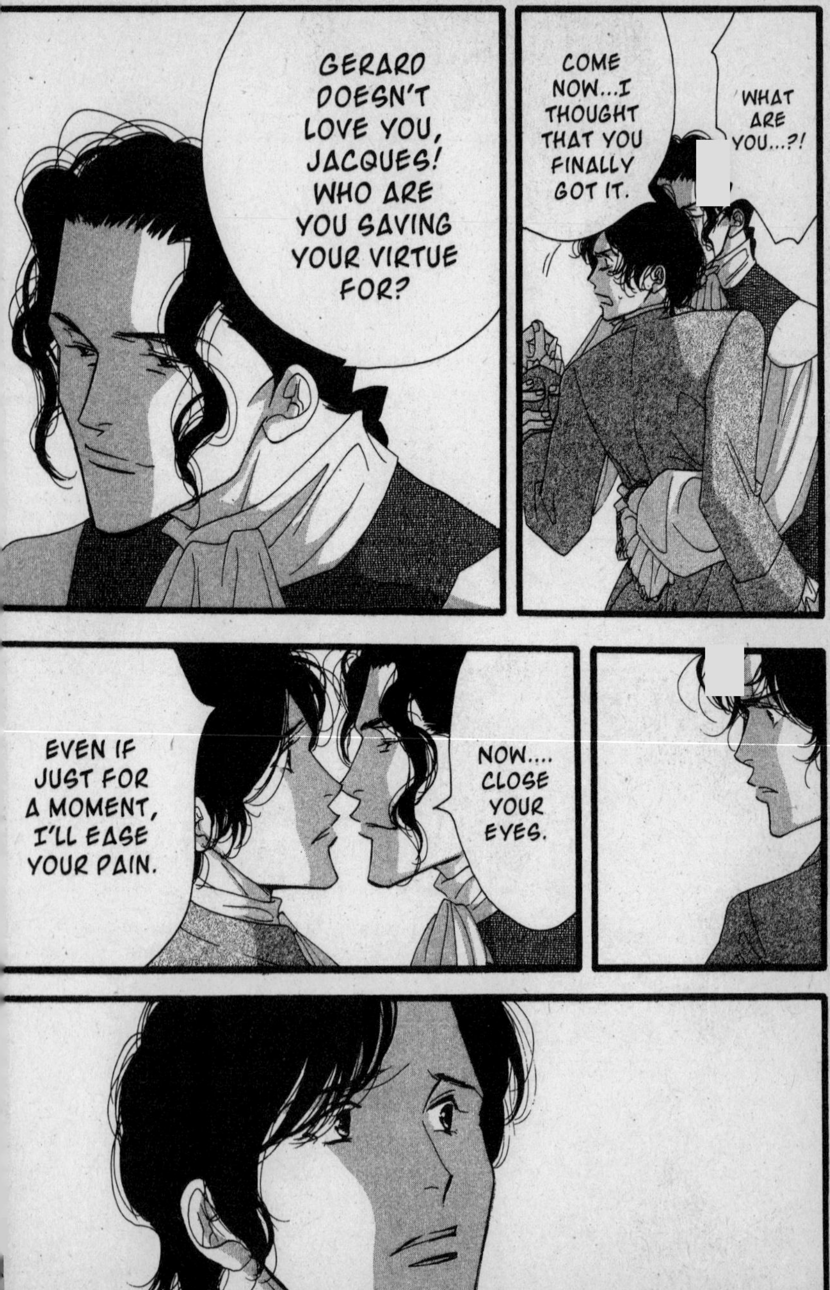
WHAT ARE YOU...?!
COME NOW...I THOUGHT THAT YOU FINALLY GOT IT.
GERARD DOESN'T LOVE YOU, JACQUES! WHO ARE YOU SAVING YOUR VIRTUE FOR?
NOW.... CLOSE YOUR EYES.
EVEN IF JUST FOR A MOMENT, I'LL EASE YOUR PAIN.

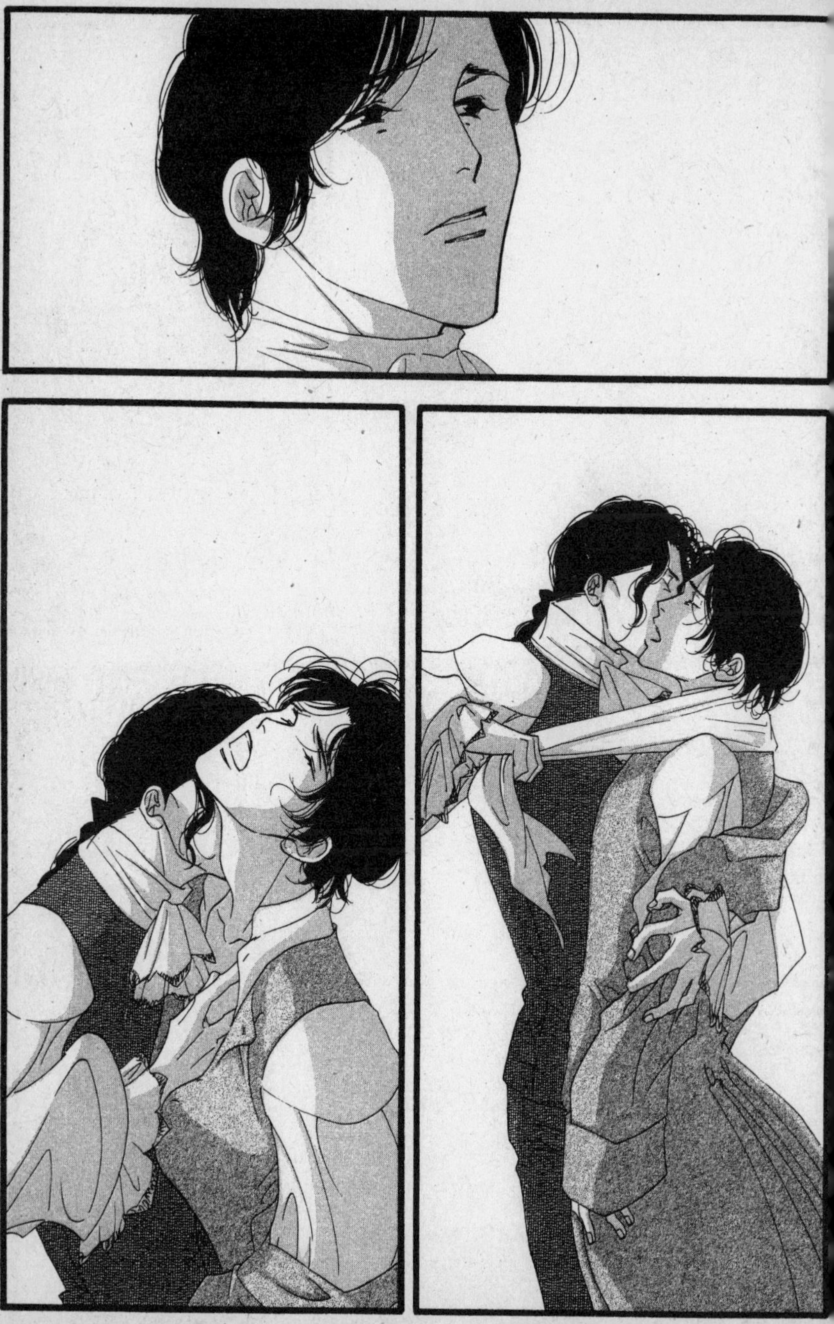

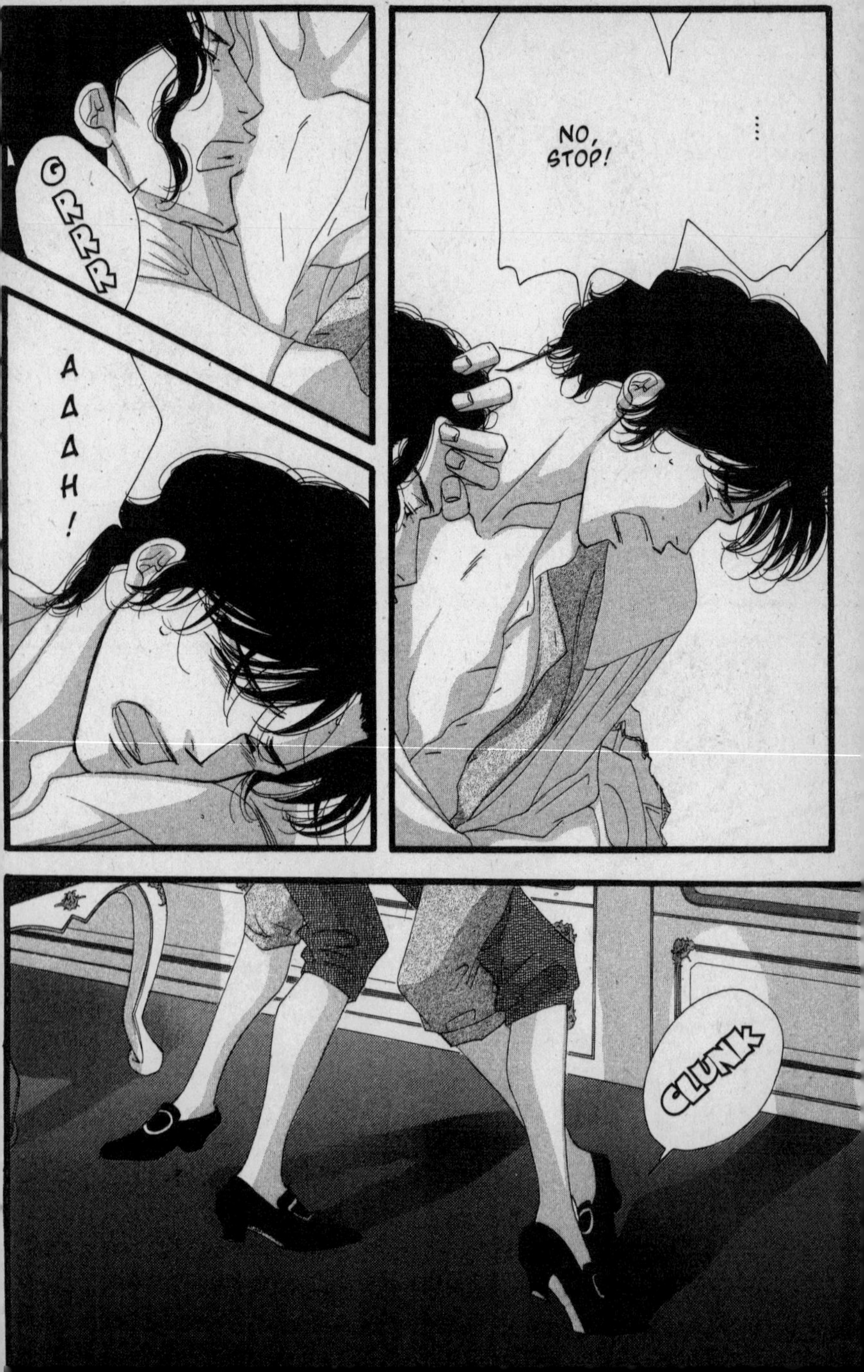
....
NO, STOP!
GRRRR
AAAAH!
CLUNK

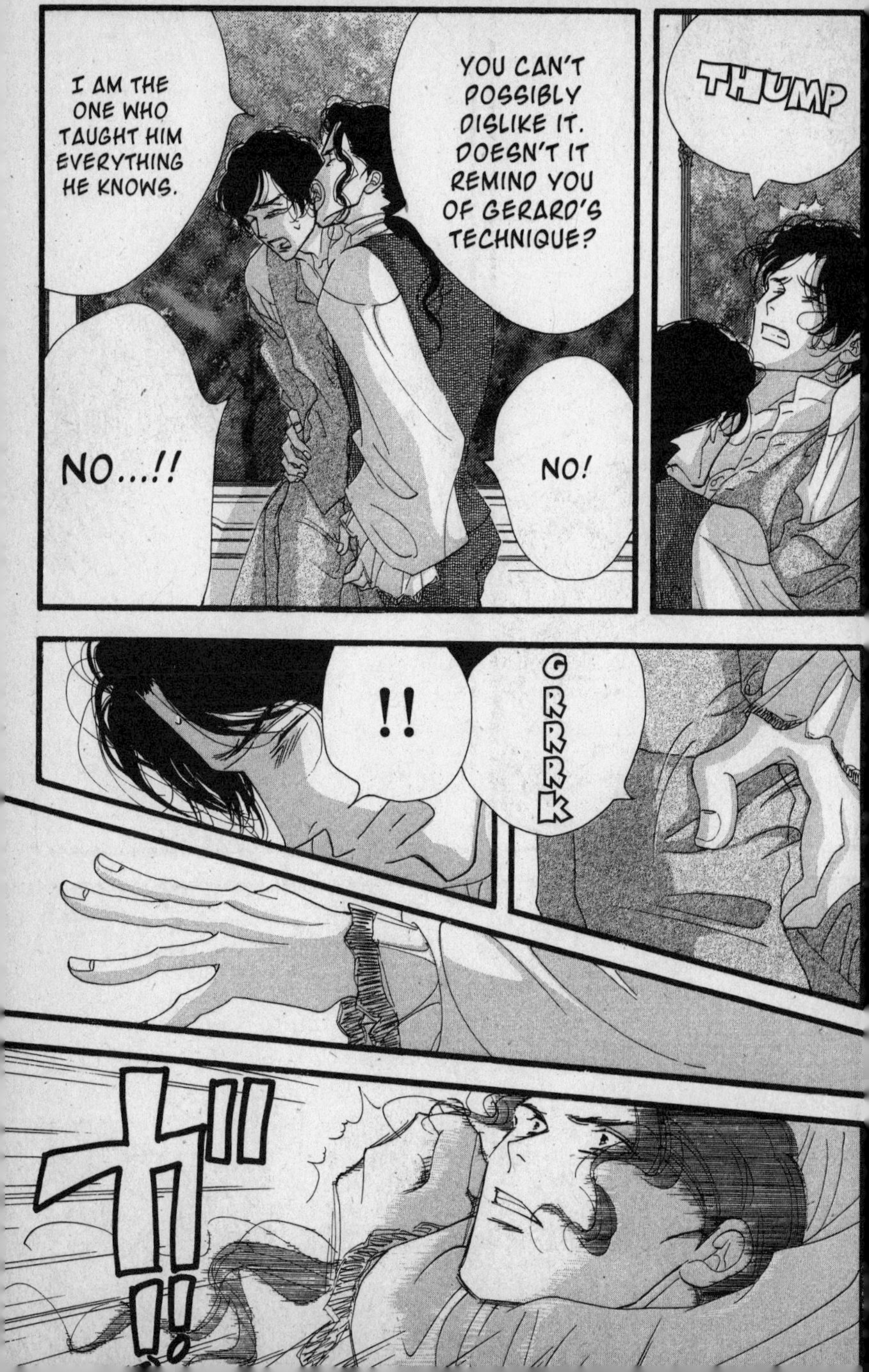
THUMP
YOU CAN'T POSSIBLY DISLIKE IT. DOESN'T IT REMIND YOU OF GERARD'S TECHNIQUE?
I AM THE ONE WHO TAUGHT HIM EVERYTHING HE KNOWS.
NO!
NO...!!
GRRRK
!!

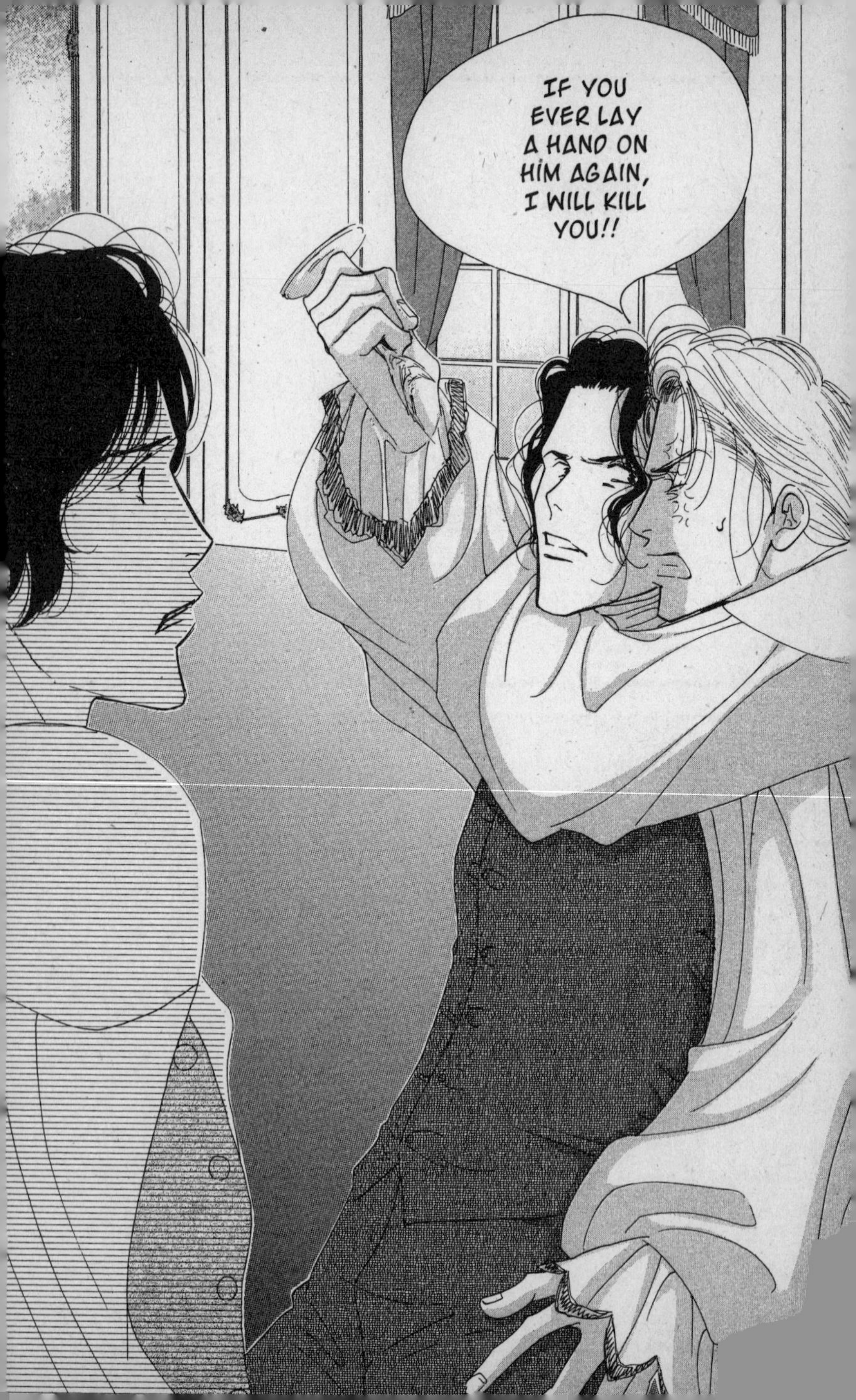
IF YOU EVER LAY A HAND ON HIM AGAIN, I WILL KILL YOU!!

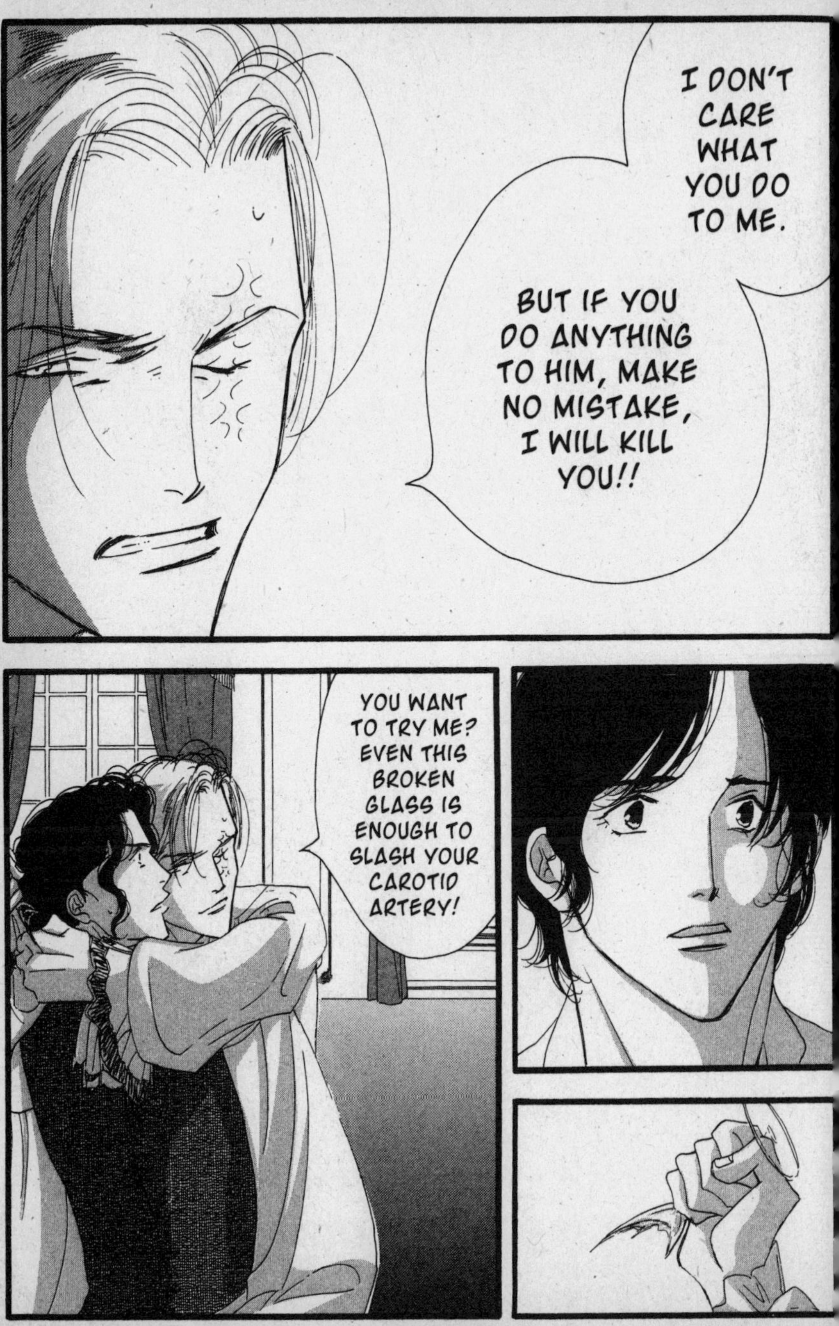
I DON'T CARE WHAT YOU DO TO ME.
BUT IF YOU DO ANYTHING TO HIM, MAKE NO MISTAKE, I WILL KILL YOU!!
YOU WANT TO TRY ME? EVEN THIS BROKEN GLASS IS ENOUGH TO SLASH YOUR CAROTID ARTERY!

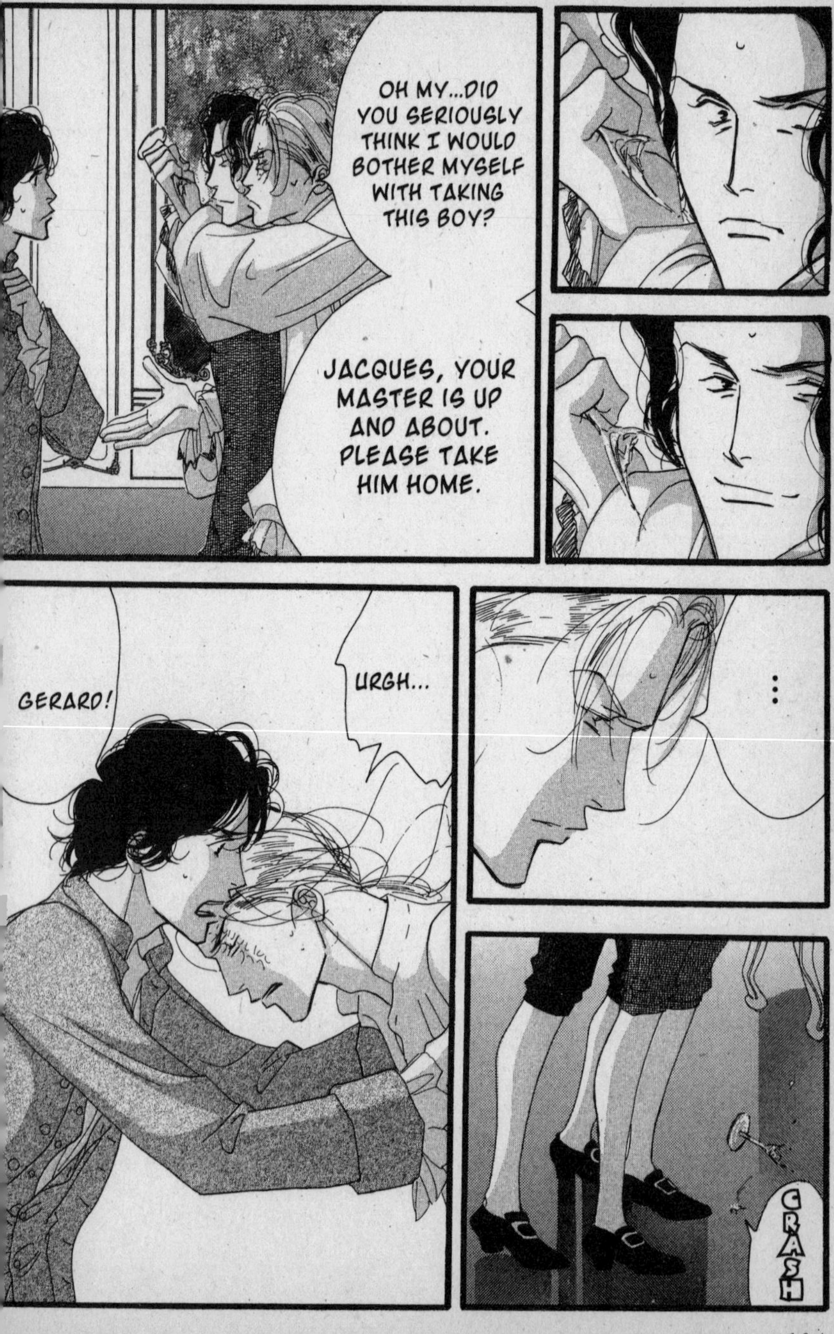
OH MY...DID YOU SERIOUSLY THINK I WOULD BOTHER MYSELF WITH TAKING THIS BOY?
JACQUES, YOUR MASTER IS UP AND ABOUT. PLEASE TAKE HIM HOME.
...
CRASH
URGH...
GERARD!

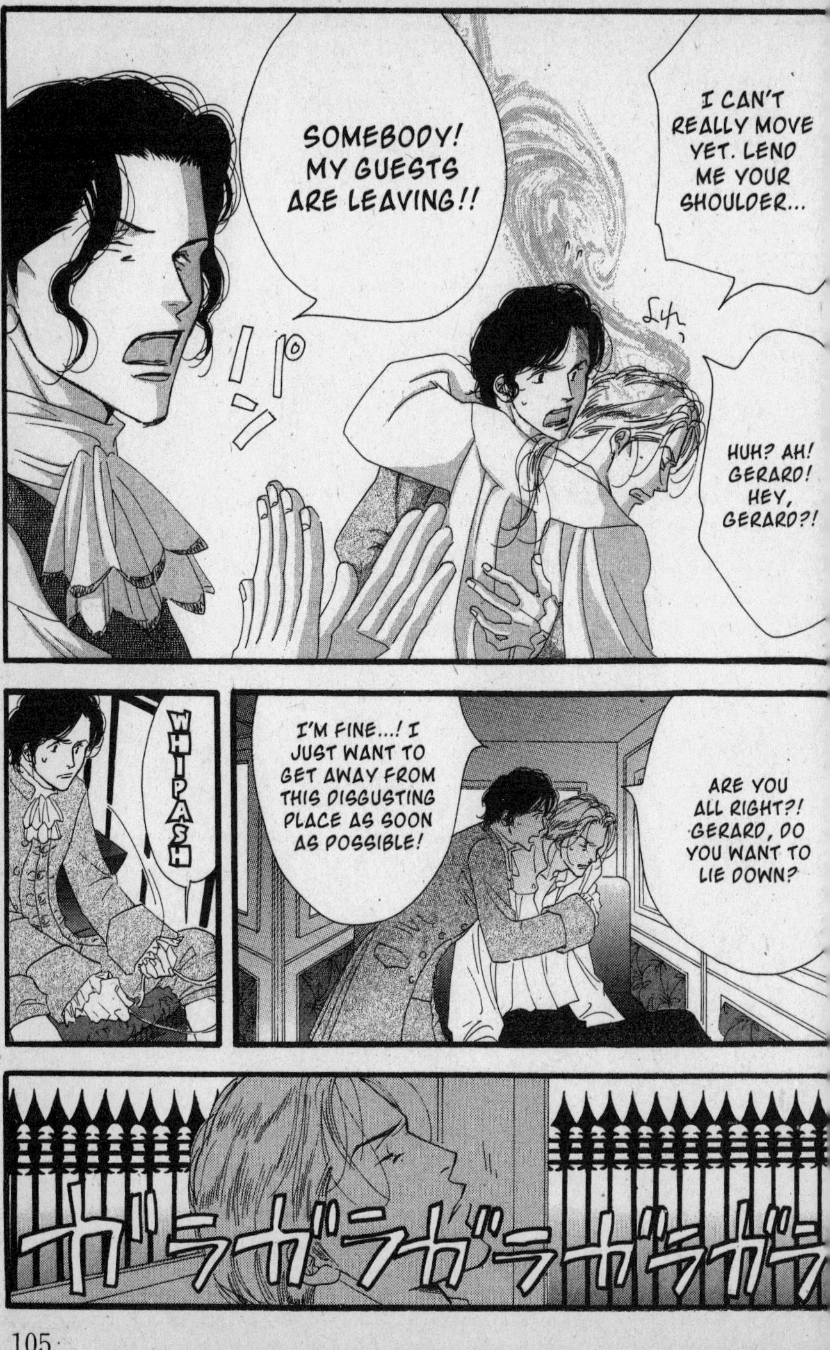
I CAN'T REALLY MOVE YET. LEND ME YOUR SHOULDER...
SOMEBODY! MY GUESTS ARE LEAVING!!
HUH? AH! GERARD! HEY, GERARD?!
ARE YOU ALL RIGHT?! GERARD, DO YOU WANT TO LIE DOWN?
I'M FINE...! I JUST WANT TO GET AWAY FROM THIS DISGUSTING PLACE AS SOON AS POSSIBLE!
WHIPASH
ガラガラガラガラガラ

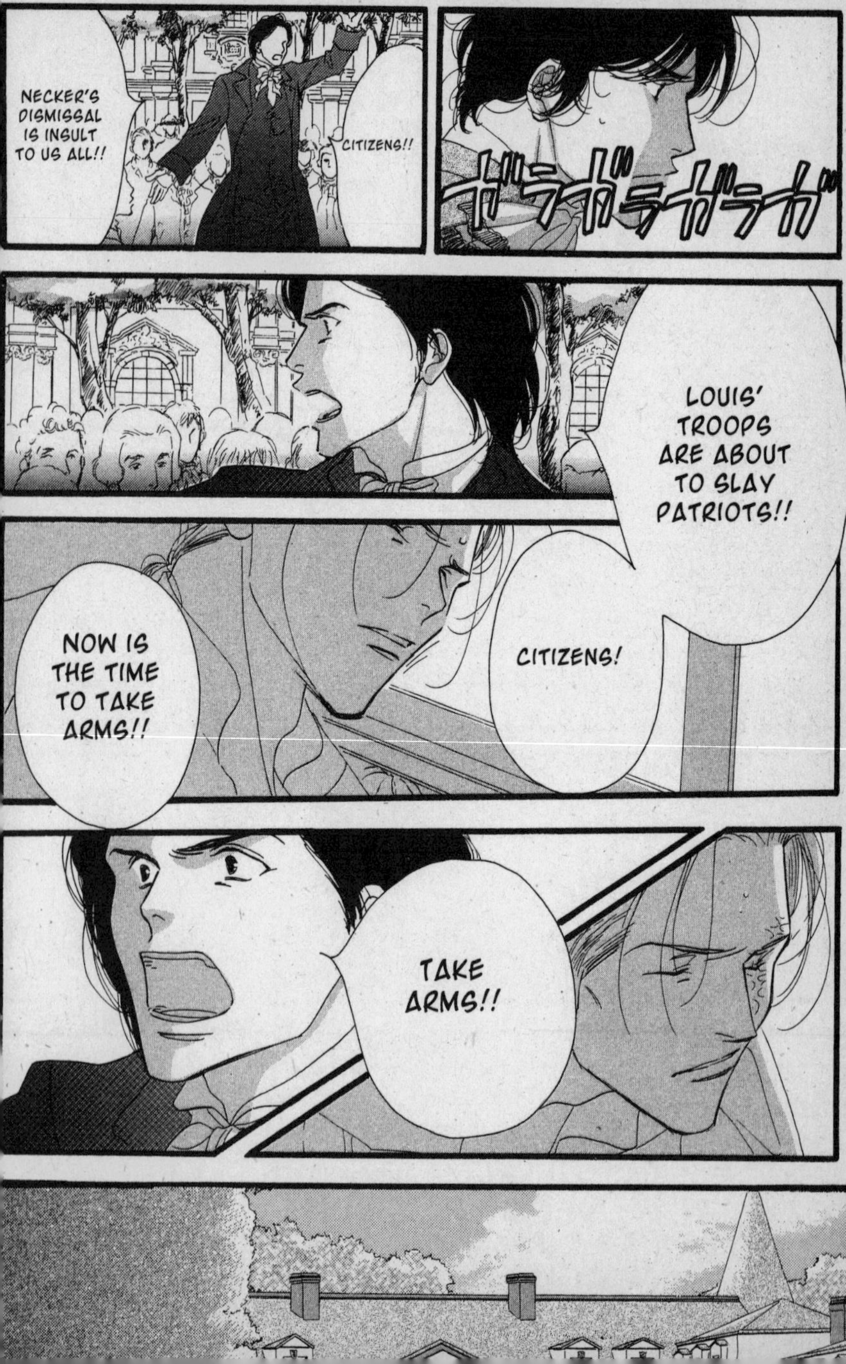
ガラガラガラガ
CITIZENS!!
NECKER'S DISMISSAL IS INSULT TO US ALL!!
LOUIS' TROOPS ARE ABOUT TO SLAY PATRIOTS!!
CITIZENS!
NOW IS THE TIME TO TAKE ARMS!!
TAKE ARMS!!

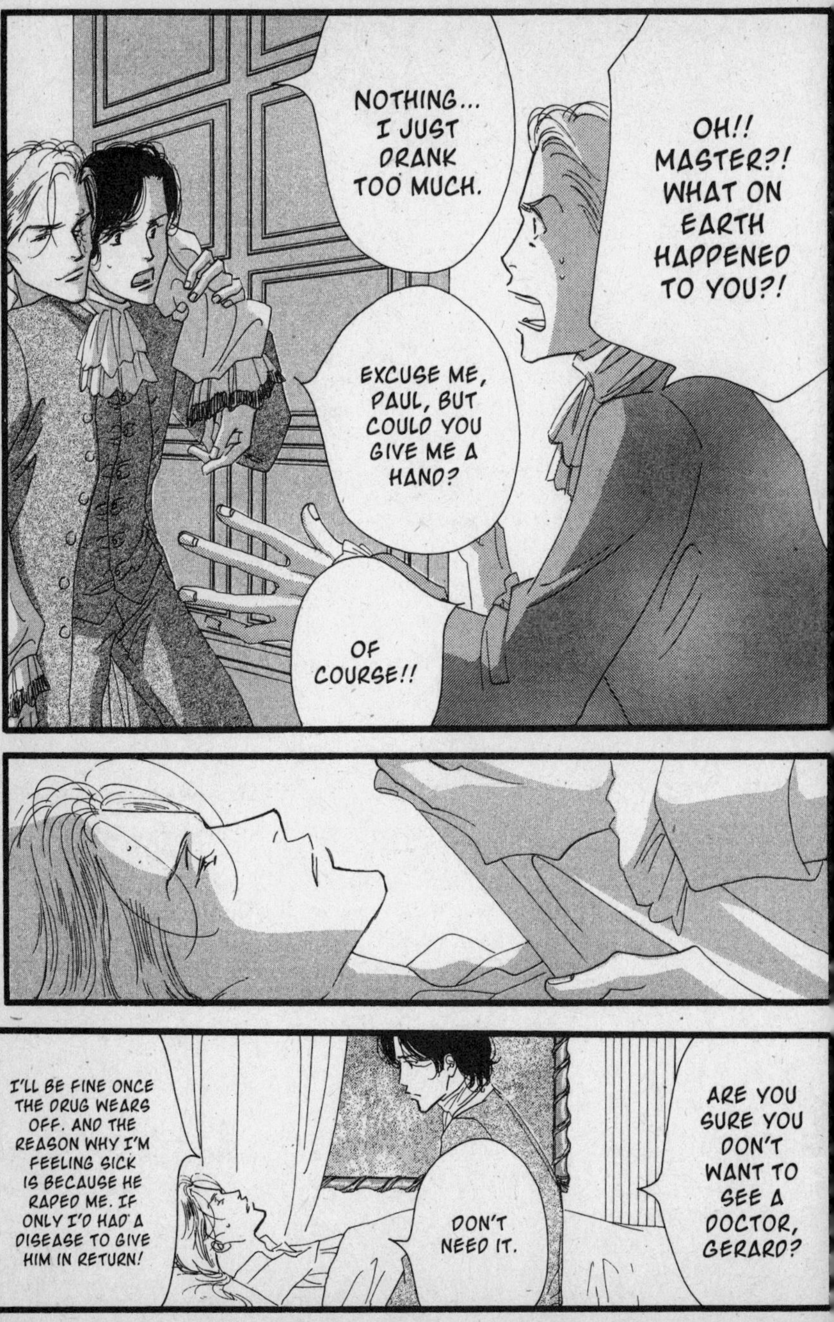
OH!! MASTER?! WHAT ON EARTH HAPPENED TO YOU?!
NOTHING... I JUST DRANK TOO MUCH.
EXCUSE ME, PAUL, BUT COULD YOU GIVE ME A HAND?
OF COURSE!!
ARE YOU SURE YOU DON'T WANT TO SEE A DOCTOR, GERARD?
DON'T NEED IT.
I'LL BE FINE ONCE THE DRUG WEARS OFF. AND THE REASON WHY I'M FEELING SICK IS BECAUSE HE RAPED ME. IF ONLY I'D HAD A DISEASE TO GIVE HIM IN RETURN!

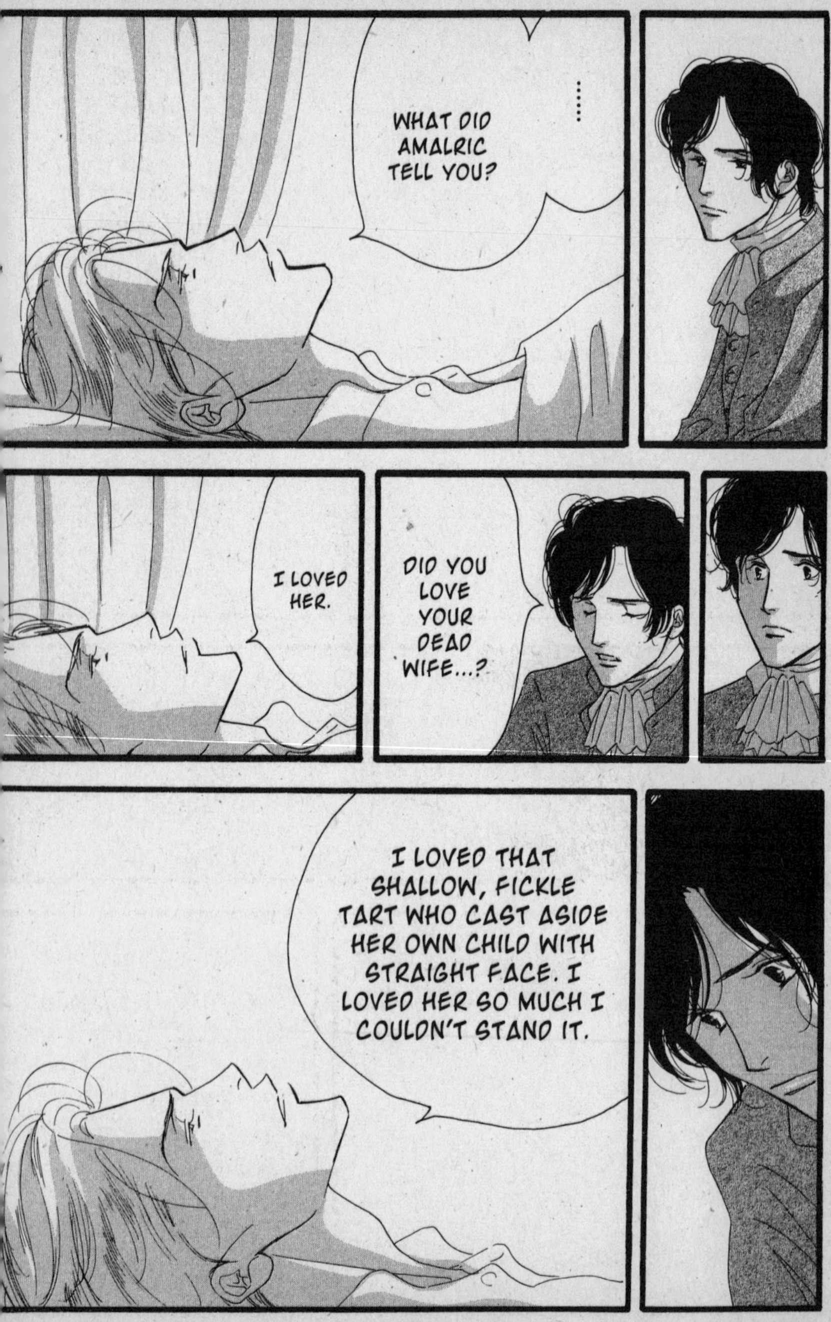
......
WHAT DID AMALRIC TELL YOU?
DID YOU LOVE YOUR DEAD WIFE...?
I LOVED HER.
I LOVED THAT SHALLOW, FICKLE TART WHO CAST ASIDE HER OWN CHILD WITH STRAIGHT FACE. I LOVED HER SO MUCH I COULDN'T STAND IT.

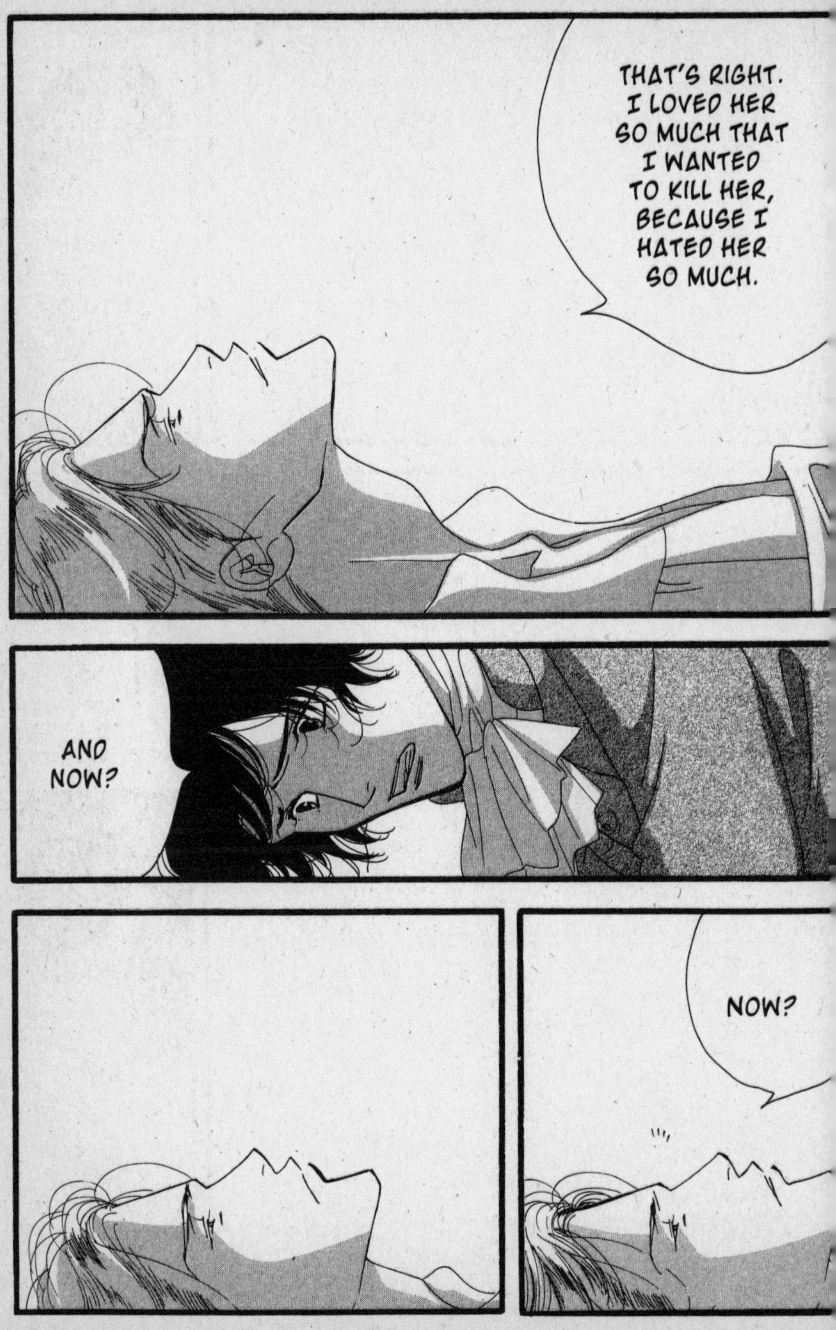
THAT'S RIGHT. I LOVED HER SO MUCH THAT I WANTED TO KILL HER, BECAUSE I HATED HER SO MUCH.
AND NOW?
NOW?

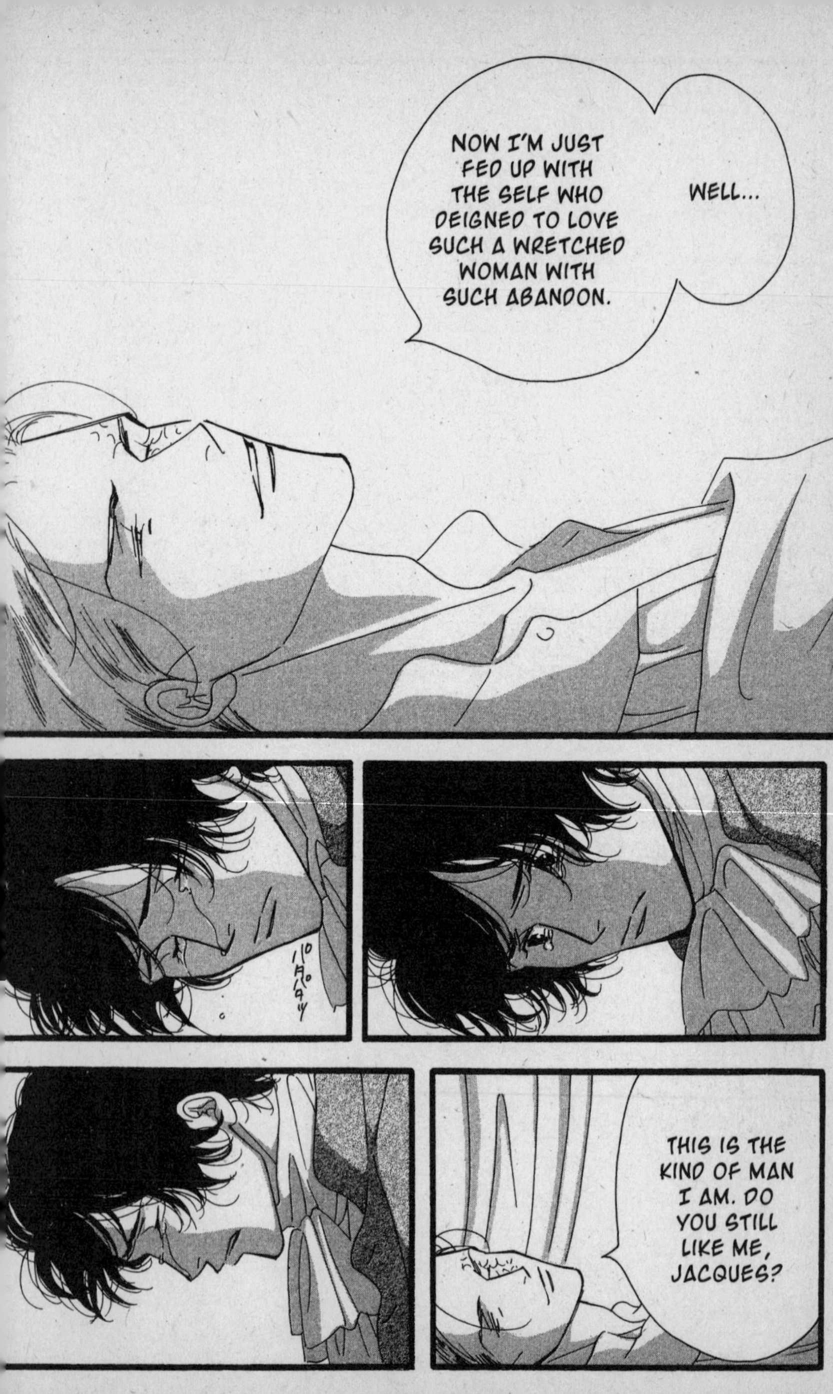
WELL...
NOW I'M JUST FED UP WITH THE SELF WHO DEIGNED TO LOVE SUCH A WRETCHED WOMAN WITH SUCH ABANDON.
THIS IS THE KIND OF MAN I AM. DO YOU STILL LIKE ME, JACQUES?

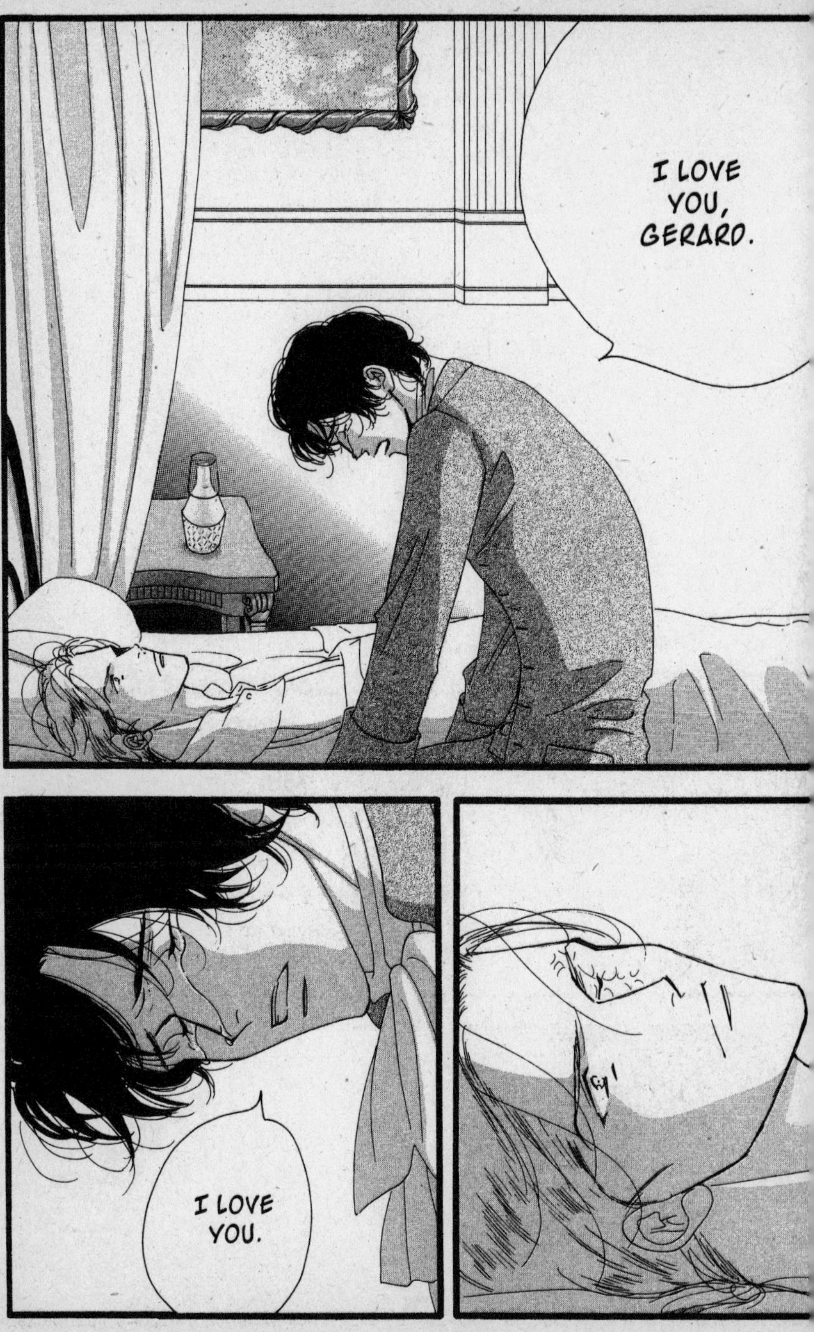
I LOVE YOU, GERARD.
I LOVE YOU.

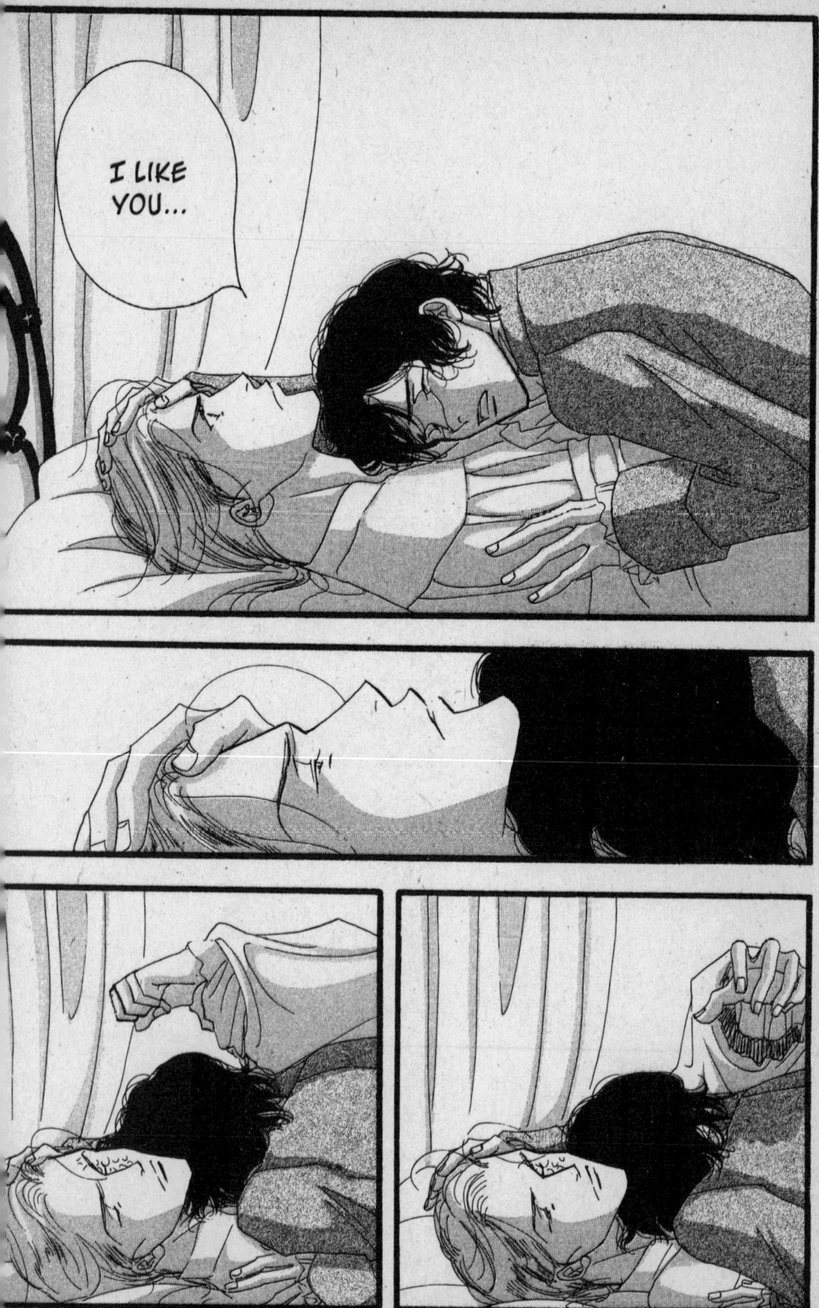
I LIKE YOU...

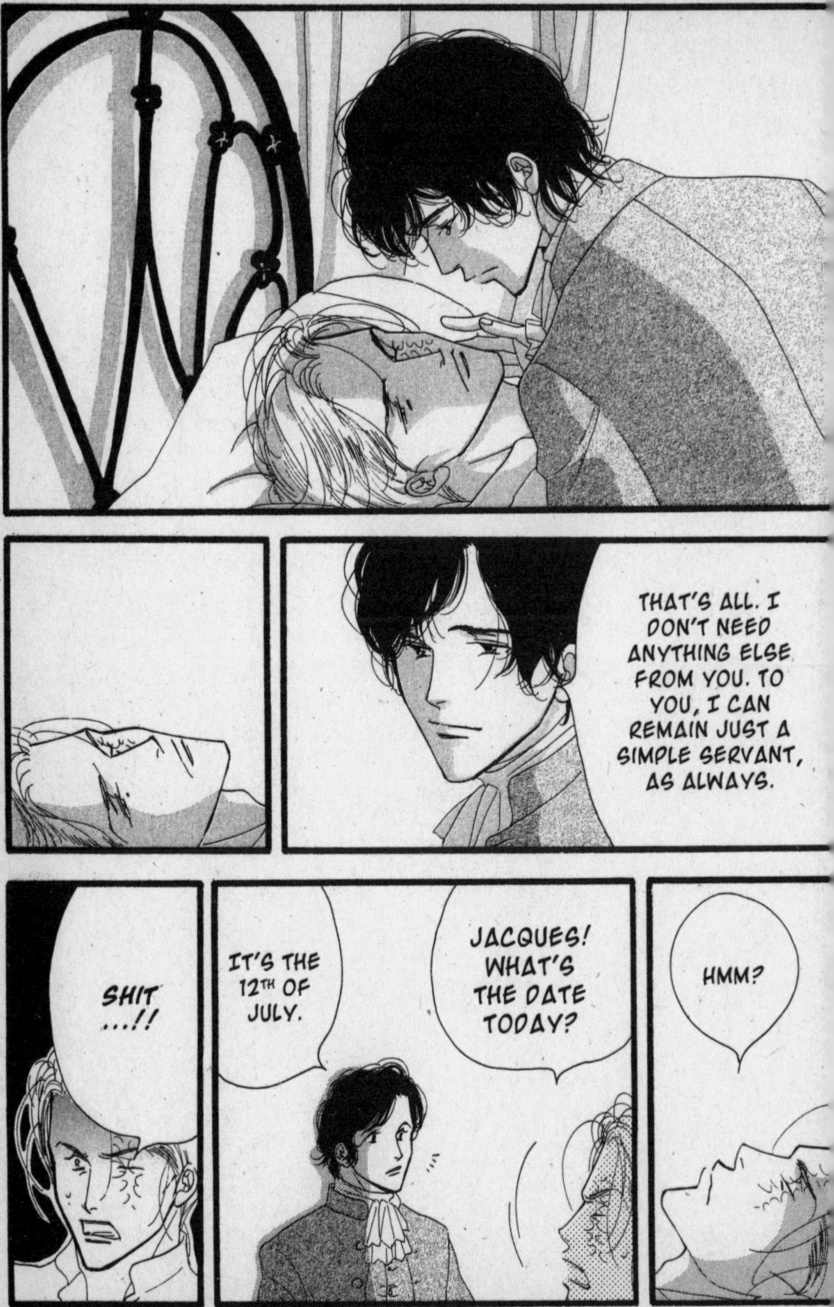
THAT'S ALL. I DON'T NEED ANYTHING ELSE FROM YOU. TO YOU, I CAN REMAIN JUST A SIMPLE SERVANT, AS ALWAYS.
HMM?
JACQUES! WHAT'S THE DATE TODAY?
IT'S THE 12TH OF JULY.
SHIT ...!!

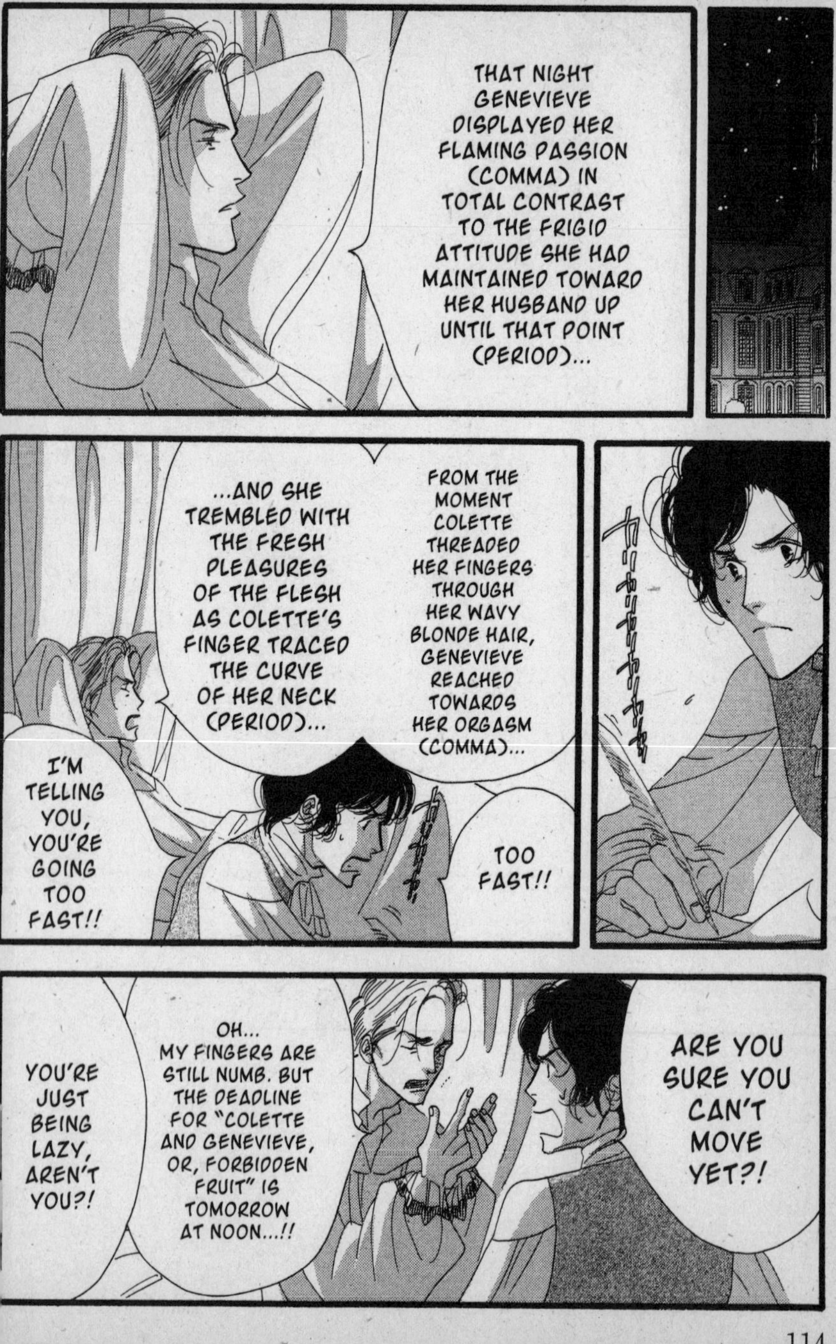
THAT NIGHT GENEVIEVE DISPLAYED HER FLAMING PASSION (COMMA) IN TOTAL CONTRAST TO THE FRIGID ATTITUDE SHE HAD MAINTAINED TOWARD HER HUSBAND UP UNTIL THAT POINT (PERIOD)...
FROM THE MOMENT COLETTE THREADED HER FINGERS THROUGH HER WAVY BLONDE HAIR, GENEVIEVE REACHED TOWARDS HER ORGASM (COMMA)...
...AND SHE TREMBLED WITH THE FRESH PLEASURES OF THE FLESH AS COLETTE'S FINGER TRACED THE CURVE OF HER NECK (PERIOD)...
TOO FAST!!
I'M TELLING YOU, YOU'RE GOING TOO FAST!!
ARE YOU SURE YOU CAN'T MOVE YET?!
OH... MY FINGERS ARE STILL NUMB. BUT THE DEADLINE FOR "COLETTE AND GENEVIEVE, OR, FORBIDDEN FRUIT" IS TOMORROW AT NOON...!!
YOU'RE JUST BEING LAZY, AREN'T YOU?!

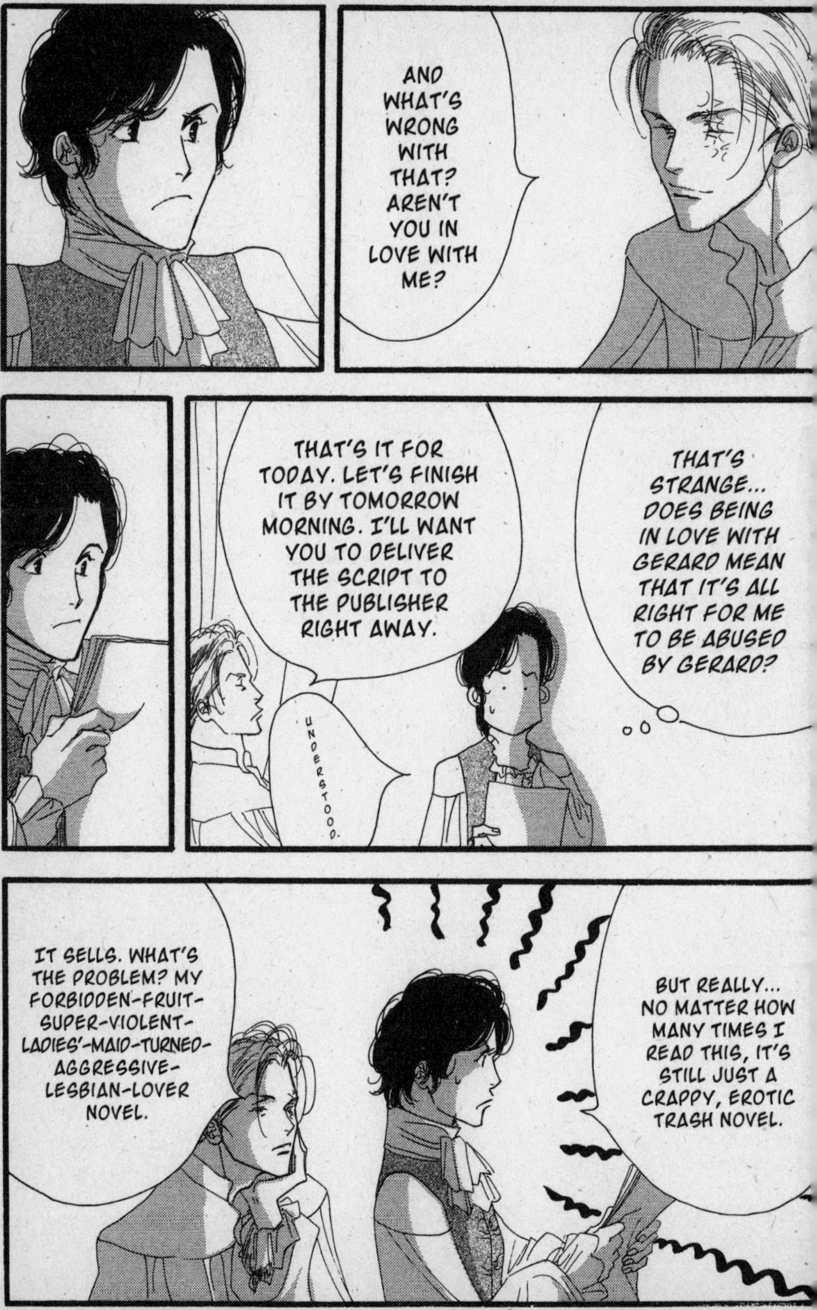
AND WHAT'S WRONG WITH THAT? AREN'T YOU IN LOVE WITH ME?
THAT'S STRANGE... DOES BEING IN LOVE WITH GERARD MEAN THAT IT'S ALL RIGHT FOR ME TO BE ABUSED BY GERARD?
THAT'S IT FOR TODAY. LET'S FINISH IT BY TOMORROW MORNING. I'LL WANT YOU TO DELIVER THE SCRIPT TO THE PUBLISHER RIGHT AWAY.
UNDERSTOOD.
BUT REALLY... NO MATTER HOW MANY TIMES I READ THIS, IT'S STILL JUST A CRAPPY, EROTIC TRASH NOVEL.
IT SELLS. WHAT'S THE PROBLEM? MY FORBIDDEN-FRUIT-SUPER-VIOLENT-LADIES'-MAID-TURNED-AGGRESSIVE-LESBIAN-LOVER NOVEL.

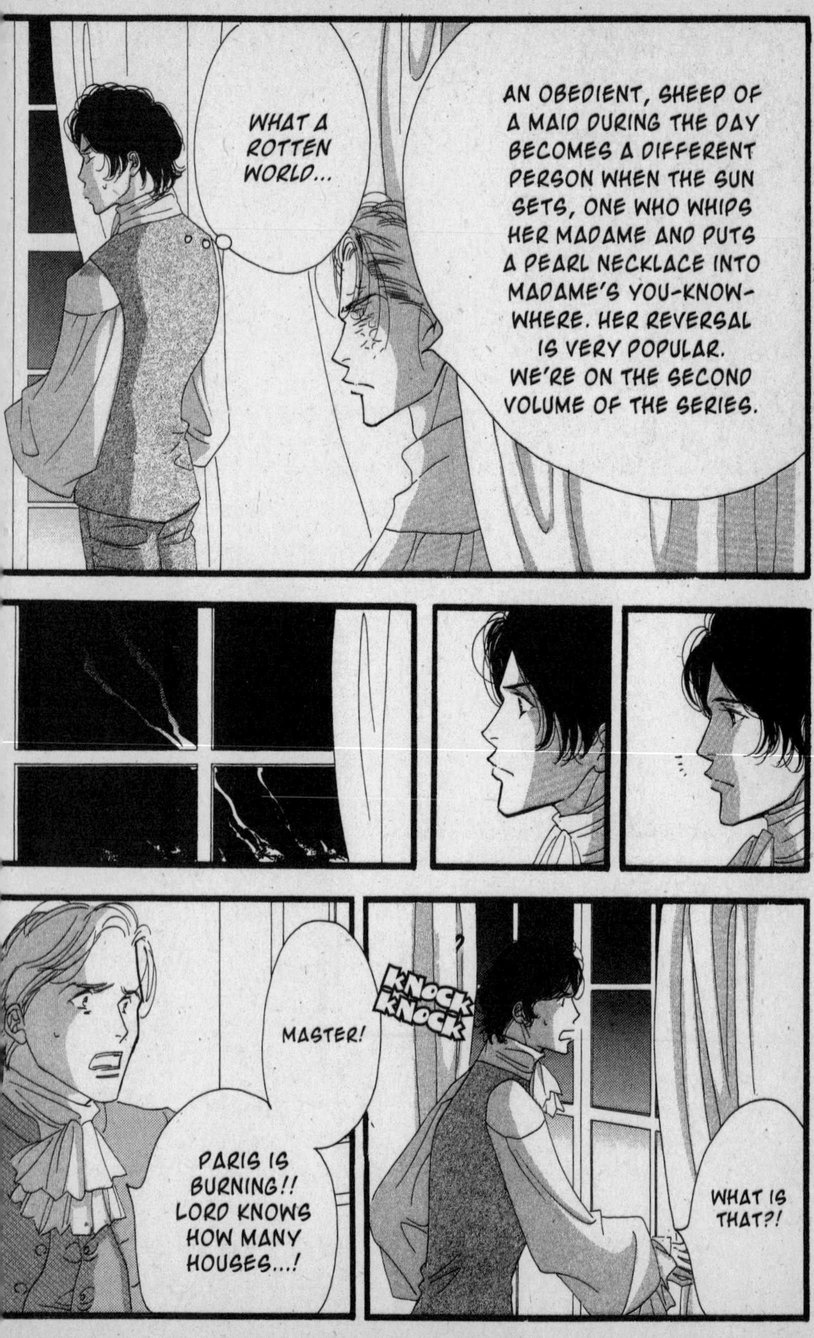
AN OBEDIENT, SHEEP OF A MAID DURING THE DAY BECOMES A DIFFERENT PERSON WHEN THE SUN SETS, ONE WHO WHIPS HER MADAME AND PUTS A PEARL NECKLACE INTO MADAME'S YOU-KNOW-WHERE. HER REVERSAL IS VERY POPULAR. WE'RE ON THE SECOND VOLUME OF THE SERIES.
WHAT A ROTTEN WORLD...
KNOCK KNOCK
WHAT IS THAT?!
MASTER!
PARIS IS BURNING!! LORD KNOWS HOW MANY HOUSES...!

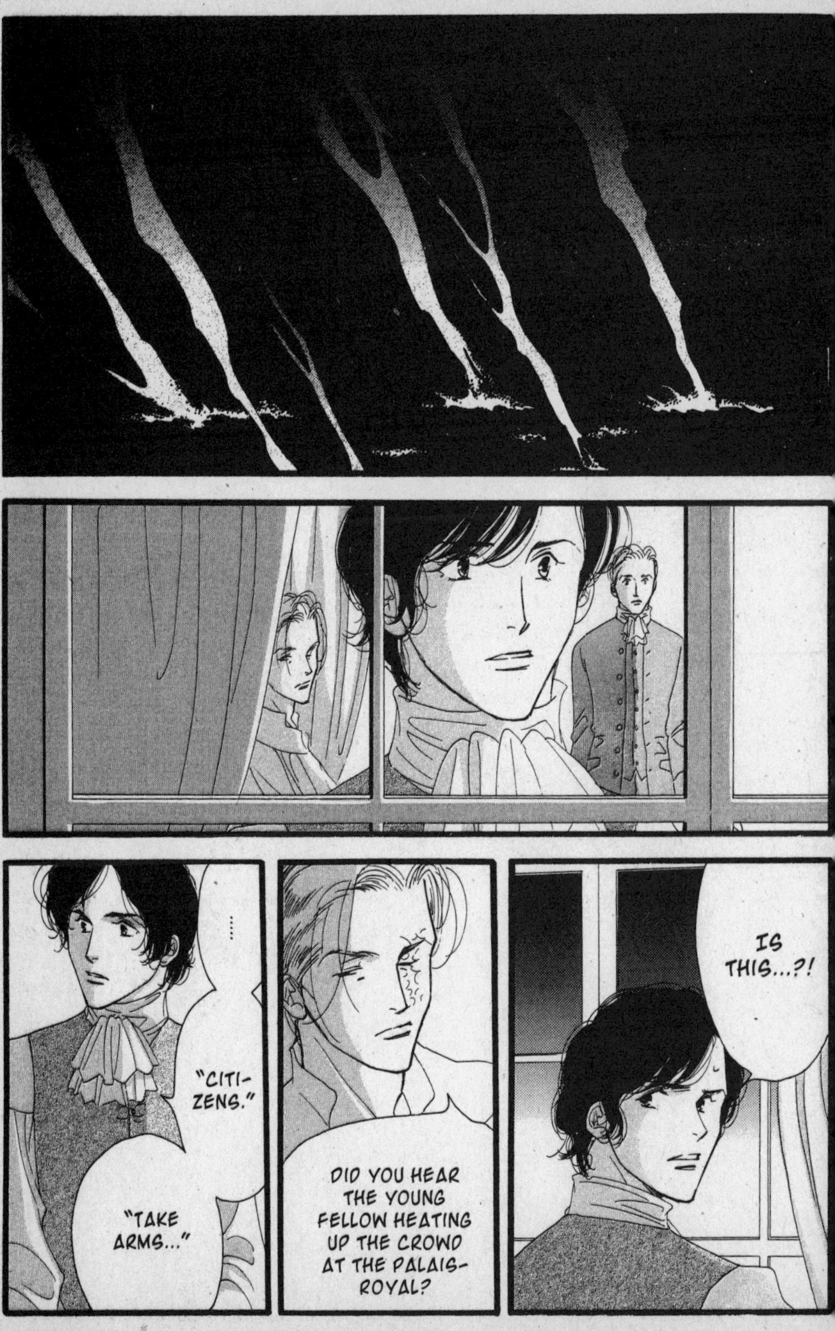
IS THIS...?!
DID YOU HEAR THE YOUNG FELLOW HEATING UP THE CROWD AT THE PALAIS-ROYAL?
....
"CITI-ZENS."
"TAKE ARMS..."

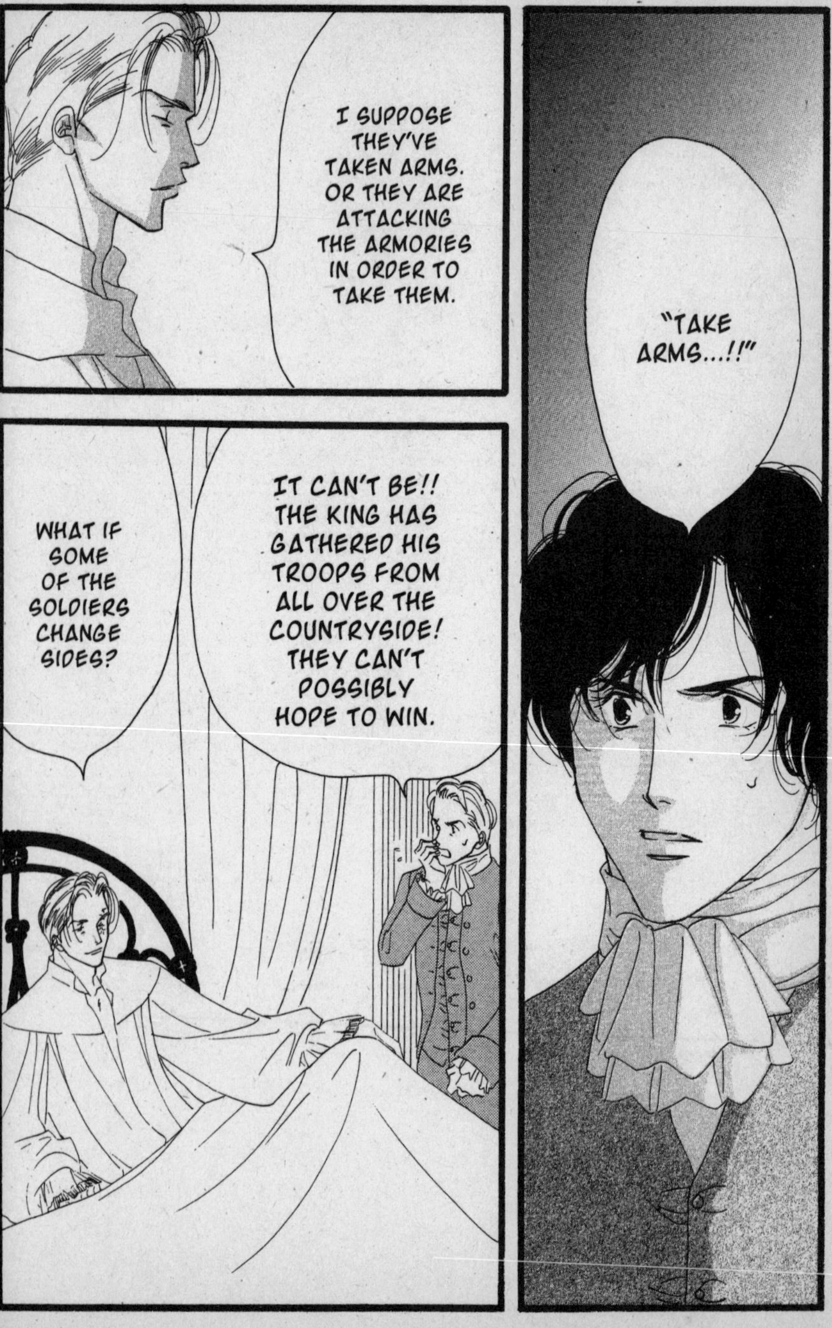
"TAKE ARMS...!!"
I SUPPOSE THEY'VE TAKEN ARMS. OR THEY ARE ATTACKING THE ARMORIES IN ORDER TO TAKE THEM.
IT CAN'T BE!! THE KING HAS GATHERED HIS TROOPS FROM ALL OVER THE COUNTRYSIDE! THEY CAN'T POSSIBLY HOPE TO WIN.
WHAT IF SOME OF THE SOLDIERS CHANGE SIDES?

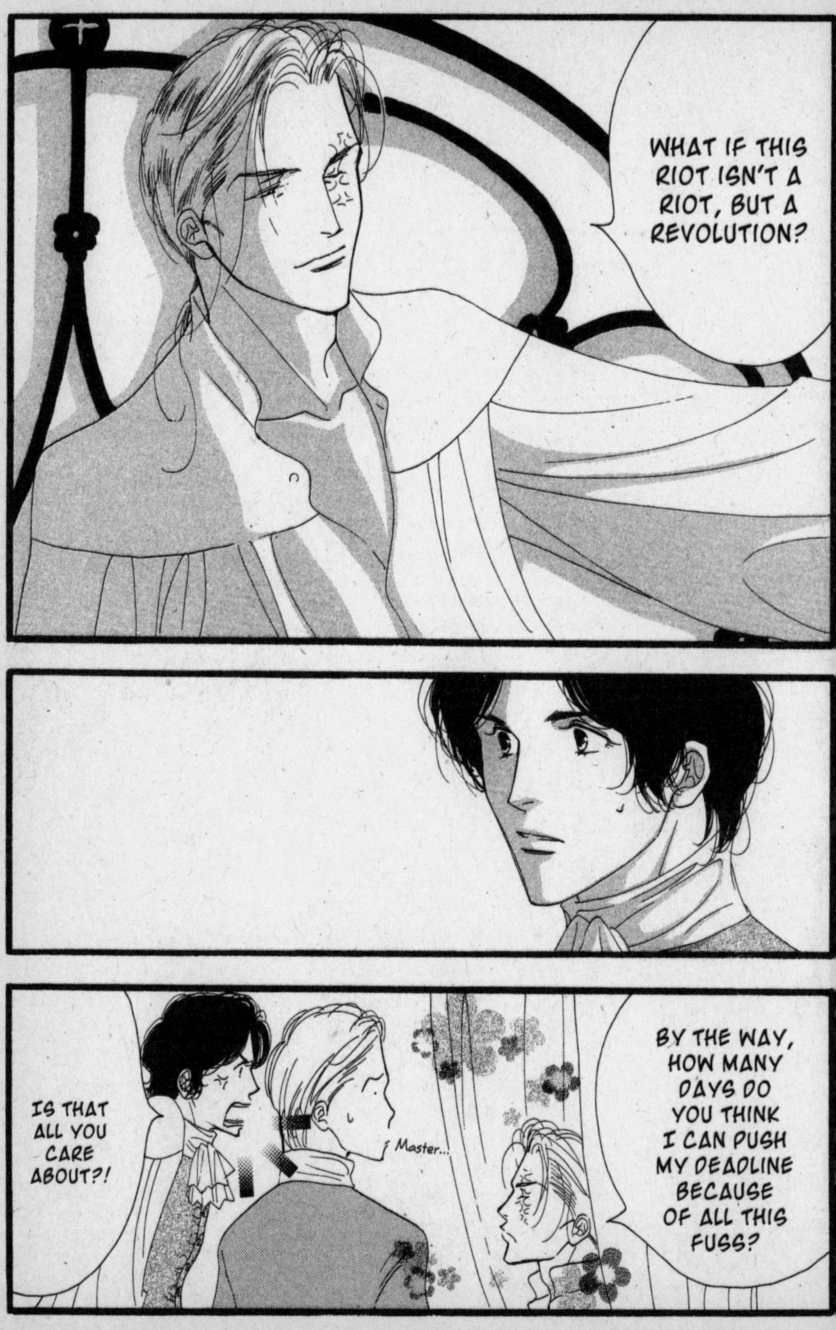
WHAT IF THIS RIOT ISN'T A RIOT, BUT A REVOLUTION?
BY THE WAY, HOW MANY DAYS DO YOU THINK I CAN PUSH MY DEADLINE BECAUSE OF ALL THIS FUSS?
Master...
IS THAT ALL YOU CARE ABOUT?!

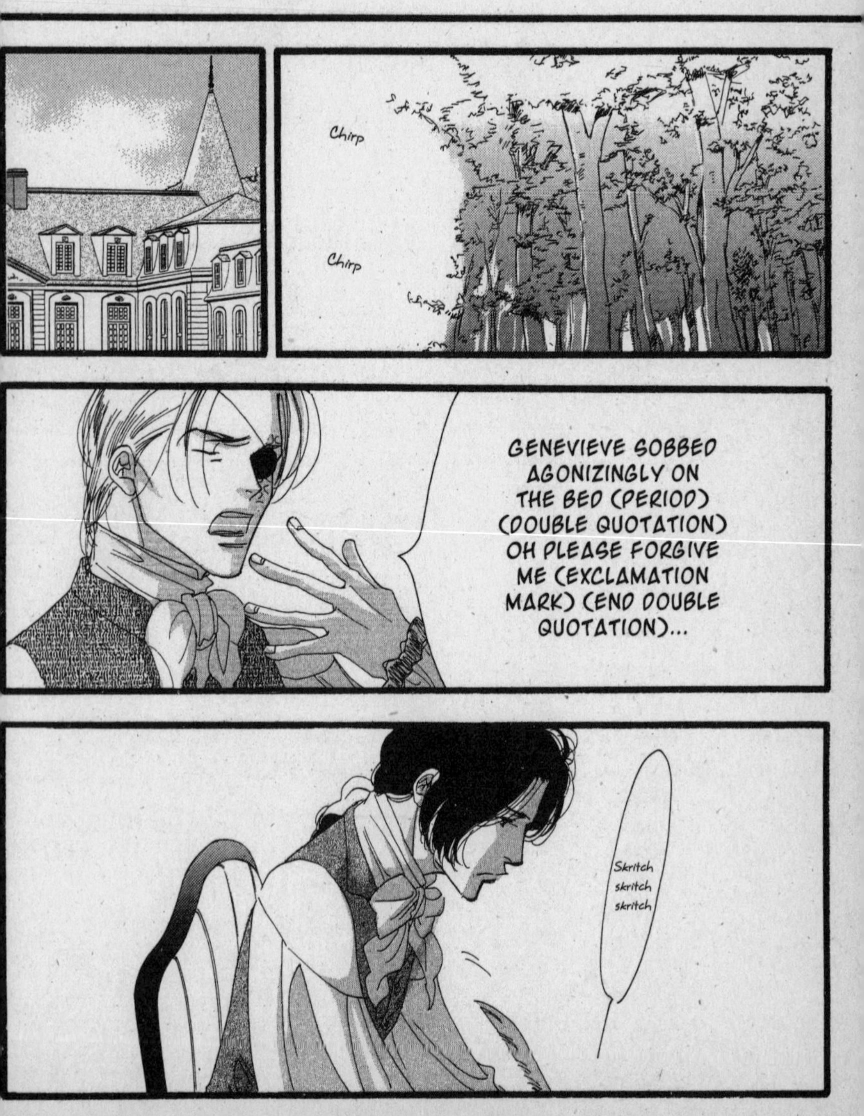
Chirp
Chirp
GENEVIEVE SOBBED AGONIZINGLY ON THE BED (PERIOD) (DOUBLE QUOTATION) OH PLEASE FORGIVE ME (EXCLAMATION MARK) (END DOUBLE QUOTATION)...
Skritch skritch skritch

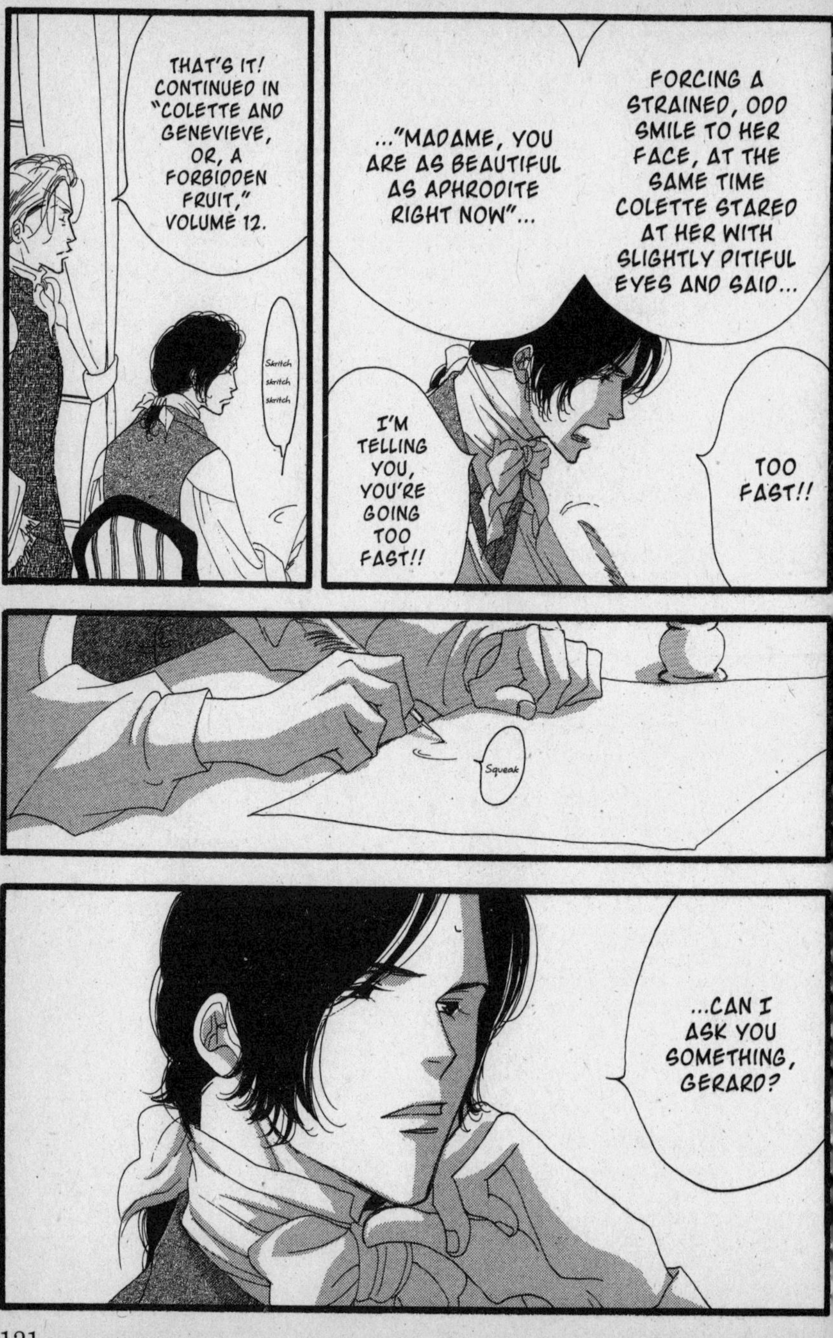
FORCING A STRAINED, ODD SMILE TO HER FACE, AT THE SAME TIME COLETTE STARED AT HER WITH SLIGHTLY PITIFUL EYES AND SAID...
..."MADAME, YOU ARE AS BEAUTIFUL AS APHRODITE RIGHT NOW"...
TOO FAST!!
I'M TELLING YOU, YOU'RE GOING TOO FAST!!
THAT'S IT! CONTINUED IN "COLETTE AND GENEVIEVE, OR, A FORBIDDEN FRUIT," VOLUME 12.
Skritch skritch skritch
Squeak
...CAN I ASK YOU SOMETHING, GERARD?

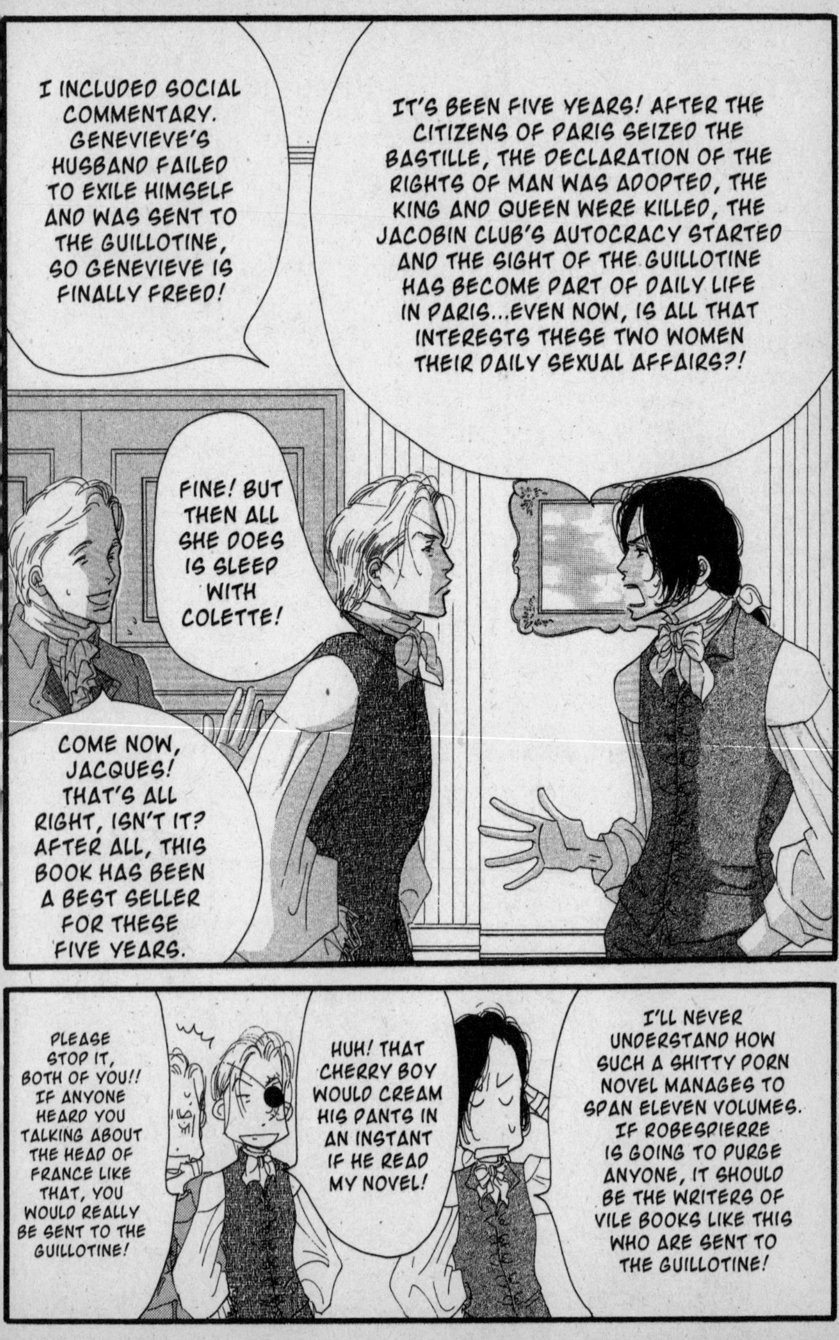
IT'S BEEN FIVE YEARS! AFTER THE CITIZENS OF PARIS SEIZED THE BASTILLE, THE DECLARATION OF THE RIGHTS OF MAN WAS ADOPTED, THE KING AND QUEEN WERE KILLED, THE JACOBIN CLUB'S AUTOCRACY STARTED AND THE SIGHT OF THE GUILLOTINE HAS BECOME PART OF DAILY LIFE IN PARIS...EVEN NOW, IS ALL THAT INTERESTS THESE TWO WOMEN THEIR DAILY SEXUAL AFFAIRS?!
I INCLUDED SOCIAL COMMENTARY. GENEVIEVE'S HUSBAND FAILED TO EXILE HIMSELF AND WAS SENT TO THE GUILLOTINE, SO GENEVIEVE IS FINALLY FREED!
FINE! BUT THEN ALL SHE DOES IS SLEEP WITH COLETTE!
COME NOW, JACQUES! THAT'S ALL RIGHT, ISN'T IT? AFTER ALL, THIS BOOK HAS BEEN A BEST SELLER FOR THESE FIVE YEARS.
I'LL NEVER UNDERSTAND HOW SUCH A SHITTY PORN NOVEL MANAGES TO SPAN ELEVEN VOLUMES. IF ROBESPIERRE IS GOING TO PURGE ANYONE, IT SHOULD BE THE WRITERS OF VILE BOOKS LIKE THIS WHO ARE SENT TO THE GUILLOTINE!
HUH! THAT CHERRY BOY WOULD CREAM HIS PANTS IN AN INSTANT IF HE READ MY NOVEL!
PLEASE STOP IT, BOTH OF YOU!! IF ANYONE HEARD YOU TALKING ABOUT THE HEAD OF FRANCE LIKE THAT, YOU WOULD REALLY BE SENT TO THE GUILLOTINE!

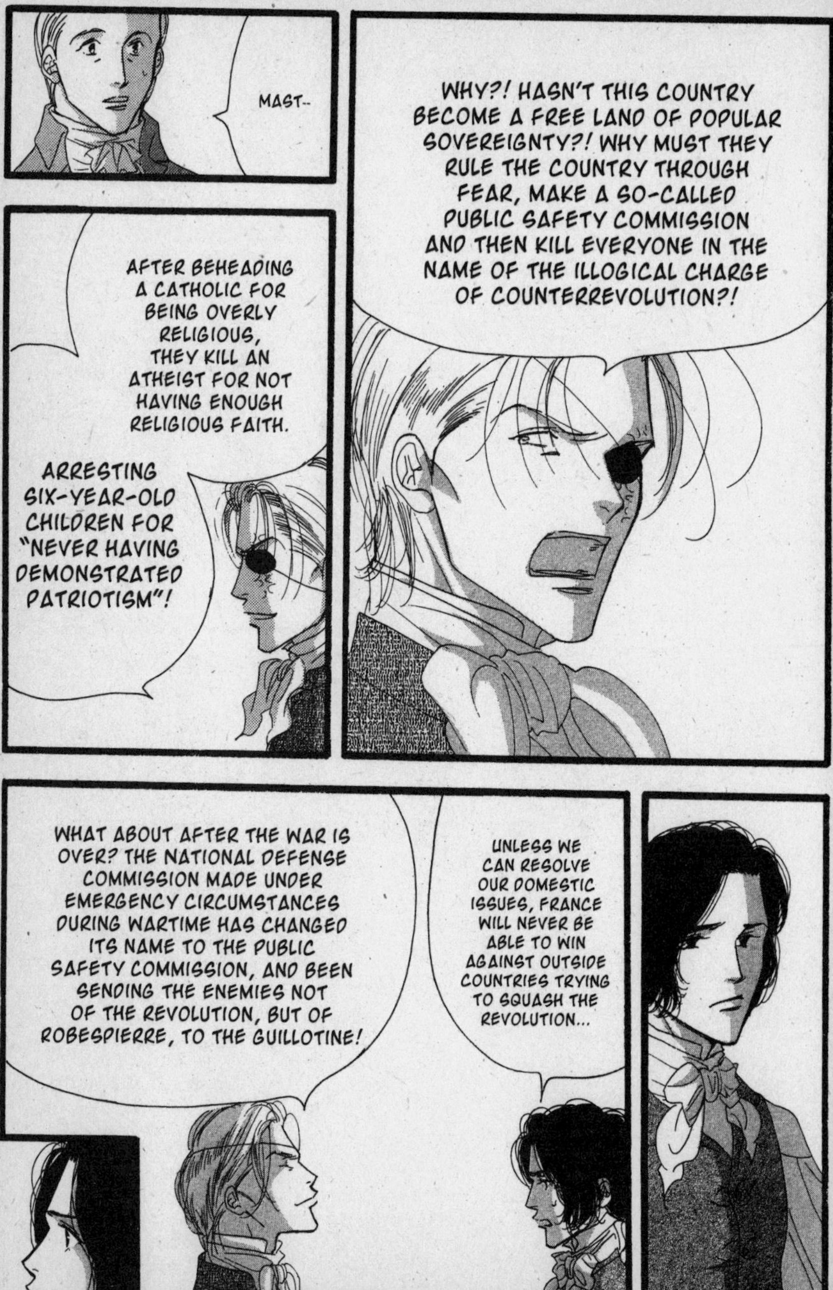
WHY?! HASN'T THIS COUNTRY BECOME A FREE LAND OF POPULAR SOVEREIGNTY?! WHY MUST THEY RULE THE COUNTRY THROUGH FEAR, MAKE A SO-CALLED PUBLIC SAFETY COMMISSION AND THEN KILL EVERYONE IN THE NAME OF THE ILLOGICAL CHARGE OF COUNTERREVOLUTION?!
MAST--
AFTER BEHEADING A CATHOLIC FOR BEING OVERLY RELIGIOUS, THEY KILL AN ATHEIST FOR NOT HAVING ENOUGH RELIGIOUS FAITH.
ARRESTING SIX-YEAR-OLD CHILDREN FOR "NEVER HAVING DEMONSTRATED PATRIOTISM"!
UNLESS WE CAN RESOLVE OUR DOMESTIC ISSUES, FRANCE WILL NEVER BE ABLE TO WIN AGAINST OUTSIDE COUNTRIES TRYING TO SQUASH THE REVOLUTION...
WHAT ABOUT AFTER THE WAR IS OVER? THE NATIONAL DEFENSE COMMISSION MADE UNDER EMERGENCY CIRCUMSTANCES DURING WARTIME HAS CHANGED ITS NAME TO THE PUBLIC SAFETY COMMISSION, AND BEEN SENDING THE ENEMIES NOT OF THE REVOLUTION, BUT OF ROBESPIERRE, TO THE GUILLOTINE!

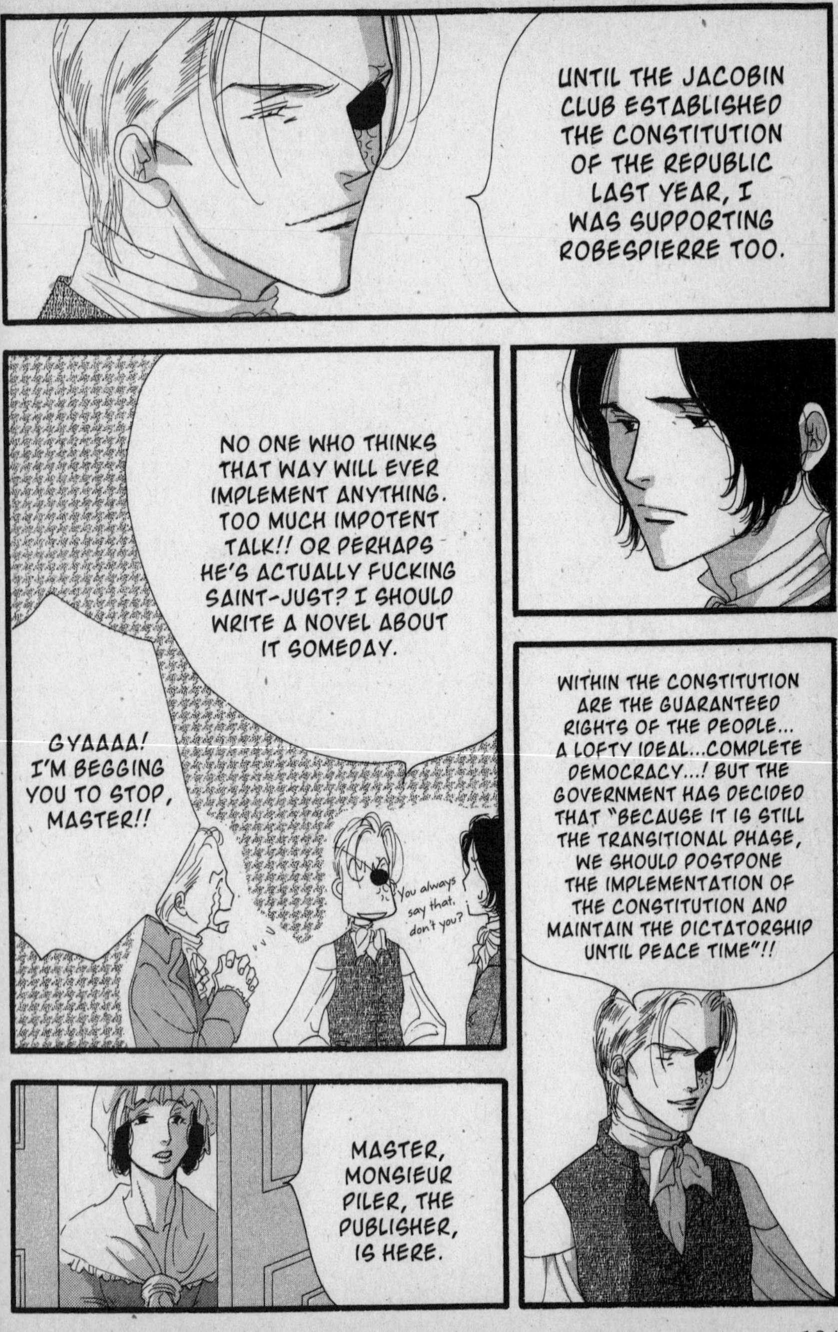
UNTIL THE JACOBIN CLUB ESTABLISHED THE CONSTITUTION OF THE REPUBLIC LAST YEAR, I WAS SUPPORTING ROBESPIERRE TOO.
WITHIN THE CONSTITUTION ARE THE GUARANTEED RIGHTS OF THE PEOPLE... A LOFTY IDEAL...COMPLETE DEMOCRACY...! BUT THE GOVERNMENT HAS DECIDED THAT "BECAUSE IT IS STILL THE TRANSITIONAL PHASE, WE SHOULD POSTPONE THE IMPLEMENTATION OF THE CONSTITUTION AND MAINTAIN THE DICTATORSHIP UNTIL PEACE TIME"!!
NO ONE WHO THINKS THAT WAY WILL EVER IMPLEMENT ANYTHING. TOO MUCH IMPOTENT TALK!! OR PERHAPS HE'S ACTUALLY FUCKING SAINT-JUST? I SHOULD WRITE A NOVEL ABOUT IT SOMEDAY.
GYAAAA! I'M BEGGING YOU TO STOP, MASTER!!
You always say that, don't you?
MASTER, MONSIEUR PILER, THE PUBLISHER, IS HERE.

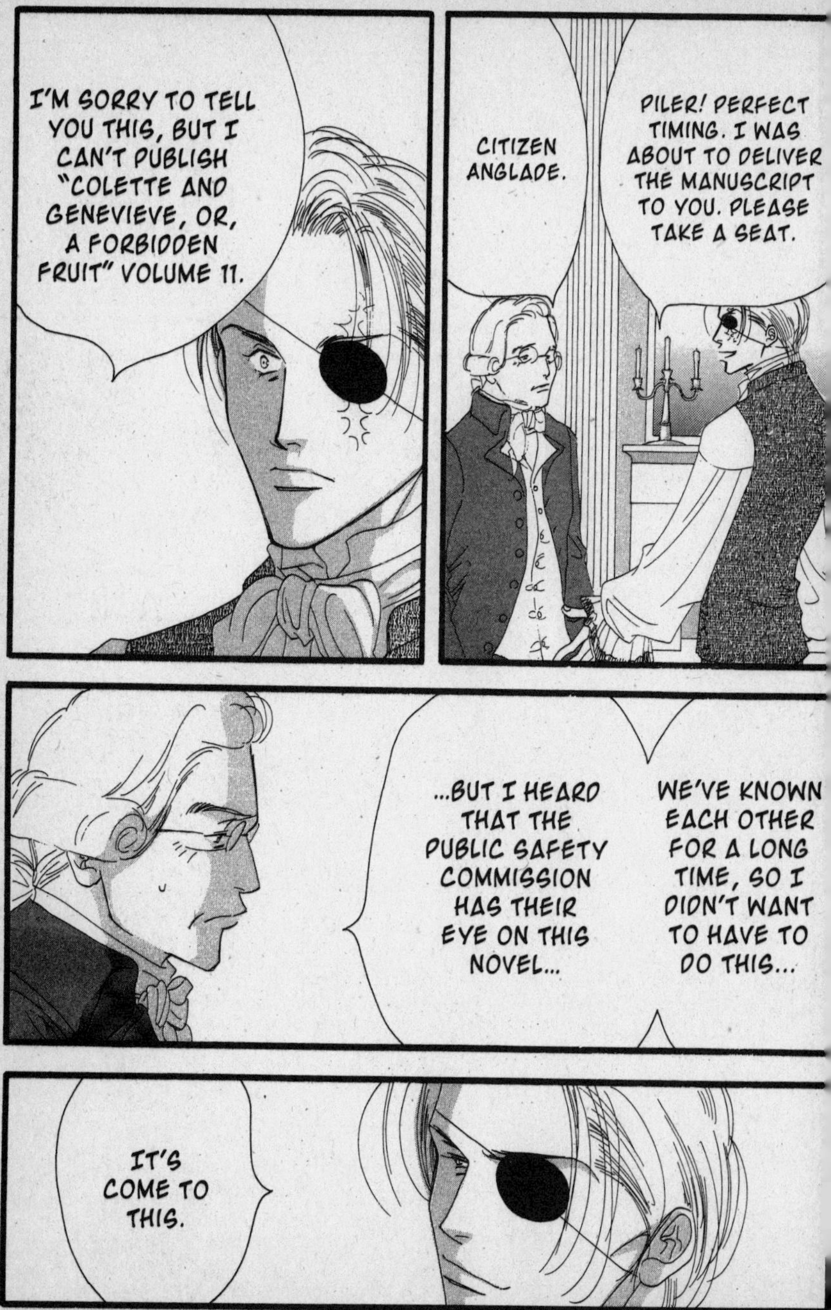
PILER! PERFECT TIMING. I WAS ABOUT TO DELIVER THE MANUSCRIPT TO YOU. PLEASE TAKE A SEAT.
CITIZEN ANGLADE.
I'M SORRY TO TELL YOU THIS, BUT I CAN'T PUBLISH "COLETTE AND GENEVIEVE, OR, A FORBIDDEN FRUIT" VOLUME 11.
WE'VE KNOWN EACH OTHER FOR A LONG TIME, SO I DIDN'T WANT TO HAVE TO DO THIS...
...BUT I HEARD THAT THE PUBLIC SAFETY COMMISSION HAS THEIR EYE ON THIS NOVEL...
IT'S COME TO THIS.

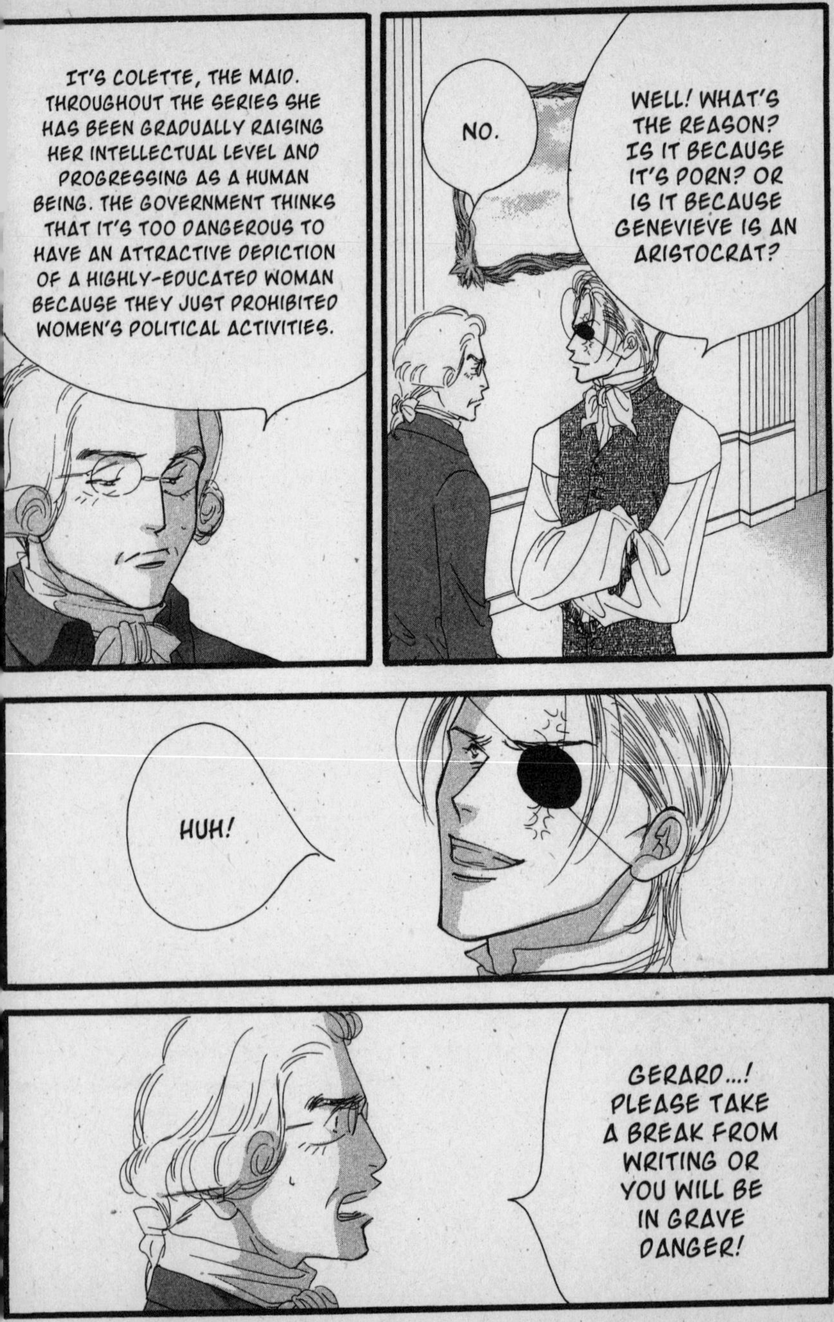
NO.
WELL! WHAT'S THE REASON? IS IT BECAUSE IT'S PORN? OR IS IT BECAUSE GENEVIEVE IS AN ARISTOCRAT?
IT'S COLETTE, THE MAID. THROUGHOUT THE SERIES SHE HAS BEEN GRADUALLY RAISING HER INTELLECTUAL LEVEL AND PROGRESSING AS A HUMAN BEING. THE GOVERNMENT THINKS THAT IT'S TOO DANGEROUS TO HAVE AN ATTRACTIVE DEPICTION OF A HIGHLY-EDUCATED WOMAN BECAUSE THEY JUST PROHIBITED WOMEN'S POLITICAL ACTIVITIES.
HUH!
GERARD...! PLEASE TAKE A BREAK FROM WRITING OR YOU WILL BE IN GRAVE DANGER!

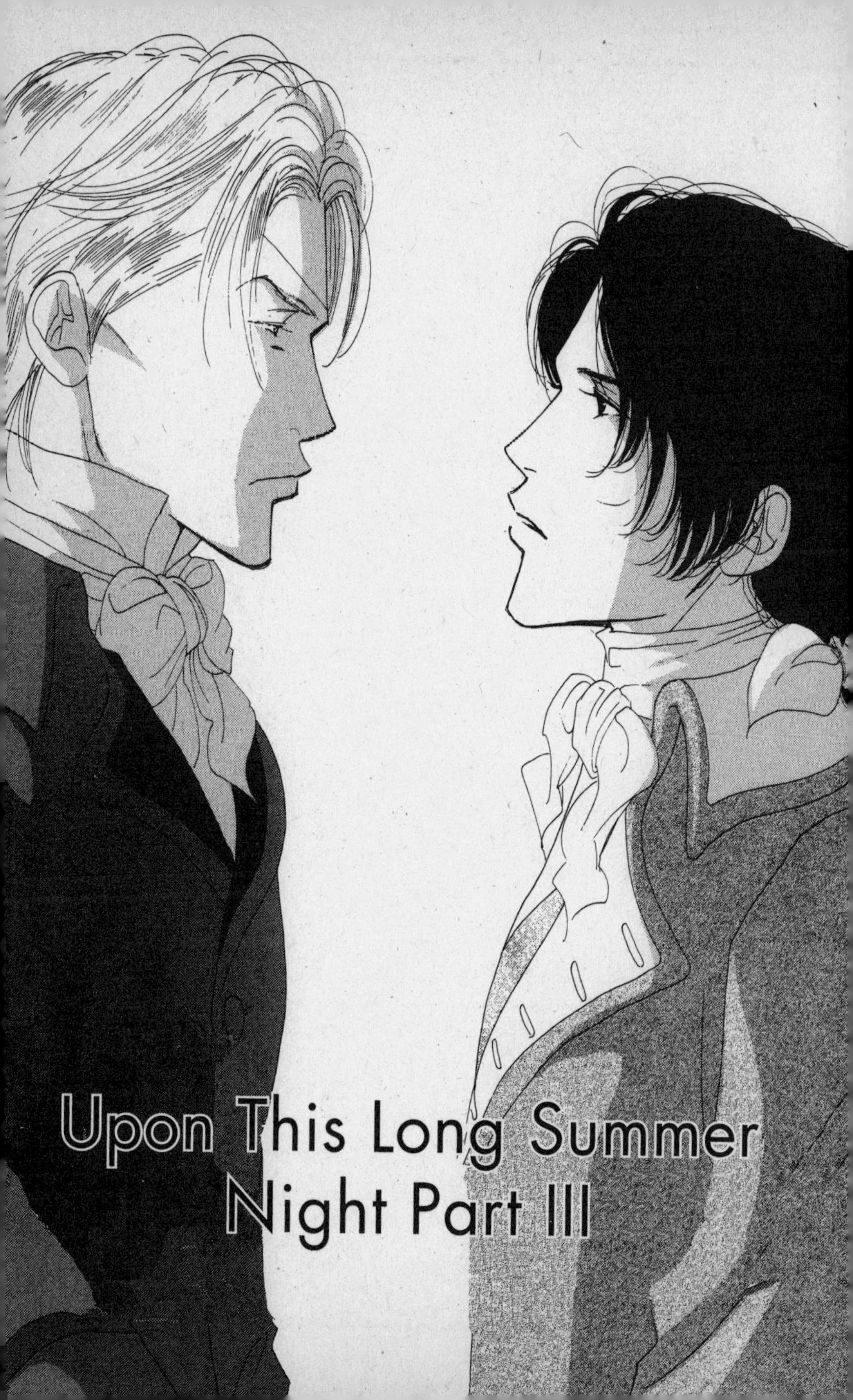
Upon This Long Summer Night Part III

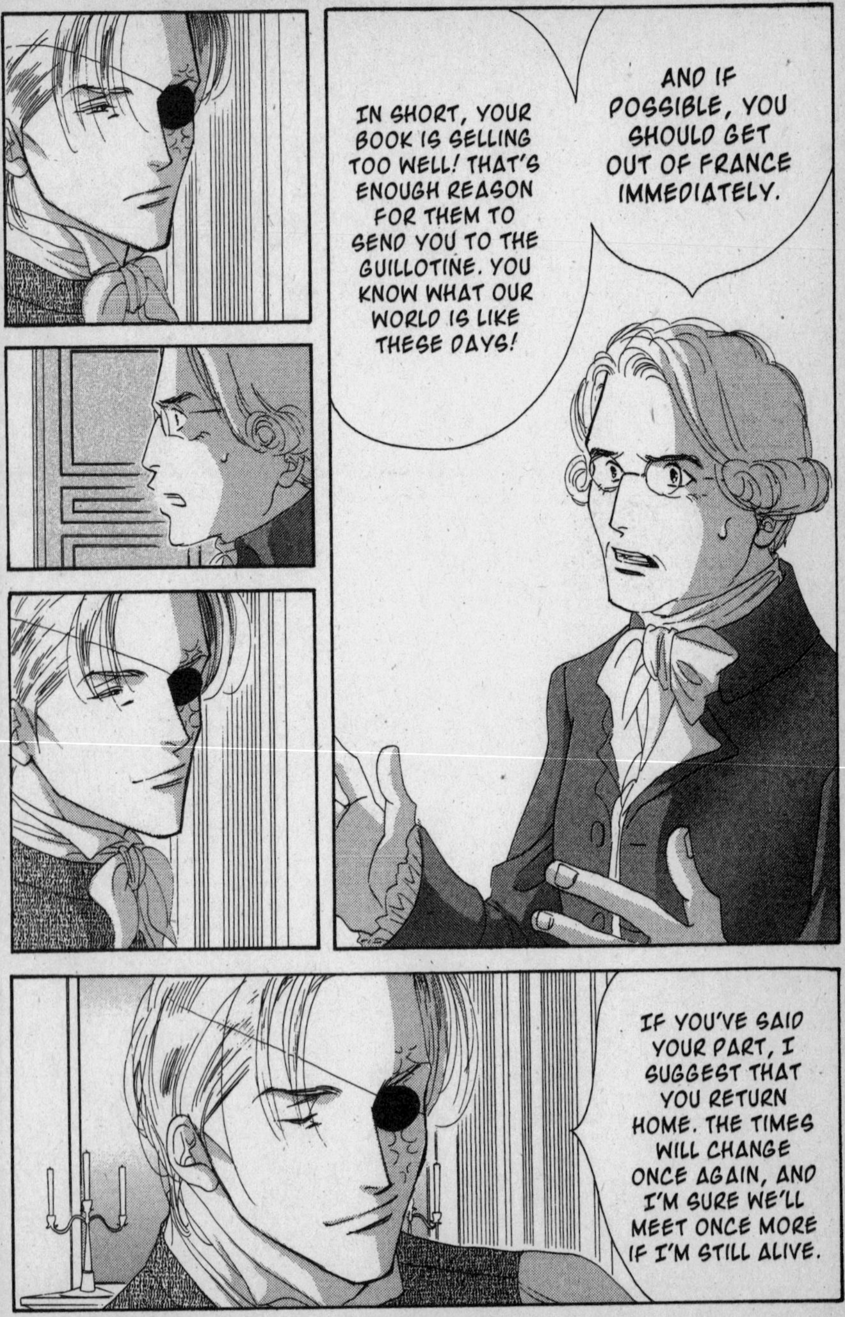
AND IF POSSIBLE, YOU SHOULD GET OUT OF FRANCE IMMEDIATELY.
IN SHORT, YOUR BOOK IS SELLING TOO WELL! THAT'S ENOUGH REASON FOR THEM TO SEND YOU TO THE GUILLOTINE. YOU KNOW WHAT OUR WORLD IS LIKE THESE DAYS!
IF YOU'VE SAID YOUR PART, I SUGGEST THAT YOU RETURN HOME. THE TIMES WILL CHANGE ONCE AGAIN, AND I'M SURE WE'LL MEET ONCE MORE IF I'M STILL ALIVE.

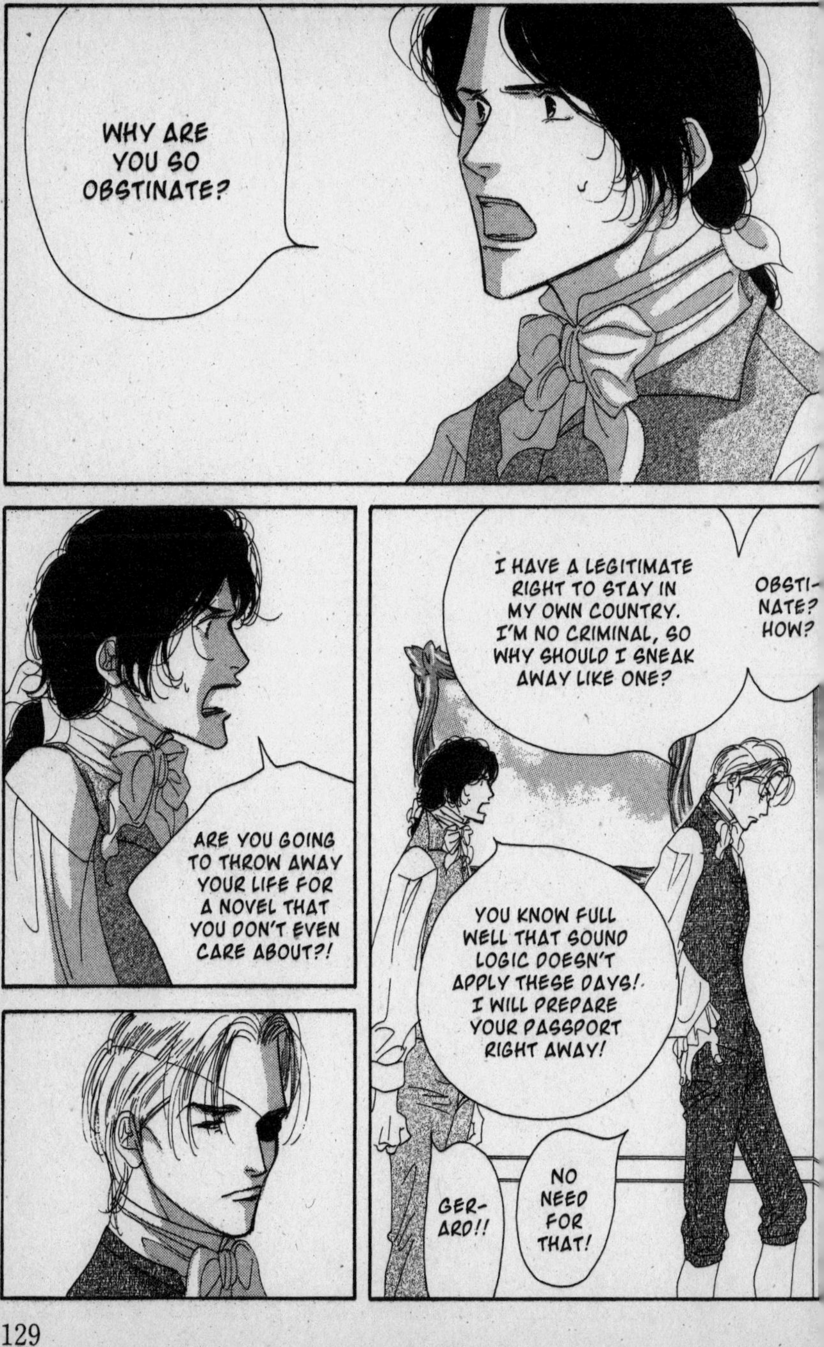
WHY ARE YOU SO OBSTINATE?
OBSTINATE? HOW?
I HAVE A LEGITIMATE RIGHT TO STAY IN MY OWN COUNTRY. I'M NO CRIMINAL, SO WHY SHOULD I SNEAK AWAY LIKE ONE?
YOU KNOW FULL WELL THAT SOUND LOGIC DOESN'T APPLY THESE DAYS! I WILL PREPARE YOUR PASSPORT RIGHT AWAY!
NO NEED FOR THAT!
GERARD!!
ARE YOU GOING TO THROW AWAY YOUR LIFE FOR A NOVEL THAT YOU DON'T EVEN CARE ABOUT?!

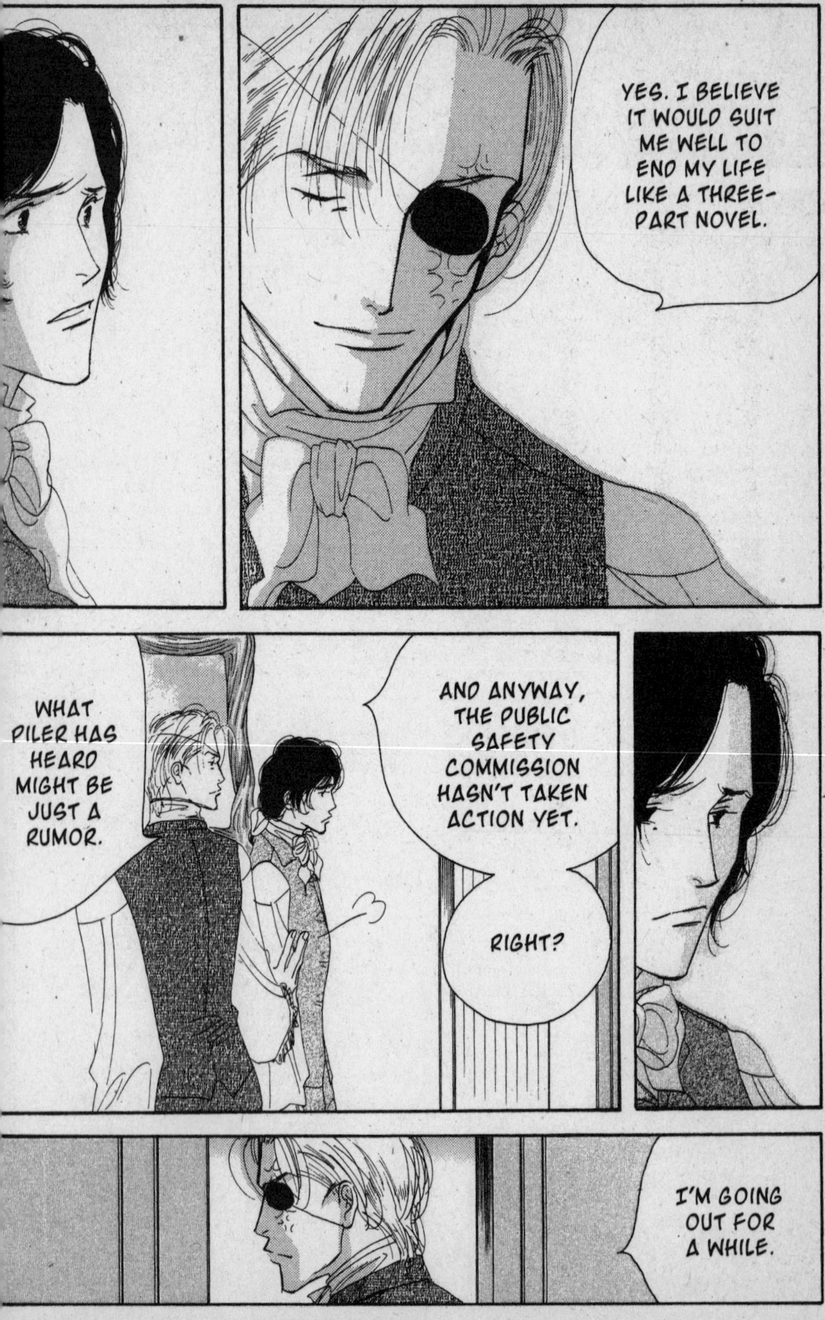
YES. I BELIEVE IT WOULD SUIT ME WELL TO END MY LIFE LIKE A THREE-PART NOVEL.
WHAT PILER HAS HEARD MIGHT BE JUST A RUMOR.
AND ANYWAY, THE PUBLIC SAFETY COMMISSION HASN'T TAKEN ACTION YET.
RIGHT?
I'M GOING OUT FOR A WHILE.

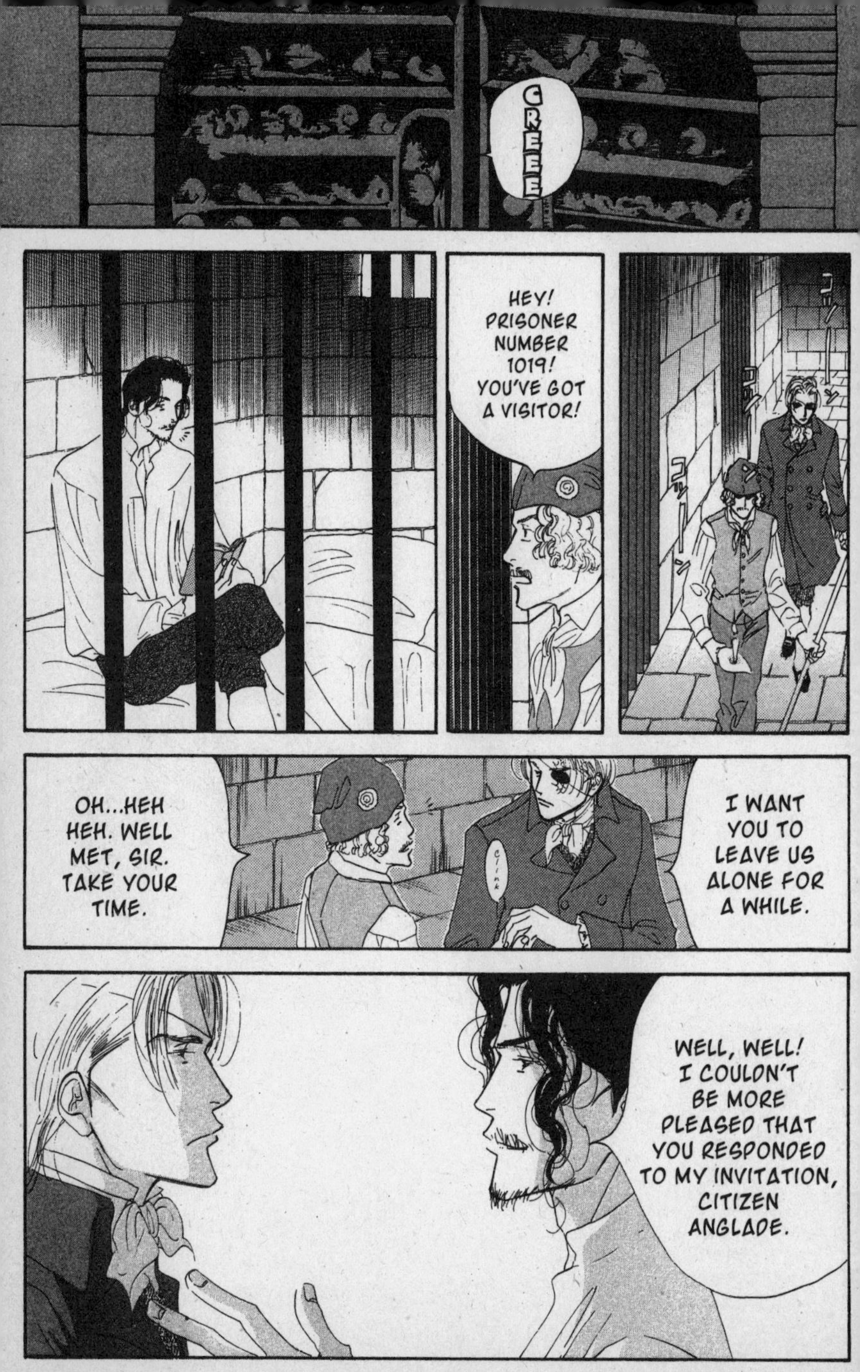
CREEE
HEY! PRISONER NUMBER 1019! YOU'VE GOT A VISITOR!
I WANT YOU TO LEAVE US ALONE FOR A WHILE.
Clink
OH...HEH HEH. WELL MET, SIR. TAKE YOUR TIME.
WELL, WELL! I COULDN'T BE MORE PLEASED THAT YOU RESPONDED TO MY INVITATION, CITIZEN ANGLADE.

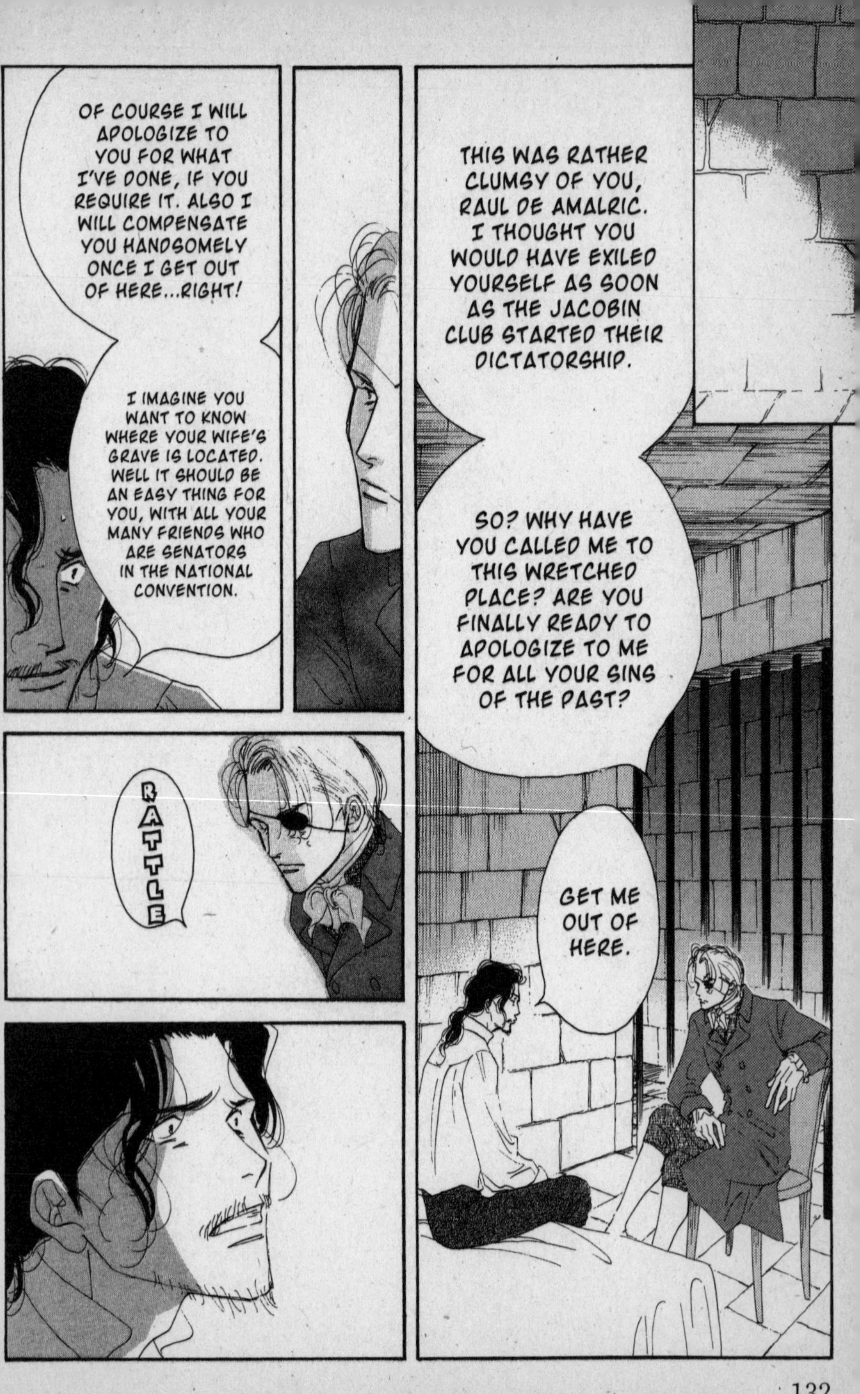
THIS WAS RATHER CLUMSY OF YOU, RAUL DE AMALRIC. I THOUGHT YOU WOULD HAVE EXILED YOURSELF AS SOON AS THE JACOBIN CLUB STARTED THEIR DICTATORSHIP.
SO? WHY HAVE YOU CALLED ME TO THIS WRETCHED PLACE? ARE YOU FINALLY READY TO APOLOGIZE TO ME FOR ALL YOUR SINS OF THE PAST?
GET ME OUT OF HERE.
I IMAGINE YOU WANT TO KNOW WHERE YOUR WIFE'S GRAVE IS LOCATED. WELL IT SHOULD BE AN EASY THING FOR YOU, WITH ALL YOUR MANY FRIENDS WHO ARE SENATORS IN THE NATIONAL CONVENTION.
OF COURSE I WILL APOLOGIZE TO YOU FOR WHAT I'VE DONE, IF YOU REQUIRE IT. ALSO I WILL COMPENSATE YOU HANDSOMELY ONCE I GET OUT OF HERE...RIGHT!
RATTLE

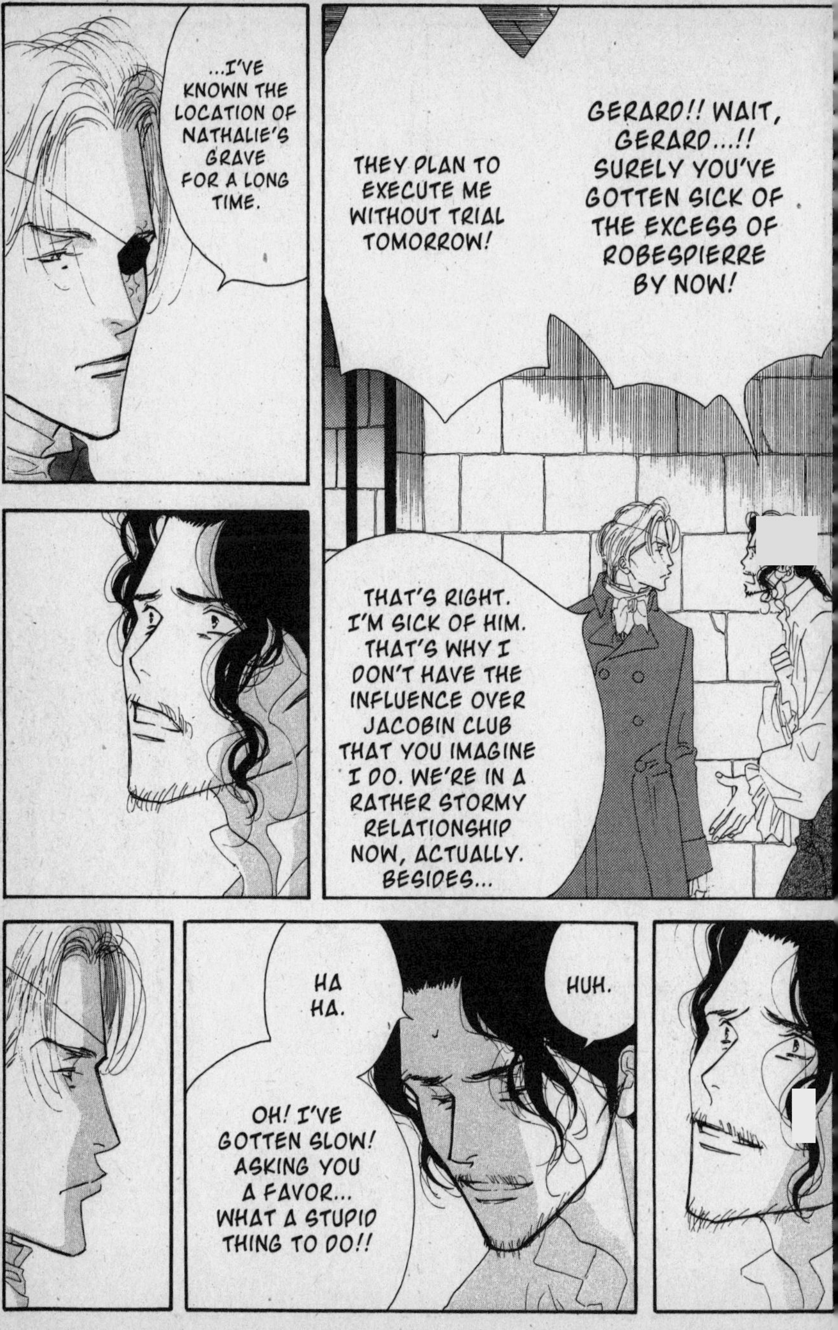
GERARD!! WAIT, GERARD...!! SURELY YOU'VE GOTTEN SICK OF THE EXCESS OF ROBESPIERRE BY NOW!
THEY PLAN TO EXECUTE ME WITHOUT TRIAL TOMORROW!
THAT'S RIGHT. I'M SICK OF HIM. THAT'S WHY I DON'T HAVE THE INFLUENCE OVER JACOBIN CLUB THAT YOU IMAGINE I DO. WE'RE IN A RATHER STORMY RELATIONSHIP NOW, ACTUALLY. BESIDES...
...I'VE KNOWN THE LOCATION OF NATHALIE'S GRAVE FOR A LONG TIME.
HUH.
HA HA.
OH! I'VE GOTTEN SLOW! ASKING YOU A FAVOR... WHAT A STUPID THING TO DO!!

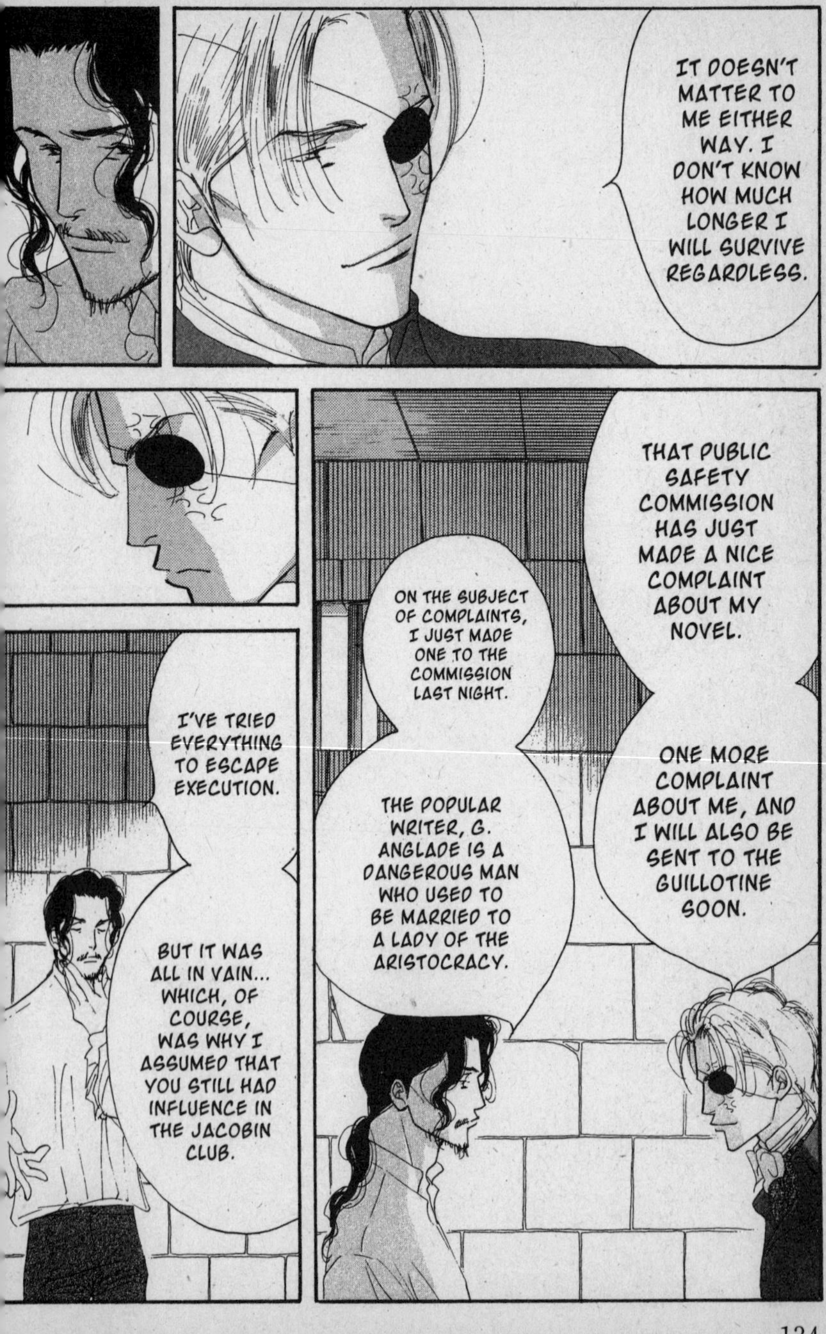
IT DOESN'T MATTER TO ME EITHER WAY. I DON'T KNOW HOW MUCH LONGER I WILL SURVIVE REGARDLESS.
THAT PUBLIC SAFETY COMMISSION HAS JUST MADE A NICE COMPLAINT ABOUT MY NOVEL.
ONE MORE COMPLAINT ABOUT ME, AND I WILL ALSO BE SENT TO THE GUILLOTINE SOON.
ON THE SUBJECT OF COMPLAINTS, I JUST MADE ONE TO THE COMMISSION LAST NIGHT.
THE POPULAR WRITER, G. ANGLADE IS A DANGEROUS MAN WHO USED TO BE MARRIED TO A LADY OF THE ARISTOCRACY.
I'VE TRIED EVERYTHING TO ESCAPE EXECUTION.
BUT IT WAS ALL IN VAIN... WHICH, OF COURSE, WAS WHY I ASSUMED THAT YOU STILL HAD INFLUENCE IN THE JACOBIN CLUB.

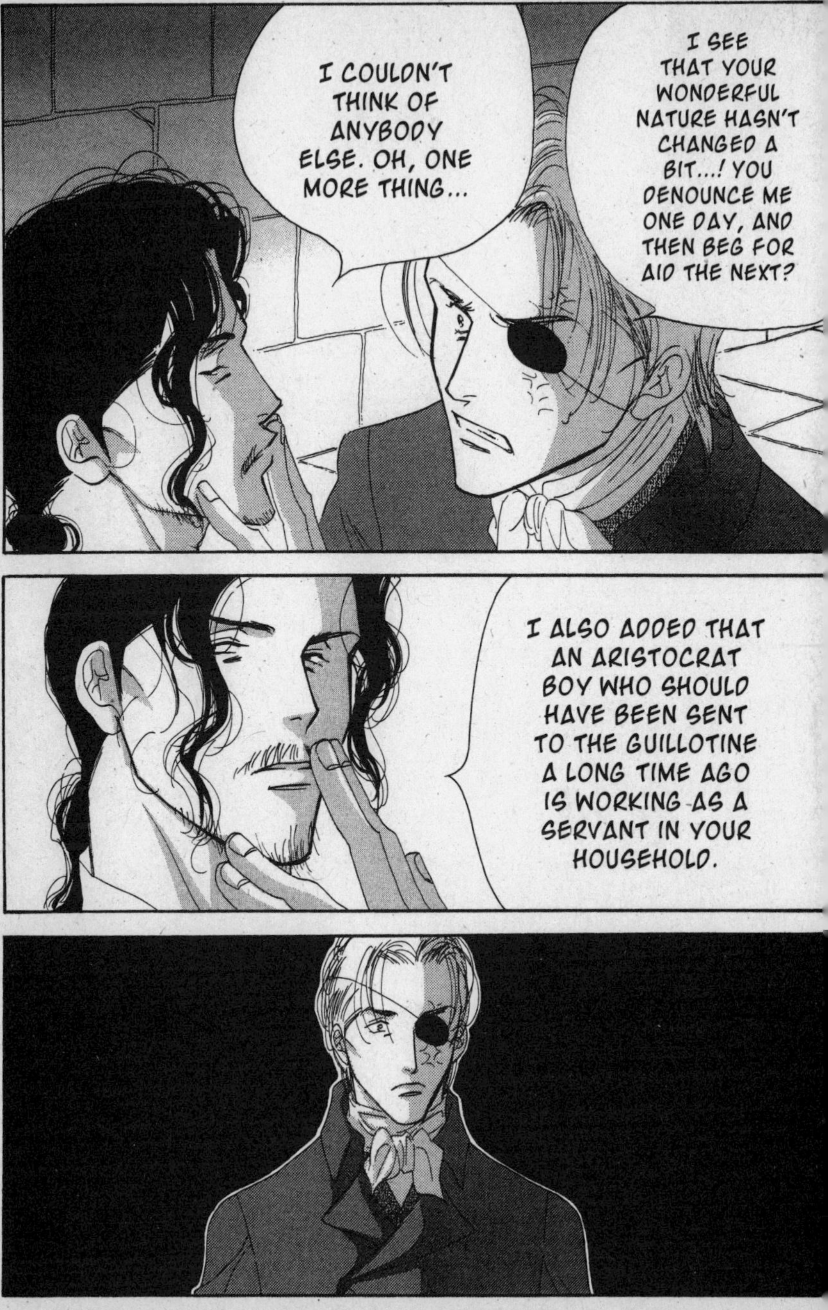
I SEE THAT YOUR WONDERFUL NATURE HASN'T CHANGED A BIT...! YOU DENOUNCE ME ONE DAY, AND THEN BEG FOR AID THE NEXT?
I COULDN'T THINK OF ANYBODY ELSE. OH, ONE MORE THING...
I ALSO ADDED THAT AN ARISTOCRAT BOY WHO SHOULD HAVE BEEN SENT TO THE GUILLOTINE A LONG TIME AGO IS WORKING AS A SERVANT IN YOUR HOUSEHOLD.

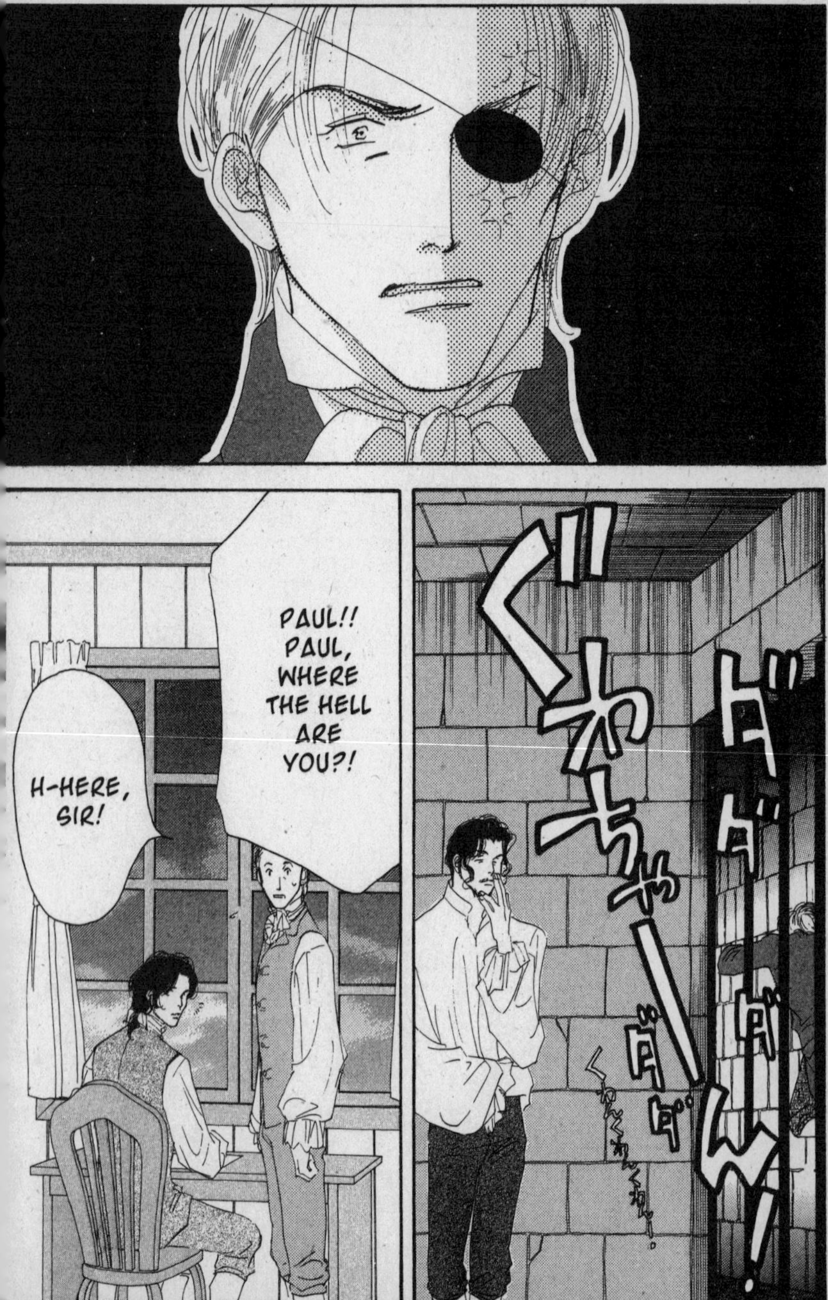
PAUL!! PAUL, WHERE THE HELL ARE YOU?!
H-HERE, SIR!

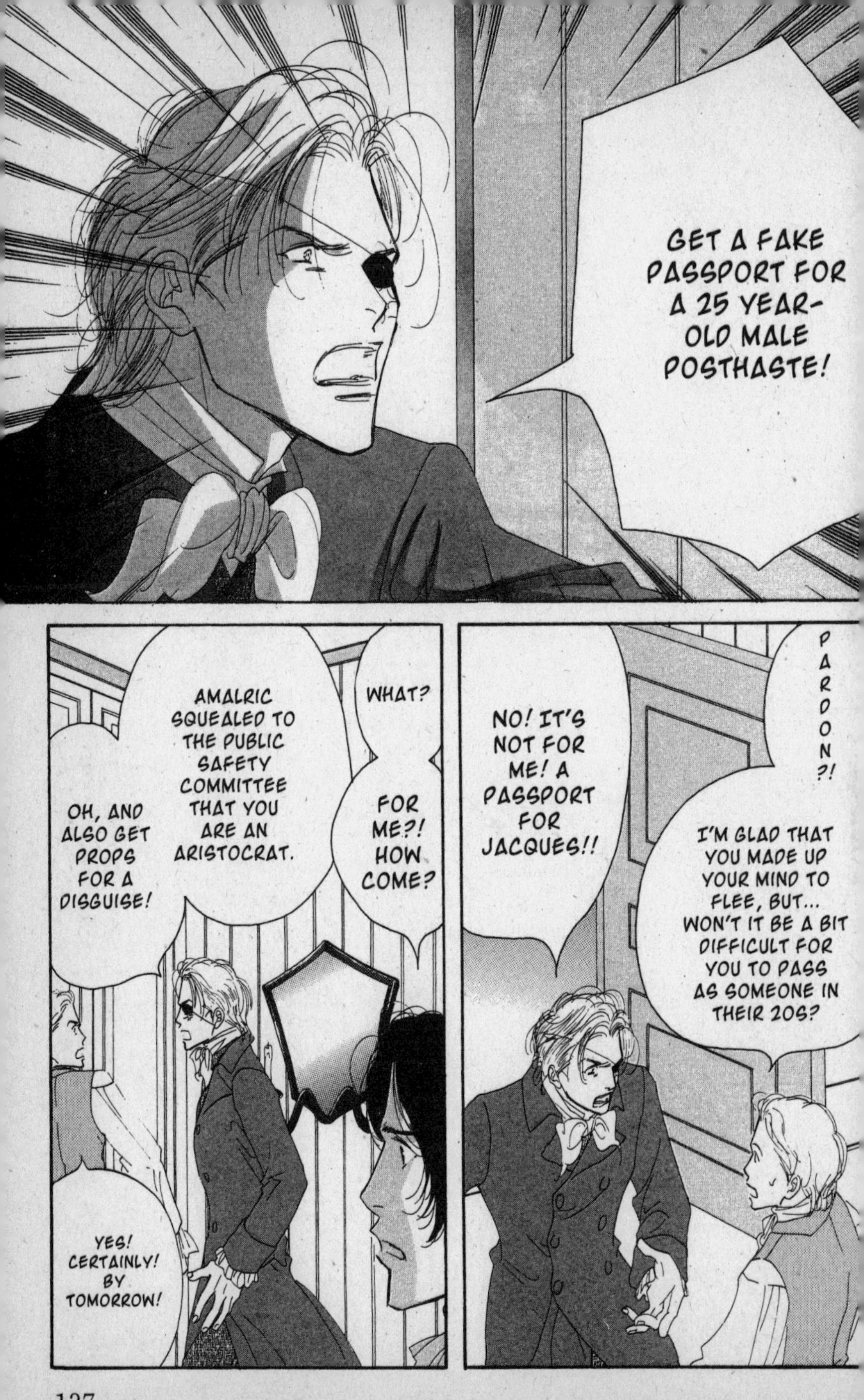
GET A FAKE PASSPORT FOR A 25 YEAR-OLD MALE POSTHASTE!
PARDOON?!
I'M GLAD THAT YOU MADE UP YOUR MIND TO FLEE, BUT... WON'T IT BE A BIT DIFFICULT FOR YOU TO PASS AS SOMEONE IN THEIR 20S?
NO! IT'S NOT FOR ME! A PASSPORT FOR JACQUES!!
WHAT?
FOR ME?! HOW COME?
AMALRIC SQUEALED TO THE PUBLIC SAFETY COMMITTEE THAT YOU ARE AN ARISTOCRAT.
OH, AND ALSO GET PROPS FOR A DISGUISE!
YES! CERTAINLY! BY TOMORROW!

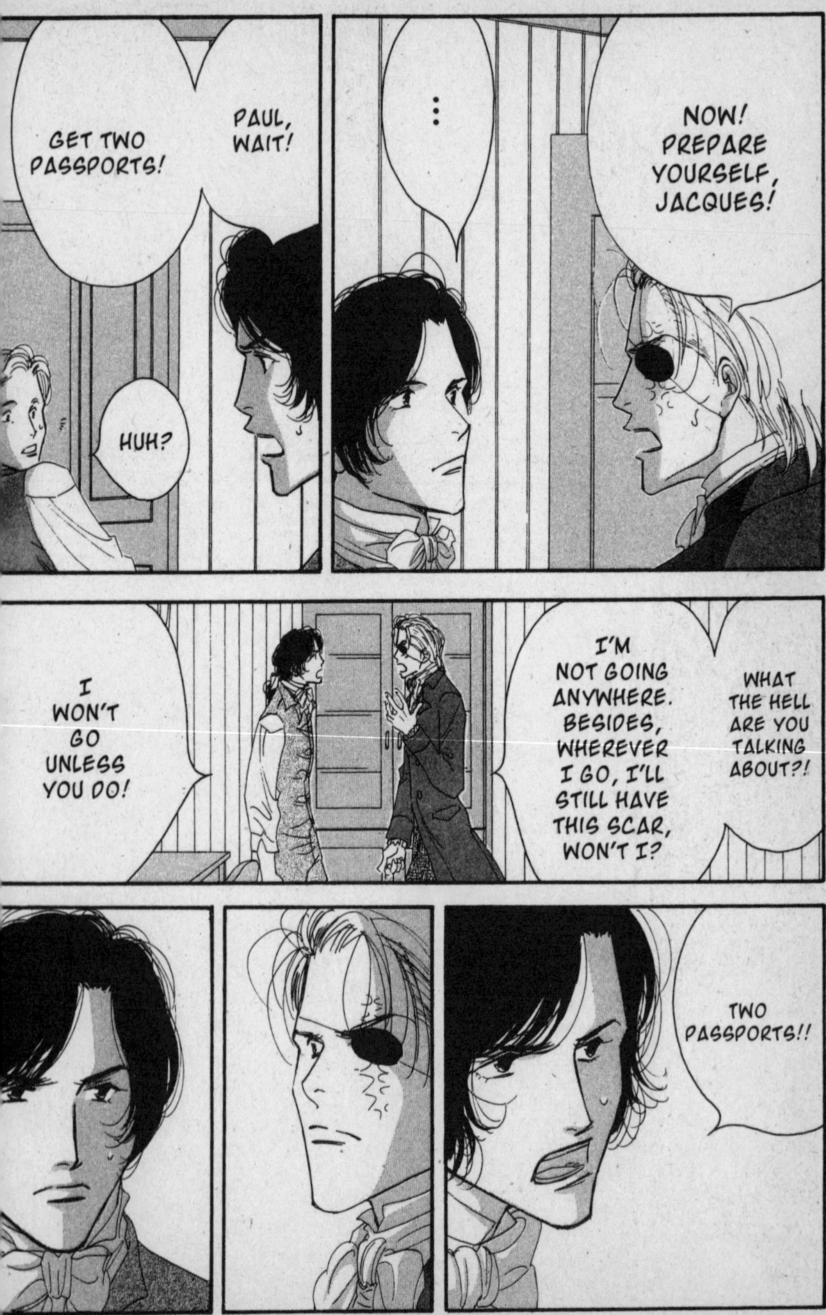
NOW! PREPARE YOURSELF, JACQUES!
...
PAUL, WAIT!
GET TWO PASSPORTS!
HUH?
WHAT THE HELL ARE YOU TALKING ABOUT?!
I'M NOT GOING ANYWHERE. BESIDES, WHEREVER I GO, I'LL STILL HAVE THIS SCAR, WON'T I?
I WON'T GO UNLESS YOU DO!
TWO PASSPORTS!!

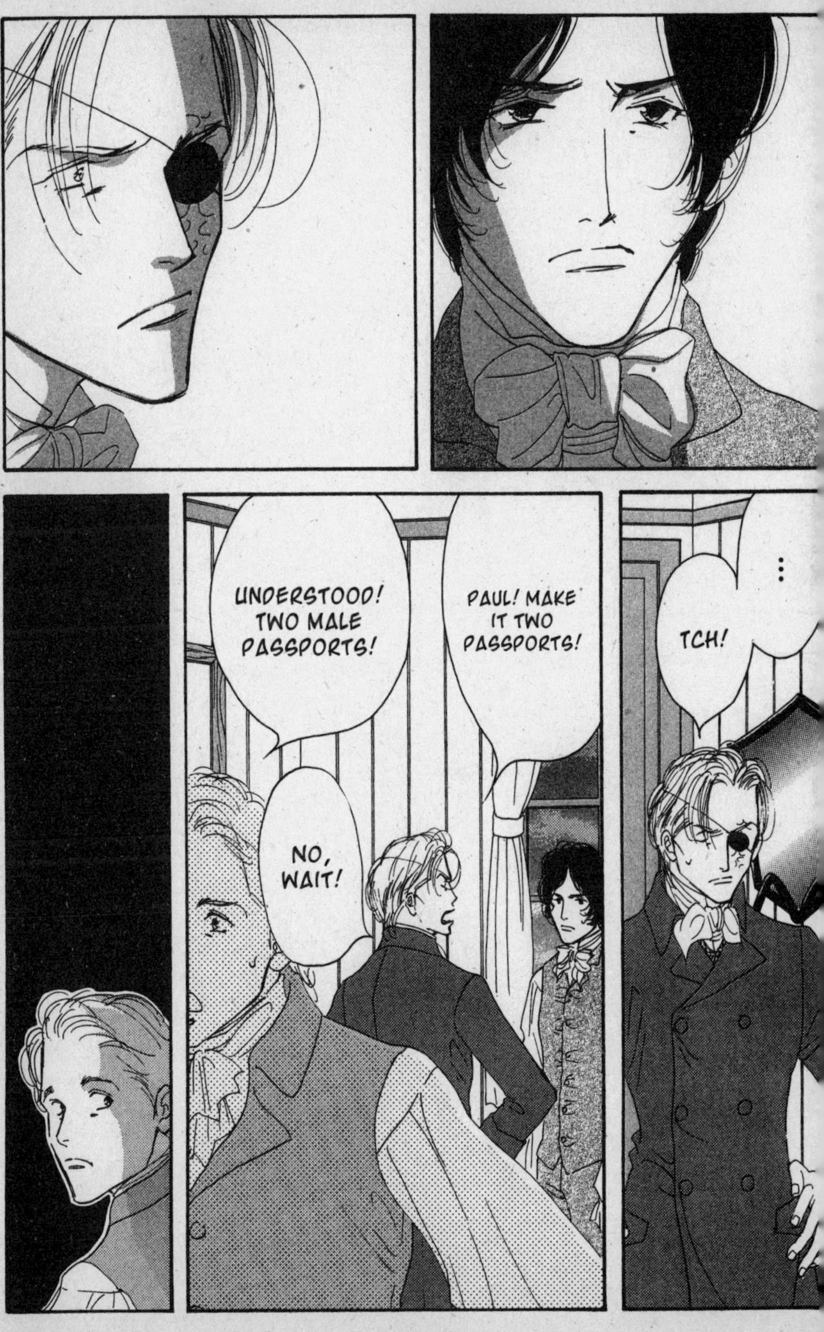
...
TCH!
PAUL! MAKE IT TWO PASSPORTS!
UNDERSTOOD! TWO MALE PASSPORTS!
NO, WAIT!

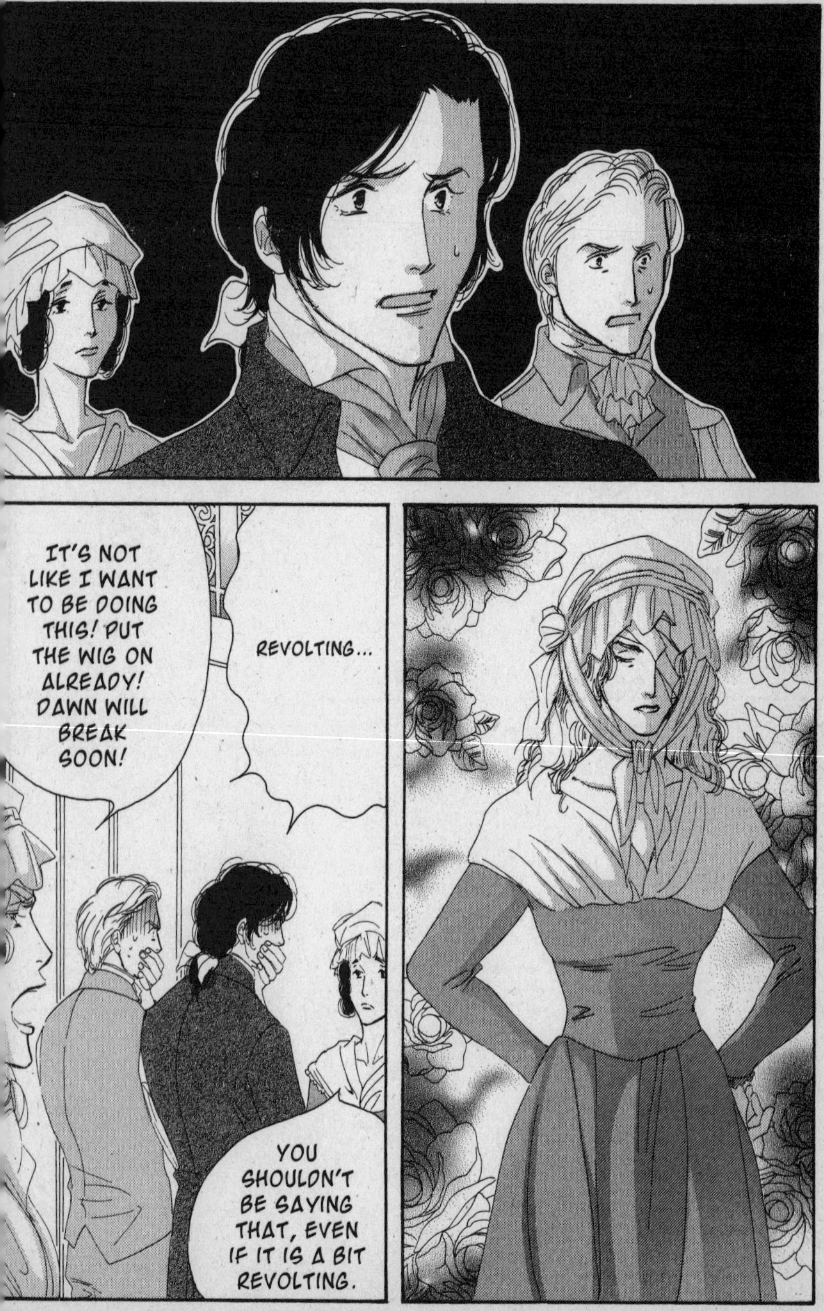
REVOLTING...
IT'S NOT LIKE I WANT TO BE DOING THIS! PUT THE WIG ON ALREADY! DAWN WILL BREAK SOON!
YOU SHOULDN'T BE SAYING THAT, EVEN IF IT IS A BIT REVOLTING.

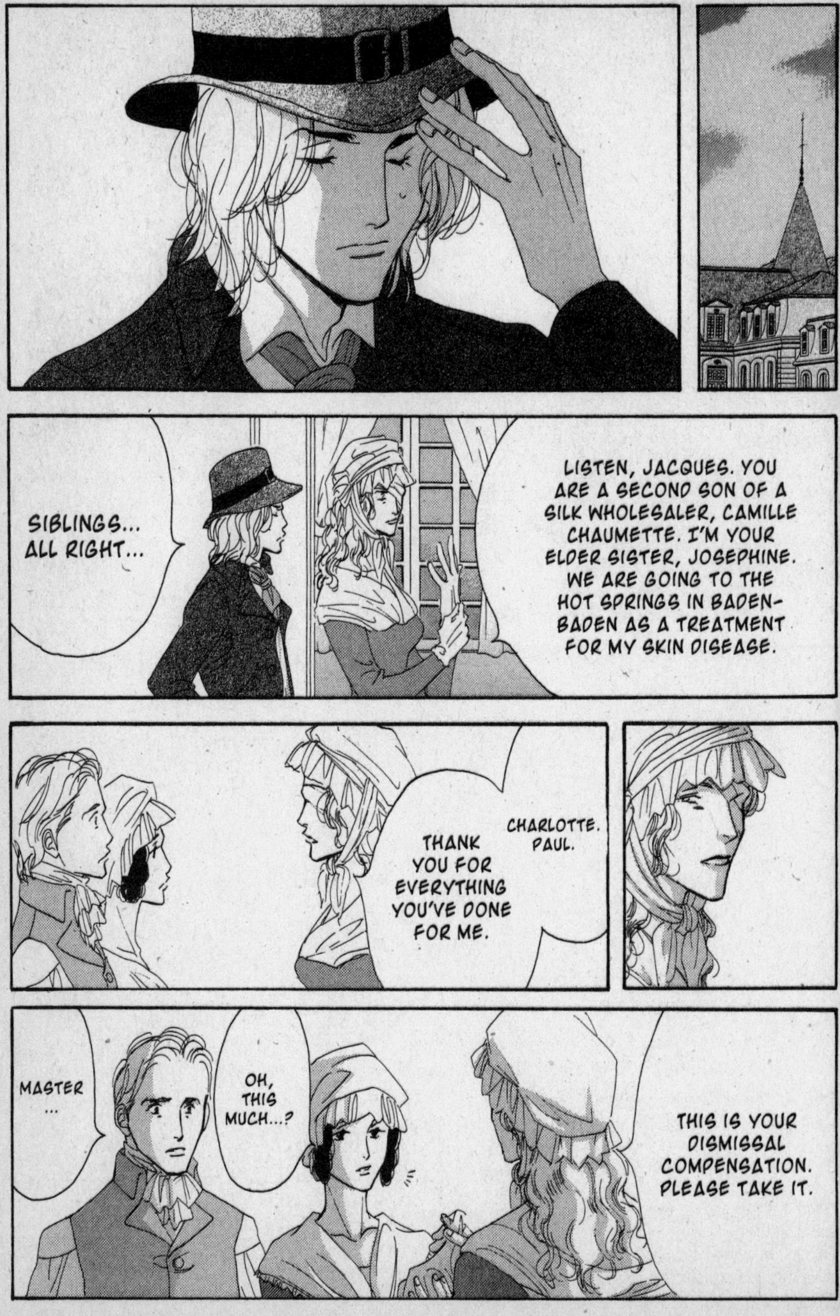
LISTEN, JACQUES. YOU ARE A SECOND SON OF A SILK WHOLESALER, CAMILLE CHAUMETTE. I'M YOUR ELDER SISTER, JOSEPHINE. WE ARE GOING TO THE HOT SPRINGS IN BADEN-BADEN AS A TREATMENT FOR MY SKIN DISEASE.
SIBLINGS... ALL RIGHT...
CHARLOTTE. PAUL.
THANK YOU FOR EVERYTHING YOU'VE DONE FOR ME.
THIS IS YOUR DISMISSAL COMPENSATION. PLEASE TAKE IT.
OH, THIS MUCH...?
MASTER ...

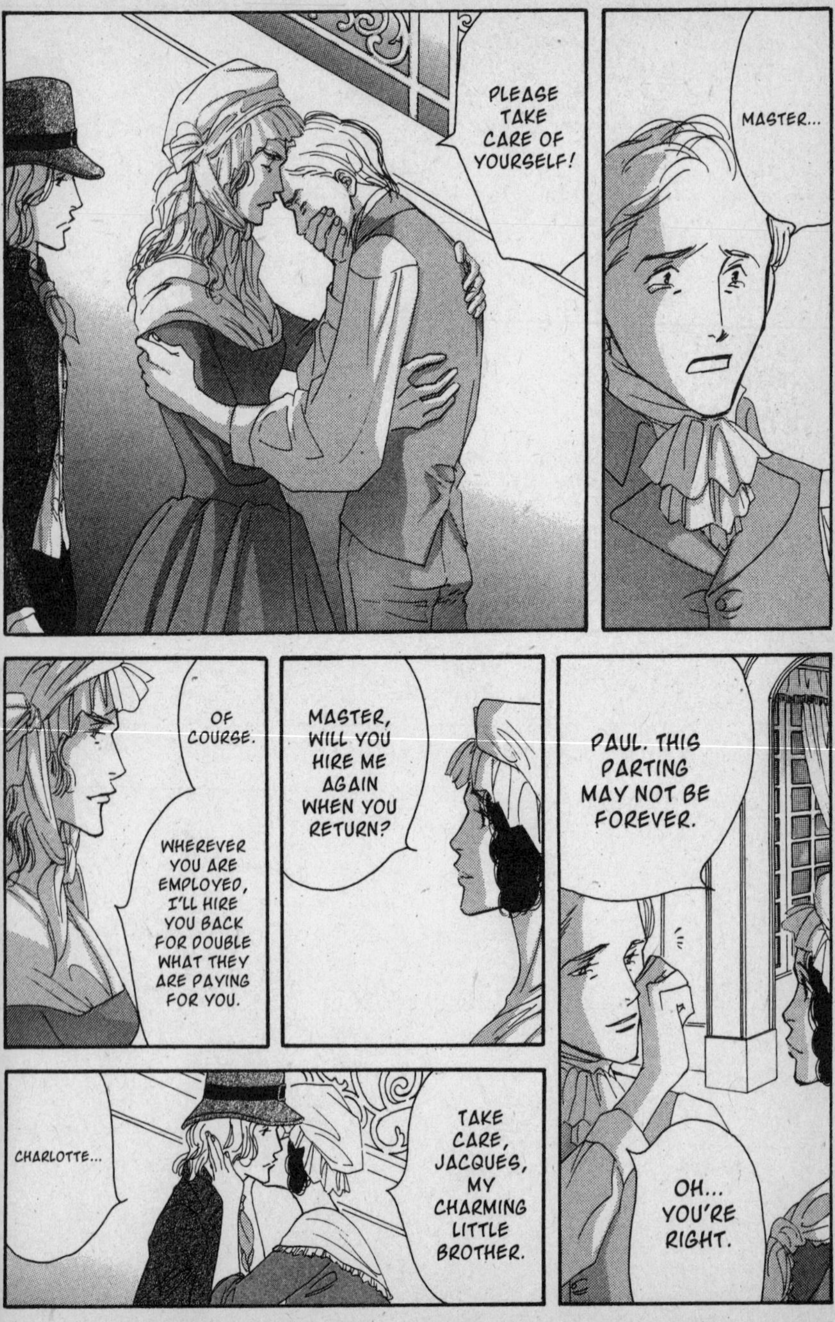
MASTER...
PLEASE TAKE CARE OF YOURSELF!
PAUL. THIS PARTING MAY NOT BE FOREVER.
OH... YOU'RE RIGHT.
MASTER, WILL YOU HIRE ME AGAIN WHEN YOU RETURN?
OF COURSE.
WHEREVER YOU ARE EMPLOYED, I'LL HIRE YOU BACK FOR DOUBLE WHAT THEY ARE PAYING FOR YOU.
TAKE CARE, JACQUES, MY CHARMING LITTLE BROTHER.
CHARLOTTE...

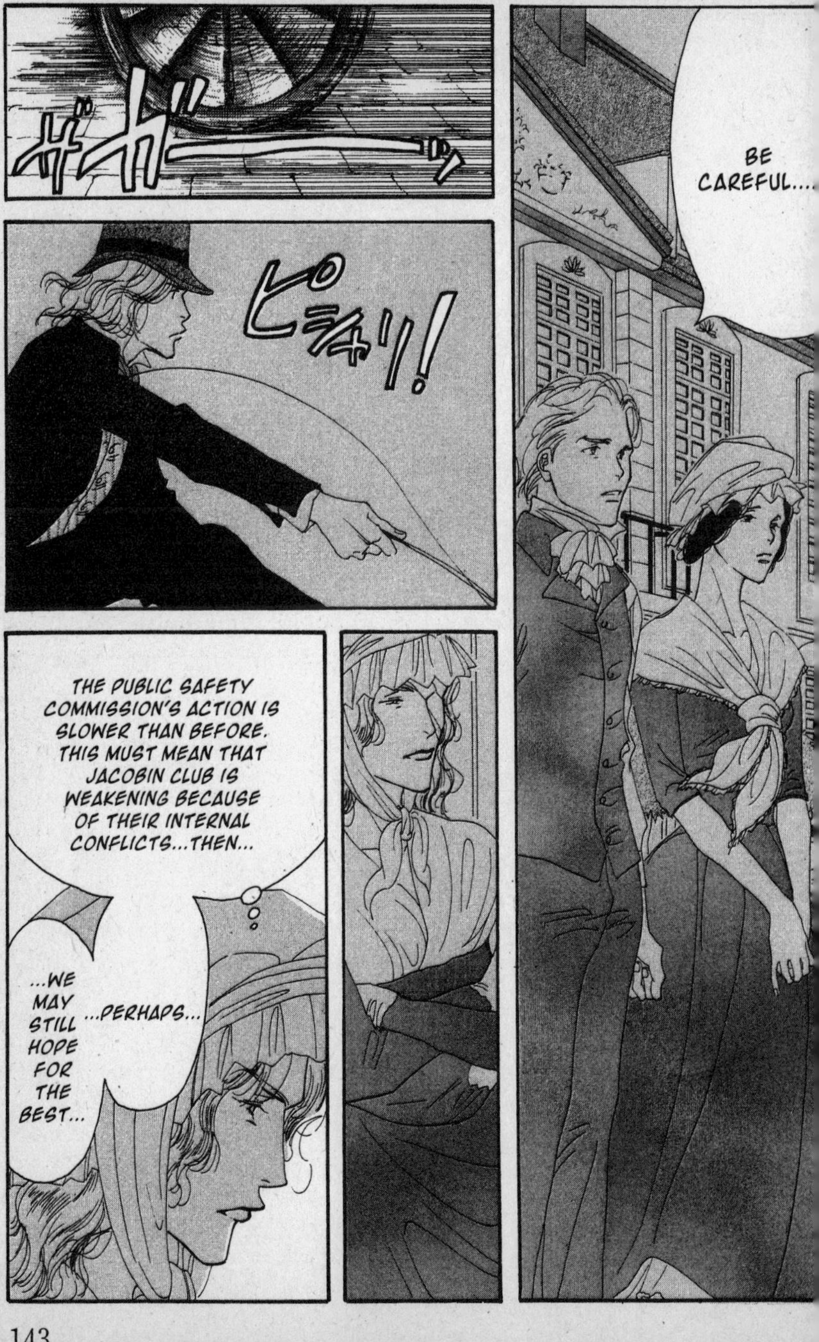
BE CAREFUL....
ザガーッ
ピシャリ!
THE PUBLIC SAFETY COMMISSION'S ACTION IS SLOWER THAN BEFORE. THIS MUST MEAN THAT JACOBIN CLUB IS WEAKENING BECAUSE OF THEIR INTERNAL CONFLICTS...THEN...
...PERHAPS...
...WE MAY STILL HOPE FOR THE BEST...

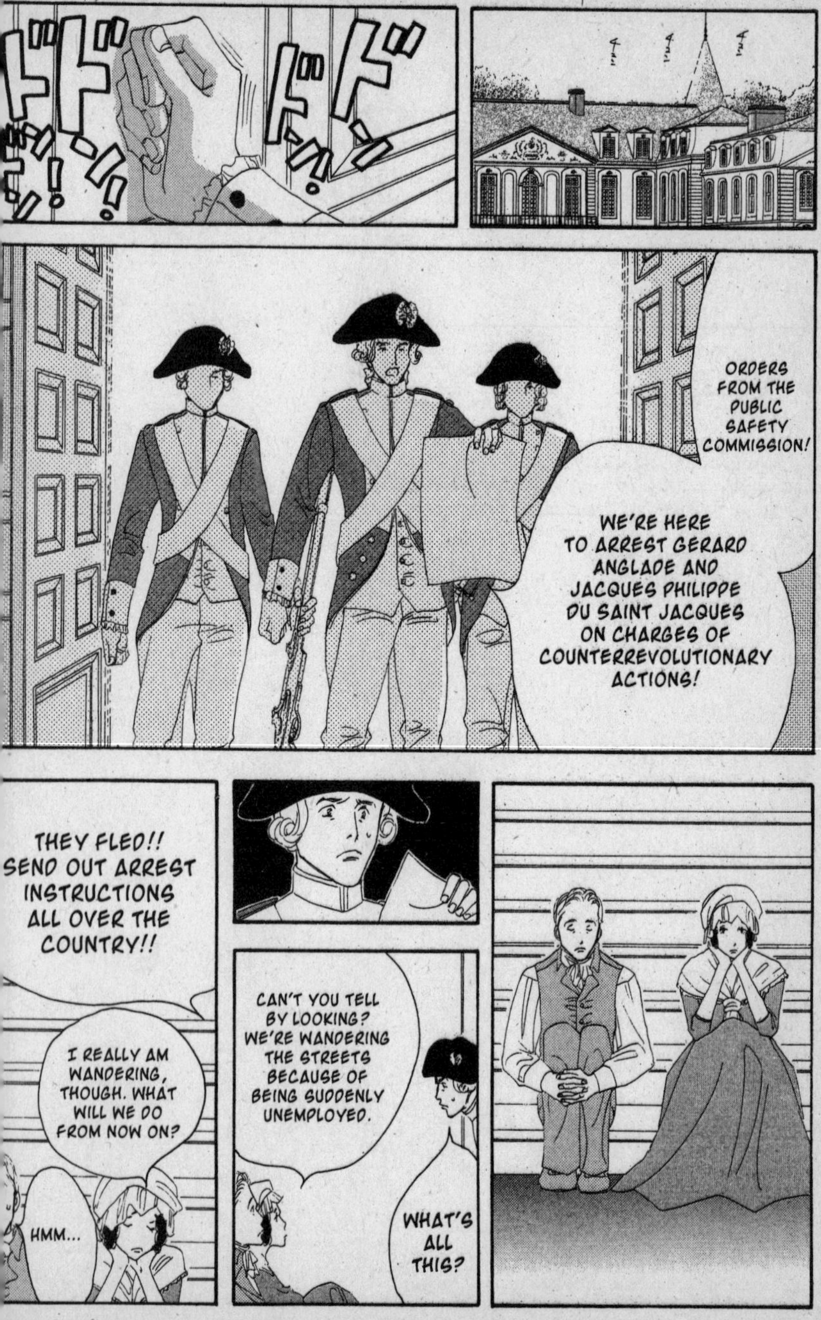
ORDERS FROM THE PUBLIC SAFETY COMMISSION!
WE'RE HERE TO ARREST GERARD ANGLADE AND JACQUES PHILIPPE DU SAINT JACQUES ON CHARGES OF COUNTERREVOLUTIONARY ACTIONS!
CAN'T YOU TELL BY LOOKING? WE'RE WANDERING THE STREETS BECAUSE OF BEING SUDDENLY UNEMPLOYED.
WHAT'S ALL THIS?
THEY FLED!! SEND OUT ARREST INSTRUCTIONS ALL OVER THE COUNTRY!!
I REALLY AM WANDERING, THOUGH. WHAT WILL WE DO FROM NOW ON?
HMM...

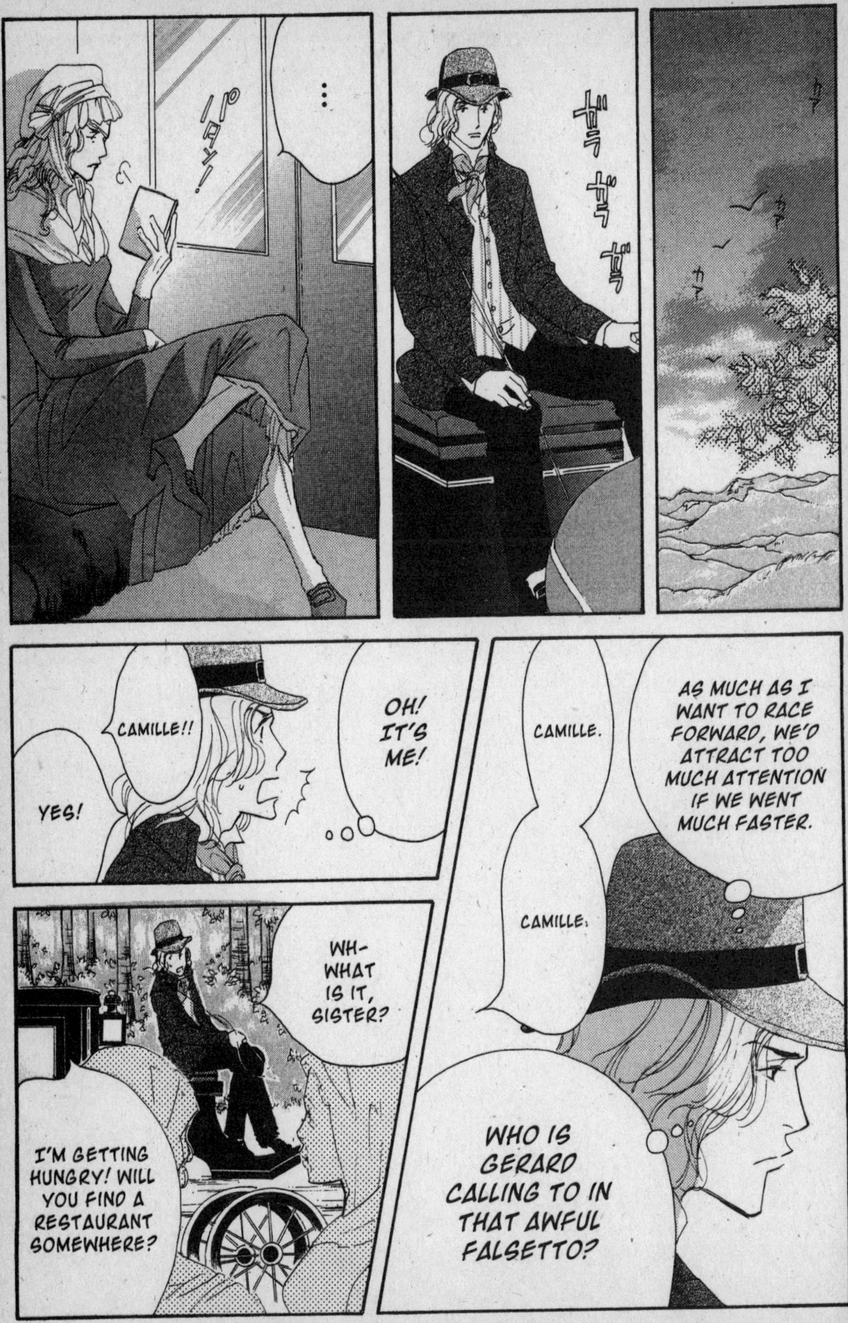
ガラ ガラ ガラ
…
パタン!
AS MUCH AS I WANT TO RACE FORWARD, WE'D ATTRACT TOO MUCH ATTENTION IF WE WENT MUCH FASTER.
CAMILLE.
CAMILLE.
WHO IS GERARD CALLING TO IN THAT AWFUL FALSETTO?
OH! IT'S ME!
CAMILLE!!
YES!
WH-WHAT IS IT, SISTER?
I'M GETTING HUNGRY! WILL YOU FIND A RESTAURANT SOMEWHERE?

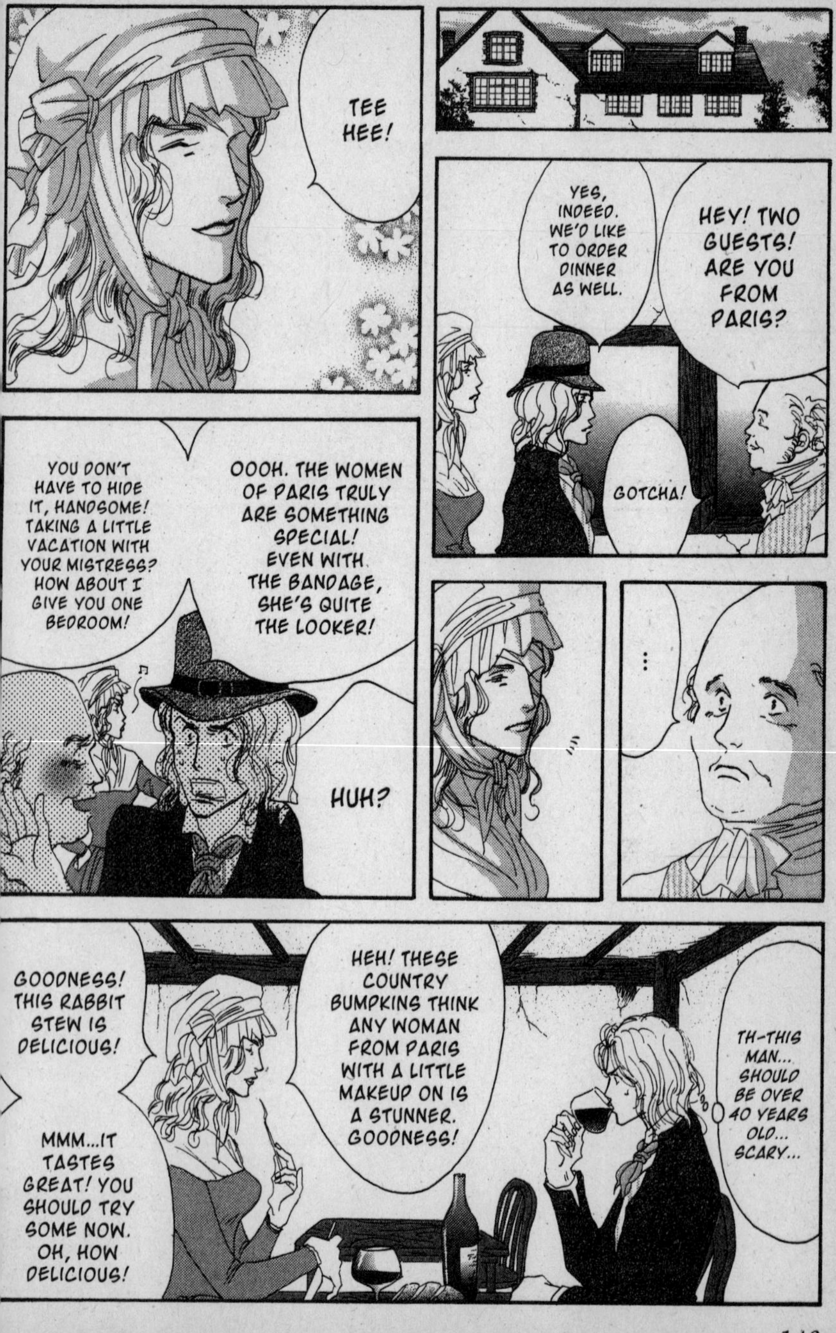
HEY! TWO GUESTS! ARE YOU FROM PARIS?
YES, INDEED. WE'D LIKE TO ORDER DINNER AS WELL.
GOTCHA!
TEE HEE!
OOOH. THE WOMEN OF PARIS TRULY ARE SOMETHING SPECIAL! EVEN WITH THE BANDAGE, SHE'S QUITE THE LOOKER!
YOU DON'T HAVE TO HIDE IT, HANDSOME! TAKING A LITTLE VACATION WITH YOUR MISTRESS? HOW ABOUT I GIVE YOU ONE BEDROOM!
HUH?
...
TH-THIS MAN... SHOULD BE OVER 40 YEARS OLD... SCARY...
HEH! THESE COUNTRY BUMPKINS THINK ANY WOMAN FROM PARIS WITH A LITTLE MAKEUP ON IS A STUNNER. GOODNESS!
GOODNESS! THIS RABBIT STEW IS DELICIOUS!
MMM...IT TASTES GREAT! YOU SHOULD TRY SOME NOW. OH, HOW DELICIOUS!

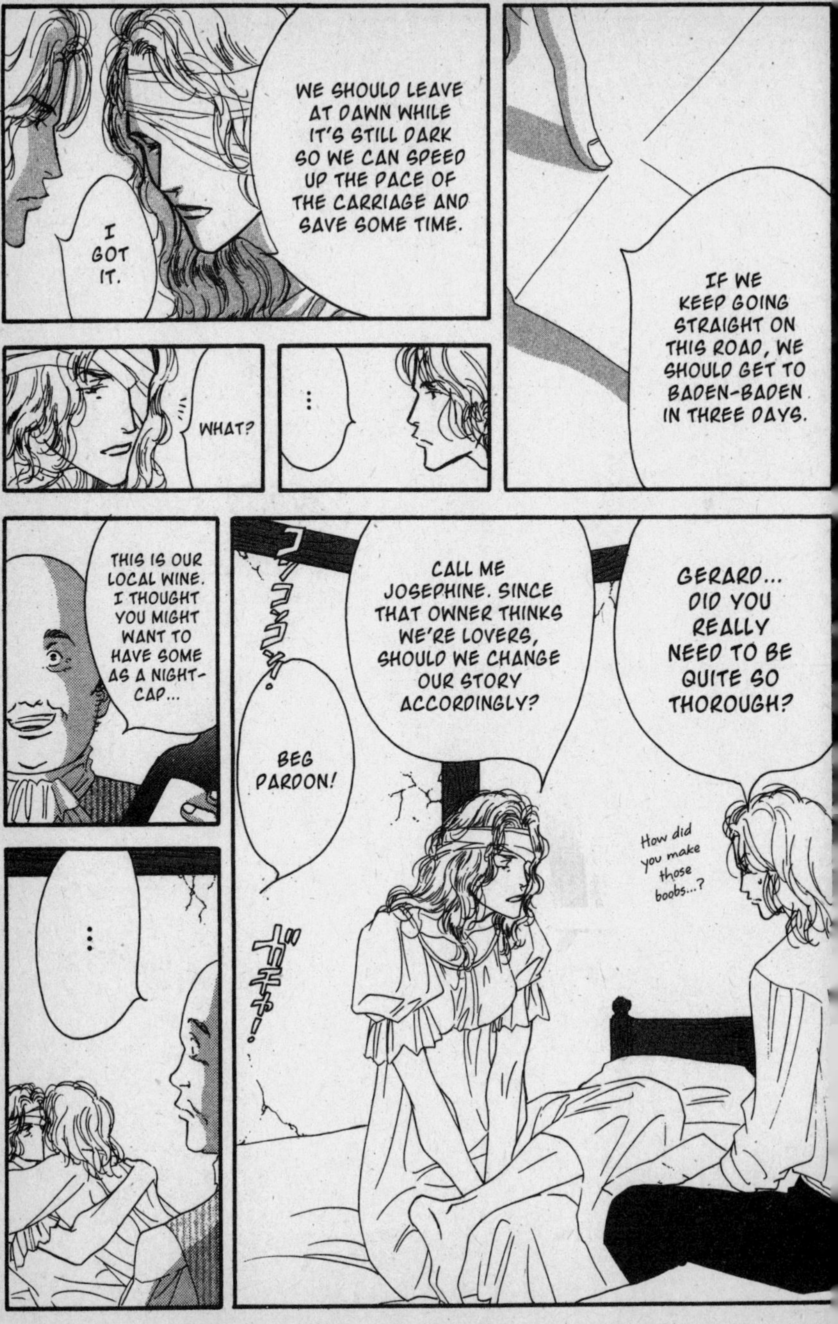
IF WE KEEP GOING STRAIGHT ON THIS ROAD, WE SHOULD GET TO BADEN-BADEN IN THREE DAYS.
WE SHOULD LEAVE AT DAWN WHILE IT'S STILL DARK SO WE CAN SPEED UP THE PACE OF THE CARRIAGE AND SAVE SOME TIME.
I GOT IT.
...
WHAT?
GERARD... DID YOU REALLY NEED TO BE QUITE SO THOROUGH?
How did you make those boobs...?
CALL ME JOSEPHINE. SINCE THAT OWNER THINKS WE'RE LOVERS, SHOULD WE CHANGE OUR STORY ACCORDINGLY?
BEG PARDON!
THIS IS OUR LOCAL WINE. I THOUGHT YOU MIGHT WANT TO HAVE SOME AS A NIGHT-CAP...
...

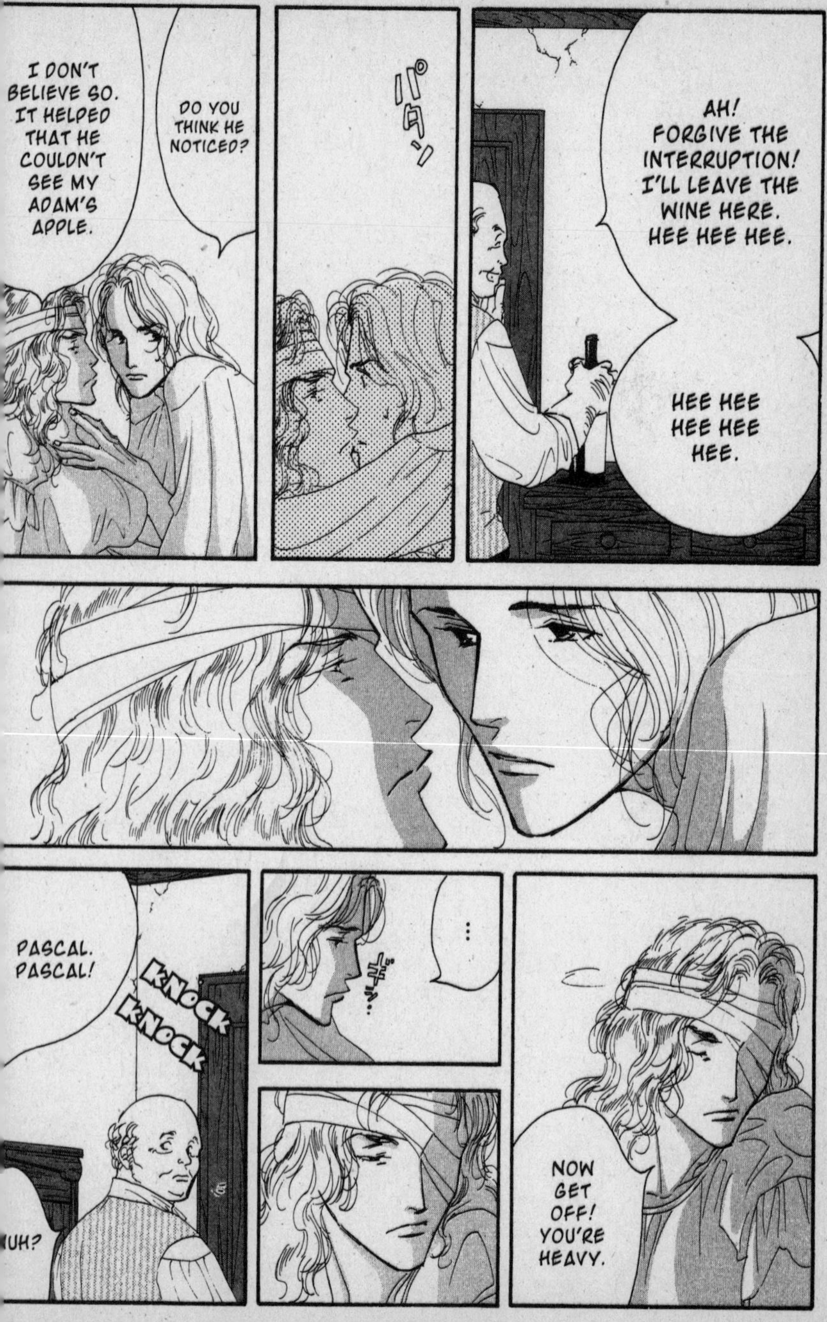
AH! FORGIVE THE INTERRUPTION! I'LL LEAVE THE WINE HERE. HEE HEE HEE.
HEE HEE HEE HEE HEE.
パタン
DO YOU THINK HE NOTICED?
I DON'T BELIEVE SO. IT HELPED THAT HE COULDN'T SEE MY ADAM'S APPLE.
NOW GET OFF! YOU'RE HEAVY.
...
PASCAL. PASCAL!
KNOCK
KNOCK
UH?

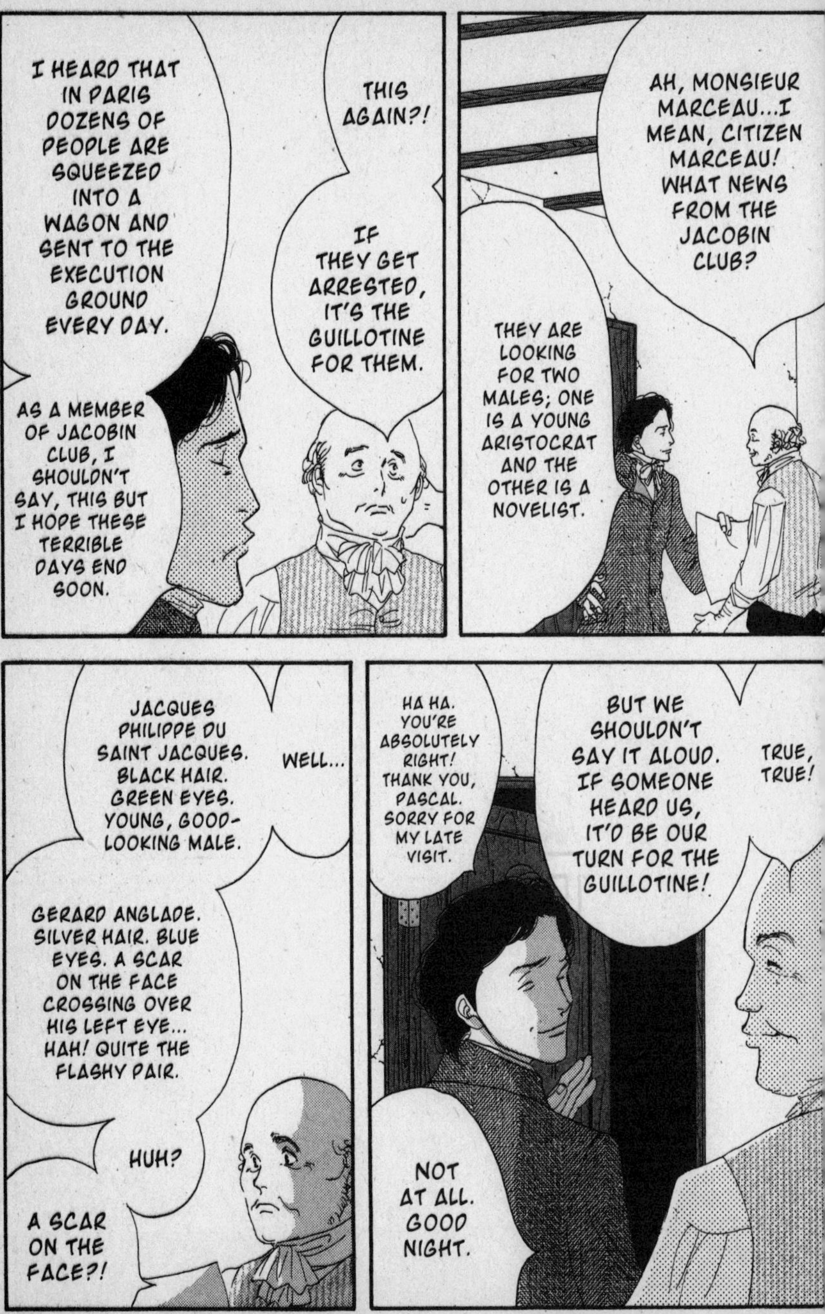
AH, MONSIEUR MARCEAU...I MEAN, CITIZEN MARCEAU! WHAT NEWS FROM THE JACOBIN CLUB?
THEY ARE LOOKING FOR TWO MALES; ONE IS A YOUNG ARISTOCRAT AND THE OTHER IS A NOVELIST.
THIS AGAIN?!
IF THEY GET ARRESTED, IT'S THE GUILLOTINE FOR THEM.
I HEARD THAT IN PARIS DOZENS OF PEOPLE ARE SQUEEZED INTO A WAGON AND SENT TO THE EXECUTION GROUND EVERY DAY.
AS A MEMBER OF JACOBIN CLUB, I SHOULDN'T SAY, THIS BUT I HOPE THESE TERRIBLE DAYS END SOON.
TRUE, TRUE!
BUT WE SHOULDN'T SAY IT ALOUD. IF SOMEONE HEARD US, IT'D BE OUR TURN FOR THE GUILLOTINE!
HA HA. YOU'RE ABSOLUTELY RIGHT! THANK YOU, PASCAL. SORRY FOR MY LATE VISIT.
NOT AT ALL. GOOD NIGHT.
WELL...
JACQUES PHILIPPE DU SAINT JACQUES. BLACK HAIR. GREEN EYES. YOUNG, GOOD-LOOKING MALE.
GERARD ANGLADE. SILVER HAIR. BLUE EYES. A SCAR ON THE FACE CROSSING OVER HIS LEFT EYE... HAH! QUITE THE FLASHY PAIR.
HUH?
A SCAR ON THE FACE?!

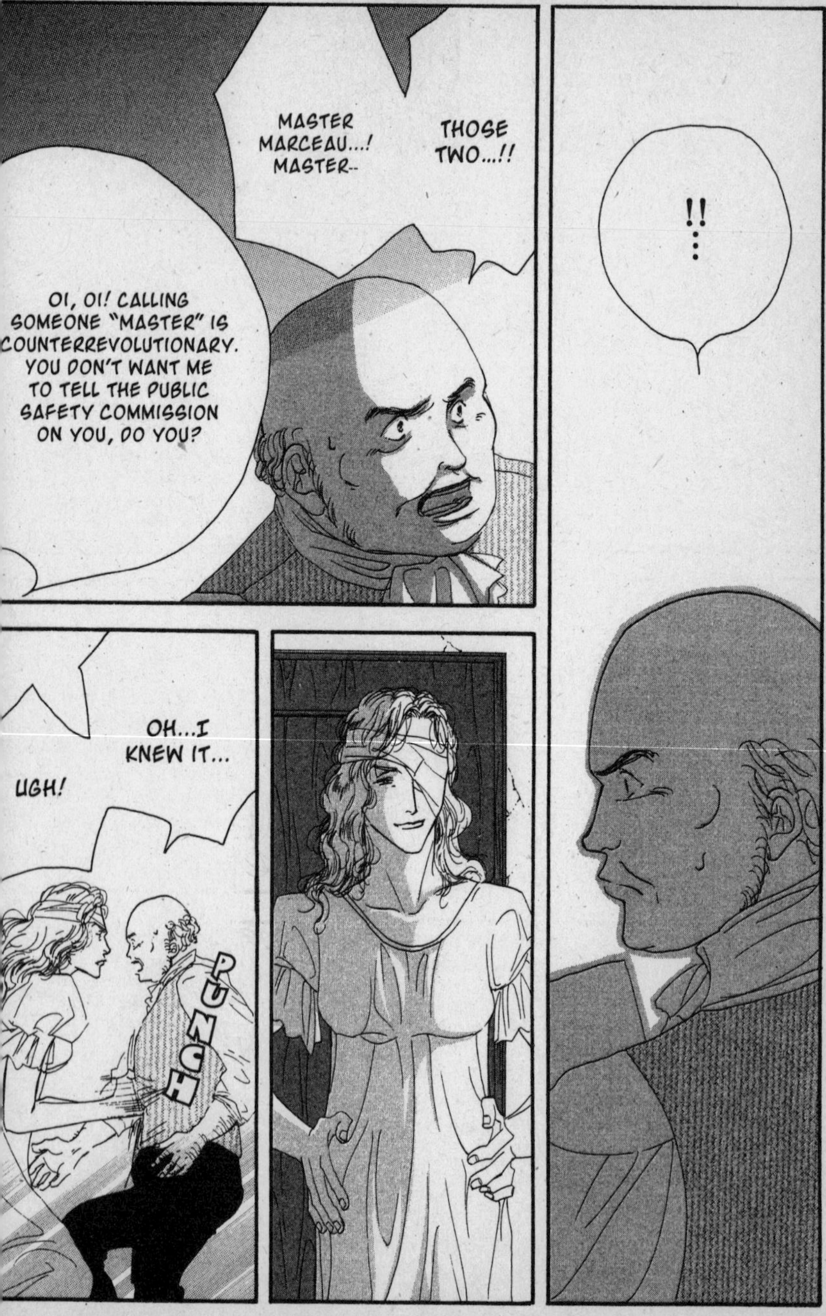
!!...
THOSE TWO...!!
MASTER MARCEAU...! MASTER--
OI, OI! CALLING SOMEONE "MASTER" IS COUNTERREVOLUTIONARY. YOU DON'T WANT ME TO TELL THE PUBLIC SAFETY COMMISSION ON YOU, DO YOU?
OH...I KNEW IT...
UGH!
PUNCH

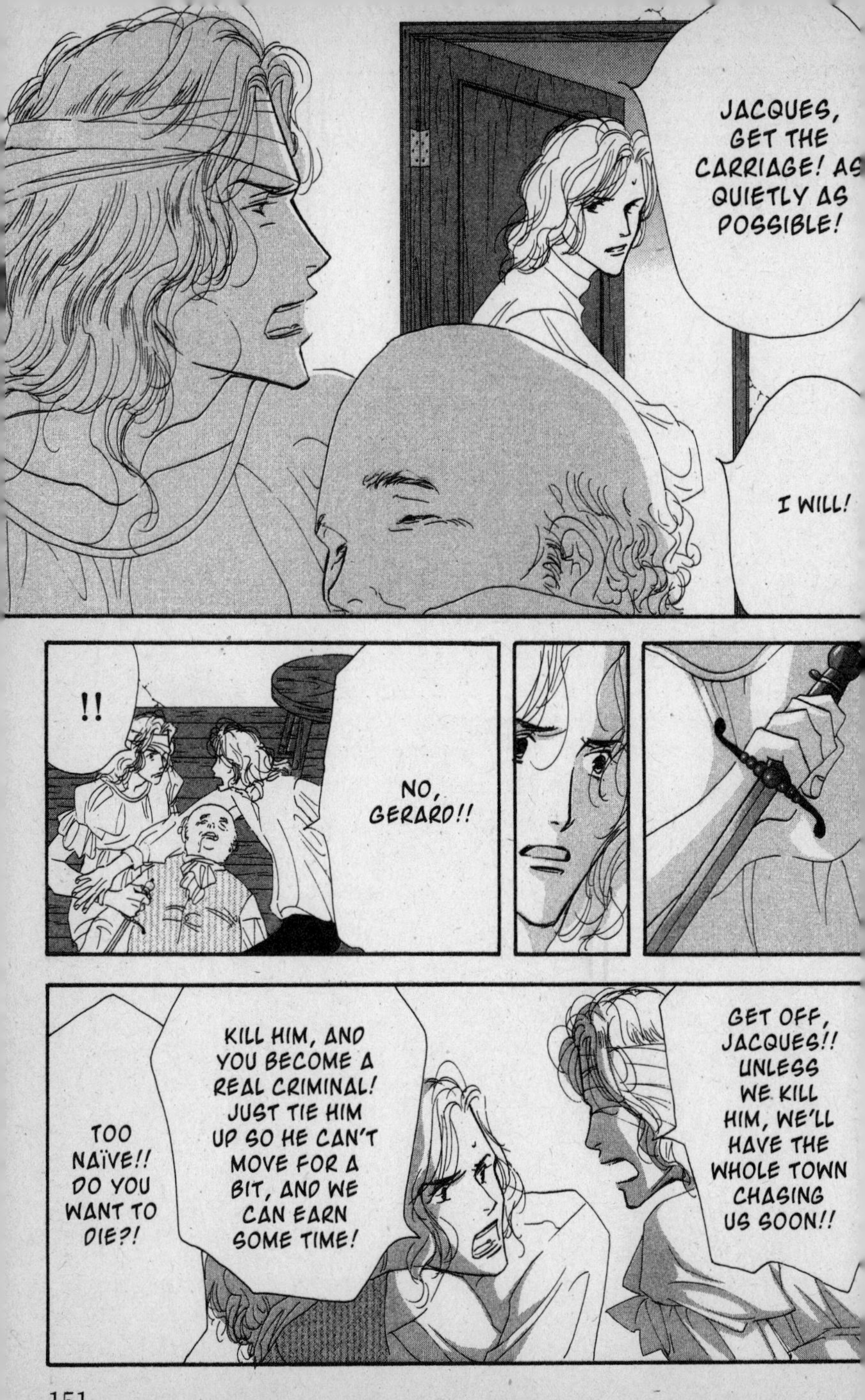
JACQUES, GET THE CARRIAGE! AS QUIETLY AS POSSIBLE!
I WILL!
NO, GERARD!!
!!
GET OFF, JACQUES!! UNLESS WE KILL HIM, WE'LL HAVE THE WHOLE TOWN CHASING US SOON!!
KILL HIM, AND YOU BECOME A REAL CRIMINAL! JUST TIE HIM UP SO HE CAN'T MOVE FOR A BIT, AND WE CAN EARN SOME TIME!
TOO NAÏVE!! DO YOU WANT TO DIE?!

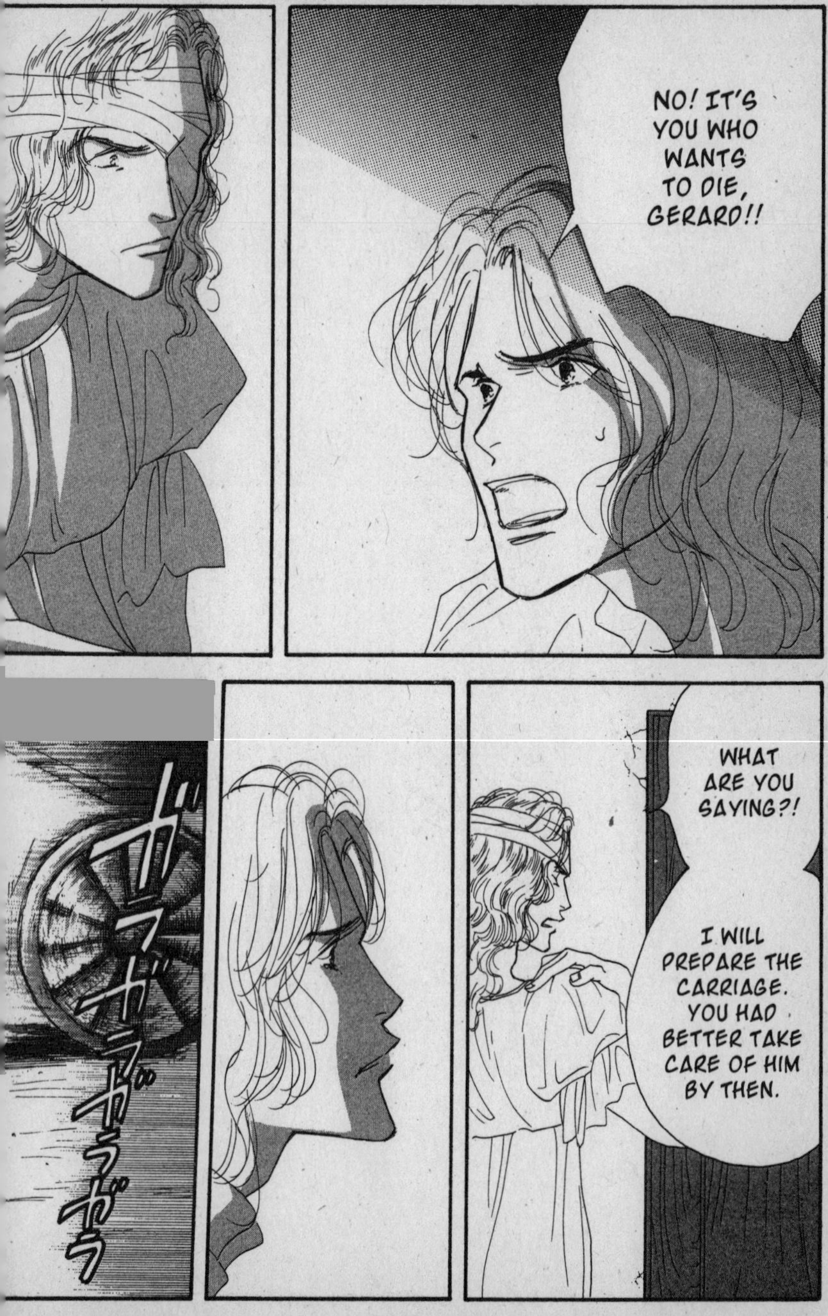
NO! IT'S YOU WHO WANTS TO DIE, GERARD!!
WHAT ARE YOU SAYING?!
I WILL PREPARE THE CARRIAGE. YOU HAD BETTER TAKE CARE OF HIM BY THEN.

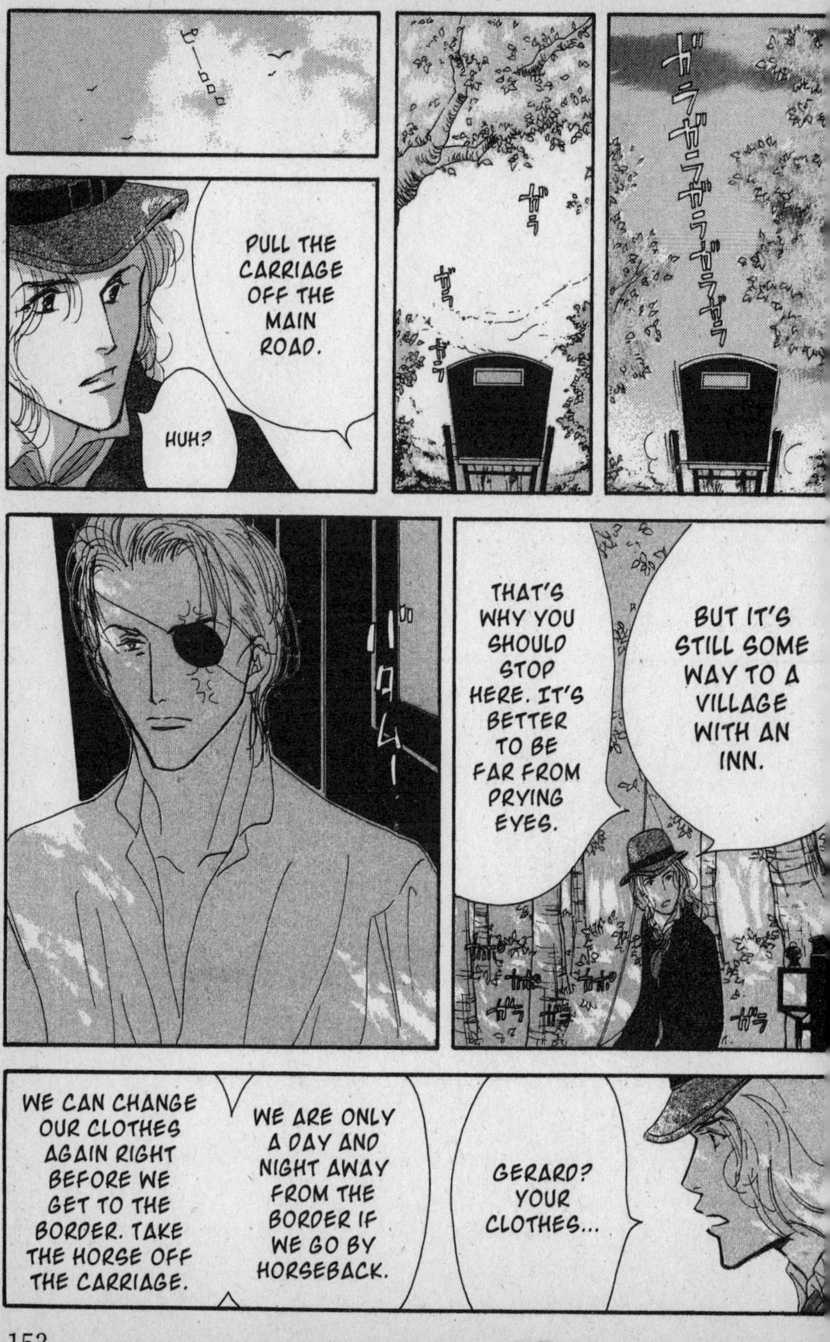
PULL THE CARRIAGE OFF THE MAIN ROAD.
HUH?
BUT IT'S STILL SOME WAY TO A VILLAGE WITH AN INN.
THAT'S WHY YOU SHOULD STOP HERE. IT'S BETTER TO BE FAR FROM PRYING EYES.
GERARD? YOUR CLOTHES...
WE ARE ONLY A DAY AND NIGHT AWAY FROM THE BORDER IF WE GO BY HORSEBACK.
WE CAN CHANGE OUR CLOTHES AGAIN RIGHT BEFORE WE GET TO THE BORDER. TAKE THE HORSE OFF THE CARRIAGE.

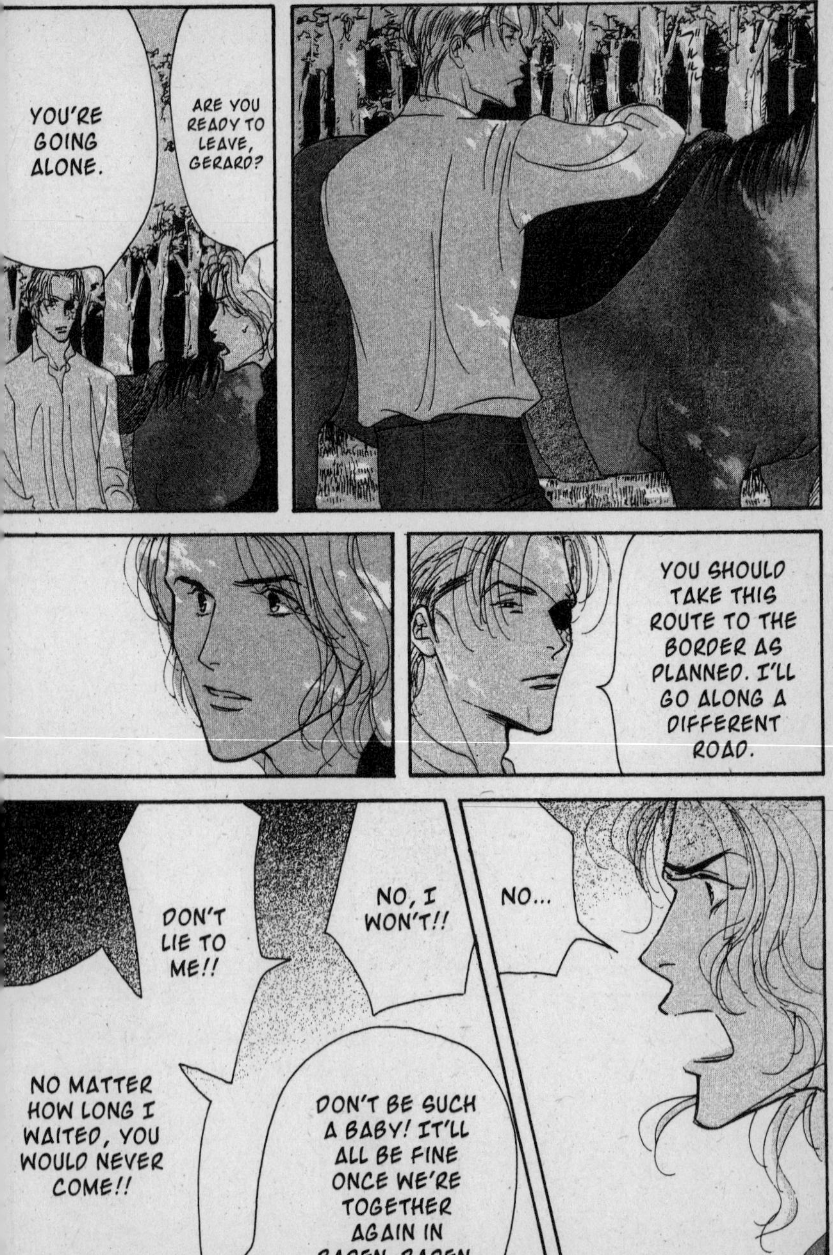
ARE YOU READY TO LEAVE, GERARD?
YOU'RE GOING ALONE.
YOU SHOULD TAKE THIS ROUTE TO THE BORDER AS PLANNED. I'LL GO ALONG A DIFFERENT ROAD.
NO...
NO, I WON'T!!
DON'T LIE TO ME!!
DON'T BE SUCH A BABY! IT'LL ALL BE FINE ONCE WE'RE TOGETHER AGAIN IN BADEN-BADEN.
NO MATTER HOW LONG I WAITED, YOU WOULD NEVER COME!!

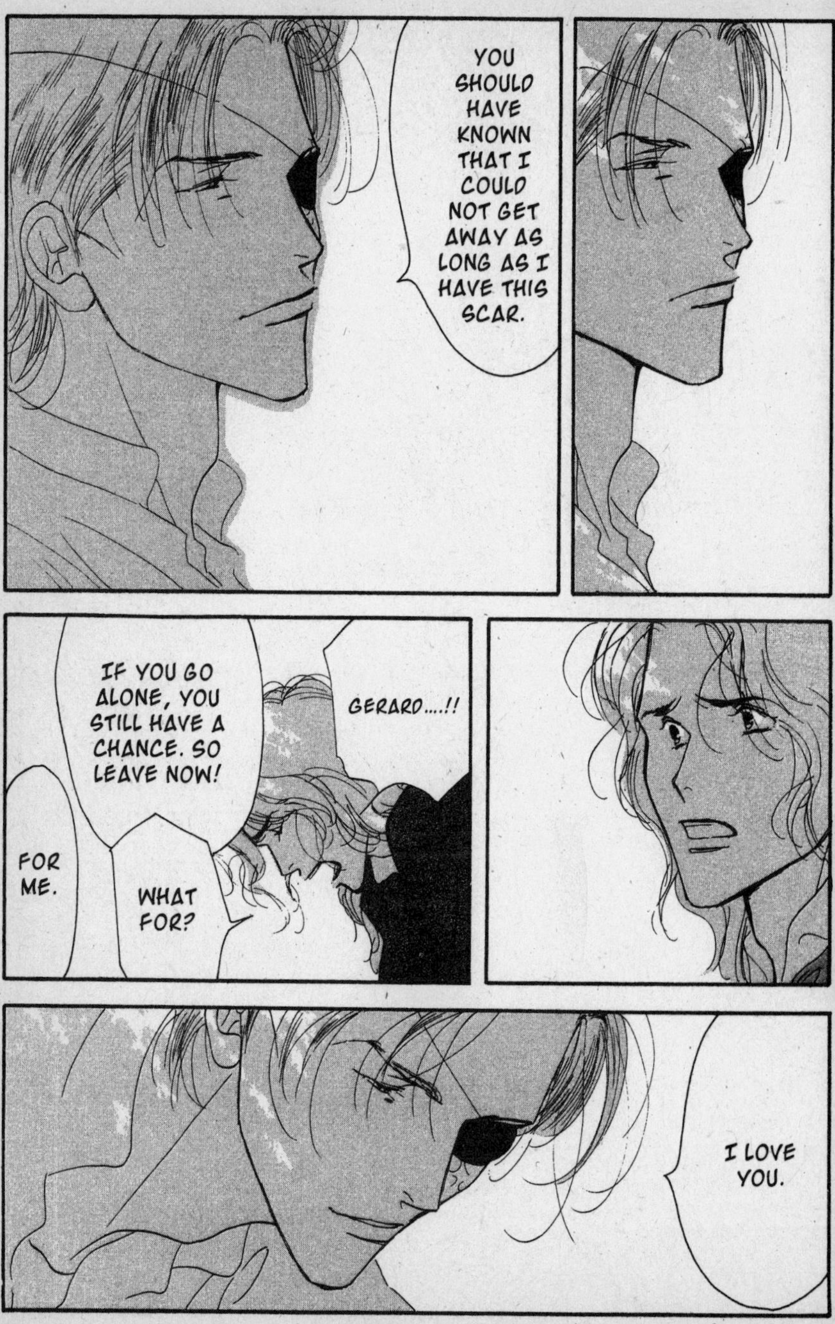
YOU SHOULD HAVE KNOWN THAT I COULD NOT GET AWAY AS LONG AS I HAVE THIS SCAR.
GERARD....!!
IF YOU GO ALONE, YOU STILL HAVE A CHANCE. SO LEAVE NOW!
WHAT FOR?
FOR ME.
I LOVE YOU.

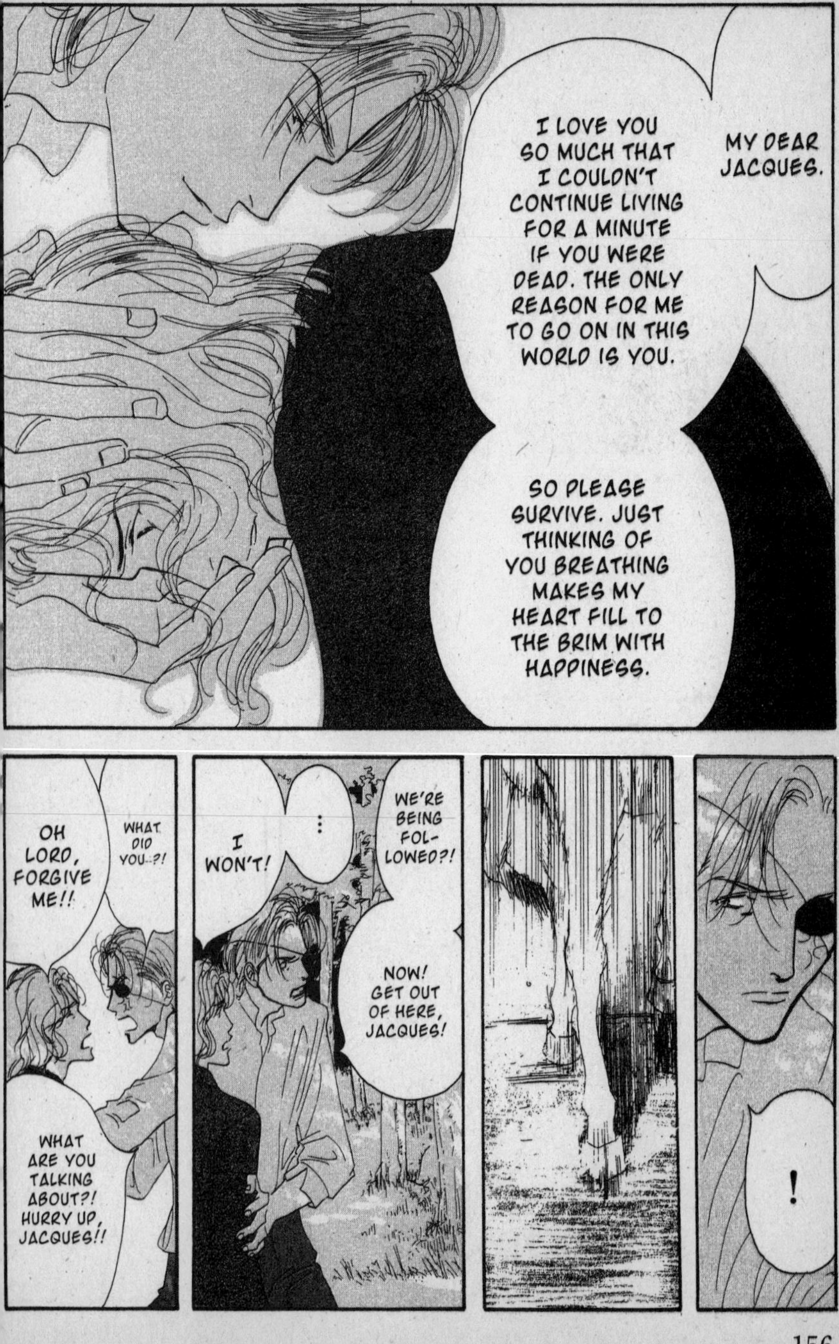
MY DEAR JACQUES.
I LOVE YOU SO MUCH THAT I COULDN'T CONTINUE LIVING FOR A MINUTE IF YOU WERE DEAD. THE ONLY REASON FOR ME TO GO ON IN THIS WORLD IS YOU.
SO PLEASE SURVIVE. JUST THINKING OF YOU BREATHING MAKES MY HEART FILL TO THE BRIM WITH HAPPINESS.
!
WE'RE BEING FOL-LOWED?!
...
I WON'T!
NOW! GET OUT OF HERE, JACQUES!
WHAT DID YOU...?!
OH LORD, FORGIVE ME!!
WHAT ARE YOU TALKING ABOUT?! HURRY UP, JACQUES!!

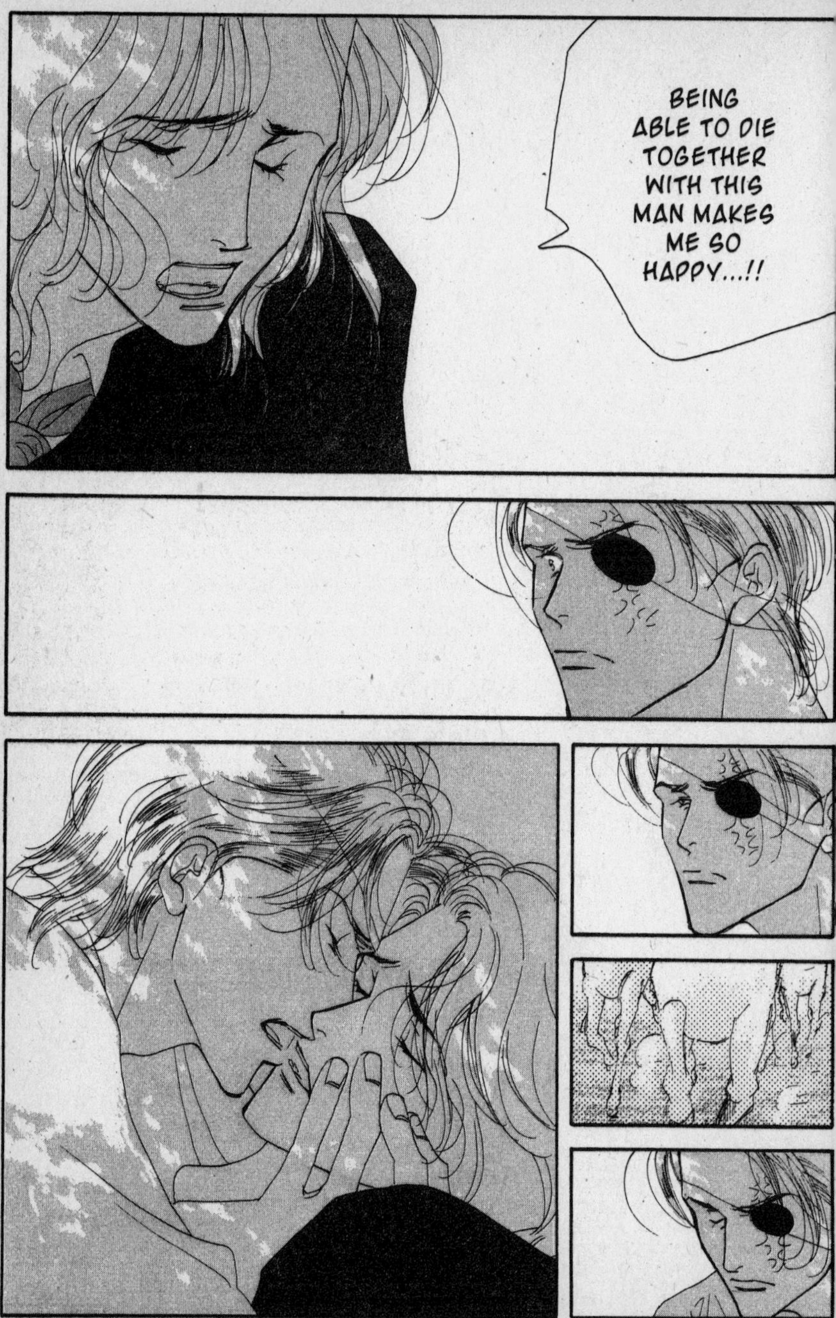
BEING ABLE TO DIE TOGETHER WITH THIS MAN MAKES ME SO HAPPY...!!

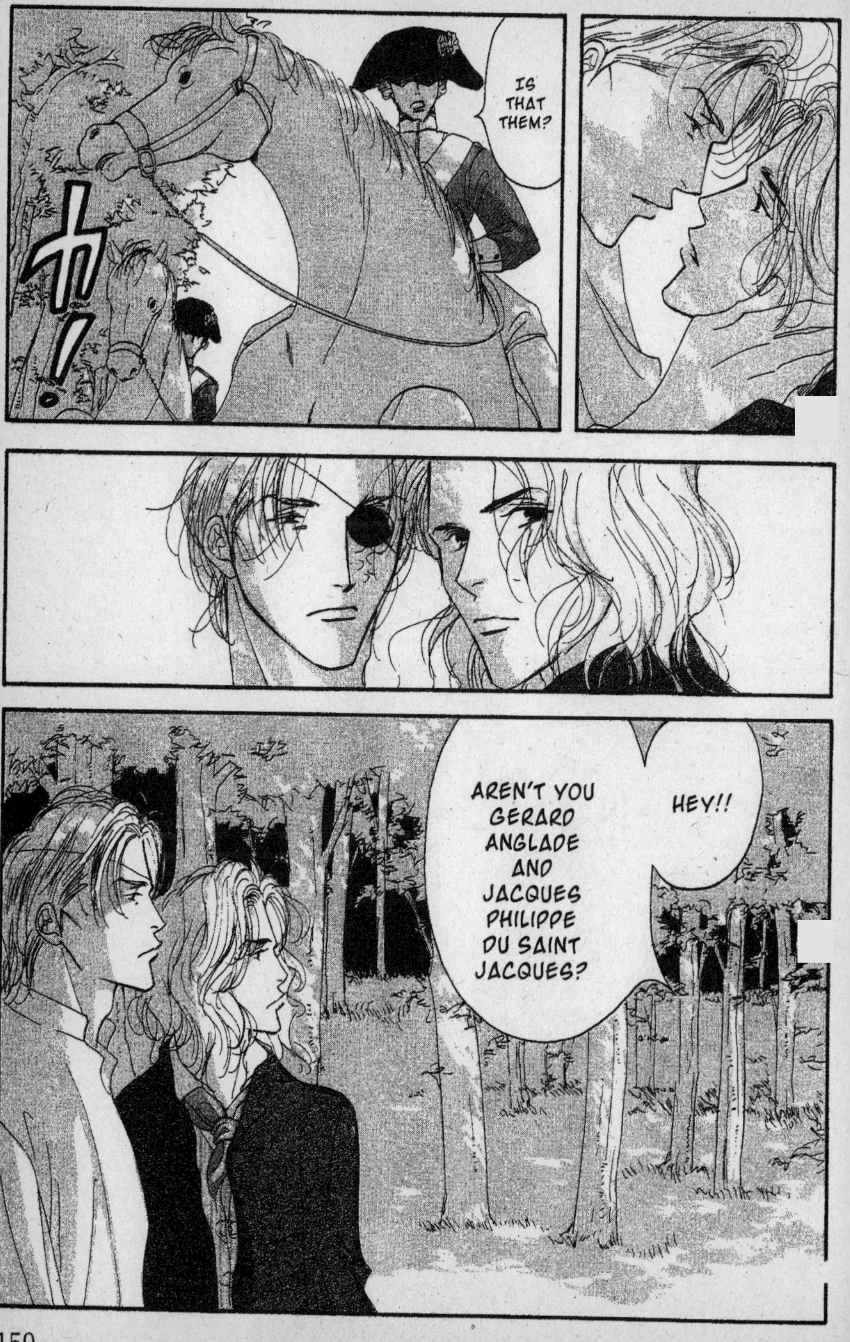
IS THAT THEM?
HEY!!
AREN'T YOU GERARD ANGLADE AND JACQUES PHILIPPE DU SAINT JACQUES?

GÉRARD ET JACQUES

GERARD ET JACQUES

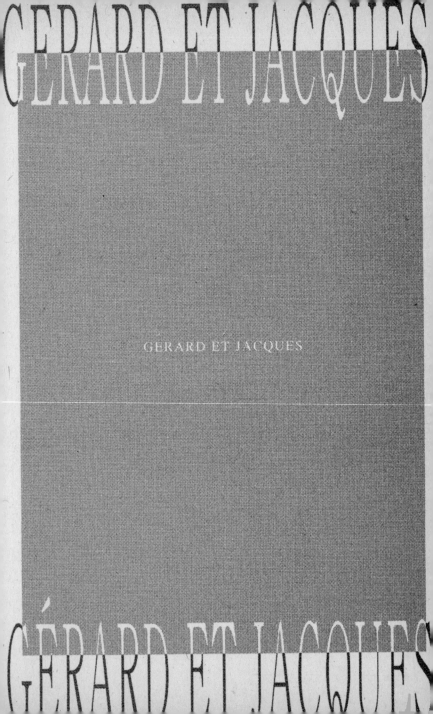

GÉRARD ET JACQUES

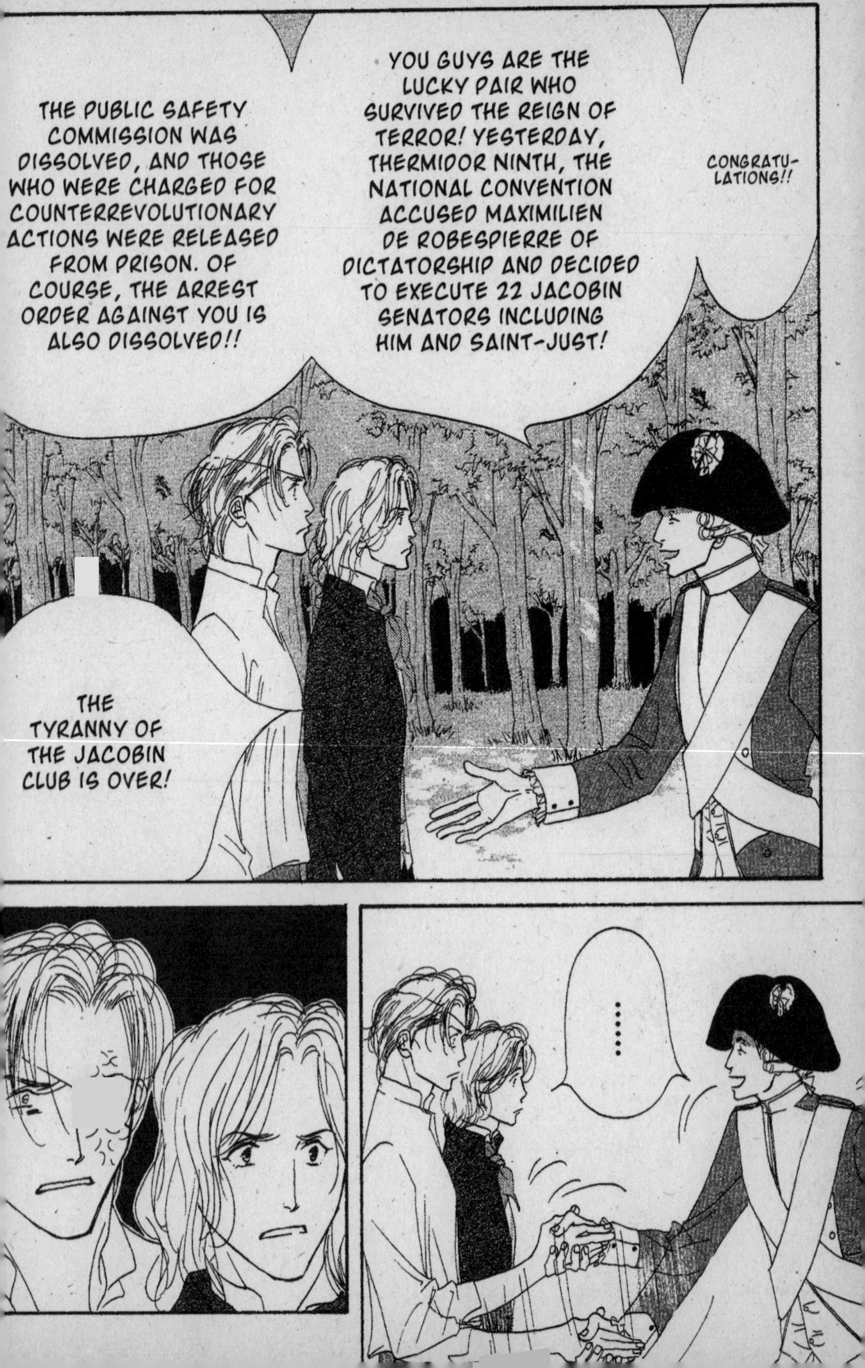
CONGRATU-LATIONS!!
YOU GUYS ARE THE LUCKY PAIR WHO SURVIVED THE REIGN OF TERROR! YESTERDAY, THERMIDOR NINTH, THE NATIONAL CONVENTION ACCUSED MAXIMILIEN DE ROBESPIERRE OF DICTATORSHIP AND DECIDED TO EXECUTE 22 JACOBIN SENATORS INCLUDING HIM AND SAINT-JUST!
THE PUBLIC SAFETY COMMISSION WAS DISSOLVED, AND THOSE WHO WERE CHARGED FOR COUNTERREVOLUTIONARY ACTIONS WERE RELEASED FROM PRISON. OF COURSE, THE ARREST ORDER AGAINST YOU IS ALSO DISSOLVED!!
THE TYRANNY OF THE JACOBIN CLUB IS OVER!
......

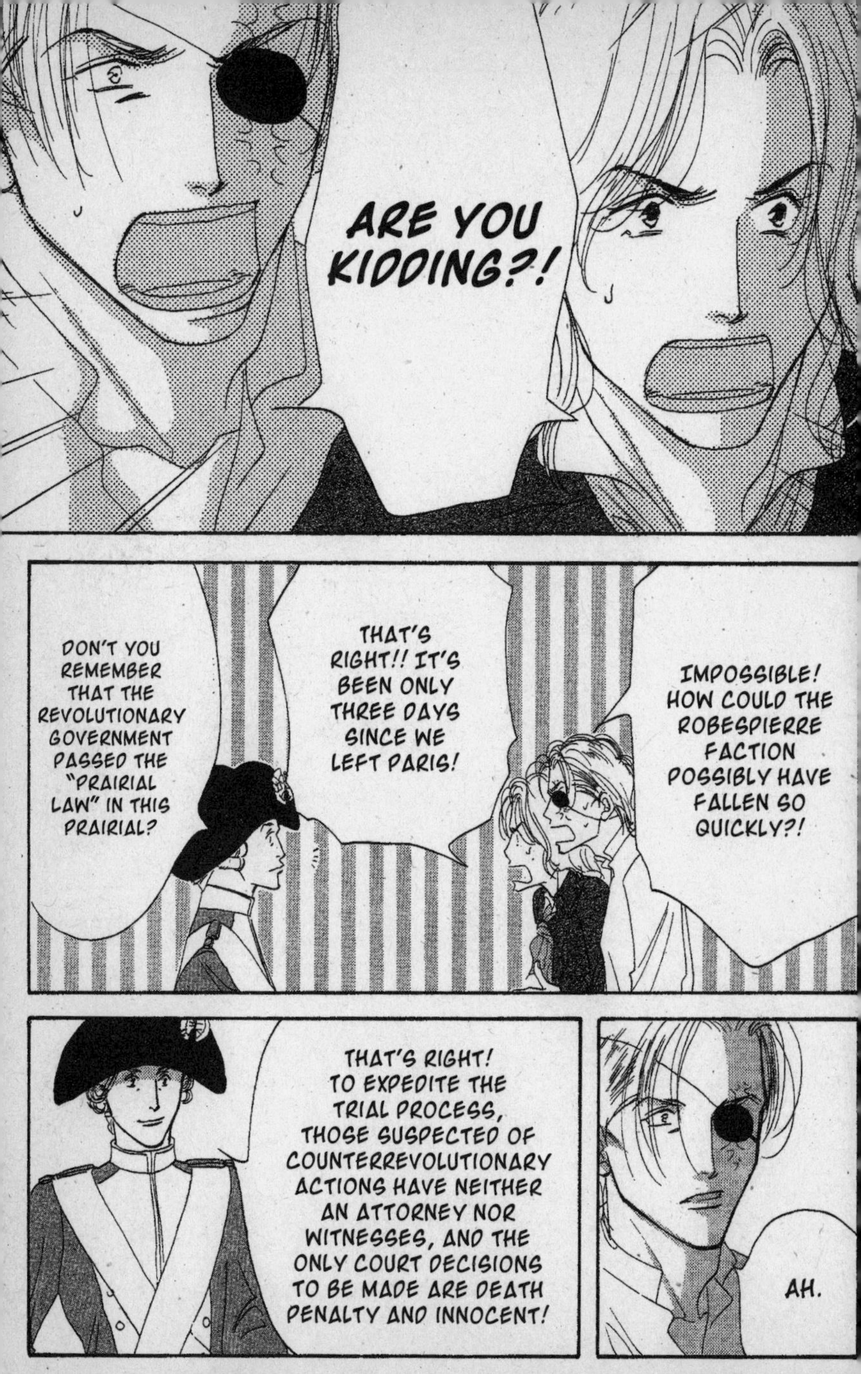
ARE YOU KIDDING?!
IMPOSSIBLE! HOW COULD THE ROBESPIERRE FACTION POSSIBLY HAVE FALLEN SO QUICKLY?!
THAT'S RIGHT!! IT'S BEEN ONLY THREE DAYS SINCE WE LEFT PARIS!
DON'T YOU REMEMBER THAT THE REVOLUTIONARY GOVERNMENT PASSED THE "PRAIRIAL LAW" IN THIS PRAIRIAL?
AH.
THAT'S RIGHT! TO EXPEDITE THE TRIAL PROCESS, THOSE SUSPECTED OF COUNTERREVOLUTIONARY ACTIONS HAVE NEITHER AN ATTORNEY NOR WITNESSES, AND THE ONLY COURT DECISIONS TO BE MADE ARE DEATH PENALTY AND INNOCENT!

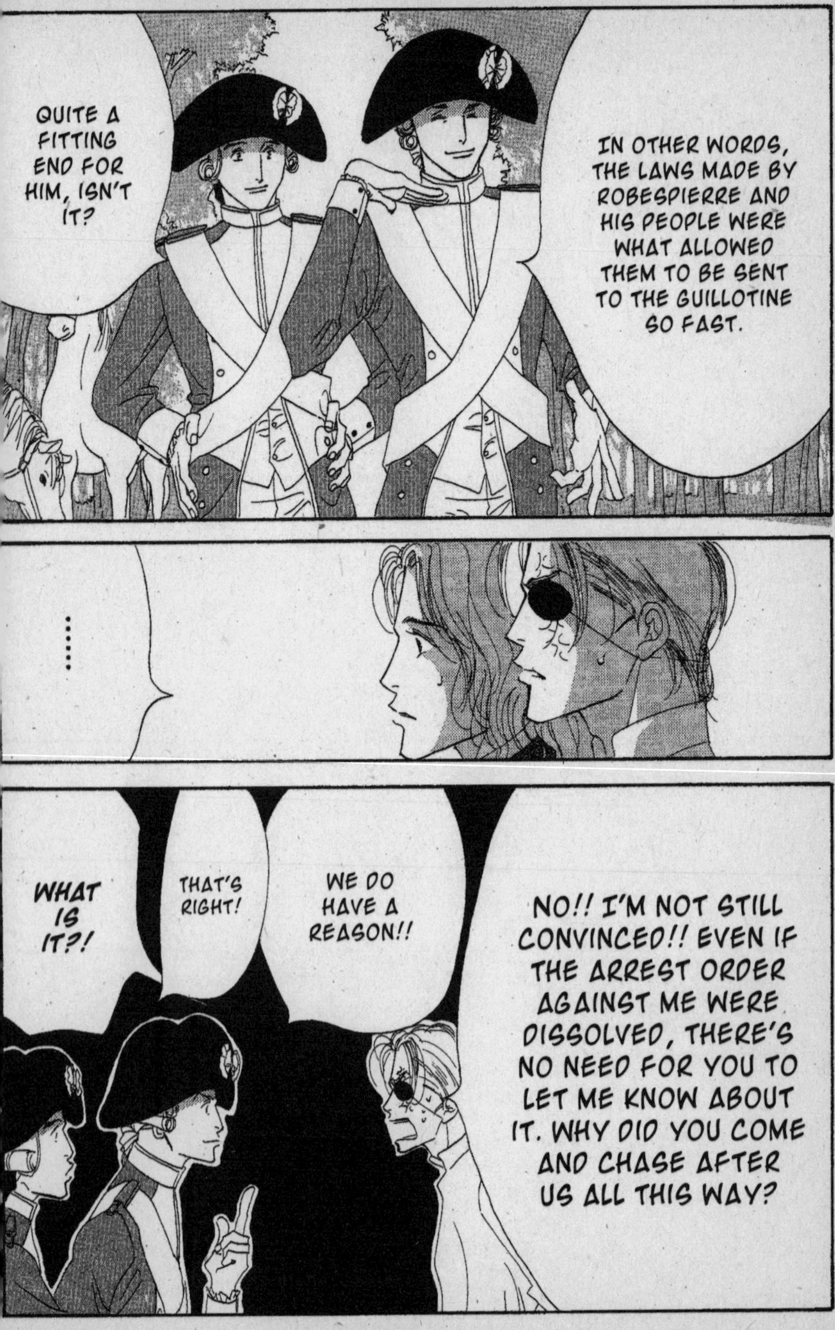
IN OTHER WORDS, THE LAWS MADE BY ROBESPIERRE AND HIS PEOPLE WERE WHAT ALLOWED THEM TO BE SENT TO THE GUILLOTINE SO FAST.
QUITE A FITTING END FOR HIM, ISN'T IT?
......
NO!! I'M NOT STILL CONVINCED!! EVEN IF THE ARREST ORDER AGAINST ME WERE DISSOLVED, THERE'S NO NEED FOR YOU TO LET ME KNOW ABOUT IT. WHY DID YOU COME AND CHASE AFTER US ALL THIS WAY?
WE DO HAVE A REASON!!
THAT'S RIGHT!
WHAT IS IT?!

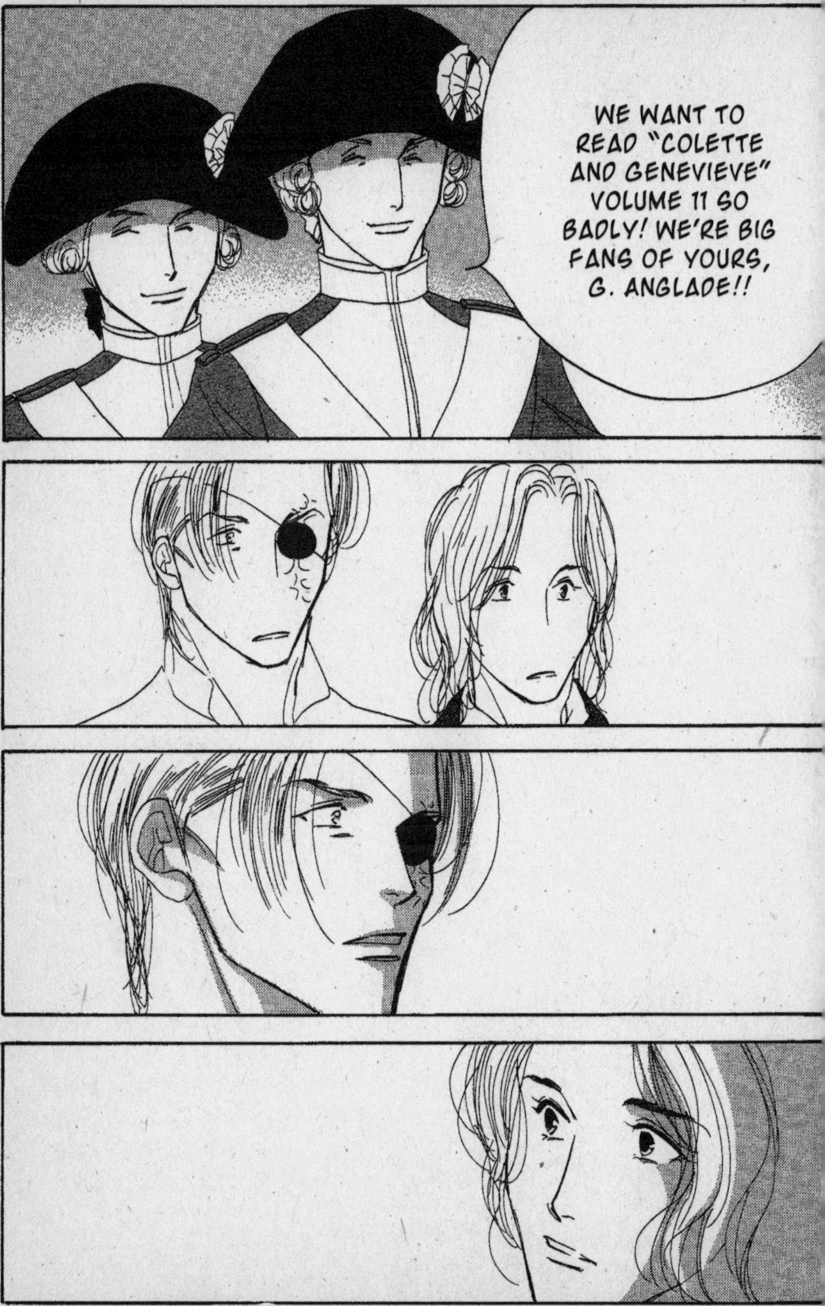
WE WANT TO READ "COLETTE AND GENEVIEVE" VOLUME 11 SO BADLY! WE'RE BIG FANS OF YOURS, G. ANGLADE!!

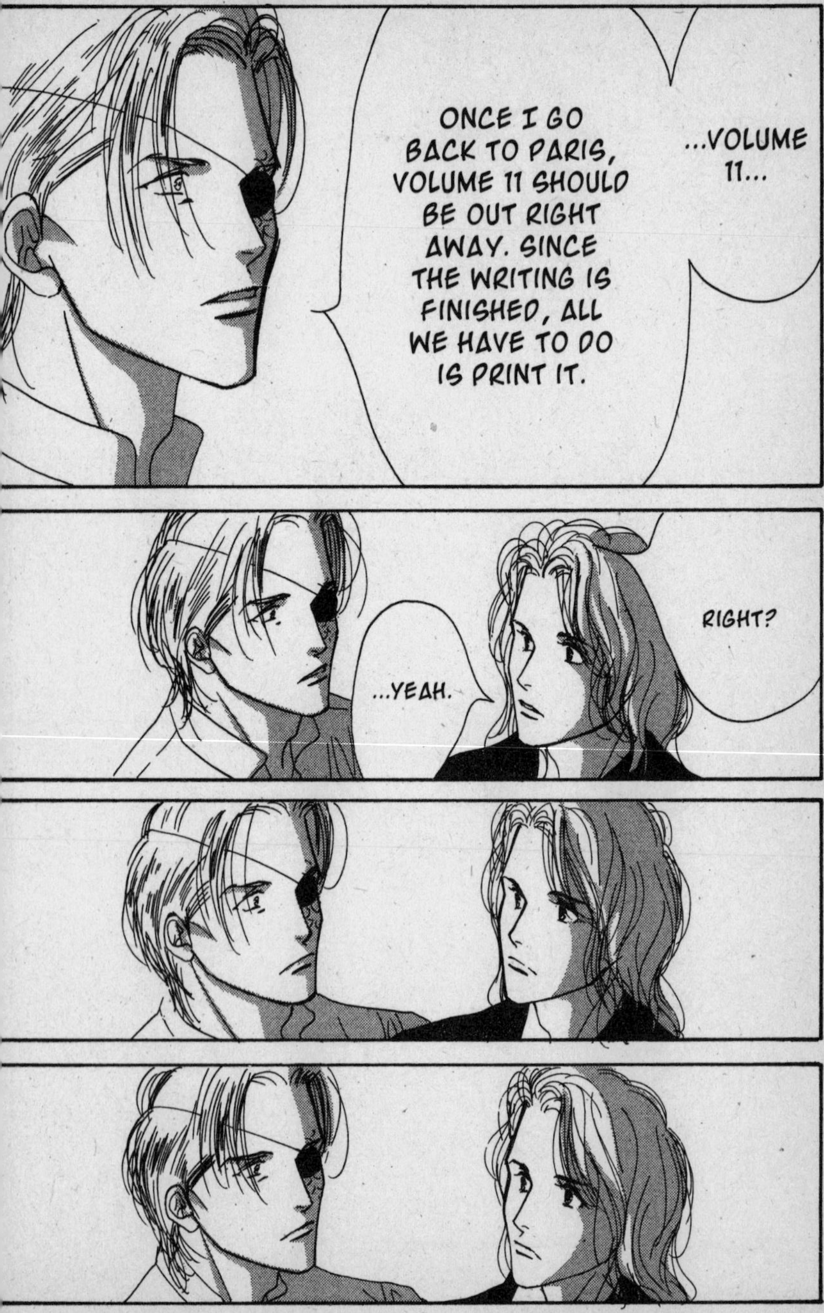
...VOLUME 11...
ONCE I GO BACK TO PARIS, VOLUME 11 SHOULD BE OUT RIGHT AWAY. SINCE THE WRITING IS FINISHED, ALL WE HAVE TO DO IS PRINT IT.
RIGHT?
...YEAH.

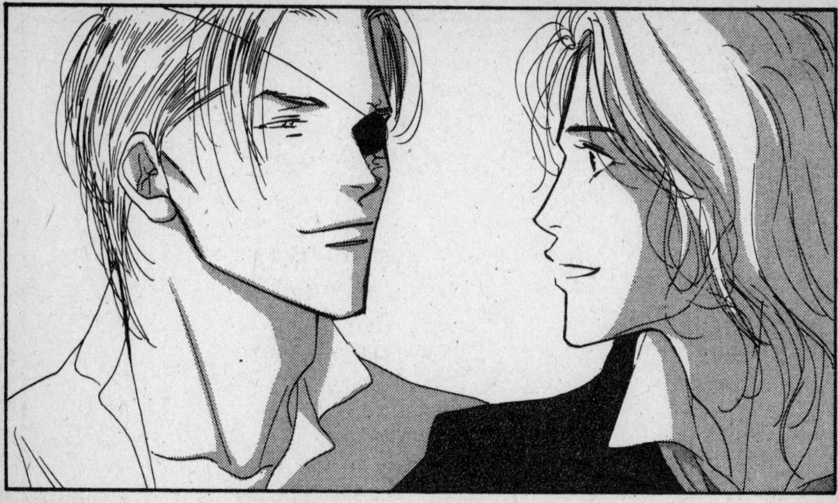
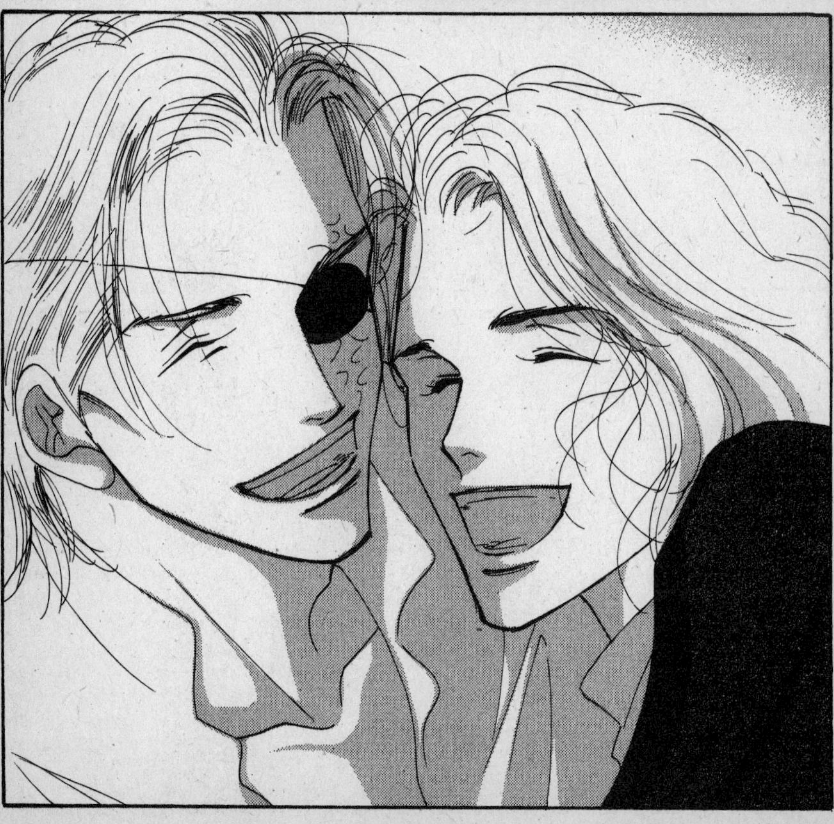

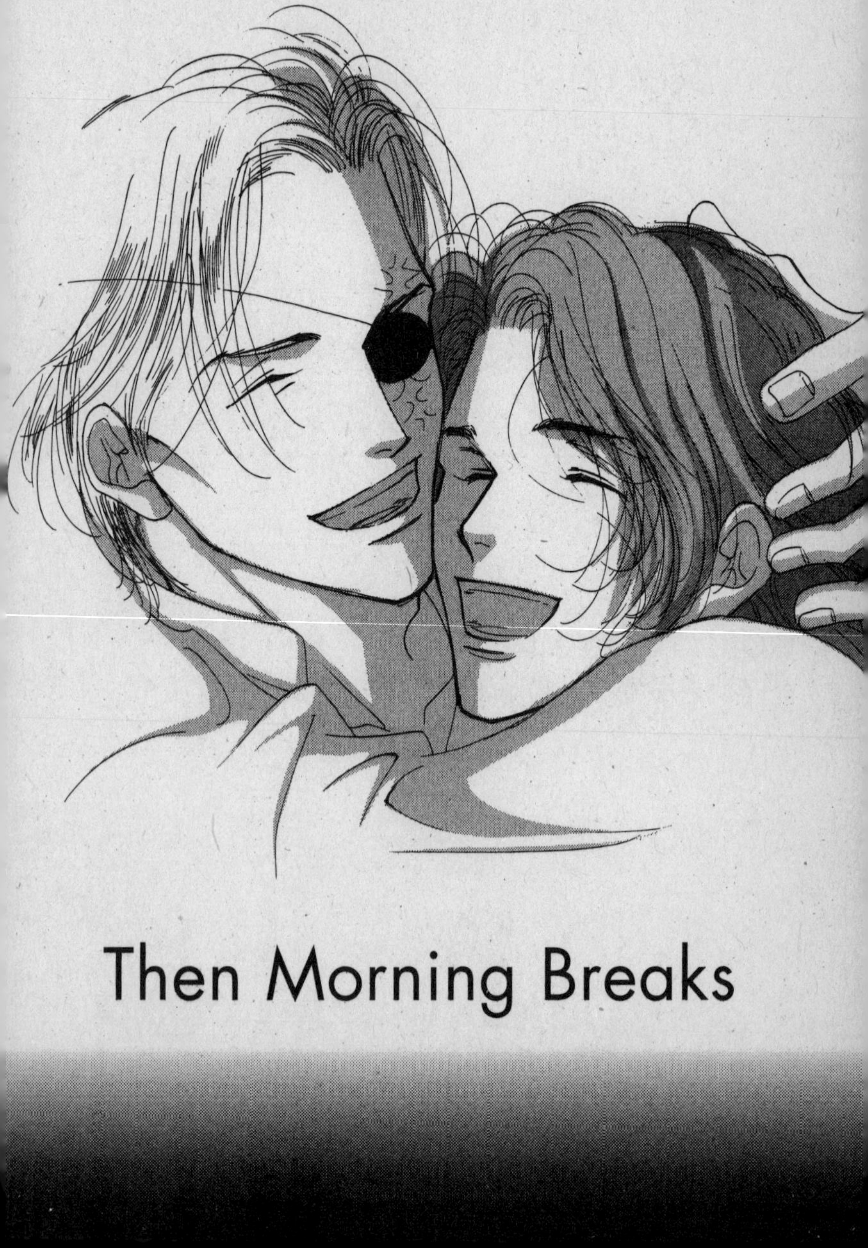

Then Morning Breaks

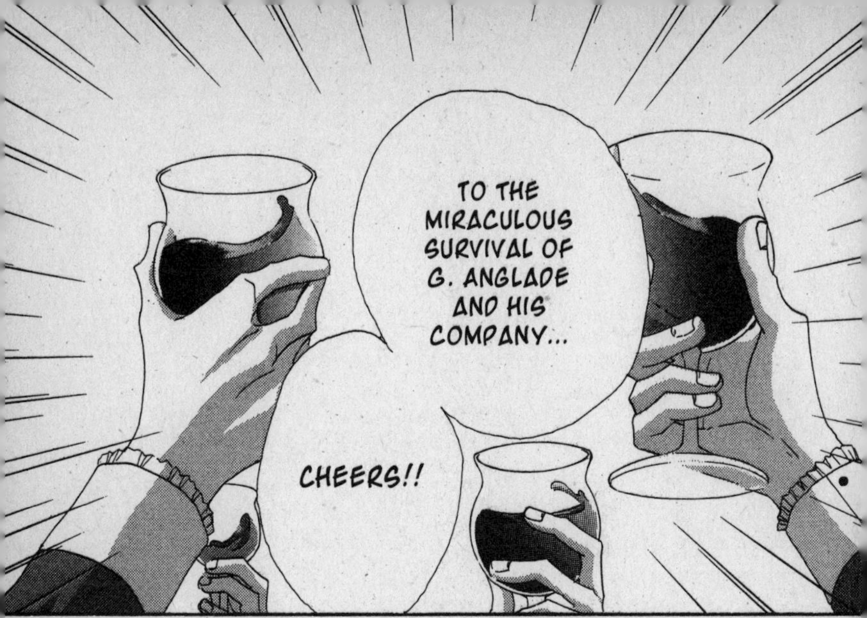
TO THE MIRACULOUS SURVIVAL OF G. ANGLADE AND HIS COMPANY...
CHEERS!!

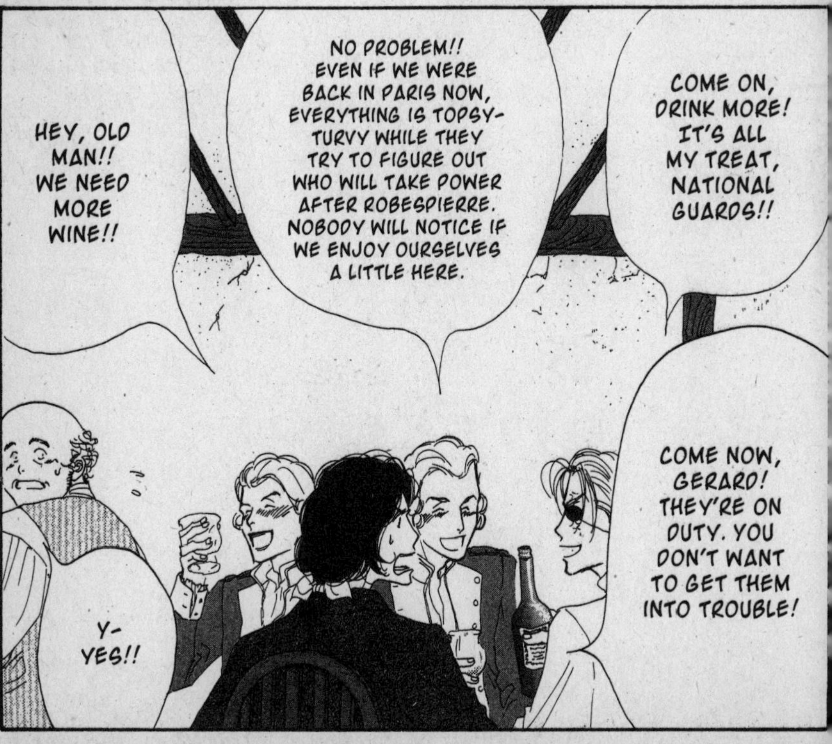
COME ON, DRINK MORE! IT'S ALL MY TREAT, NATIONAL GUARDS!!
NO PROBLEM!! EVEN IF WE WERE BACK IN PARIS NOW, EVERYTHING IS TOPSY-TURVY WHILE THEY TRY TO FIGURE OUT WHO WILL TAKE POWER AFTER ROBESPIERRE. NOBODY WILL NOTICE IF WE ENJOY OURSELVES A LITTLE HERE.
HEY, OLD MAN!! WE NEED MORE WINE!!
COME NOW, GERARD! THEY'RE ON DUTY. YOU DON'T WANT TO GET THEM INTO TROUBLE!
Y-YES!!

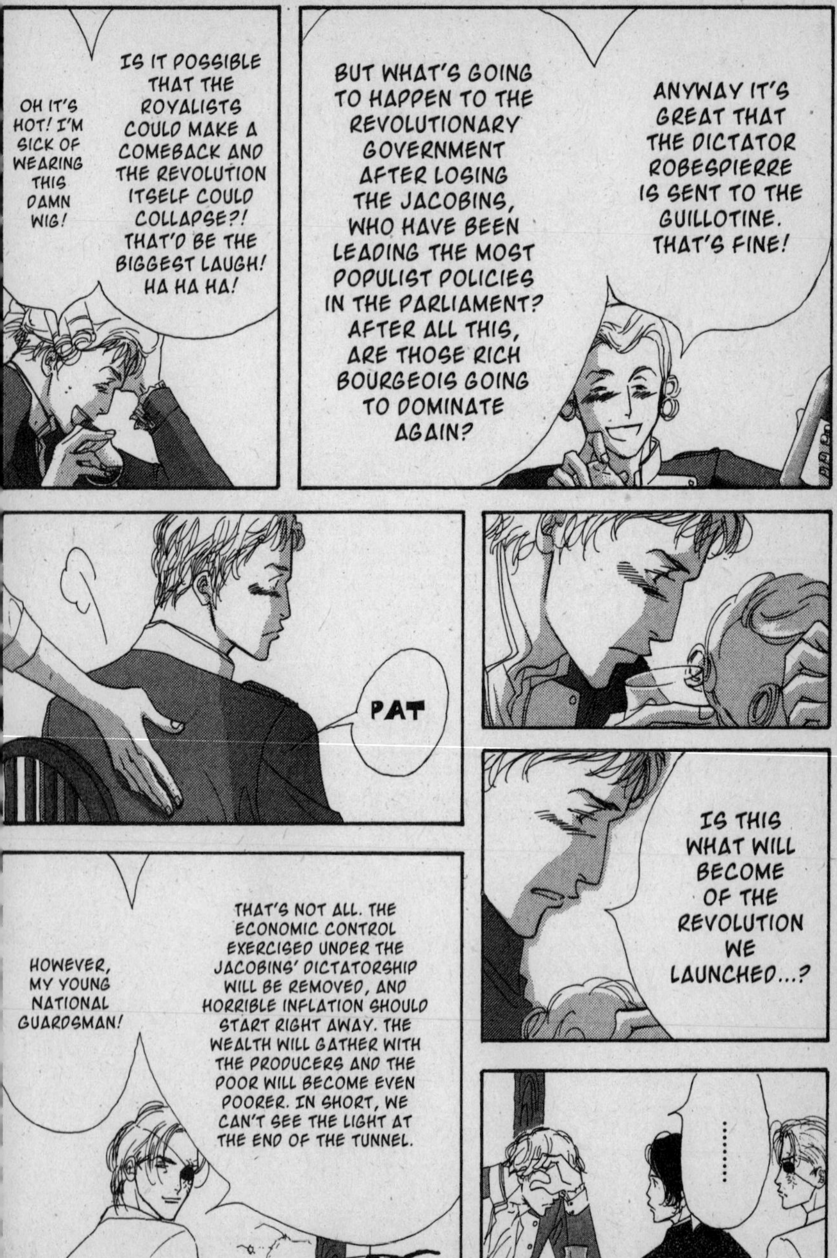

ANYWAY IT'S GREAT THAT THE DICTATOR ROBESPIERRE IS SENT TO THE GUILLOTINE. THAT'S FINE!
BUT WHAT'S GOING TO HAPPEN TO THE REVOLUTIONARY GOVERNMENT AFTER LOSING THE JACOBINS, WHO HAVE BEEN LEADING THE MOST POPULIST POLICIES IN THE PARLIAMENT? AFTER ALL THIS, ARE THOSE RICH BOURGEOIS GOING TO DOMINATE AGAIN?
IS IT POSSIBLE THAT THE ROYALISTS COULD MAKE A COMEBACK AND THE REVOLUTION ITSELF COULD COLLAPSE?! THAT'D BE THE BIGGEST LAUGH! HA HA HA!
OH IT'S HOT! I'M SICK OF WEARING THIS DAMN WIG!
IS THIS WHAT WILL BECOME OF THE REVOLUTION WE LAUNCHED...?
......
PAT
THAT'S NOT ALL. THE ECONOMIC CONTROL EXERCISED UNDER THE JACOBINS' DICTATORSHIP WILL BE REMOVED, AND HORRIBLE INFLATION SHOULD START RIGHT AWAY. THE WEALTH WILL GATHER WITH THE PRODUCERS AND THE POOR WILL BECOME EVEN POORER. IN SHORT, WE CAN'T SEE THE LIGHT AT THE END OF THE TUNNEL.
HOWEVER, MY YOUNG NATIONAL GUARDSMAN!

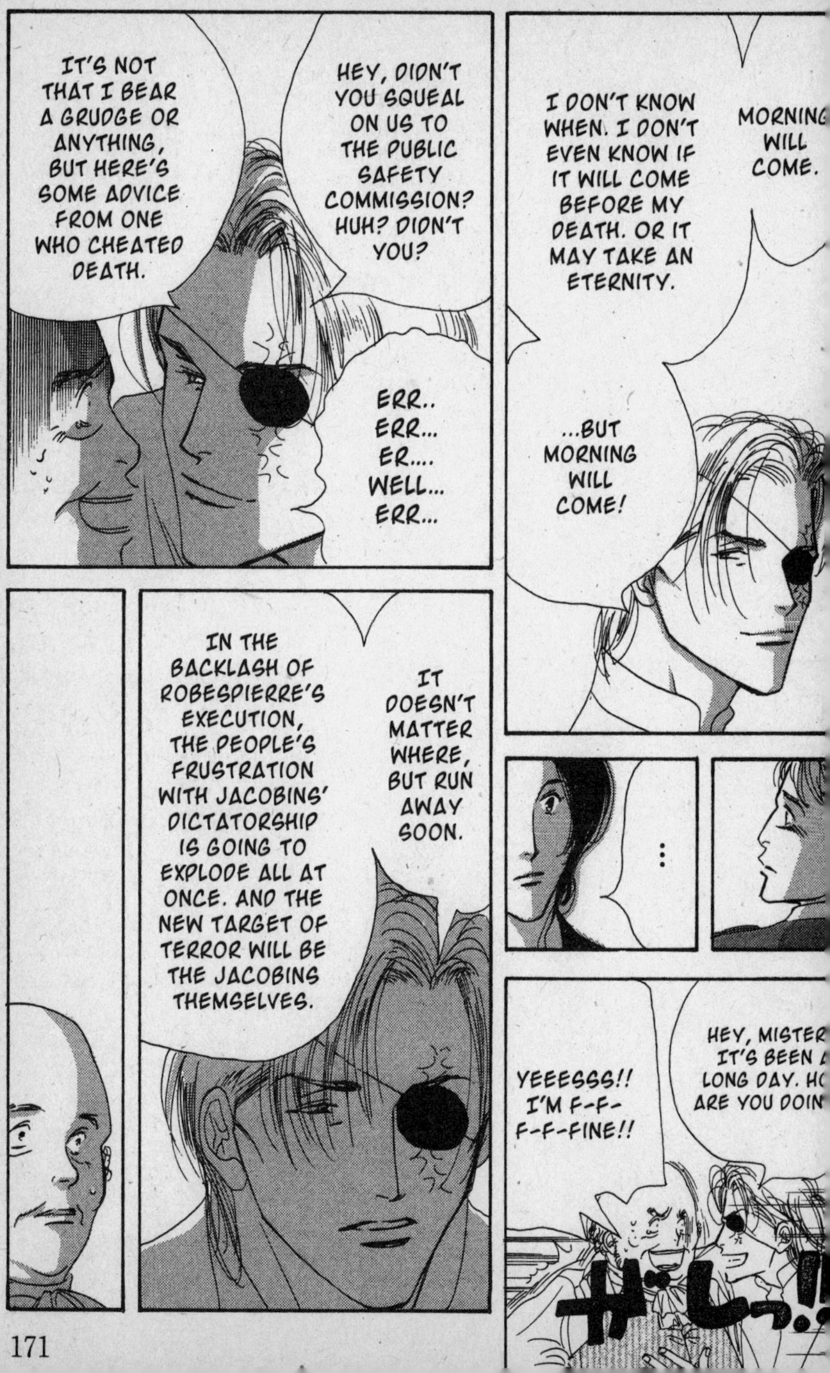
IT'S NOT THAT I BEAR A GRUDGE OR ANYTHING, BUT HERE'S SOME ADVICE FROM ONE WHO CHEATED DEATH.
HEY, DIDN'T YOU SQUEAL ON US TO THE PUBLIC SAFETY COMMISSION? HUH? DIDN'T YOU?
ERR.. ERR... ER.... WELL... ERR...
IN THE BACKLASH OF ROBESPIERRE'S EXECUTION, THE PEOPLE'S FRUSTRATION WITH JACOBINS' DICTATORSHIP IS GOING TO EXPLODE ALL AT ONCE. AND THE NEW TARGET OF TERROR WILL BE THE JACOBINS THEMSELVES.
IT DOESN'T MATTER WHERE, BUT RUN AWAY SOON.
I DON'T KNOW WHEN. I DON'T EVEN KNOW IF IT WILL COME BEFORE MY DEATH. OR IT MAY TAKE AN ETERNITY.
MORNING WILL COME.
...BUT MORNING WILL COME!
...
HEY, MISTER IT'S BEEN LONG DAY. H ARE YOU DOIN
YEEESSS!! I'M F-F-F-F-FINE!!
ガしっ!!

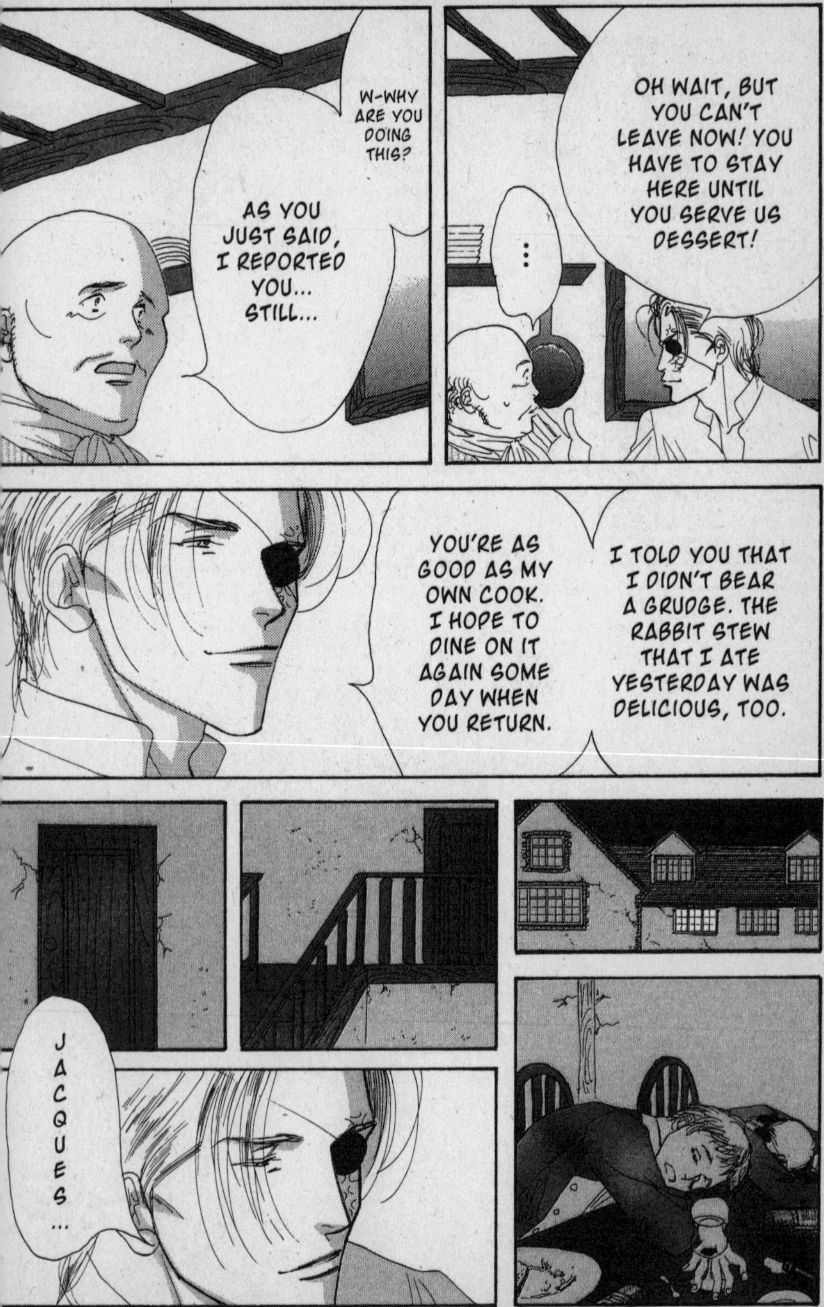
OH WAIT, BUT YOU CAN'T LEAVE NOW! YOU HAVE TO STAY HERE UNTIL YOU SERVE US DESSERT!
...
W-WHY ARE YOU DOING THIS?
AS YOU JUST SAID, I REPORTED YOU... STILL...
I TOLD YOU THAT I DIDN'T BEAR A GRUDGE. THE RABBIT STEW THAT I ATE YESTERDAY WAS DELICIOUS, TOO.
YOU'RE AS GOOD AS MY OWN COOK. I HOPE TO DINE ON IT AGAIN SOME DAY WHEN YOU RETURN.
JACQUES...

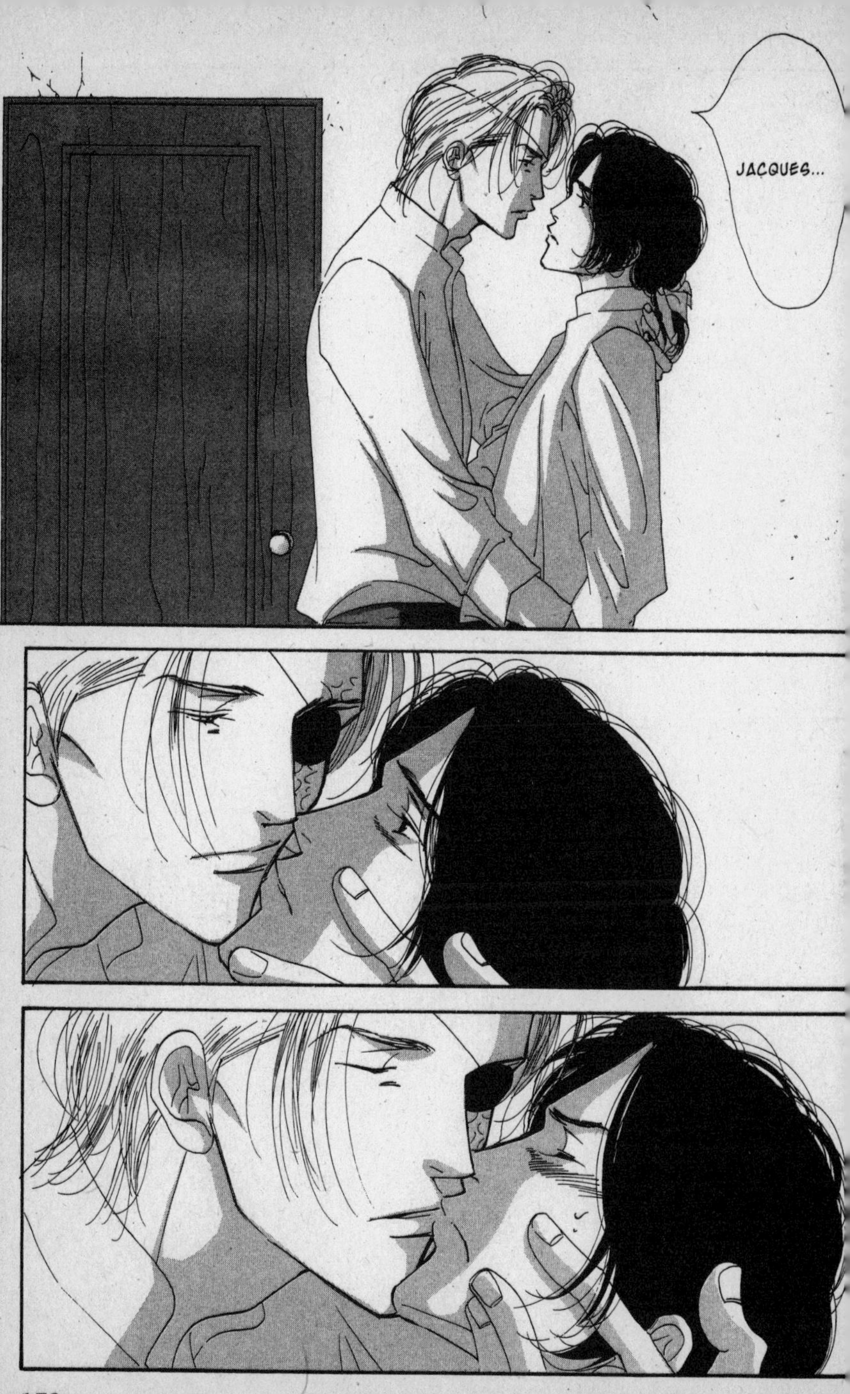
JAÇQUES...

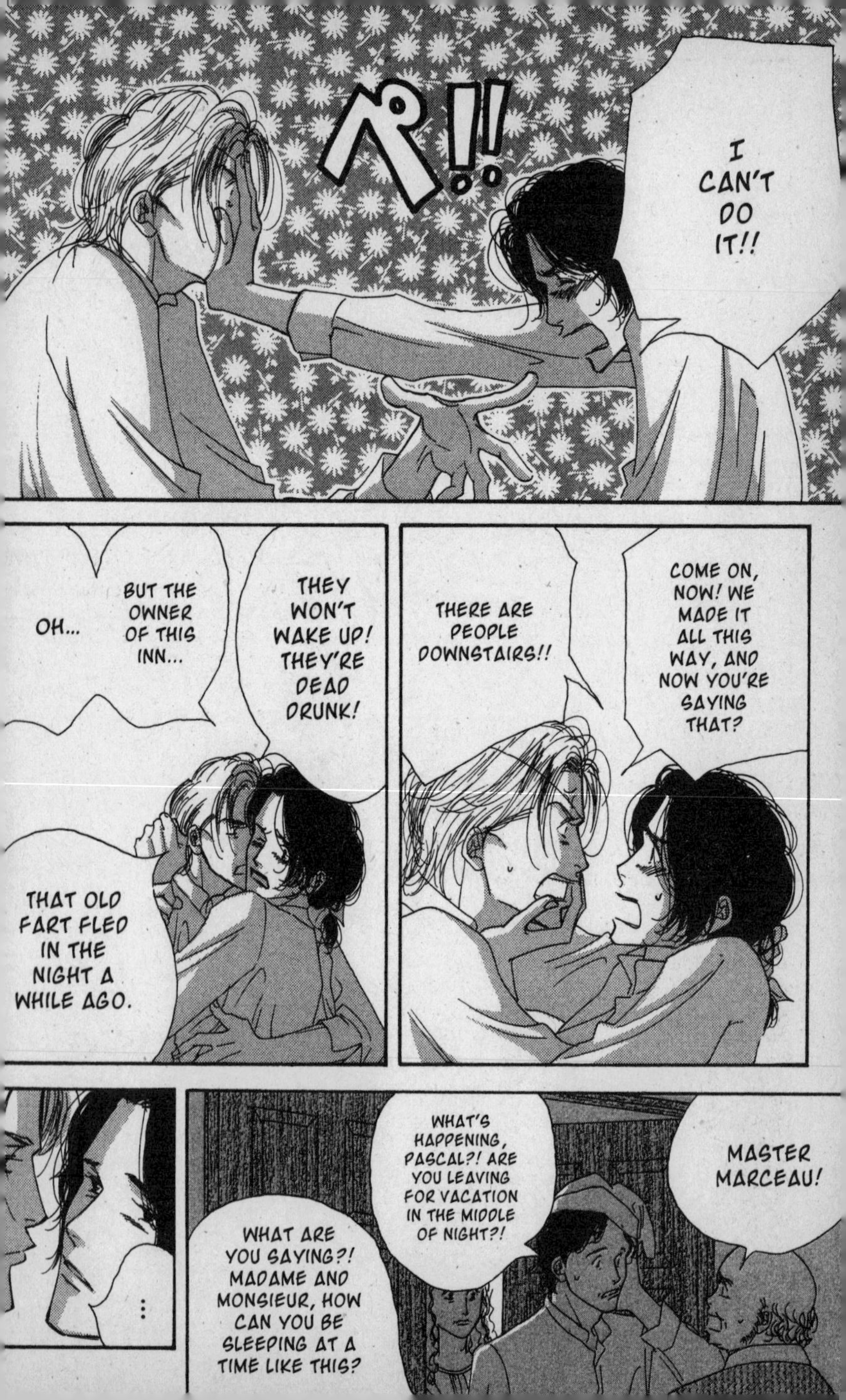
I CAN'T DO IT!!
ペ!!
COME ON, NOW! WE MADE IT ALL THIS WAY, AND NOW YOU'RE SAYING THAT?
THERE ARE PEOPLE DOWNSTAIRS!!
THEY WON'T WAKE UP! THEY'RE DEAD DRUNK!
BUT THE OWNER OF THIS INN...
OH...
THAT OLD FART FLED IN THE NIGHT A WHILE AGO.
MASTER MARCEAU!
WHAT'S HAPPENING, PASCAL?! ARE YOU LEAVING FOR VACATION IN THE MIDDLE OF NIGHT?!
WHAT ARE YOU SAYING?! MADAME AND MONSIEUR, HOW CAN YOU BE SLEEPING AT A TIME LIKE THIS?
...

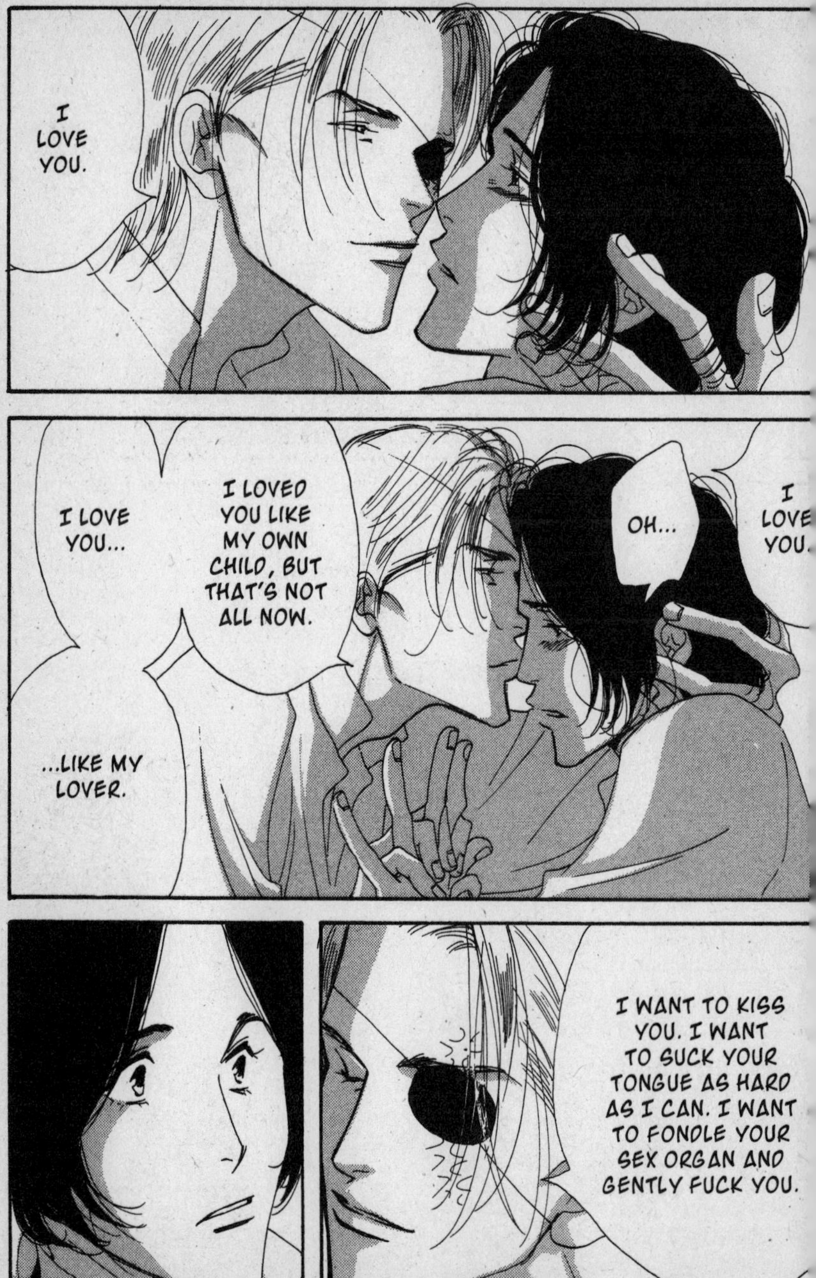
I LOVE YOU.
I LOVE YOU.
OH...
I LOVED YOU LIKE MY OWN CHILD, BUT THAT'S NOT ALL NOW.
I LOVE YOU...
...LIKE MY LOVER.
I WANT TO KISS YOU. I WANT TO SUCK YOUR TONGUE AS HARD AS I CAN. I WANT TO FONDLE YOUR SEX ORGAN AND GENTLY FUCK YOU.

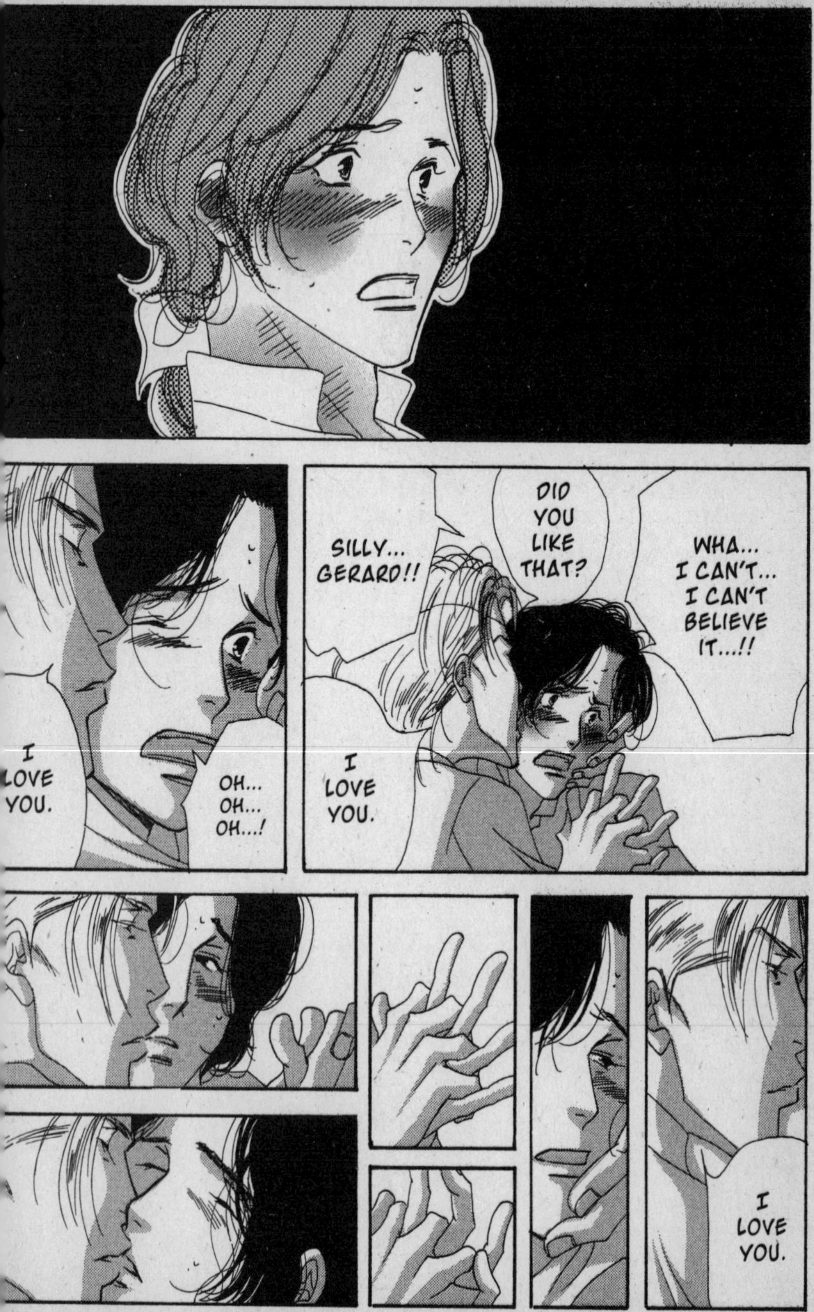
WHA... I CAN'T... I CAN'T BELIEVE IT...!!
DID YOU LIKE THAT?
SILLY... GERARD!!
I LOVE YOU.
OH... OH... OH...!
I LOVE YOU.
I LOVE YOU.

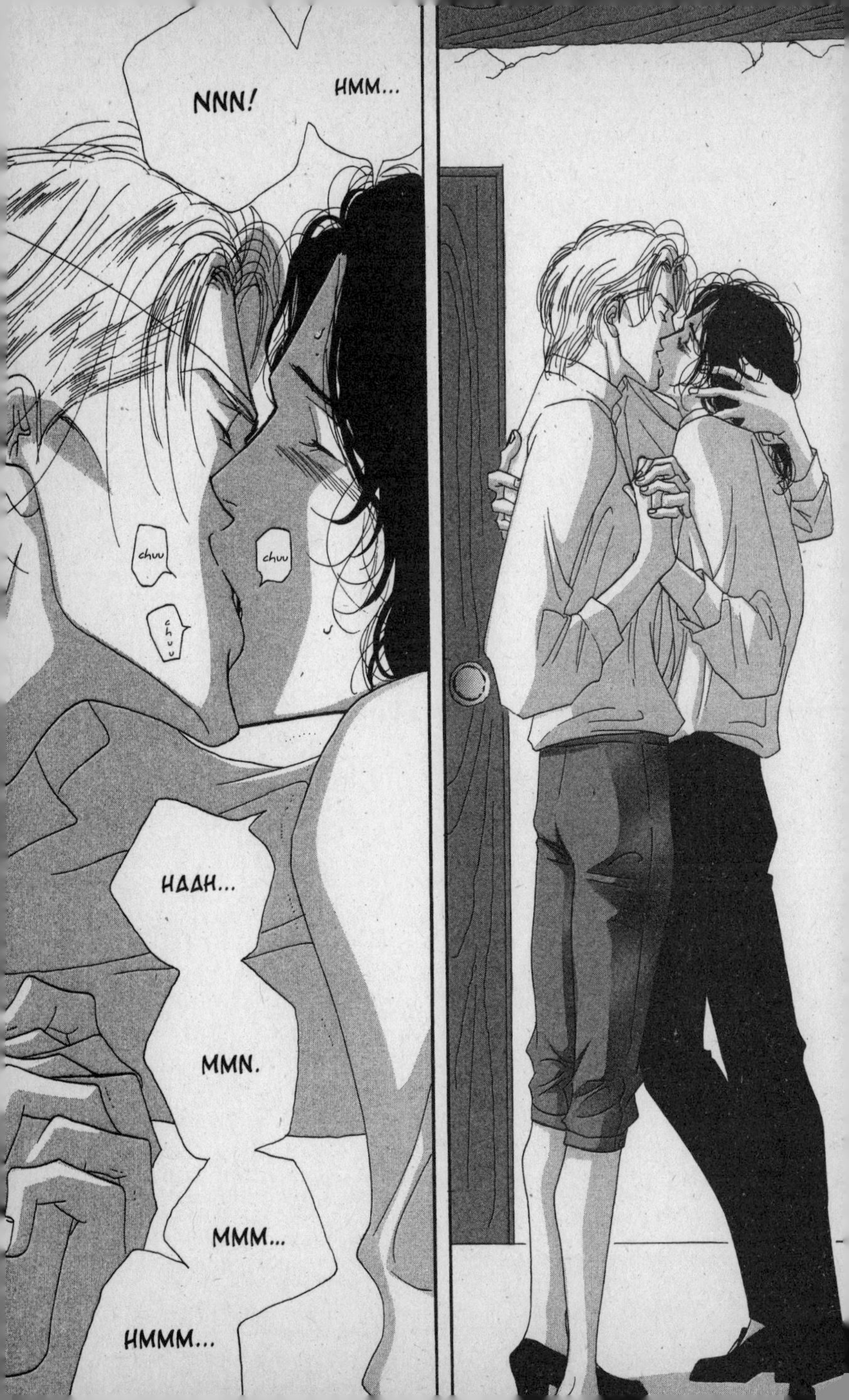
HMM...
NNN!
chuu
chuu
chuu
HAAH...
MMN.
MMM...
HMMM...

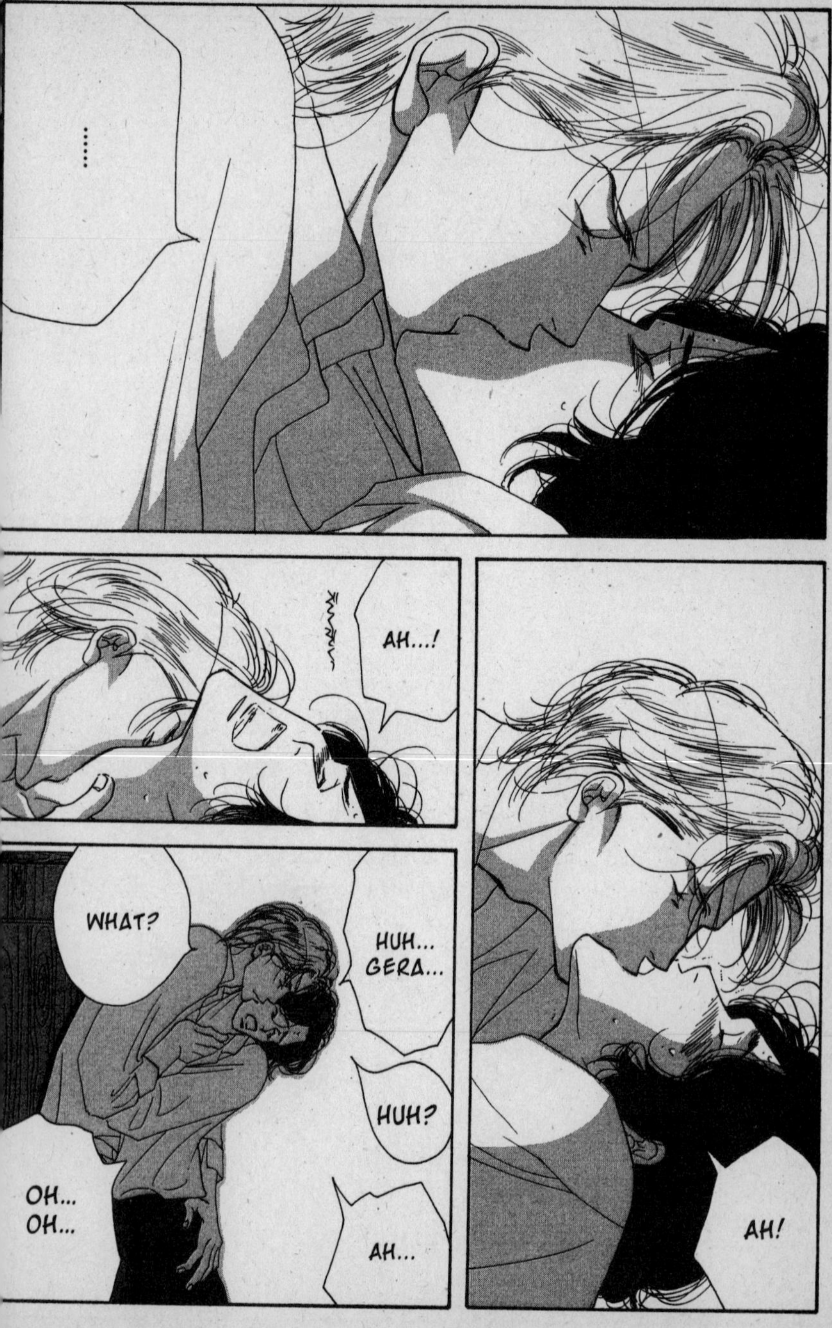
......
AH!
AH...!
HUH... GERA...
WHAT?
HUH?
AH...
OH... OH...

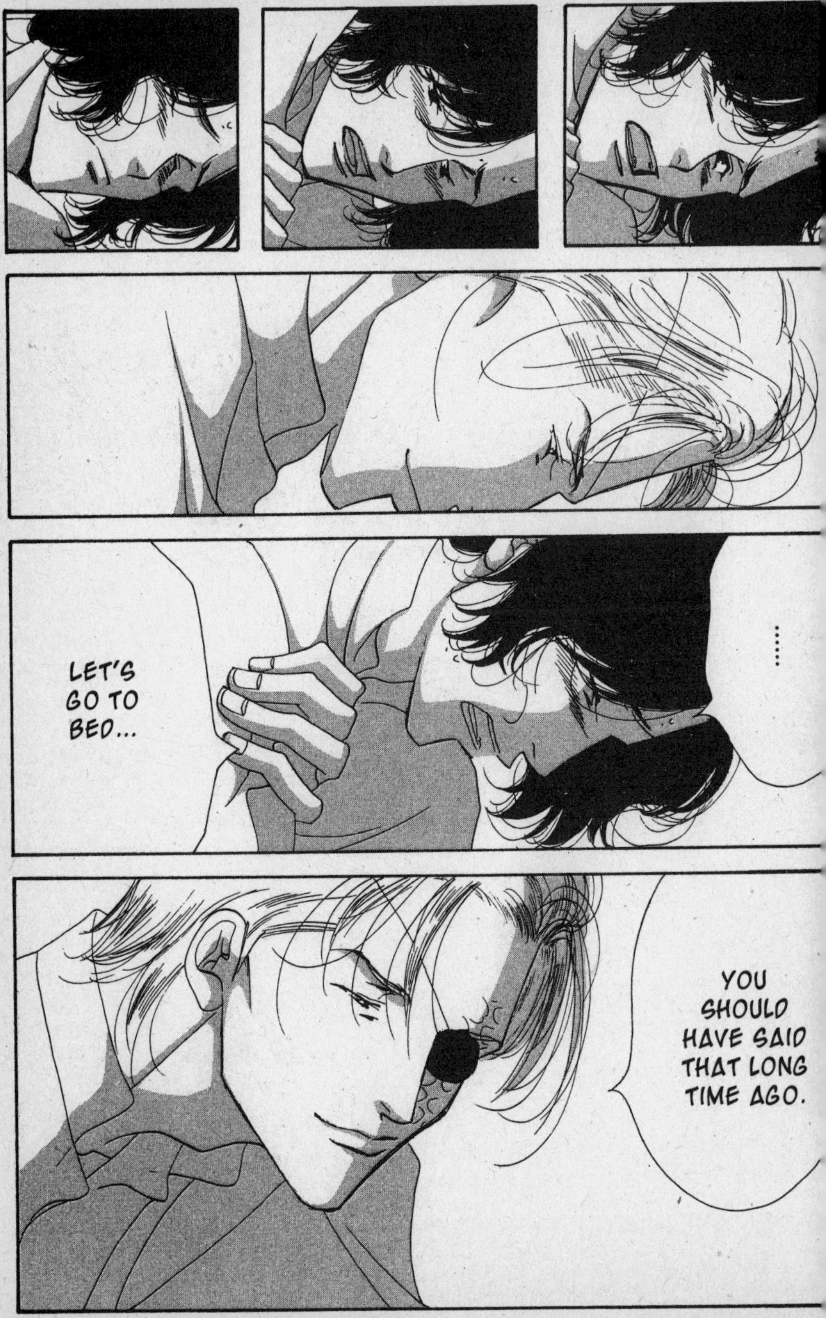
......
LET'S GO TO BED...
YOU SHOULD HAVE SAID THAT LONG TIME AGO.

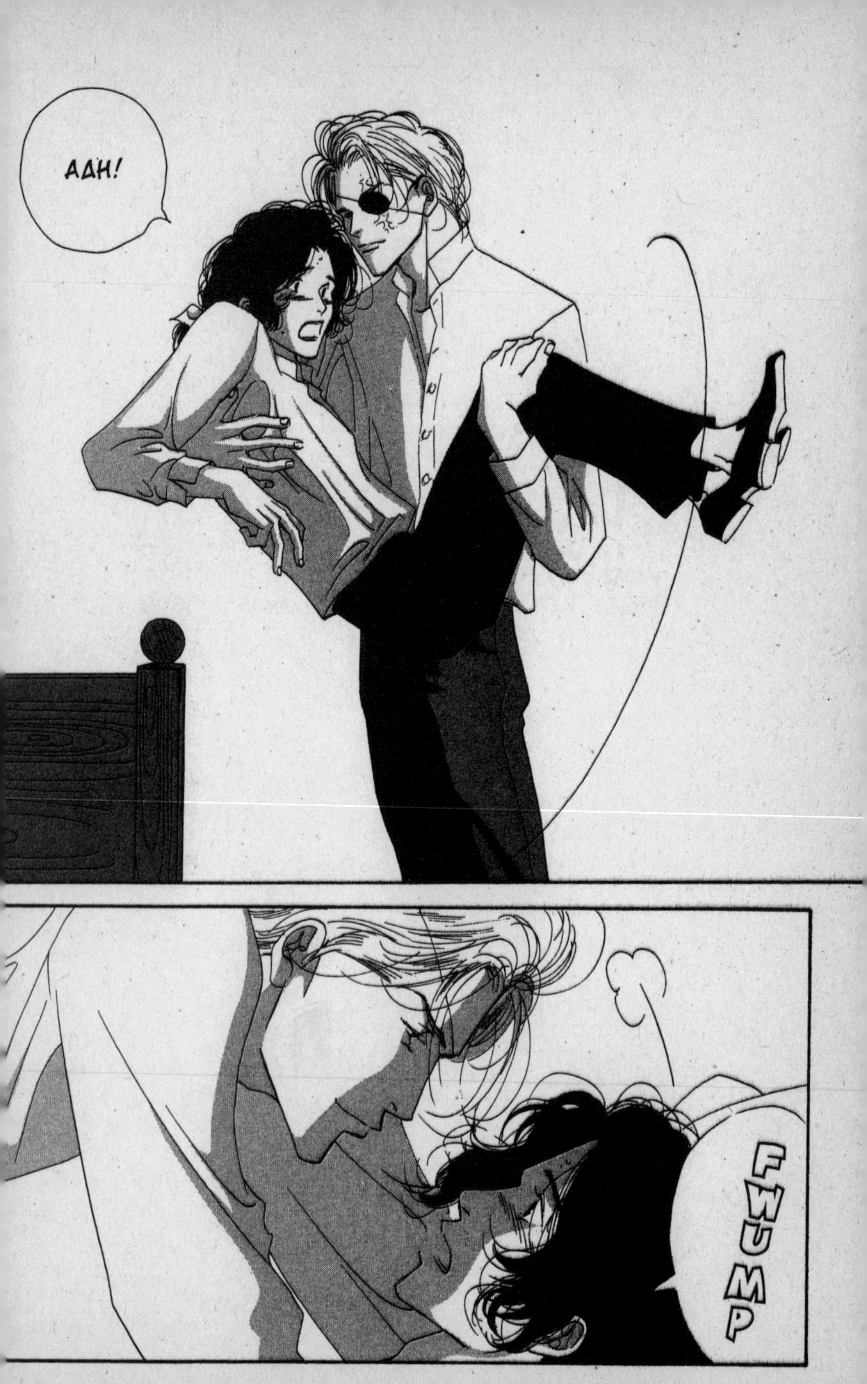
AAH!
FWUMP

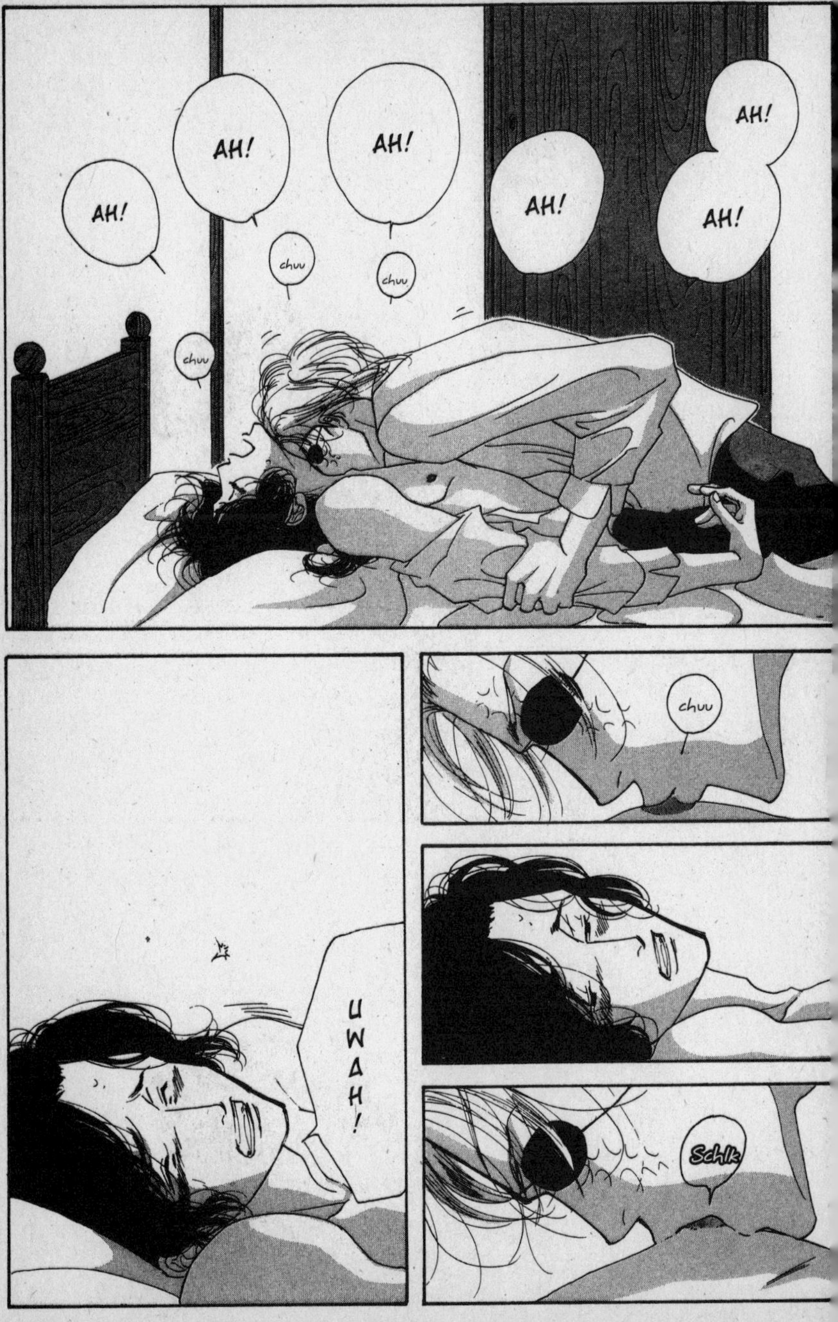
AH!
AH!
AH!
AH!
chuu
AH!
chuu
AH!
chuu
chuu
Schlk
UWAH!

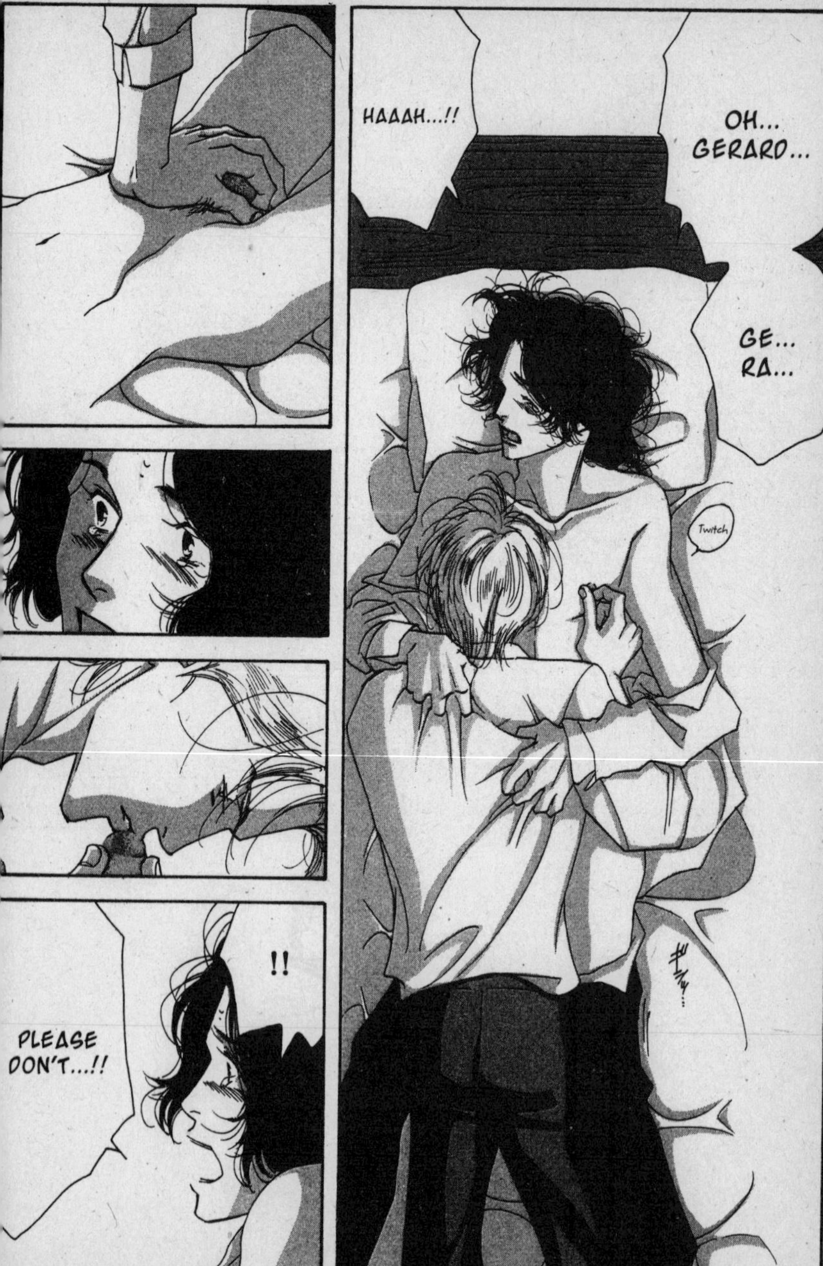
OH... GERARD...
HAAAH...!!
GE... RA...
Twitch
!!
PLEASE DON'T...!!

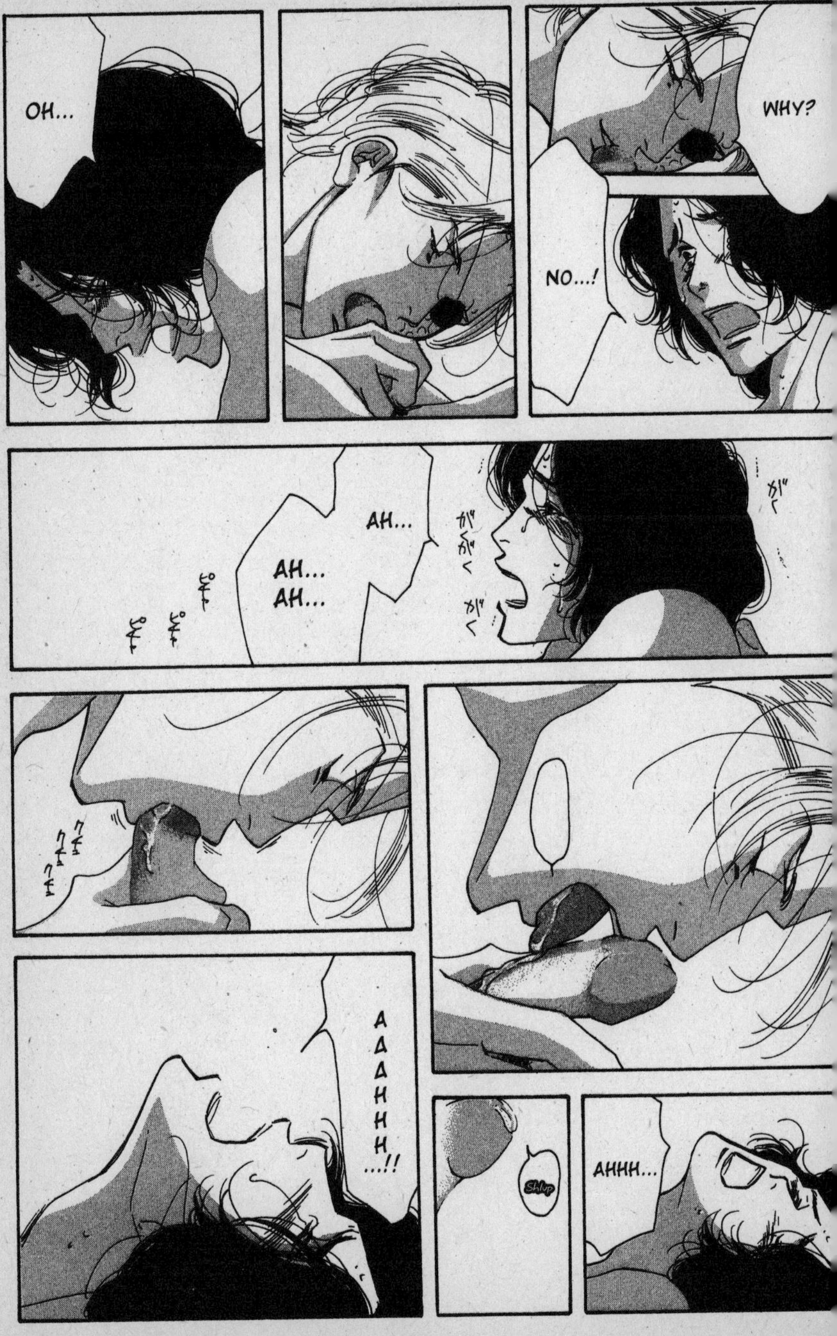
WHY?
NO...!
OH...
AH...
AH...
AH...
AHHH...
Shlup
AAAHHHH...!!

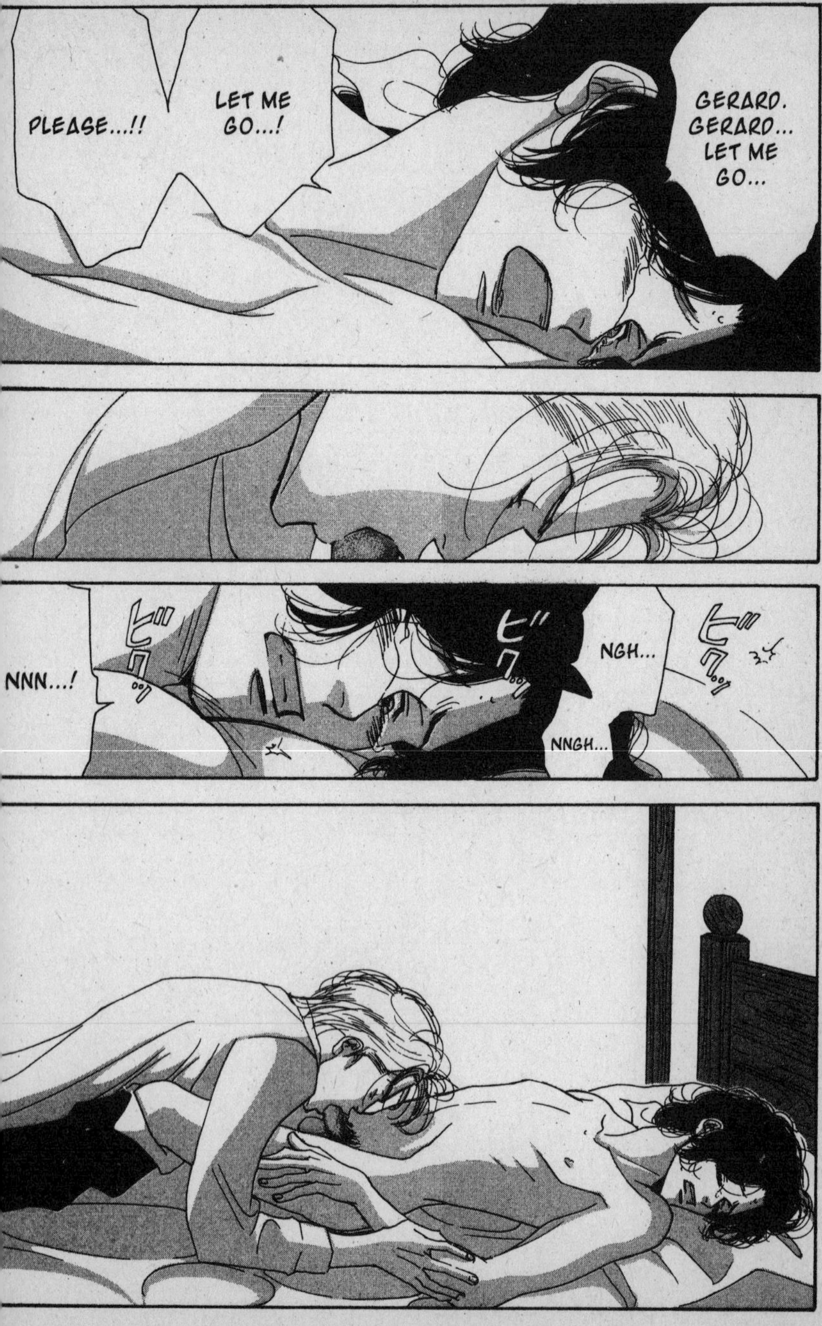
GERARD. GERARD... LET ME GO...
LET ME GO...!
PLEASE...!!
ビクッ
NGH...
ビクッ
NNGH...
ビクッ
NNN...!

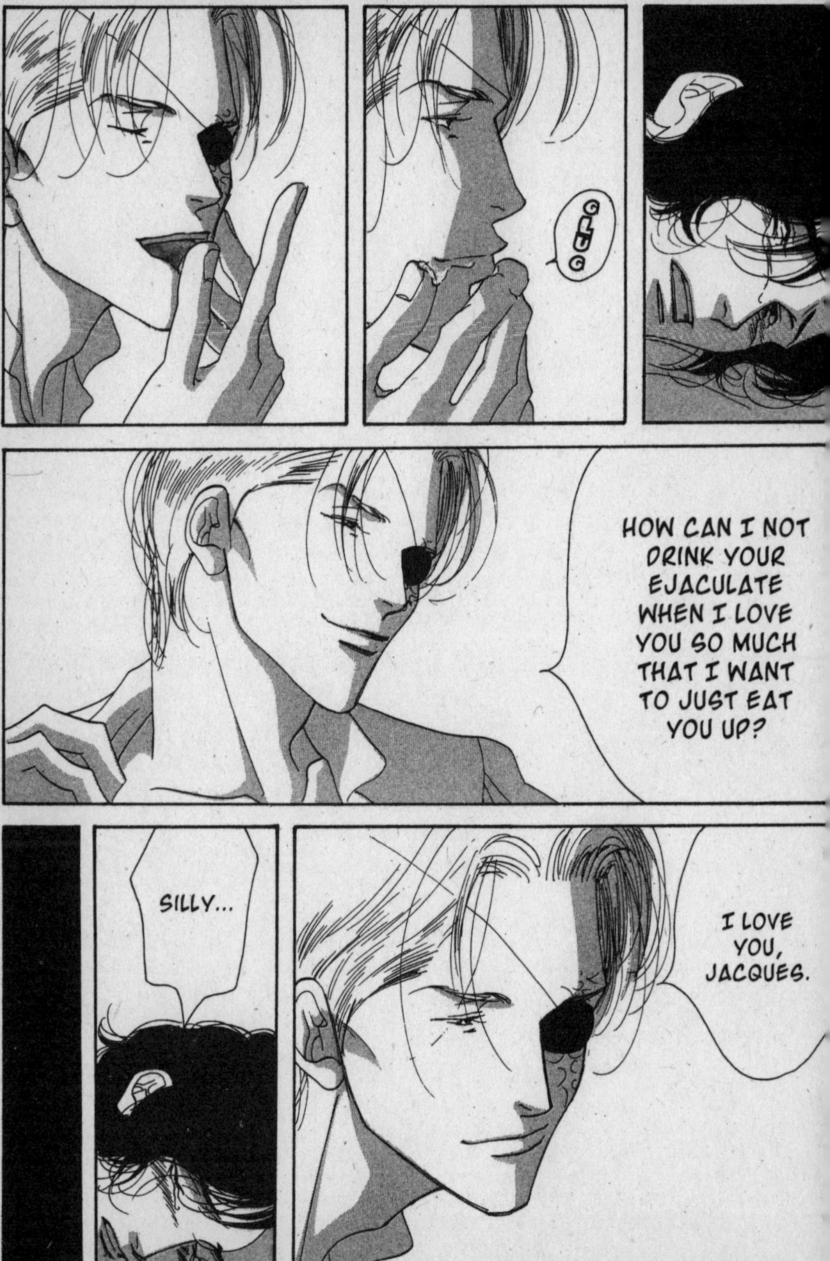
GLUG
HOW CAN I NOT DRINK YOUR EJACULATE WHEN I LOVE YOU SO MUCH THAT I WANT TO JUST EAT YOU UP?
I LOVE YOU, JACQUES.
SILLY...

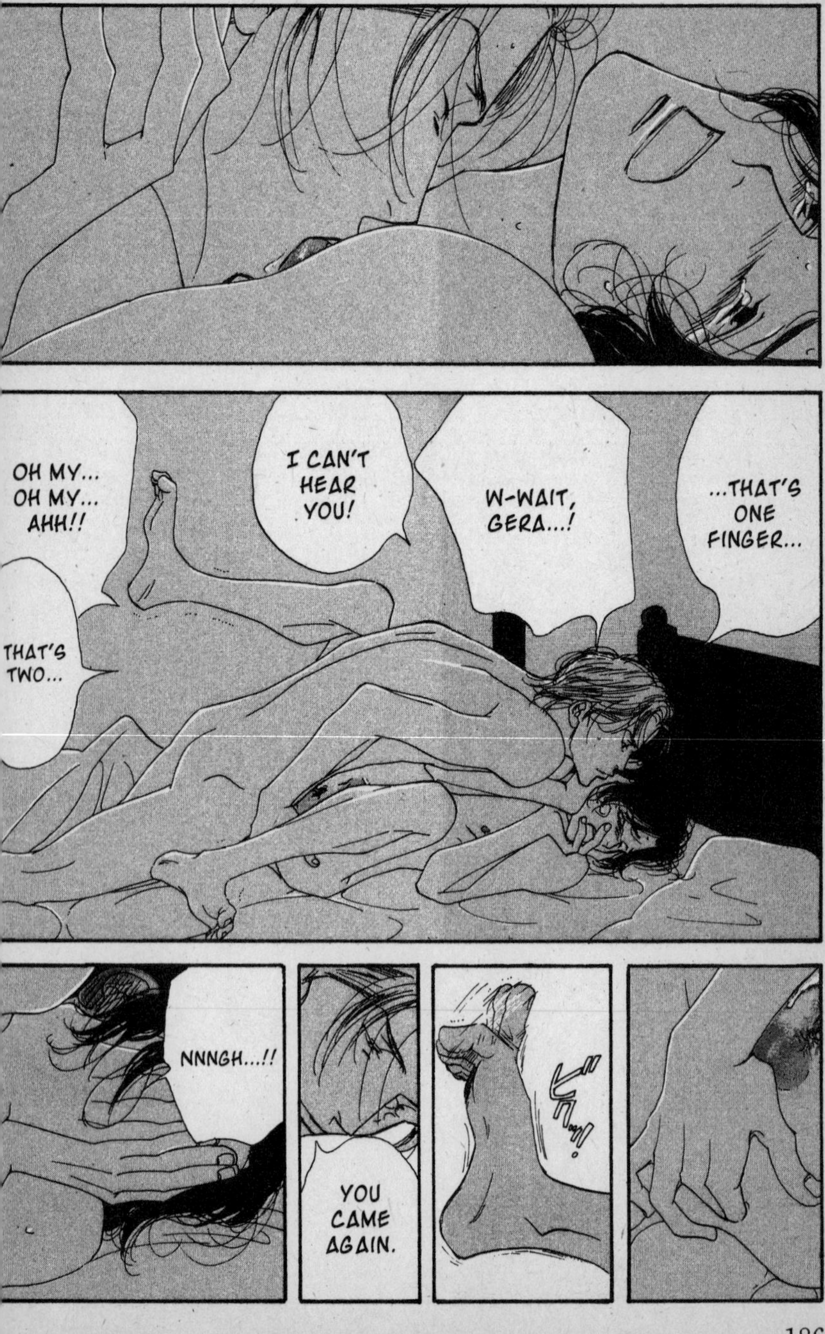
...THAT'S ONE FINGER...
W-WAIT, GERA...!
I CAN'T HEAR YOU!
OH MY... OH MY... AHH!!
THAT'S TWO...
YOU CAME AGAIN.
NNNGH...!!

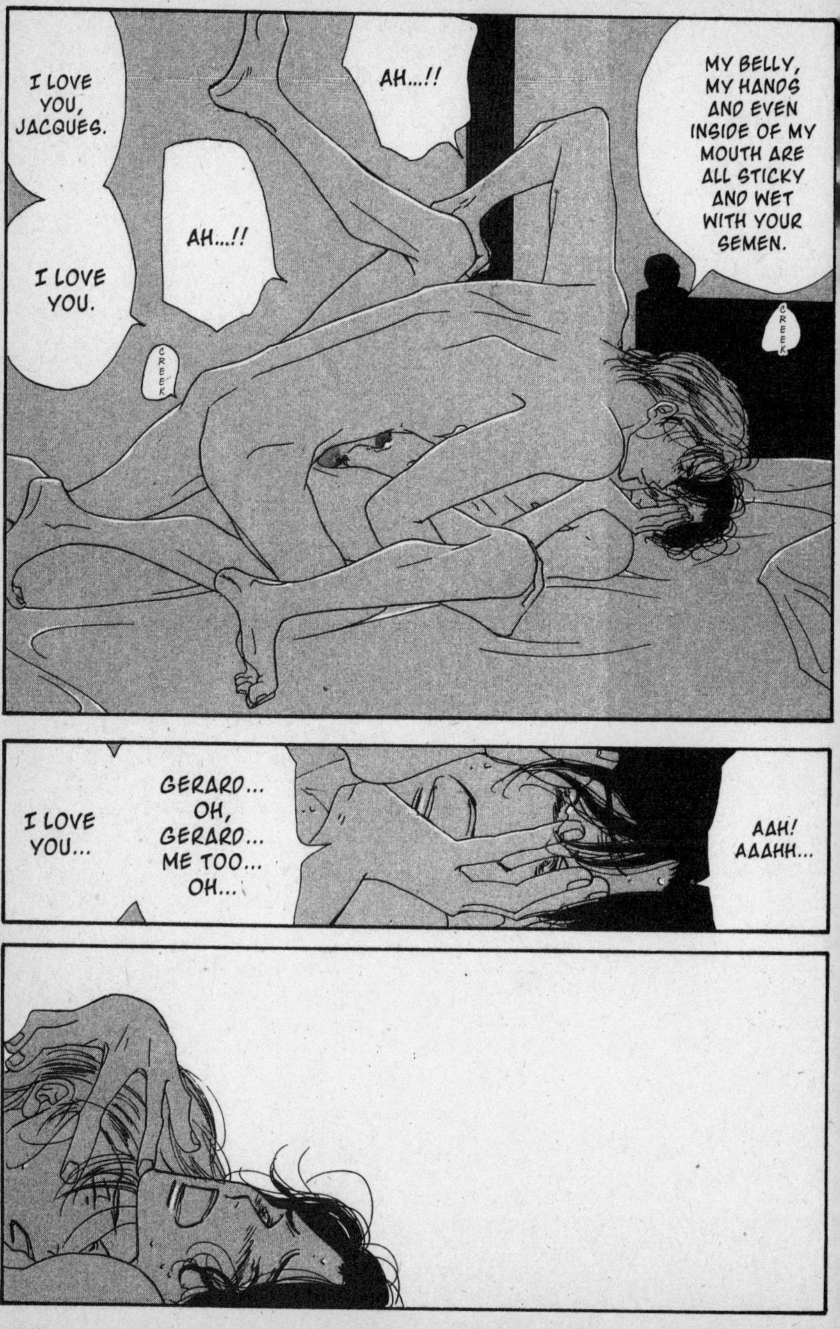

MY BELLY, MY HANDS AND EVEN INSIDE OF MY MOUTH ARE ALL STICKY AND WET WITH YOUR SEMEN.
CREEK
AH...!!
AH...!!
I LOVE YOU, JACQUES.
I LOVE YOU.
CREEK
AAH! AAAHH...
GERARD... OH, GERARD... ME TOO... OH...
I LOVE YOU...

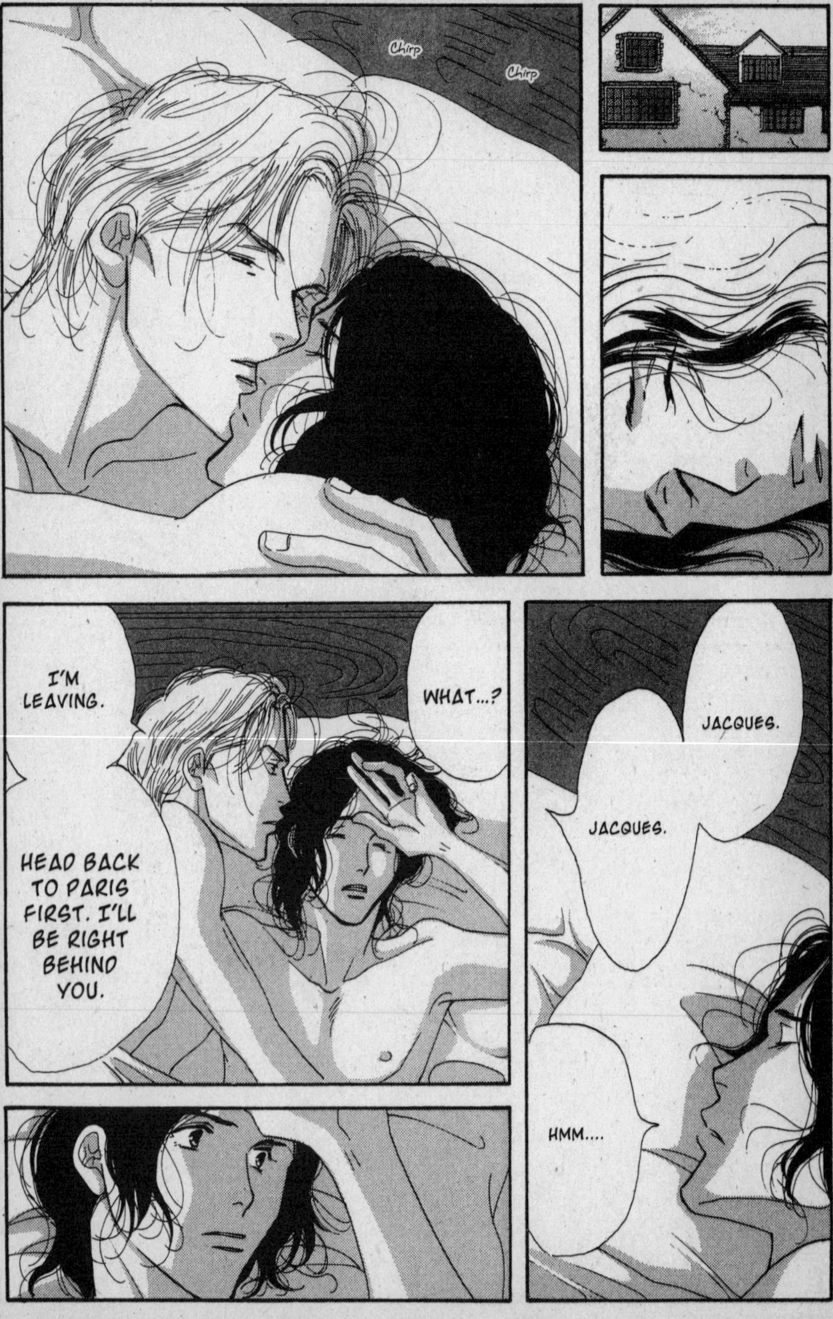
Chirp
Chirp
JACQUES.
JACQUES.
HMM....
WHAT...?
I'M LEAVING.
HEAD BACK TO PARIS FIRST. I'LL BE RIGHT BEHIND YOU.

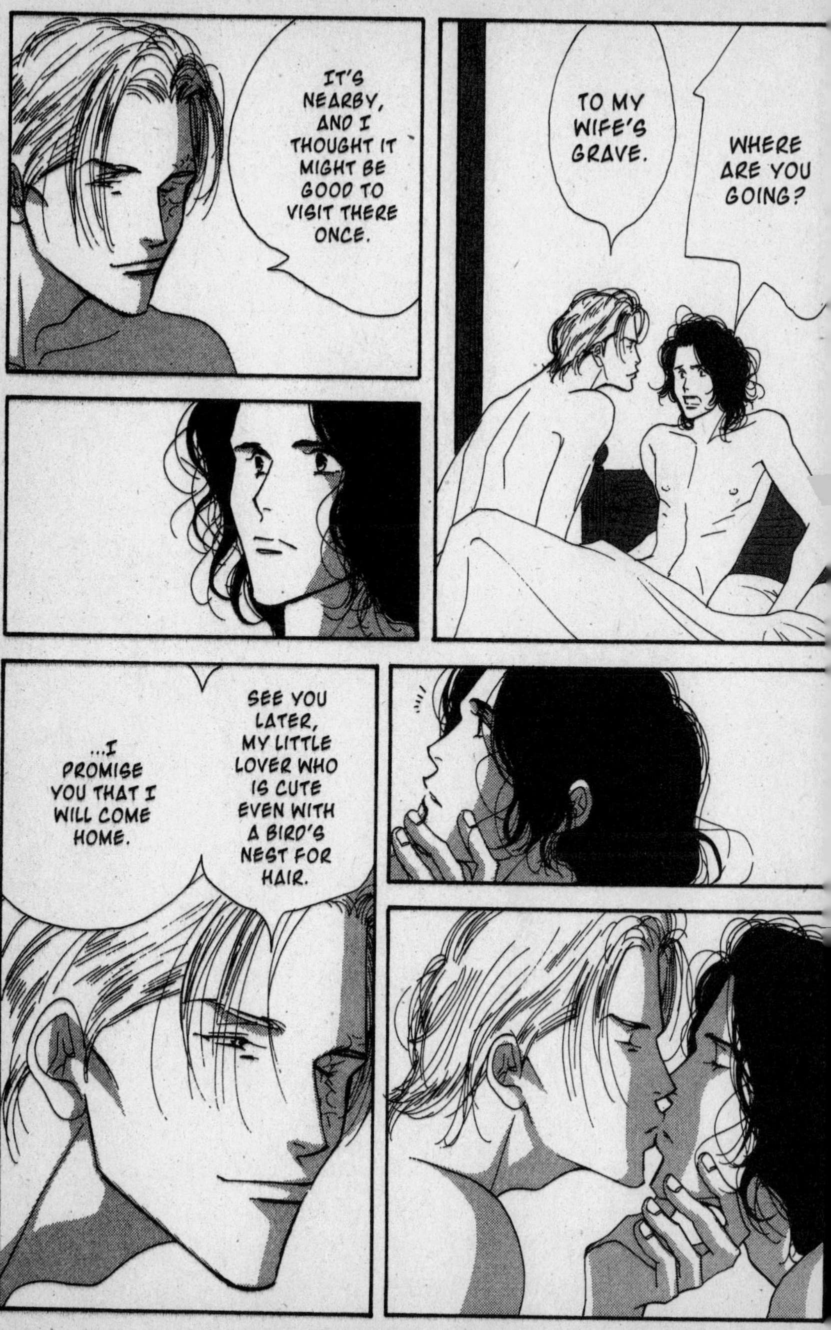
WHERE ARE YOU GOING?
TO MY WIFE'S GRAVE.
IT'S NEARBY, AND I THOUGHT IT MIGHT BE GOOD TO VISIT THERE ONCE.
SEE YOU LATER, MY LITTLE LOVER WHO IS CUTE EVEN WITH A BIRD'S NEST FOR HAIR.
...I PROMISE YOU THAT I WILL COME HOME.

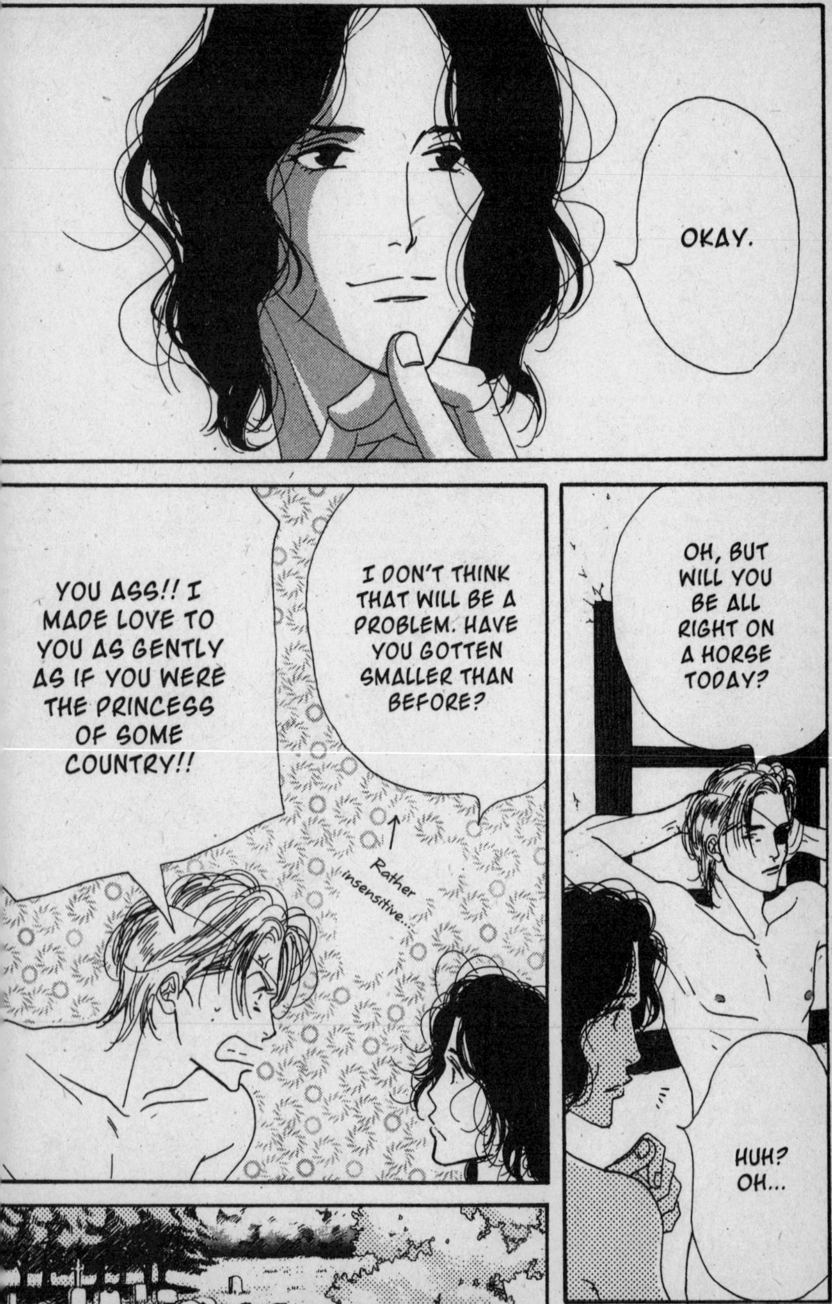
OKAY.
OH, BUT WILL YOU BE ALL RIGHT ON A HORSE TODAY?
HUH? OH...
I DON'T THINK THAT WILL BE A PROBLEM. HAVE YOU GOTTEN SMALLER THAN BEFORE?
Rather insensitive...
YOU ASS!! I MADE LOVE TO YOU AS GENTLY AS IF YOU WERE THE PRINCESS OF SOME COUNTRY!!

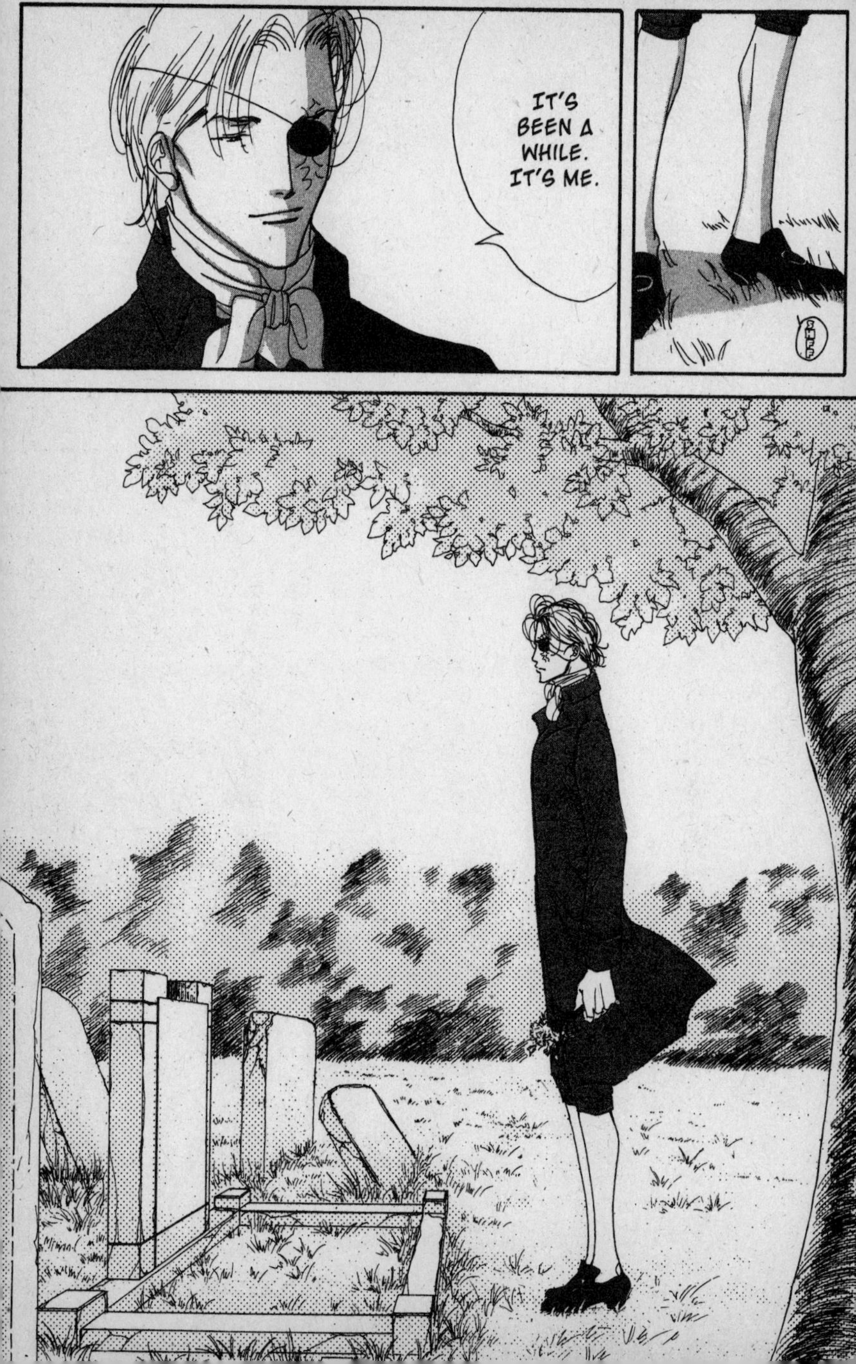
SHFF
IT'S BEEN A WHILE. IT'S ME.

THE NATIONAL GUARDS TOLD ME THAT RAUL DE AMALRIC WAS SENT TO THE GUILLOTINE JUST BEFORE ROBESPIERRE WAS ARRESTED.
SERVED HIM RIGHT...
I SUPPOSE I SHOULD SAY?
NO...
I WOULD FORGIVE HIM EVEN IF HE WERE ALIVE.
ROBESPIERRE, WHO BECAME A DICTATOR WITH ROUSSEAU'S DREAM IN HIS HEART, THE MEGALOMANIACAL PUBLIC SAFETY COMMISSION, THAT POOR OWNER OF THE INN....

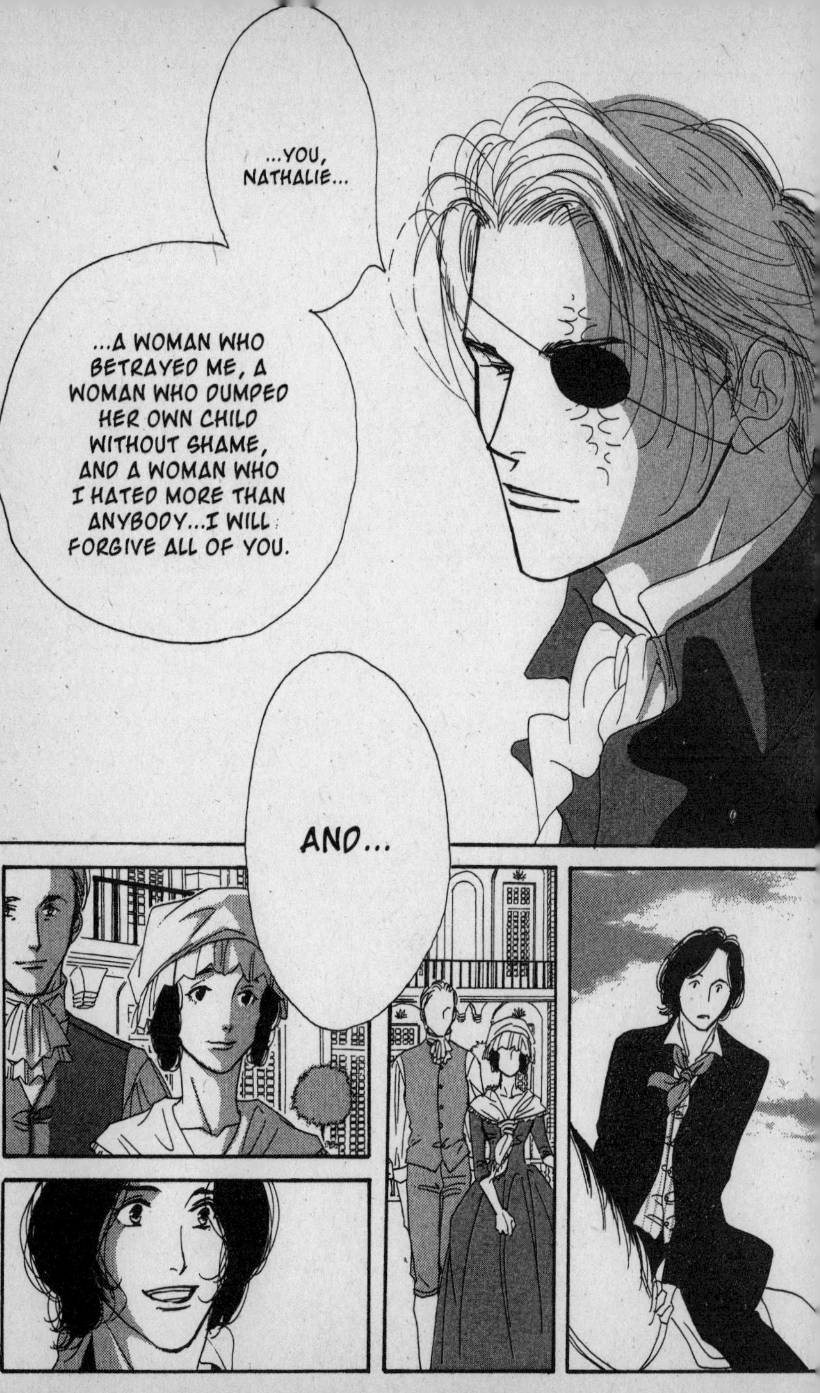
...YOU, NATHALIE...
...A WOMAN WHO BETRAYED ME, A WOMAN WHO DUMPED HER OWN CHILD WITHOUT SHAME, AND A WOMAN WHO I HATED MORE THAN ANYBODY...I WILL FORGIVE ALL OF YOU.
AND...

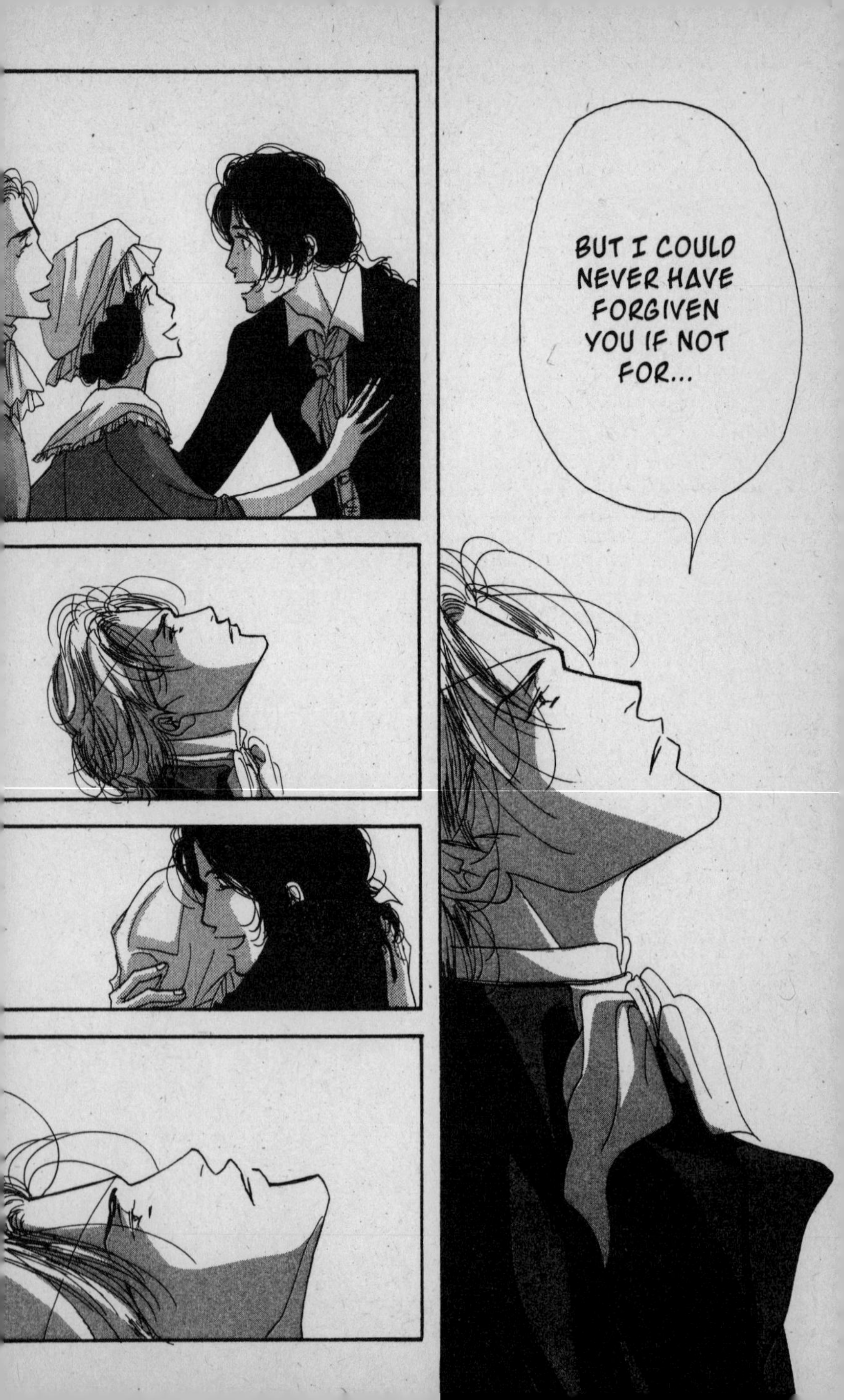
BUT I COULD NEVER HAVE FORGIVEN YOU IF NOT FOR...

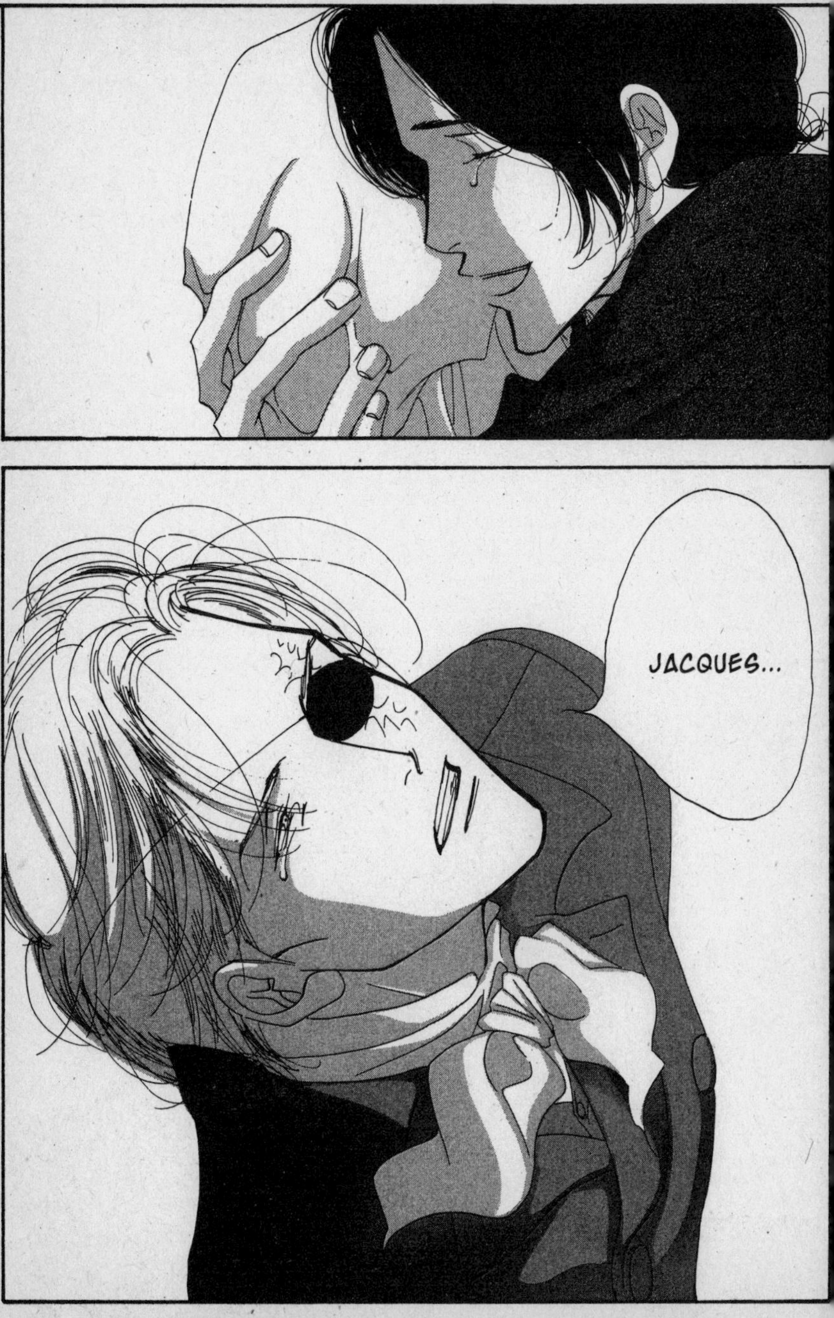
JACQUES...

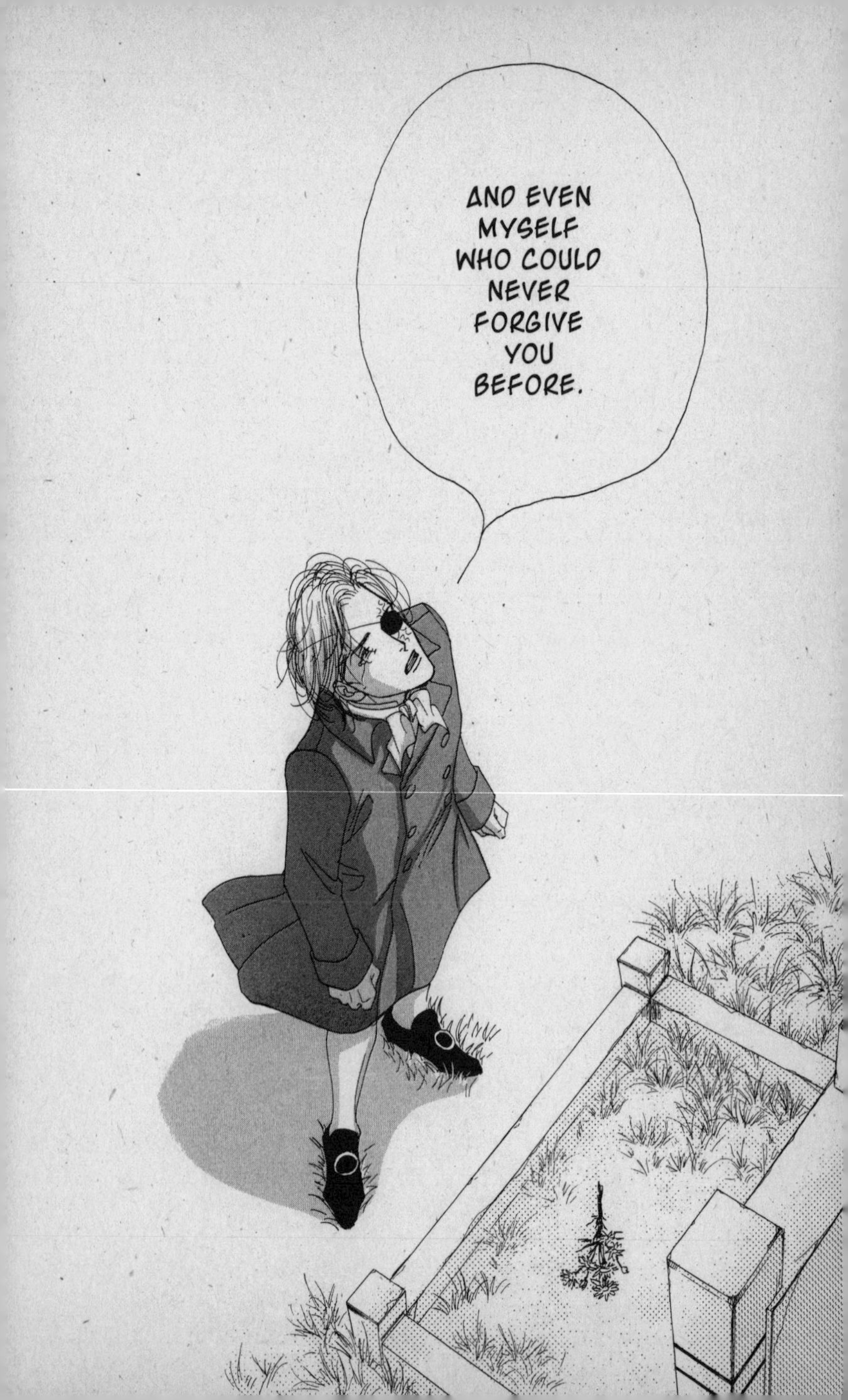
AND EVEN MYSELF WHO COULD NEVER FORGIVE YOU BEFORE.

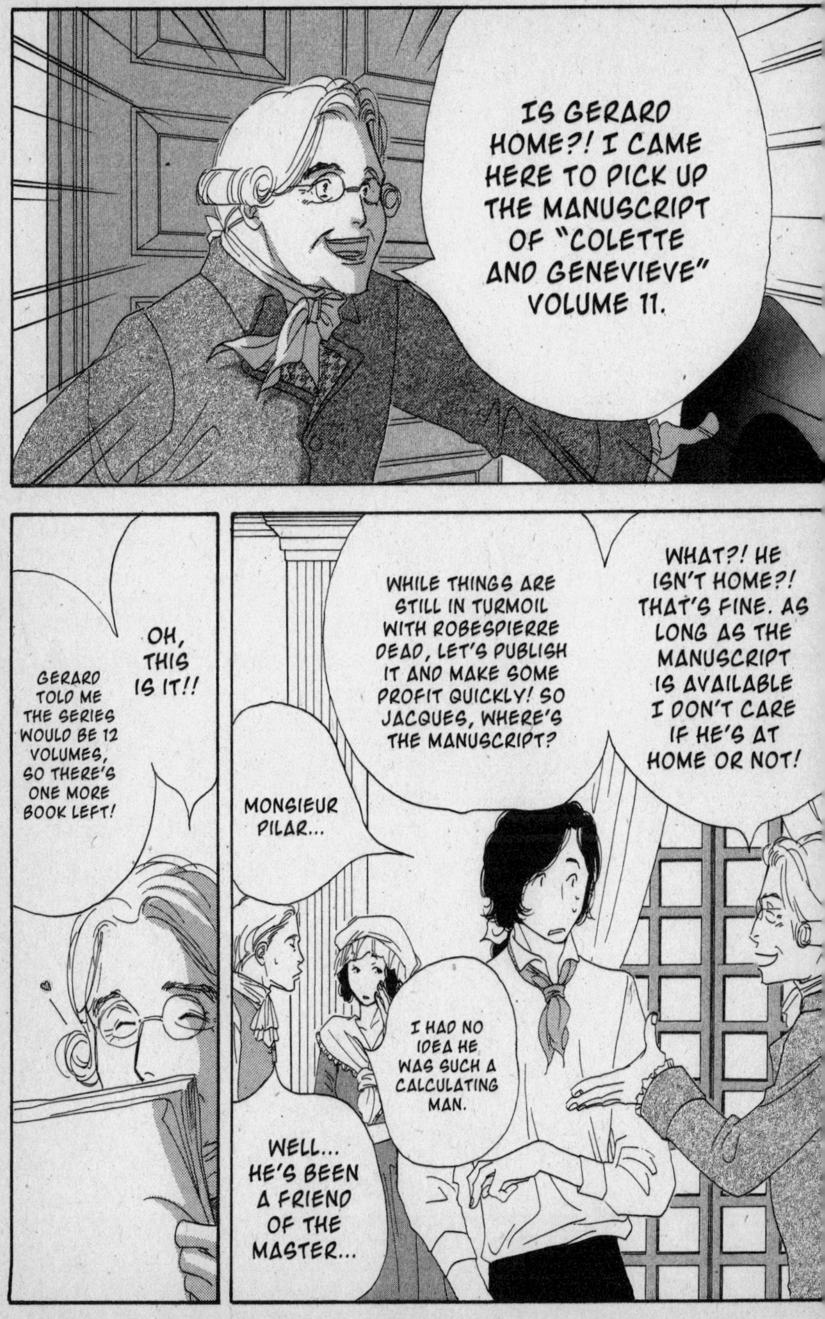
IS GERARD HOME?! I CAME HERE TO PICK UP THE MANUSCRIPT OF "COLETTE AND GENEVIEVE" VOLUME 11.
WHAT?! HE ISN'T HOME?! THAT'S FINE. AS LONG AS THE MANUSCRIPT IS AVAILABLE I DON'T CARE IF HE'S AT HOME OR NOT!
WHILE THINGS ARE STILL IN TURMOIL WITH ROBESPIERRE DEAD, LET'S PUBLISH IT AND MAKE SOME PROFIT QUICKLY! SO JACQUES, WHERE'S THE MANUSCRIPT?
MONSIEUR PILAR...
I HAD NO IDEA HE WAS SUCH A CALCULATING MAN.
WELL... HE'S BEEN A FRIEND OF THE MASTER...
OH, THIS IS IT!!
GERARD TOLD ME THE SERIES WOULD BE 12 VOLUMES, SO THERE'S ONE MORE BOOK LEFT!

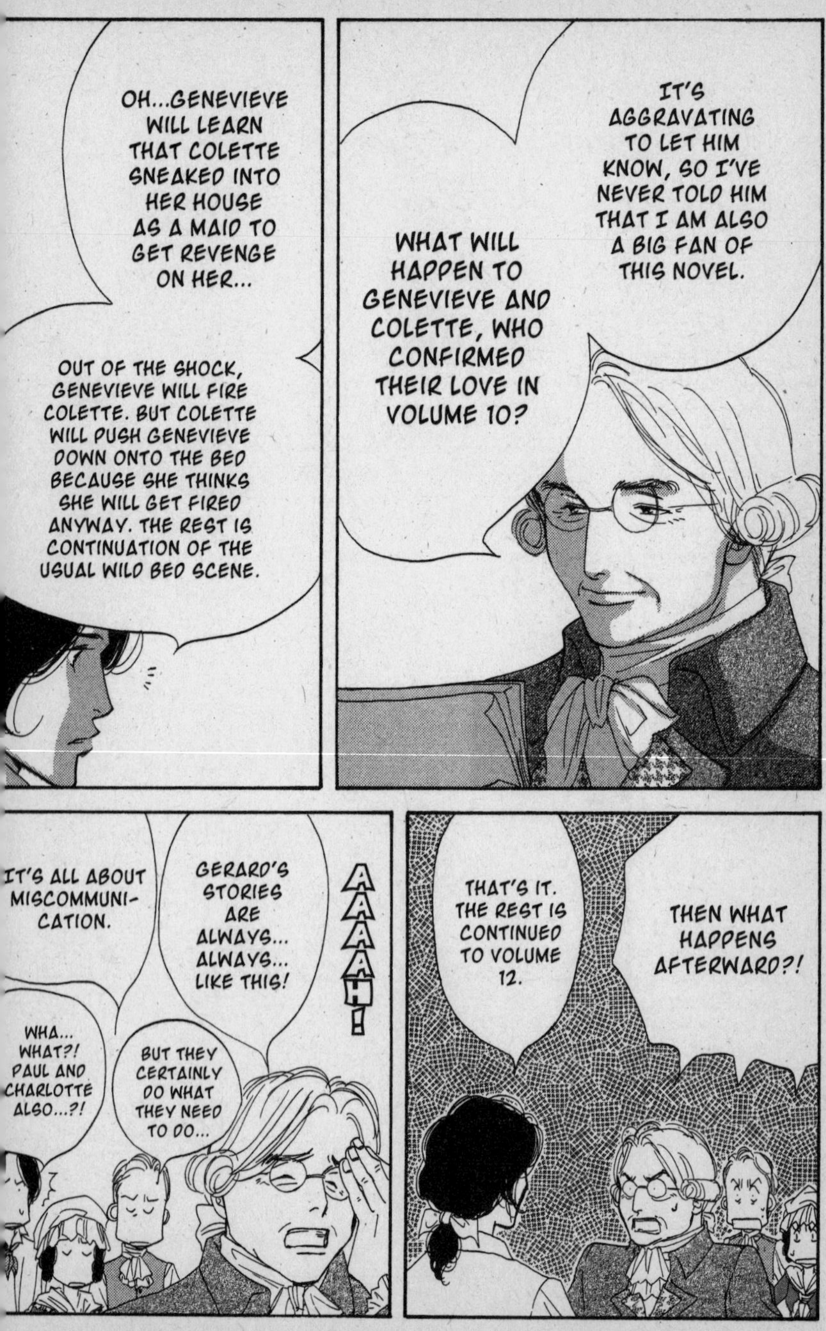
IT'S AGGRAVATING TO LET HIM KNOW, SO I'VE NEVER TOLD HIM THAT I AM ALSO A BIG FAN OF THIS NOVEL.
WHAT WILL HAPPEN TO GENEVIEVE AND COLETTE, WHO CONFIRMED THEIR LOVE IN VOLUME 10?
OH...GENEVIEVE WILL LEARN THAT COLETTE SNEAKED INTO HER HOUSE AS A MAID TO GET REVENGE ON HER...
OUT OF THE SHOCK, GENEVIEVE WILL FIRE COLETTE. BUT COLETTE WILL PUSH GENEVIEVE DOWN ONTO THE BED BECAUSE SHE THINKS SHE WILL GET FIRED ANYWAY. THE REST IS CONTINUATION OF THE USUAL WILD BED SCENE.
THEN WHAT HAPPENS AFTERWARD?!
THAT'S IT. THE REST IS CONTINUED TO VOLUME 12.
AAAAH!
GERARD'S STORIES ARE ALWAYS... ALWAYS... LIKE THIS!
IT'S ALL ABOUT MISCOMMUNICATION.
BUT THEY CERTAINLY DO WHAT THEY NEED TO DO...
WHA... WHAT?! PAUL AND CHARLOTTE ALSO...?!

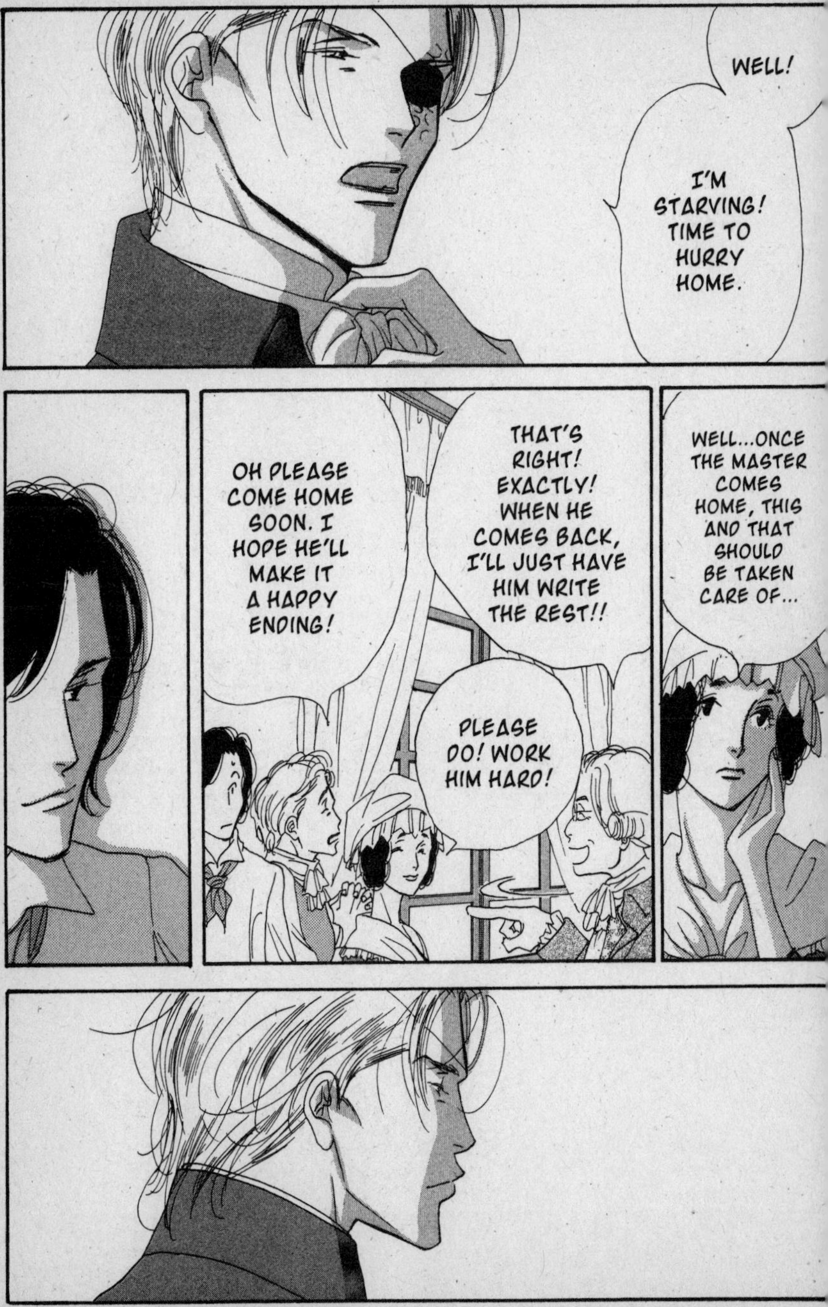
WELL!
I'M STARVING! TIME TO HURRY HOME.
WELL...ONCE THE MASTER COMES HOME, THIS AND THAT SHOULD BE TAKEN CARE OF...
THAT'S RIGHT! EXACTLY! WHEN HE COMES BACK, I'LL JUST HAVE HIM WRITE THE REST!!
OH PLEASE COME HOME SOON. I HOPE HE'LL MAKE IT A HAPPY ENDING!
PLEASE DO! WORK HIM HARD!

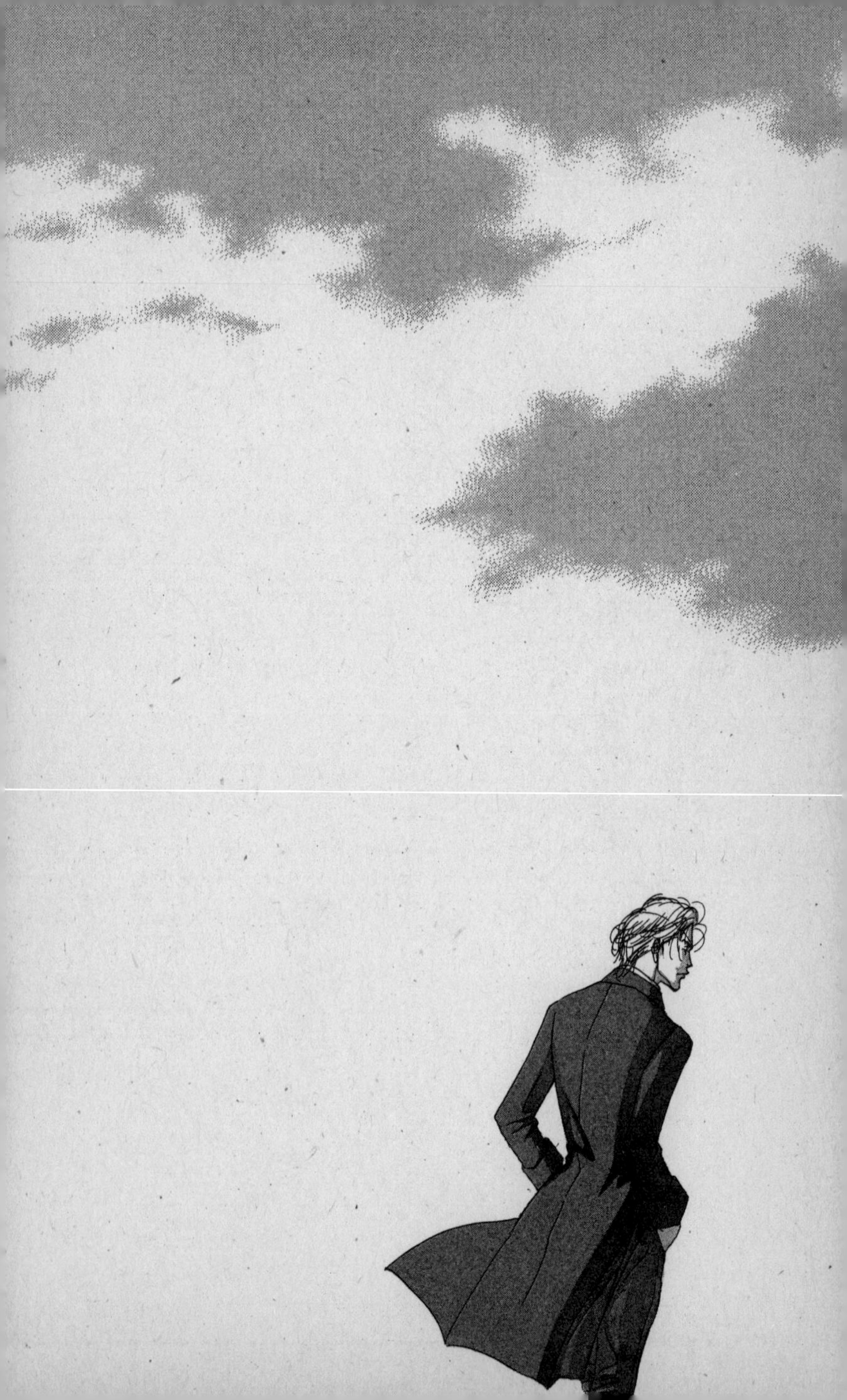

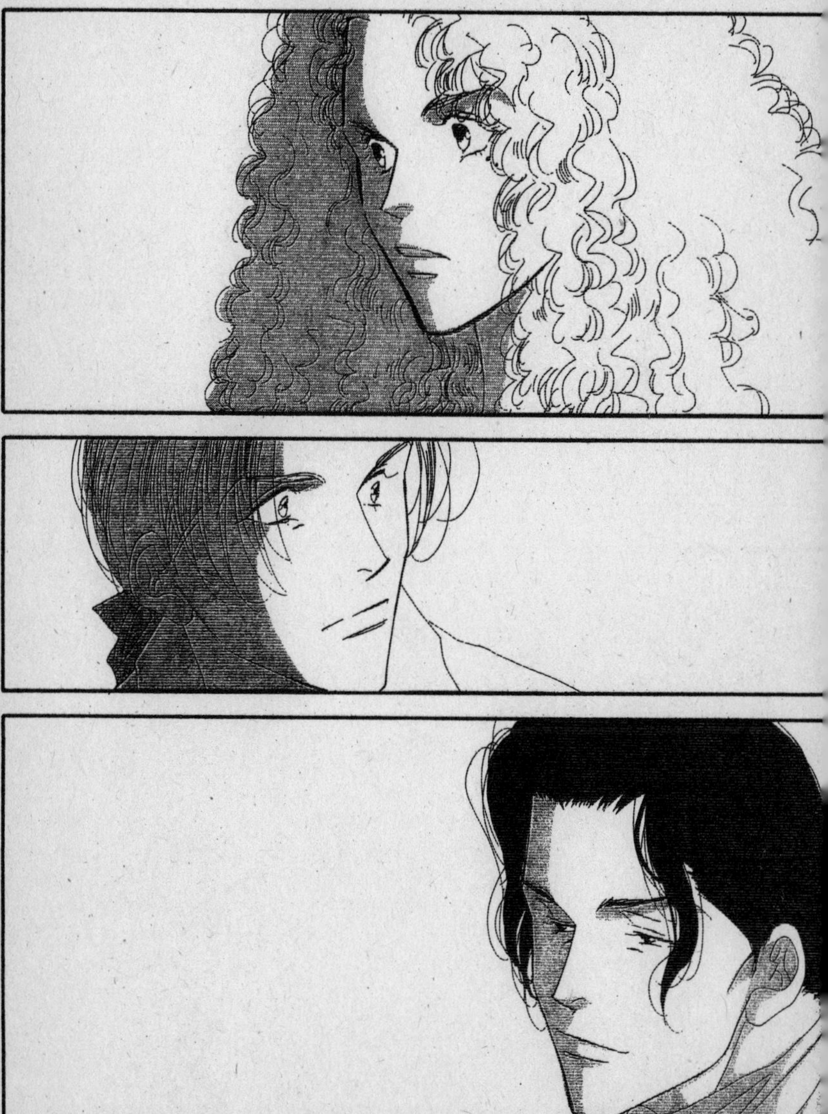

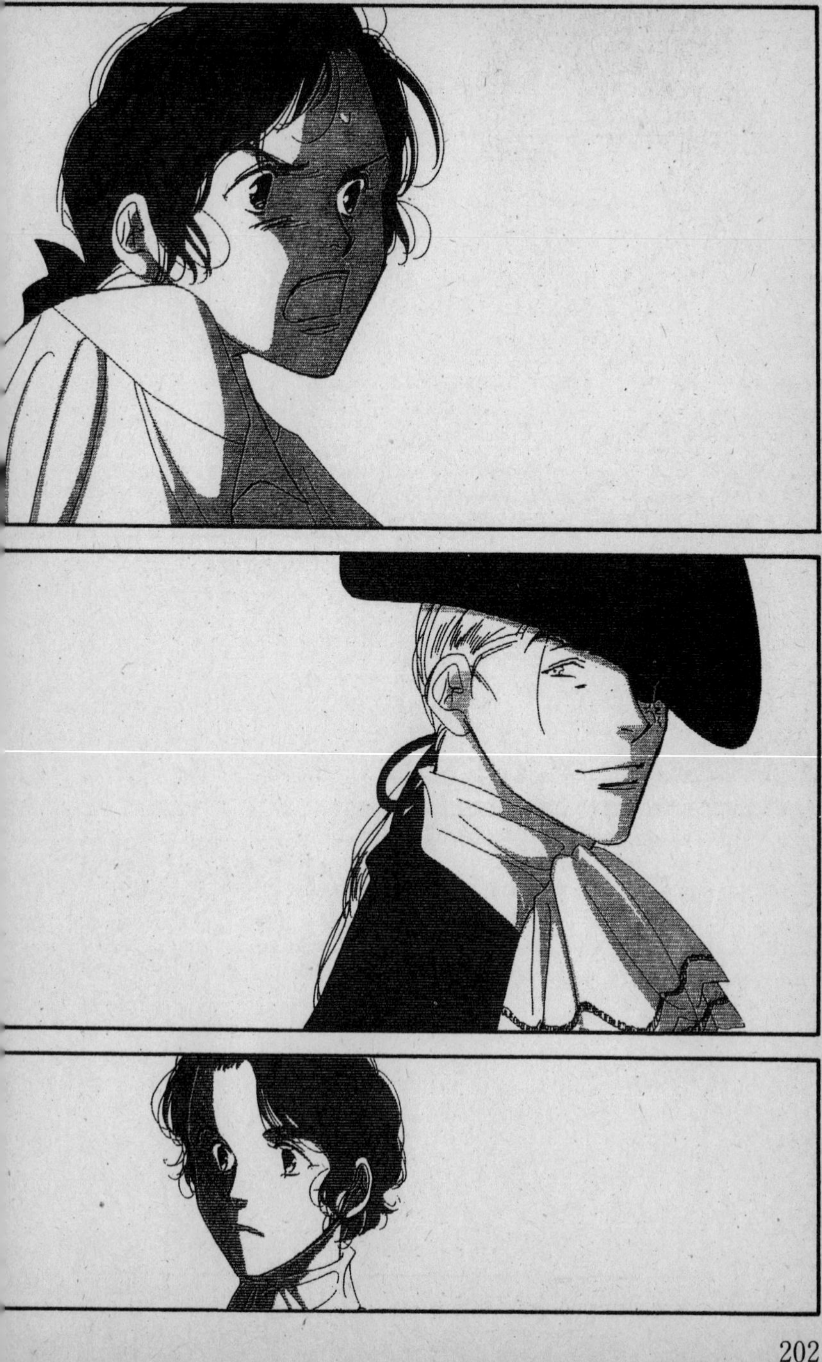

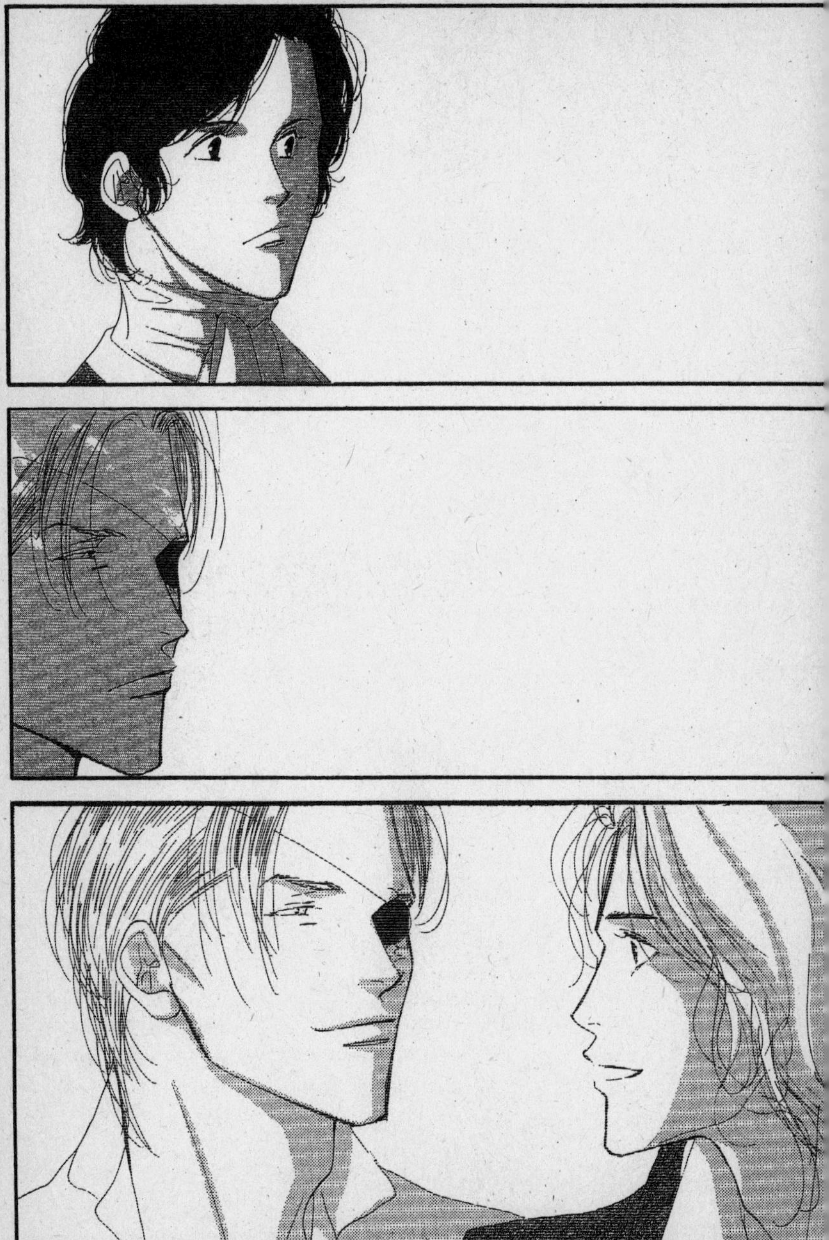

Fin.

Gerard & Jacques
Created by Fumi Yoshinaga

© 2001 Fumi Yoshinaga. All Rights Reserved. First published in Japan in 2001 by
BIBLOS Co., Ltd. Tokyo. English publication rights arranged through BIBLOS Co., Ltd.

English text copyright © 2006 BLU

ISBN: 1-59816-542-9

First Printing: December 2006
10 9 8 7 6 5 4 3 2 1
Printed in the USA

The Moon and Sandals

Vol. 1

月とサンダル

See me After CLASS!

THE MOON & SANDALS 1 © 1996 Fumi Yoshinaga. All rights reserved. First published in Japan in 1996 by HOBUNSHA CO., LTD. Tokyo

ISBN# 978-1-56970-802-9 SRP $12.95

June
by DMP

As a newly appointed high school teacher, Ida has yet to gain confidence in his abilities. His insecurity grows worse when he feels someone staring intensely at him during class. The piercing eyes belong to a tall, intimidating student – Koichi Kobayashi. What exactly should Ida do about it? Is it discontent that fuels Kobayashi's sultry gaze… or could it be something else?

Written and Illustrated by:
Fumi Yoshinaga

On Sale 02-28-2007
junemanga.com

Where schoolwork is the last thing you need to worry about...

When Keita is admitted to the prestigous all-boys school Bell Liberty Academy, his life gets turned upside down!

Filled with the hottest cast of male students ever put together, this highly anticipated boys' love series drawn by You Higuri (*Gorgeous Carat*) is finally here!

stop

blu manga are published in the original japanese format

go to the other side and begin reading